"WHAT REALLY FASCINATED (THE KILLER) WAS THE HUNT, THE ADVENTURE OF SEARCHING OUT HIS VICTIMS. AND . . . POSSESSING THEM PHYSICALLY AS ONE WOULD POSSESS A POTTED PLANT, A PAINTING, OR A PORSCHE. OWNING, AS IT WERE, THIS INDIVIDUAL . . ."

The man who said this was Ted Bundy, from the Death Row cell where he waits for the courts to decide his final fate, and where he still receives love letters and sex letters from adoring women and "Bundy groupies."

The killer he was talking about is himself. . . .

# THE ONLY
# LIVING WITNESS

**"FRIGHTENING . . . A FASCINATING PICTURE OF A MADMAN AS SEEN THROUGH THE EYES OF A MADMAN."**
—*Houston Chronicle*

**"TERRIFYING, BIZARRELY FASCINATING** . . . written with gut-wrenching immediacy."
—*Saturday Review*

*(Please ___ ___ ___ ___ ___ ___ ___ cal acclaim . . .)*

# THE ONLY LIVING WITNESS

by
### Stephen G. Michaud
### Hugh Aynesworth

A SIGNET BOOK

NEW AMERICAN LIBRARY

This is an authorized reprint of a hardcover edition published by
Linden Press/Simon & Schuster.

For information address Linden Press/Simon & Schuster, a Simon & Schuster Division
of Gulf & Western Corporation, Simon & Schuster Building, Rockefeller Center,
1230 Avenue of the Americas, New York, New York 10020.

To the memories
of Lynn Callison, Larry Grove,
and Richard Boeth.

Society wants to believe it can identify evil people, or bad or harmful people, but it's not practical. There are no stereotypes.

The thing is that some people are just psychologically less ready for failure than others.

—Theodore Robert Bundy

# The Women

### Mary Adams, 18

Battered 1/4/74 in her basement bedroom in Seattle. Survived after several months in a coma.

### Lynda Ann Healy, 21

Disappeared 2/1/74 from her basement bedroom in Seattle. Body found (with Susan Rancourt, Roberta Parks, and Brenda Ball) 3/75 on Taylor Mountain, 20 miles east of Seattle. Forensic indication: bludgeoned.

### Donna Gail Manson, 19

Disappeared 3/12/74 in Olympia. Body never found.

### Susan Rancourt, 18

Disappeared 4/17/74 in Ellensburg. Body found 3/75 on Taylor Mountain. Forensic indication: bludgeoned.

### Roberta Kathleen Parks, 22

Disappeared in Corvallis, Oregon, 5/6/74. Body found 3/75 on Taylor Mountain. Forensic indication: bludgeoned.

### Brenda Ball, 22

Disappeared 6/1/74 from a tavern in Burien. Body found 3/75 on Taylor Mountain. Forensic indication: bludgeoned.

### Georgann Hawkins, 18

Disappeared from behind her sorority house in Seattle 6/11/74. Body never found.

### Janice Ott, 23

Disappeared from Lake Sammamish 7/14/74. Body found 9/74 four miles northeast of the park. Forensic indication: strangled or bludgeoned.

### Denise Naslund, 19

Disappeared from Lake Sammamish 7/14/74. Body found 9/74 four miles northeast of the park. Forensic indication: strangled or bludgeoned.

### Carol Valenzuela, 20

Disappeared 8/2/74 in Vancouver. Body found 10/74, along with remains of unidentified female in her late teens or early twenties, some miles south of Olympia. Forensic indication: strangled.

## UTAH

### Nancy Wilcox, 16

Disappeared 10/2/74 in Holladay. Body never found.

### Melissa Smith, 17

Disappeared 10/18/74 in Midvale. Body found ten days later in Summit Park, a few miles from Salt Lake City. Forensic indication: strangled and bludgeoned.

### Laura Aime, 17

Disappeared 10/31/74 south of Lehi. Body found 11/74 in the Wasatch mountains. Forensic indication: strangled and bludgeoned.

### Debra Kent, 17

Disappeared from high school in Bountiful 11/8/74. Body never found.

### Carol DaRonch, 19

Survived attempted abduction same night as Kent disappearance.

### Nancy Baird, 21

Disappeared 7/1/75 from a service station in Farmington. Body never found.

## COLORADO

### Caryn Campbell, 23

Disappeared from a Snowmass lodge 1/12/75. Body found a month later off Owl Creek Road between Snowmass and Aspen. Forensic indication: bludgeoned.

### Julie Cunningham, 26

Disappeared from a downtown street in Vail 3/15/75. Body never found.

### Denise Oliverson, 25

Disappeared while riding bicycle in Grand Junction 4/6/75. Body never found.

---

## FLORIDA

---

### Lisa Levy, 20

Clubbed to death in Chi Omega sorority house, Florida State University in Tallahassee, 1/15/78.

### Margaret Bowman, 21

Clubbed to death in Chi Omega sorority house 1/15/78.

### Kathy Kleiner, 21

Battered during attack at Chi Omega sorority house 1/15/78.

### Karen Chandler, 21

Battered during attack at Chi Omega sorority house 1/15/78.

### Cheryl Thomas, 21

Battered at her apartment, minutes after the Chi Omega murders, 1/15/78.

### Kimberly Leach, 12

Disappeared 2/9/78 from a junior high school in Lake City, Florida. Body found 4/78 in Suwannee State Park, 32 miles west of Lake City. Forensic indication: homicidal violence, neck region.

# Prologue

I LAST SAW Ted Bundy on a miserable day in early June. The Florida sun came up hot in the morning; there was a feel of bloat in the air, a rank sponginess that shortens the breath and makes the skin feel dirty, prickly.

Hugh and I drove southeast from the Quality Inn in Lake City along State Highway 100 toward the maximum security prison near the remote hamlet of Raiford. It is a thirty-five-mile trip through the middle of north-central Florida, a flat, unrewarding stretch of scraggly pine trees and truck farms. This is not the Florida of Miami Beach hotels, Disney World, and orange groves. This landscape is rural and mostly poor and has much more in common with the backwaters of southern Georgia than it does with the tourist country that begins farther down the Florida peninsula toward Orlando.

We passed a convenience store that serves free coffee to highway patrolmen. A bit farther along the straight two-lane highway is the town of Lulu with its tiny post office and well-attended Baptist church. A good deal of praying and singing (and sometimes stomping and hollering) in the name of the Lord goes on in this part of Florida. On the car radio that morning, there was a choice of farm reports, country music, and gospel hours.

A massive tractor trailer zoomed by. Around Lulu, the country people are accustomed to the roar of the big rigs as they barrel up and down Highway 100. They are also accustomed to the splotches of fur, feathers, and spines squashed flat into the pavement under the truckers' wheels. Buzzards and nimble crows work Highway 100 like so many Eighth Avenue hookers with one eye on their business and the other on the lookout for The Man. As a car or truck approaches, the scavengers fly straight up and just high enough to clear the vehicle's roof. Then they alight again on the roadway. Once in a while, the slower birds will

1

misjudge a truck's height, or fail to notice another tall truck just behind it.

It was only eight-thirty in the morning, but already waves of heat shimmered up from the highway. We turned, and the road opened onto a broad plain. To the right is the Union Correctional Institution, which is in Union County, and then the Florida State Prison itself, just a rifle shot away across the New River in Bradford County. Prison cattle stood motionless along the roadside, stupefied by the heat and humidity. Their milk, which the prisoners consume, is often redolent of soil. Interspersed with the cows were inmate work gangs out with their uniformed guards, who cradled shotguns and wore sunglasses that coruscated in the bright morning light.

It was a banal vision of purgatory, the sullen, shuffling cons toiling under a heavy sun that glinted hard at them from their keepers' shielded eyes. This stasis and timeless futility is common to all prisons; it only seemed more pronounced that day because of our mood. Hugh was hacking and wheezing from a respiratory infection exacerbated by too many cigarettes and the lung-clogging density of the air. My brain was cottony from a hangover and my stomach churned from too much black coffee and aspirin. When we arrived at the prison itself, both my hands were cramped and sore from clutching the steering wheel, as if I'd been hanging from it.

For months, I had been coming to the prison to see Ted. Each time I drove up, I would be accosted by a blue-clad trusty leaning on a rake in the parking lot and wanting to know if I was an attorney. This day, to my surprise, the importuning felons were missing. And gone, too, were the raucous seagulls that in the springtime wheel and screech above the prison kitchens or stand nattering at one another under the guard towers. Many inmates will swear that they are served creamed chicken with suspicious frequency during seagull season.

The tedium of prison life and prolonged isolation's regressive effect on personality are in large part responsible for such fears. Many convicts retreat into juvenile narcissism; they will exercise their bodies with monkish devotion, immerse themselves in dietary and nutritional literature, and spend hours in careful, loving scrutiny of their hair, their skin, their teeth, their hands and feet.

Ironically, this neurotic self-absorption is fostered by an environment which—apart from the threat of violence and the influence of drugs and alcohol—is physically the healthiest most prisoners have ever known. In some respects, a prison is a hothouse. The inmates vegetate like exotic flora. They lead orderly lives, consume a balanced diet, and are protected in their isolation from most contagious diseases and the majority of the modern world's mundane threats to psychic well-being. Much more sinister forces shape them.

Convicts generally do not age as quickly as do people on the outside. Nevertheless, their health is a constant preoccupation. Some inmates at the Florida State Prison are persuaded that beef liver from the prison slaughterhouse, freshly butchered and stuffed hot from the animal into a plastic bag, is a favored masturbatory vessel among the kitchen workers. As a result, many prisoners refuse to eat the beef liver for psycho-hygienic reasons.

More feared and gossiped about than the food, however, is the prison medical staff. One story widely credited inside the walls has an inmate being given an injection for an abscessed tooth. The needle misses and he develops an ear infection. After surgery, he goes deaf in that ear and the infection spreads to his other ear. During a second operation, the doctor fumbles with his scalpel and puts out the prisoner's eye. Eventually, the man is returned to his cell; he is deaf, blind in one eye, and missing one arm due to complications following an improper administration of anesthetics.

The swamp thrum of a billion insects greeted Hugh and me as we walked from our rental car toward the prison itself. Ahead was a pastel lime-colored structure enclosed by a double row of high cyclone fences topped with barbed wire. Between the two fences is an open area once patrolled by guard dogs. The fearsome-looking Dobermans and German shepherds have been retired ever since a pair of the animals accompanied a group of prisoners on an attempted escape.

Theodore Robert Bundy is among the more than 1,400 felons housed at the Florida State Prison. He and 180 or so other inmates are kept in Q,R,S, or T wings, the lock-down blocks of the longest Death Row in the United States. These men do not mingle with the general population of the prison; in Ted's case, that would mean almost certain assault by fellow inmates whose rough notions of justice prescribe no mercy for so-called baby rapers. Instead, Ted and the rest of the men on The Row spend almost all their time alone in individual cells awaiting the day when, as the story has it, a guard will place a taut rubber band around the inmate's penis, pack cotton wadding up his rectum, and lead him down to Old Sparky for electrocution. John

Spenkelink was executed in Florida State Prison (Ted later would occupy his cell) in the spring of 1979. The day Spenkelink was put to death a popular Jacksonville disc jockey aired a recording of sizzling bacon and dedicated it to the doomed man.

Bundy went to Death Row that summer after he was convicted in a Miami courtroom for the "Chi Omega killings." It was a sensational trial, the first on national television. Two hundred and fifty reporters with an audience on five continents applied for working-press credentials. Above Edward D. Cowart's fourth-floor courtroom in the Dade County Metropolitan Justice Building, an elaborate media center was established to handle the crush of newspeople. And ABC News underwrote a special satellite hookup that brought the trial into an estimated forty million American homes.

Center stage was the defendant himself—arguably the profoundest enigma in the history of U.S. criminal justice. Handsome, arrogant, and articulate, he drew scores of rapt groupies to the jammed court each day. Some were cookie-cutter blondes desperate to catch Ted's eye. Then there were the blue-haired and dewlapped geriatrics come over from their retirement bungalows along the lower stretches of Collins Avenue, hoping to catch a glimpse of the young man whom the newspapers were calling the "Love-Bite Killer."

Here was no two-bit loner or galumphing yokel with a mean streak. Ted was the mediagenic thirty-two-year-old former law student from Tacoma, Washington, his mother's darling, and a Republican of faintly liberal stripe whose confident manner and political acumen, some thought, might have taken him to the governor's mansion and beyond. Yet locked within him, or so the state contended, was a depravity off the scale of human understanding. And he was on trial for the sickening penultimate spasm of an alleged four-year cross-country murder binge that had left dozens of young women violated, mangled, and dead.

Bundy, charged prosecutor Larry Simpson, had come silently in the early morning hours of Super Bowl Sunday 1978 to the upstairs bedrooms of the Chi Omega sorority house on the campus of Florida State University in Tallahassee. There, with the agitated purposefulness of a shark in feeding frenzy, he hunted from room to room with an oak club.

He fled before the urge was spent, but in a scant few minutes two girls were murdered and two others lay battered senseless. One victim was found with her brain exposed from a blow to her forehead. He had sodomized the other dead girl with a Clairol hair spray bottle. Evidence showed that at the moment of her death, he bit at her right nipple, nearly tearing it from her breast. Then he rolled her over and sank his teeth twice into her left buttock, leaving an angry wound.

Paramedics led one of the stunned survivors from her bed holding a plastic pail beneath her chin to catch the gush of blood from her shattered mouth.

Then, as the police arrived at this scene of carnage, there came a report from less than three blocks away; another sleeping coed had been savaged in her duplex apartment. She would survive, but only because the arrhythmic thumping of her attacker's club had been loud enough to awaken her neighbors, who frightened the assailant away.

A month later, on February 15, 1978, Ted Bundy was captured in Pensacola, Florida. He was charged with the Chi Omega slaughter, and subsequently also indicted for the kidnap and murder of twelve-year-old Kimberly Diane Leach, a Lake City, Florida, schoolgirl whom he'd abducted six days before his arrest. A jury would conclude that Ted killed her and then dumped her partially clad body under an abandoned hog shed, where it was found nearly two months later. It was the unofficial surmise of some forensic experts that Kimberly's throat had been slit and that a knife had been taken to her genital organs.

The man who committed these outrages was regarded by those who knew him as sincere, bright, often courtly around women. He has a high intelligent forehead and a straight patrician nose inherited from his doting mother. Under even brows that he sometimes plucks, his expressive eyes can be a gentle blue, and together with a sensitive mouth have created the illusion of depth to his nature. More than once a woman has used the word "beautiful" to describe Ted Bundy.

Ted's male friends admired him; they detected a power in him. Older men marked him for his solid, conventional turn of mind, and his look of purpose. Several of them treated Bundy as if he were a likable and deserving nephew or a younger brother.

His case—or cases—was a terrible shock to these people. Long before a national audience was to be fascinated and mystified by his story, Ted's friends in Washington State, and then Utah, were incredulous at news reports alleging that he was a mass killer, an incubus who alone and undetected had murdered untold numbers of innocent girls.

At first his friends clung to the belief that some dreadful error had been made. Yet an unmistakable pattern finally did emerge, a pattern of death and sorrow wrought by a man of manifest gentility and hideous covert longings.

So diabolically crafty had he been in his first years of killing that what was known of the deaths was more guess and inference than anything else. It appeared that the girls had been either strangled or bludgeoned, or both. They were all young, and most of them were college girls. He often stalked them first, then approached them on a pretext. In a matter of seconds, they were gone. Only one young woman was known to have escaped him, and the circumstances of that assault suggested that he silenced his prey quickly after luring them to him.

He drove hundreds of miles with their dead or unconscious bodies in his car and dumped the girls at preselected forest sites where they were stripped and left for predators to devour. By the time most of them were found, their remains had totally decomposed. Their skulls and skeletons, some showing telltale striations left by gnawing animals, were often strewn for several hundred yards. What little physical evidence there was indicated rape and mutilation. The caved-in skulls attested that he had delivered blows of tremendous force and fury.

Had Ted Bundy fit the public's stereotype of the mass murderer, the identifiable lunatic, these tragedies might not have provoked the terror that they did. But as one of Bundy's friends later explained to me, "Ted was one of us." He shattered the comfortable preconceptions about who is capable of such monstrosities, presenting a mass killer both gross to contemplate and wholesome to behold; a likable, lovable homicidal mutant.

Yet even this perception of Ted was false, or at best superficial. All it did was recognize in horror and fascination that the stereotype is a vain assumption. "People," said Bob Dekle, the Florida assistant state attorney who prosecuted Bundy for the murder of Kim Leach, "think a criminal is a hunchbacked, cross-eyed little monster slithering through the dark, leaving a trail of slime. They're human beings."

But within Ted Bundy, human being, that slithering hunchback lives, residing behind what one eminent psychiatrist has termed a psychopath's "mask of sanity." The mask is a fabrication and nothing more, but it is impenetrable by even the most skilled doctor of the mind. In Ted, the cross-eyed creature lurks on a different plane of existence and can only be seen by means of a tautology; its presence must be inferred before it can be found.

Thus, the only doctor who did not assume Ted Bundy was a killer was also the only doctor not to conclude he was mentally disturbed. Once the assumption of guilt was made, nearly all the classic symptoms of psychopathology were identified and duly noted. But before that time, no one saw it, because no one could see it behind the mask. Ted alone—and only partially—understands the hunchback.

It allowed Bundy to hide reality from others and to deny it to himself. It also gave him a preternatural power to manipulate, a capacity whose effect was akin to magic. It was this power that made him such an effective killer and so impossible to track down. It was a key to his two successful escapes from Colorado jails.

And he used it to bind women to him. Over the years, several would be physically intimate with him and many, many more wished they could be. He has inspired passionate love and hopeless love, such as the sort felt by his wife, Carole Boone. She married him after he was condemned to death and later bore him a daughter.

The press stories about Ted have stressed his normalcy, his intellect, his attractiveness, his Republicanism. For the most part, these stories ignored or failed to report that Bundy was a compulsive nail biter and nose picker, that he was only middling bright (I.Q. 124), that he was at best a fair student in college and a failure in law school, that he was essentially untraveled and poorly read, that he stuttered when nervous and had acquired only a surface sophistication. Against a backdrop of mass insane homicide, Ted instead emerged as a variety of criminal genius, a nearly fictive character who wasn't stereotypically a loner or a loser—because he didn't *look* like one—and so must be something else: the incarnation of Evil.

Even the closer profiles of him, some well researched, others based upon presumed personal knowledge of Ted, are suffused with a variety of awe at his works. There have been extensive articles in the *Reader's Digest, The New York Times Magazine, Rolling Stone, Cosmopolitan,* and elsewhere. To date, four books have appeared. Each attempted to fathom the essential mystery of the man, and each found a slightly different Theodore Robert Bundy: the "Killer Next Door," the "Deliberate Stranger," the "Stranger Beside Me," and the "Phantom Prince."

Each book entertains the possibility, or concludes, that Ted is in some way deranged. Each offers evidence of this and insights into his story. But ultimately, each writer had to confront unaided Ted's unlit interior realm, his Golgotha. At its edge, each was foiled as we were. As we were, that is, until the day we met the hunchback.

Hugh and I followed a tortuous route to this confrontation, a journey that began in 1978 with a call from my agent. She told me that Ted Bundy, the noted alleged murderer, wanted to tell his story in a book. There was interest in such a project among publishers, she said. We could expect an adequate advance. Furthermore, Bundy understood that *he* was legally unable to benefit financially from the proposed book, but he did stipulate that the authors make a contribution to a charitable organization founded to aid indigent prisoners.

At the time, I was working for *Business Week* magazine. Years before, I had covered several murders and kidnappings while working for *Newsweek* magazine, most notably the 1973 Houston, Texas, case of homosexual killer Dean Corll, who, with two young accomplices, tortured and murdered perhaps thirty small boys. Mass killers, however, were hardly my specialty.

After some reflection, I called Hugh in Dallas, where he was then based as chief investigator for the ABC newsmagazine program *20/20*. I had worked for Aynesworth in Houston when he was the *Newsweek* bureau chief there. He had assigned me to the Corll case, and through it and several other stories Hugh had taught me a good deal of what I know about reporting. Given the sheer complexity of the Bundy case—unlike most killer stories it stretched across both time and geography and would involve reporting in several states—Hugh was the perfect partner. His reportorial experience with criminals and cops extended back to the Clutter murder case, the 1959 slaughter of a west Kansas farm family that Truman Capote turned into his masterpiece, *In Cold Blood*.

We agreed to take on Ted's story together, totally unprepared for where it would lead us.

The first surprise was mine:

Ted, it turned out, had grown up not five miles from where I had lived as a youngster. He and I later determined that we knew a number of people in common. Moreover, we were both born in Burlington, Vermont; Ted in 1946, I in 1948. While still quite young, both of us were moved from the east to Tacoma, Washington. Ted at the time was an only child. I was the youngest of four. Neither of us knew his natural father, although unlike Ted I was born within the benefit of wedlock.

We both attended Tacoma public schools, were swept by the same local fads, later drank the same regional beers, and knew the same kind of girl. We are of the same general height, weight, frame, and coloring. And we're both left-handed.

I once ran down these curiosities to my sister, Susan. She asked, "Well, have you ever killed anyone?"

"No," I said.

She laughed. "That's what Ted says."

Ted contended that he was a victim of incompetent defense attorneys, poisonous pretrial publicity, and manipulated evidence. He said he was caught in a monstrous tangle of circumstance that had led him from a life of promise and public spirit to unjust prosecution, imprisonment, and three death sentences. He was, he said again and again, innocent.

There *had* been disturbing elements in both his trials. Eyewitnesses waffled and were vague. The scientific evidence was at times equivocal and produced sharply differing opinions among the experts called to testify. No fingerprints were found. In fact, in the dozens of cases from Seattle to Florida in which the police have sought to implicate Bundy there has not been a single bit of physical evidence that incontrovertibly demonstrates his involvement in anything more sinister than car theft.

This question of evidence, we would learn, was Ted's personal test of guilt and innocence, part of his complex mental apparatus that turned contention into belief, flimsy rhetoric into a creed. We would soon have to deal with that.

But at the beginning, Bundy regaled us with stories of his boyhood (he once fantasized about being adopted by Roy Rogers), his academic career (he'd thought about going into law enforcement), his loves and his frustrations. His memory was acute for details of his jail breaks, the uneven course of his schooling, and his involvement with Washington State Republican politics. He spoke of his attorneys, his judges, and his juries.

He recounted tales from the eight lockups he'd been in and shared thousands of letters he had received. Nuns, mental patients, housewives, lawyers, groupies—all total strangers—write to Ted all the time with offers of salvation, sex, money, friendship, forgiveness, and abomination. A man identifying himself as a doctor suggested that he and Ted switch brains. Another wanted to know if Bundy would agree to suspended animation rather than electrocution; the idea was for Ted to donate organs as they were needed and to be available for vivisection experiments.

Ted felt that disclosures of this nature were sufficient to our purposes. In some ways, he was his own most avid fan. He foresaw an exciting, gossipy book with naughty details such as are found in best-selling biographies of celebrities. He did not want to discuss guilt—except to deny it—and he actively sought to dissuade Hugh from investigating the cases against him.

We were of a different mind. The content of the book, as far as we were concerned, would be determined by what we learned about Ted and not just what he wanted us to learn. We talked with him not just as his biographers but also had to act as private investigators attached to his prospective appeals attorneys.

In that capacity, we would have been pleased to demonstrate Ted's innocence. Instead, Hugh and I concluded that Bundy had killed a minimum of twenty-one girls. It is possible that as many as forty were killed. In view of that, we had no interest in producing a gauzy and self-serving account spoon-fed to us by Ted.

Yet he had nothing to gain by being anything but superficially candid with us. He had been twice tried and convicted of murder in Florida; he knew that nothing he could say and no fact we could disclose would prevent the state from electrocuting him, appeals notwithstanding, probably within the next five years.

When I turned our discussions to substantive issues, Ted began hedging and lying outright to me. Not only did he have nothing exculpatory to offer, not a single credible alibi or supportable interpretation of the known facts, but he turned the interviews into a game of chutes and ladders with disingenuous pleas of faulty memory and long silences preventing me from pinning him down.

Hugh and I soon wearied of this and saw nothing further to be gained from either talking to Ted or investigating his story. But we had, over the weeks, taken note of two clues, distortions in Ted's personality that might offer the key to his mystery.

Emotionally, Ted seemed a severe case of arrested development. From all that he said and all that we now knew about his past, he might as well have been a twelve-year-old, and a precocious and bratty one at that. Whether a cause or a consequence of his mental illness, his apparent emotional retardation resulted in a diseased pre-adolescent mind directing the actions of an adult male body.

And intellectually, Ted seemed profoundly dissociative, a compartmentalizer, and thus a superb rationalizer. This, we learned, was a key to understanding his entire mental edifice.

These two traits, we felt, could explain how Ted managed to live with—while also denying—his homicidal acts. We only came to understand them just as we were preparing to leave Ted to his fantasies, his conceits, and his bizarrely selfless wife. But in light of our new perspective, we decided to try one last stratagem with him.

So extreme was his childishness that his pleas of innocence were of a character very similar to that of the little boy who'll deny wrongdoing in the face of overwhelming evidence to the contrary. The immature mind's fear of shame and opprobrium is powerful. The *sick* immature mind, hostage to its own evildoing, will remain resolutely hostile to anyone perceived as an authority figure.

So I removed the threat, joining Ted, in effect, in his sandbox. Why, I asked him, couldn't he *speculate* on the nature of a person capable of doing what Ted had been accused (and convicted) of doing? I avoided the word "confession," and emphasized instead Ted's vast firsthand knowledge gained as the suspect in all the cases, as well as his background as a former psychology student and, of course, his intelligence.

The approach would be familiar to anyone experienced with children. As long as a child is not asked to use the first-person pronoun, the confessional "I," the deed or deeds in question can be discussed. It is a kind of game with tacitly understood rules. A form of punishment or atonement can even be agreed upon, exactly what Bundy had suggested when he once offered to go to prison for the remainder of his life, so long as he wasn't forced to say, "I did it."

Ted agreed to think over my proposal, an immediate indication that we had guessed right about him. The next day, I returned to the prison and found Ted more than just amenable to the idea; he embraced it enthusiastically. This was March 27, 1980, the day I made my first tentative acquaintance with the hunchback.

Ted leaned forward in the prison interview room, lit a cigarette, and took the tape recorder in his lap. At first, I didn't understand what he was doing as, in an even, professorial tone, he began to speak of themes in modern society—violence, the treatment of women, the disintegration of the home, anonymity, stress. When I interrupted, he shushed me and told me to be patient. It was going to take a while to get into it.

Finally, he turned from the sociological to the specific, and began describing the killer. Within "this individual," he explained, there dwelt a being—Ted sometimes called it "an entity," "the disordered self," or "the malignant being." The story of "the entity's" birth came slowly, chronologically, a consistent tale of gathering psychopathy that nurtured itself on the negative energy around it. Occasionally, Ted would entertain a question, but for the most part I was there to pay for lunch, light his cigarettes, and change the tapes. He was chary on specifics and skirted many cases where, I guessed, he feared that one slip might provide the vital link. Yet, protected by his use of the third person, he forged ahead in detail to explain how thoughts about sex in general came to concentrate on sexual violence, how pornography shaped and directed the "entity," how the illness inside him drew him toward ever-increasing shows of violence, and how the killer managed to mask his disordered self from his unsuspecting friends.

As Ted familiarized me with that private dementia, he took pains in his explanations lest I develop overly simplistic ideas. He wanted me to *understand*—to the extent that I could. The killer was not a schizophrenic, Bundy iterated and reiterated. "It is truly more sophisticated than that," he cautioned.

Ted called it "a hybrid situation," a psychopathology in which the "entity" is both in and *of* the killer, not some alien presence but a purely destructive power that grew from within. Psychiatrists who have listened to these tapes tell us there is no doubt Ted was talking about himself. Critical elements of the third-person narrative could only have been drawn from first-person experience. Not trained to look for these keys, I still never doubted that I was hearing autobiography. When the hunchback emerged, it spoke directly to me.

Some revelations came wrapped in metaphor. Others he described as might a clinician. It was as if in the telling he, too, was seeing the genesis of the hunchback for the first time, and there were moments when he struggled with his subject. "How do you describe the taste of bouillabaisse?" he asked rhetorically. "Some remember clams, others mullet."

He insisted that violence was never an end in itself, that sex was almost perfunctory, and that to the extent that it was possible the victims were spared pain. Not that the "entity" was moved by any humanitarian urges; it was just that the gratification it sought lay not in the assault but in the possession of the victim.

It was increasingly clear that a child's mind had directed this homicidal rampage. The fantasies were crude, more typical of a sexually innocent twelve-year-old than of an adult sex offender. We knew that by the time he actually started killing, Ted had had several adult sexual encounters, but as he explained it to me, the disordered self, the thing inside him that impelled Ted to kill, knew females through the warp of twisted perception. Only by means of his astounding capacity to compartmentalize had Bundy been able to keep the hunchback from raging through the mask and destroying him. When at last it did, *Ted* became the hunchback. No longer its protector, he and the entity fused.

I felt that I was encountering a wholly novel form of insanity. Rather than being possessed by his illness, Ted appeared to be inhabited by it. The two, man and hunchback, interacted. Above all, I saw elements of will, *conscious* will, taking part in the creation of this entity, as if Ted had wanted to become a killer.

Seeing this, knowing this about him as we sat knee to knee in a cramped and sweltering cubicle buried in the middle of the prison, I myself began to dissociate. A wall, a necessary wall of dispassion, went up in front of me as Bundy spoke in a low voice, holding the tape recorder close to him and darting glances at the guards who periodically looked in on us through a glass pane in the door.

There were times of intense concentration when his features would freeze and a distant, stony quality came into his voice, as if the hunchback had taken corporeal form. More than once, a horizontal white line like a welt appeared across his right cheek. It fascinated me because it did not follow the contour of his face at all.

I wasn't frightened of it, at least no more so than I am at the sight of a shark behind aquarium glass. Far more disconcerting were moments such as the time I pressed Ted for an explanation of how a victim was subdued. Bundy laughed and remarked, "You, too, Steve, could make a successful mass killer. I really think you have it in you!" Like it or not, I was bound to him, if for no other reason than that I had seen the hunchback. Such distilled horror, once seen, never leaves you.

After many weeks, I could absorb no more of it. It was Hugh's turn. In the coming months, Bundy would edge closer to an outright confession than he did with me, but not before the two of them fell to snarling at each other.

Whereas my role had been to go easy on Ted, Hugh played hardball with him, and Bundy was not at all happy with Hugh's intolerance for elliptical thinking. "What gratification would there be in having intercourse with a dead girl?'' Hugh asked, to Ted's manifest displeasure. And Hugh was rankled by Ted's weary sighs meant to convey his lofty impatience with this plain-vanilla gumshoe.

He dogged Ted with questions derived from his "speculations" but obviously tending toward a synthesis with information he had gathered in the course of his investigation. Bundy bridled. "I'm not going into that," he would say. "This is already too thinly disguised. I've gone further now than I wanted to."

But that was to come. On that steamy June day in 1980 we walked with our briefcases toward the main gate and under the gaze of a guard holding a rifle high above us in the watchtower. At a signal, he opened one gate then closed it behind us. Then the inner gate creaked open and rumbled shut. A concrete walkway led to the double doors of the prison entrance itself and behind them a small waiting area. We crossed the waiting room and were greeted by a man at a control panel inside a cramped glass-enclosed booth.

His name was John Boutwell and he was a twelve-year veteran of prison employment. He was responsible for checking our briefcases and identification. Generally, this took about ten minutes—time enough to adjust to the incessant clanging of the prison doors and time enough to glance over the sports pages of the *Gainesville Sun*, which only rarely was not folded neatly on a shelf inside the booth.

John Boutwell was thorough. Routine had not dulled the sharp interest he took in our belongings, even to the point of politely asking to see the innards of our tape recorders. He always asked to see my private investigator's license, despite our first-name acquaintance. Never did he fail to compare me with my license photo and physical description printed on the front of the card.

Next, we approached a third barred gate and prepared to pass through Boutwell's metal detector. Change, pens, belts, keys, shoes, and even my glasses had to be removed. The aged machine could still be set fine enough to register a penny in a penny loafer.

Accompanied now by a guard, we walked through another clanging gate and proceeded down a long, yellowish-tan corridor with a linoleum floor kept glossy by constant inmate polishing and waxing. The walls were bare, and were it not for the sonic assault of banging metal gates echoing in front of us and behind us this part of the prison could have been mistaken for some functional and well-maintained wing of a municipal building.

Up a few steps and through yet another gate controlled by another prison employee in another glass-enclosed booth and we arrived at the center of the prison—a four-way intersection called "Grand Central." To the right, we could peer through floor-to-ceiling bars at the cell blocks opening on to either side of a long, spacious hallway. At the very end of it stood Old Sparky behind a locked door. Straight ahead was the prison laundry. And behind us were the five locked gates made of specialty steel so hard and costly to manufacture that it is too expensive now for use in new prisons.

Some inmates, mostly blacks on their way to work in the prison laundry, walked past us in silence. The oldest of them looked no more than twenty-one or twenty-two. A frightened-looking white prisoner who had killed a cop was being led in manacles by a guard who looked half asleep. With our escort, we turned left toward the Colonel's office, a suite of rooms (also protected by steel gates) in which the Colonel oversees prison security. Two of these rooms, each fitted with windows so that their occupants can be watched, are set aside as conference areas for inmates and their attorneys or investigators. It is necessary to reserve these rooms days in advance through assistant warden David Watson's office.

Outside the Colonel's office stands a bright yellow cage. In it were seven inmates. Six were young blacks wearing blue prison-issue dungarees and blue work shirts that indicated that they were from general population and would not necessarily be spending the rest of their lives in the prison. The seventh man, a white, wore an apricot-colored T-shirt over a gray sweatshirt. He was accustomed to the heat. He had on blue dungarees like the other convicts. On his sockless feet were a pair of green plastic thongs. The T-shirt meant he was from The Row.

"Hey, home boy!" he called to me as usual. "Where've you been?" The accent was southern, black.

Weeks earlier, I had responded to the same greeting with a bit of fake bravura. "Oh," I said, "it took me a while to find all those maps you asked me to bring."

Ted Bundy had not smiled. No one smiled. Mentioning anything to do with escape at Florida State Prison (where everyone thinks about it constantly) is about as wise as joking about bombs and hijackings in an airport boarding lounge. It is the sort of gaffe usually associated with "fish," or new inmates too green to know better.

Ted had been kept waiting in the cage for over two hours.

Prisoners are brought for conferences at the Colonel's office when there is a spare guard to bring them. That morning, Ted was led down about seven, and once he was safely locked in the cage, he was ignored until we arrived. Such treatment, however, is not taken as an indignity. A man accustomed to having his mail read and who must spread his cheeks and lift his scrotum almost every time he leaves or enters his cell learns meek acquiescence over time.

I could generally tell within a few minutes if it was going to be a productive session with Ted. Any of a number of things might be eating at him. He could be depressed, stoned, angry, distracted, or simply dull. This morning he was listless and grouchy; it was not likely to be a good day. I silently counted my blessings that we were only to be given a couple of hours with him. Let Hugh have those marathon days of nine-to-five nonstop interrogation.

"Have you seen Carole?" Ted asked.

That was a sore point among us. Ted's wife lived on the edge of poverty in Gainesville, from where she and her teenaged son Jamey drove each weekend to see their husband and stepfather. Ted felt we were obliged to see Carole as often as possible and to keep her up to date on everything Hugh and I did. We thought that odd, because Carole was unaware of the content of my prison talks with Ted, and we assumed that he'd rather delay the time of her knowing. Besides, we had already told her that we thought Ted was guilty, which in her universe had marked us as ignorant and contemptible. No, beneath contempt.

I told him that we had not seen her, which did not go down well. I did have a two-day-old note from Carole to him, and I handed it over. It was our policy never to read these notes, partly because we figured Carole expected us to and thus would put little of interest in them.

Ted glanced up with a faint smile at something Carole had written, and inquired as to my health. Living on The Row with three death penalties over his head, Bundy was nevertheless able to tsk-tsk about my health habits. Ted disapproves of my drinking and unbalanced diet. He once offered me a wager as to which of the two of us would die first.

I allowed that I was fine, all things considered, and the three of us settled down into a desultory talk that wound its way from guesses as to Ronald Reagan's chances of becoming President to Ted's concern over the moral climate in which Jamey was being raised. Not that Carole was a neglectful mother, but those kids around Jamey's school were experimenting with all sorts of drugs and who knew what else. We talked about some of the legal issues that might affect Ted's appeals, and he told us he thought the number of executions in the U.S. was bound to rise dramatically in the coming years. As usual when we turned to such topics, his comments were crisp and to the point. Ted loves abstractions.

Grateful that our time was so brief, Hugh and I rose unsteadily to leave. Tomorrow was another day, and perhaps it would be cooler. In truth, I didn't really care. Ted was Hugh's responsibility now, and I had a headful of impressions to sort out and many months to go before I could start to write about Ted Bundy's life. I did, however, take one last self-conscious look at his hands. They are thin, almost delicate, with tapering fingers and well-kept nails. Ted used to bite his nails, but finally broke himself of the habit in jail.

I wondered again how he had slipped those hands around girls' throats. Where was the strength that bound ligatures so tightly that skin and weapon would fuse? How had he wielded the knife and the club?

Ted introduced the "entity" to us, tried to explain it, and would then finally collapse (or better, be transformed) under the pressure of confronting it. But he could never take Hugh and me that final step to comprehension of murder of a type so grotesque as to defy imagination. We could never *know* the hunchback. We like to think that the limitation is ours. We heard it all again and again as we transcribed the tapes of our interviews at the prison. We could retell it. We could give it a context. But we could not grasp it. It was like the taste of bouillabaisse.

# ONE

WASHINGTON STATE is separated into two distinct and dissimilar zones by a spine of rugged mountains, the dramatic, volcanic Cascade Range. East of the high divide lie dry, undulating farmlands and expanses of near-desert where the summers are hot and the winters often severe. In the lower elevations west of the Cascades, the climate is milder and considerably wetter. The soil tends to be highly acidic. There is pervasive dampness and an abundance of wildlife. In these conditions an exposed corpse will rapidly disintegrate.

The dominant colors of western Washington are green, blue, white, and gray. There is the green of the vast timber forests and national parks; the blue of the lakes and salt-water inlets scraped out eons ago by monumental glaciers; white covers many of the higher mountain peaks the year around; and the sky generally is an oppressive gray from the frequent northern Pacific weather systems that wade ashore on the Olympic Peninsula, then are gentled as they wash inland to the barrier of the Cascades. The sun does not shine too often in western Washington.

Despite the chills and mists and inky mornings and evenings that in winter nearly link with one another around one o'clock in the afternoon, Washingtonians are relentlessly outdoorsy. Practically everyone, it seems, has a boat, or a camper, or a ski cabin, or lake property, or drives one of those wheeled behemoths called RV's, recreational vehicles. Camping is popular in the state. So is fishing.

Even Washington's urban population, clustered mainly in and around Seattle, is robust, overwhelmingly white, and oriented to the natural world beyond the city limits. To the native, western Washington is God's country, a semi-isolated temperate zone entire unto itself where the confusion and din and extremes of the outside world have yet to intrude. It seems so safe and clean. They say it is a good place to raise a family.

That is what James and Joyce Healy would have said before the first of February 1974. They lived in a comfortable suburb, full of fir trees, just east of Seattle. He worked for a cash register company; she was a housewife. They had three happy, well-adjusted children: a teenaged son, Robert, and daughter, Laura, and twenty-one-year-old Lynda.

Lynda was an accomplished singer, an extrovert, and her mother's favorite. She had a sweet voice, wide-set blue eyes, shoulder-length brown hair, and an even smile that conveyed poise and self-assurance. She was willowy and full of life, a senior psychology major at the University of Washington who looked forward to being a teacher. Lynda enjoyed working with children.

The previous autumn, she and four other girls had moved from dorm rooms into a two-story green frame house in Seattle's University District. Lynda had her own basement bedroom with a window. Next to it and separated by a thin plywood partition was another bedroom.

She worked as a ski-report announcer for a local radio station; to thousands of area skiers, she was the dulcet Lynda (no last names were ever given on the air) who purred to them that Paradise Valley was open, that Crystal Mountain had seven inches of new powder, that there would be night skiing at Alpenthal.

Each morning before school, she awoke and pedaled down to the radio station on her bike. It was a short trip through the pitch-black predawn of the Seattle winter. Often it would be raining, and rarely would there be many people yet stirring in the University District.

In very few American cities would a young woman take such risks, but Lynda Healy evidently felt no fear at being alone and vulnerable in the University District, where she'd lived for almost four years. She appears not to have been aware that in early January of 1974 a young woman had been attacked very near where she lived.

Like Lynda, Mary Adams†* had a basement windowed bedroom in a house which she shared with several other people. She

---

* Though all the people in this account are real, and all of the incidents entirely factual, the names of some individuals have been changed to protect their privacy. The dagger (†) symbol in the text indicates the substitution of a pseudonym for a true name.

had been sound asleep when a man had assaulted her in her bed. He had taken a heavy metal rod to her head, thrashing at her repeatedly. A speculum, or vaginal probe, of a type commonly carried by medical supply houses had been thrust brutally up inside her—a kind of frenzied, bloody "examination" that caused extensive internal injuries. Mary Adams survived after spending several months in a coma. She remembered nothing of the attack or her attacker.

On the night of January 31, 1974, Lynda Healy cooked a casserole supper for her roommates. Afterward, she accompanied one of the girls and a young man of their mutual acquaintance for a casual couple of hours of beer-drinking at Dante's, a college bar. She was home by 9:00 P.M., and in bed by eleven, having set her alarm, as always, for five-thirty. Perhaps an hour later, the girl who slept in the makeshift bedroom next to Lynda's came downstairs and went to bed herself. This housemate, a light sleeper, heard nothing then or through the night until Lynda's alarm went off in the morning—and kept ringing. Then the manager of the radio station called. Where was Lynda? She hadn't come to work. A quick check revealed she was gone; yet her bicycle was still in the house.

Lynda's roommates were concerned. As Friday wore on and there was still no sign of her, their cares turned to fear. Around four o'clock that afternoon, Lynda's mother, Joyce, called; she and the rest of the Healy family were expected over for dinner that night.

"We haven't seen Lynda all day!" one of the frightened roommates blurted into the telephone, and then fell into tears.

Joyce Healy felt ice on her spine. "Immediately," she says, "I knew there was something extremely wrong. I called the police right away."

She and her husband, Jim, met the police at Lynda's house. All the girls were gathered in the living room, and none of them would leave the room alone.

The officers were courteous, businesslike, and plainly skeptical at the possibility of foul play. Cases such as Lynda's were routine for them. Implicit in their questions was the belief that this mysterious disappearance was no mystery at all. Lynda would show up at her boyfriend's, or call to say she'd be right home.

Joyce Healy, a restrained woman, quietly explained to the police that her daughter wouldn't do that sort of thing. Not

Lynda. "Well," one policeman told her, "that's the kind that do it, the ones you don't expect."

Lynda's room was inspected. A small bloodstain was found on her pillow and bottom sheet. It was A-positive blood, Lynda's type, as was another caked red blotch discovered on her night-gown hung neatly in her closet. The official conclusion: Lynda Healy had suffered a late-night nosebleed and had gone some-where to have it attended to. Someone should check the local hospitals.

Her red knapsack and a change of clothes were gone, suggest-ing that she had left the house on her own. But missing, too, was Lynda's top bedsheet and a decorative red satin pillowcase. Also, her bed was made with distinctive "hospital" corners, which would have required pulling it away from the wall then pushing it back into place. Why, the police might have wondered, would a girl who rarely made her bed take time to do so in a medical emergency? Why remove the top sheet? Why would she take the pillowcase?

Yet based upon what was known at first, what would become the most probable theory of the case seemed ludicrous. How could someone in the dead of night enter the house, creep downstairs, overpower Lynda, wrap her in a sheet, and then carry her inert five-foot-seven, 115-pound body back up the stairs and out the door without being heard? He also would have to have carefully made her bed, hung up her nightgown, selected the change of clothes, and taken the knapsack.

Dismissing this possibility as farfetched, the police did not dust the room for fingerprints or process it for telltale hair or fiber evidence or test a semen stain found on her sheet.

For the next several months the Seattle police learned nothing more. Even after they concluded that Lynda Healy must have been taken from her room, it was several more months before the police would link her disappearance to the Adams attack. No one looked at the similar times and circumstances of the cases and made a connection. And no one was willing to advance the theory that someone, a homicidal nightstalker who perhaps was familiar with hospitals (the distinctive bed corners) and medical supplies (the speculum), had roved in the dark through the University District, hunting.

The *Seattle Times* and the *Seattle Post-Intelligencer* ran sev-eral early stories on the Healy disappearance, but their coverage fell off as the police inquiry foundered.

Then, "Answers Sought to Coed's Disappearance" greeted

readers of the *Times*'s March 29 editions, nearly two months after Lynda Healy had vanished. The story reported that on March 12, Donna Gail Manson, nineteen, had disappeared sixty miles south of Seattle on the campus of Evergreen State College in Olympia, the state capital. She was last seen at about 7:00 P.M. as she left her dorm to attend an on-campus jazz concert.

Donna Manson was a little moonstruck, a sharp contrast to the sunny and purposeful Lynda Healy. She was musical like Lynda (Donna played a flute), but she also dabbled in occultism, wrote syrupy poetry, and was fascinated by the medieval alchemists. School appears to have bored her, just as western Washington's ceaseless rain frequently depressed her.

She wasn't reported missing for five days; Donna's friends knew that a chance encounter with a new friend wasn't out of the question for her, nor would they be surprised if she decided to thumb a ride somewhere on a moment's whim. Donna had done so before. A few months earlier she had hitched south to Oregon for a few days, not bothering to say exactly where she was headed or how long she'd be gone.

Once notified that Donna was missing, the police considered the possibility of suicide; she was known to be moody. But when no suicide note or body was found and she did not return to campus, they concluded that Donna Manson had been kidnapped.

How it had happened was anyone's guess. She had walked out into a misty, gloomy night wrapped against the wet cold in her grandmother's full-length coat. The coat was a treasured possession.

Her route through the heavily forested campus would have taken her down darkened pathways where there were ample opportunities for someone to jump out and silence her.

But the police believed it happened otherwise. She almost certainly was taken from the campus, probably by car. The only logical place for her abductor to have parked was behind the auditorium where the jazz concert was held. There were too many students out that night for someone not to have noticed a man carrying a lifeless body around, so Donna must have willingly accompanied him to his car. When it happened—either before, during, or after the concert—is unknown. And just what happened to her is a mystery as well; Donna Gail Manson was never seen again.

The Healy and Manson cases resembled each other only insofar as both victims were college girls and there was not a single clue as to their fate. The dissimilarities were more striking. The two did not resemble each other: physically Lynda was tall, pretty, and filled with vitality; Donna stood five feet, weighed less than a hundred pounds, and was withdrawn by comparison. The incidents occurred sixty miles apart, in two different police jurisdictions, and were separated by forty days. One girl vanished from her bed, the other was last seen alert and on foot.

Donna Manson's disappearance received even less press attention than Lynda Healy's. So far, not the tiniest ripple of apprehension had stirred the people of western Washington.

The next attack came at Central Washington State College (CWSC) in rural Ellensburg, about 120 miles equidistantly east of Seattle and Olympia. Set down amidst the rolling eastern foothills of the Cascade Mountains, Ellensburg is close to ski areas and physically remote from the major population centers of western Washington. For much of the year, it is reached from the west by road only via the formidable, 3,010-foot-high Snoqualmie Pass on U.S. 90.

Just before nine on Sunday night, April 14, 1974, twenty-one-year-old Jane Curtis finished her work in the CWSC library and walked out the main entrance. There she encountered a shabby figure wearing a long coat and a wool cap pulled low over his head. His left arm was in a gauze cast (no sling), and she noticed his fingers were sheathed in a metal splint. The splint apparatus looked sloppily done to her, as if it had been done with one hand or was taped on.

Jane nevertheless volunteered to help the man with his load of books. He gratefully accepted her offer, and they set out for his car. Later, she was sure that the stranger could not have been taller than five feet eight or so, because she stood five-nine in her platform shoes, and he definitely seemed shorter than she was. She further remembered to the police: "He kind of looked at me sideways, kind of turned his head and looked at me funny like. His eyes seemed weird."

As they neared his car, parked amidst the tall grass in a darkened area of the campus, he complained of the pain in his arm, which he said he had broken in a skiing accident. He had hit a tree, he said.

At the passenger-side door, the man produced his key and asked Miss Curtis to unlock the car. Apprehensive, she refused; so he unlocked it himself. She recollected months later that the car was a yellow VW bug with a high-backed black front seat. The interior light did not go on as he opened the door, but she could see well enough to tell that the front passenger-side seat was totally missing. Jane Curtis was suddenly scared.

Brusquely, he ordered her into the car.

"What?" she asked.

"Oh"—his tone changed—"could you get in and start the car for me?"

With that, she turned and departed. "I sort of ran away," she told police. "Kind of fast."

Three days later, Kathleen D'Olivo stepped out of the same library door that Jane Curtis had used. Behind her on the side-walk she heard a noise. "I turned around and there was this man dropping books," Kathleen told investigators. "He was squatting, trying to pick up the books and some packages. I noticed he had a sling on one arm and a hand brace on the other. I went over and said, 'Do you need some help?'

"He said, 'Yeah, could you?' "

The man's facial features didn't register clearly with Kathleen, but she thought he was about six feet tall. She noticed that he was sloppily dressed and "kinda scrawny-looking." His hair was light brown, "kind of shaggy." She was unsure if he wore a mustache or glasses. Something told her that he had both.

Miss D'Olivo originally thought the man was headed for the library, but as she walked along with him, carrying most of his books, he turned toward a dark area where he said his car was parked. She grew suspicious, but figured that she could whack him with one of his books if he tried anything.

They arrived at his car and he produced his keys. As he unlocked the passenger-side door, he dropped them. After a moment of searching on his hands and knees, he stood up and asked Kathleen if she could help him. His sling and hand brace, he explained, made it tough to feel around on the ground.

On the way to his car, Kathleen had made sure to keep the man in front of her. Now, standing alone with him by his car—which she described to police as a shiny brown VW bug— Kathleen D'Olivo wasn't going to take any chances. "I didn't want to bend over in front of him," she reported, "so I said, 'Let's step back and see if we can see the reflection in the light.' I squatted down, and luckily I did see the reflection of the keys in the light. So I picked them up and dropped them in his hand and I said, 'Good night.' "

Moments later, Susan Elaine Rancourt wouldn't be so fortunate. She was a freshman biology major, a blue-eyed, blond-haired former cheerleader and homecoming queen known for her wholesomeness (in the family, Susan was called "Prudence Pureheart") and her sensible ways. Her father had paid for a lot of dental work, and Susan protected the investment by brushing and flossing her teeth religiously.

She was a sturdy girl; she weighed 120 pounds and was just five feet tall. And Susan was more serious-minded than most of the CWSC student population. She thought that she wanted to be a doctor or maybe a research scientist, professions that would take discipline and years of study. An A student, she had the drive and intelligence to make it, plus an engaging personal warmth and a concern for the well-being of others. The only thing that seemed to get in her way was her painful late-adolescent shyness; and Susan was working on that, too.

The night of April 17, 1974, she had been to a meeting for prospective dorm counselors. Shortly after 10:00 P.M.—about the time that Kathleen D'Olivo found the Volkswagen keys in the gravel and handed them back to the man with the cast—Susan left the counselors' meeting and headed back across the campus toward her dormitory.

She was afraid of the dark and would have been walking gingerly, since she had left her contact lenses in her room. Any sudden move or suspicious sound would have frightened her.

But a cripple in distress, helpless to carry his books, might not. With her mind on the counselors' meeting, the German-language film she wanted to see that night, and the load of laundry she'd left in the dorm washing machine, she probably was less alert to trouble than usual. What is more, her determination not to be so shy could have led her to more boldness than was her custom.

Susan did not see the movie that night. She did not pick up her laundry. And she did not return to her dorm room. The next afternoon, her roommate reported her missing to campus security officer Bill Clayton. In turn, Clayton notified his chief, Alfred Pickles.

Pickles ordered up a campus search, issued a flier (which neglected to mention the date of the disappearance), and called Susan's parents at their home in Anchorage, Alaska. The search and investigation appear to have been perfunctory; they failed to turn up Jane Curtis and Kathleen D'Olivo, who were interviewed many months later by a Seattle detective. And overall responsibility for the case was inexplicably delegated by Pickles to his secretary.

Susan's parents flew down immediately from Anchorage. They were frightened. "If it was one of my other children," Dale

Rancourt told the *Seattle Times*, "I'd just say, 'Stand by, they'll be back in two or three days.' But not Susan. She always was very careful."

He told the reporter that his eighteen-year-old daughter would have packed a suitcase if she was going to go somewhere overnight, and that she would have notified someone where she was going to be. "That," said Mr. Rancourt, "is just the kind of girl she is."

Any doubts the Rancourts might have had about Susan's disappearance were settled when Mrs. Rancourt looked in her daughter's dorm-room medicine cabinet and found Susan's dental floss. Never, under *any* circumstance, would this sensible girl with a mouthful of expensive dental work leave without her floss. That was not the kind of girl she was.

The Rancourts, like the Healys and Mansons before them and the many other families who would follow, endured the special agony of knowing and not knowing what had become of their daughter. As Joyce Healy remembers, "I went kind of crazy. All the time I thought, Oh my God! She's probably dead. But we cannot quit. We can't give up. We have to try."

The Rancourts, Healys, and Mansons posted rewards, hired private detectives, prayed, and endured press interviews in the hopes of keeping their daughters' pictures in the papers. The Rancourts tried, but failed, to get the national television networks to broadcast Susan's photograph. These efforts yielded nothing but the usual vicious crank responses, the supposed sightings of the girls, the late-night telephone calls from heavy breathers, and the offers from scam artists to return their daughters for a price.

As yet, however, no one thought the families shared a *common* problem. Although in each case foul play was by now thought probable, and in each case there were no good suspects, these were negative links, not the sort of positive signature policemen are trained to notice.

Later, when the connections were finally made, the police discovered that at least one girl a month was murdered. They had Healy for February, Manson for March, Rancourt for April, but no good candidate for May. In the cynical humor of people who have seen too much, they called their missing victim Miss May.

Her full name was Roberta Kathleen Parks.

On the night of May 6, 1974, Kathy Parks left her dormitory room at Oregon State University in Corvallis, 260 miles south of Seattle, and was last seen on her way to the student union building. She was a stunning twenty-two-year-old blonde who majored in religion. A sensitive girl who recovered slowly from emotional shocks, Kathy had that week quarreled by telephone with her father and then learned from her sister in Spokane that he had suffered a heart attack. Friends said Kathy was deeply depressed the day of her disappearance.

Her moodiness led police at first to believe that Kathy, like Donna Manson, might have killed herself. For a week after she was reported missing, they searched the vicinity for her body, even dragging a nearby river bottom.

When they found nothing, a flier was issued and sent to regional police agencies, just as similar data sheets had been routinely issued for the three previous victims. It was all routine. An agency like the Seattle police received notices of missing or presumed dead young women at a rate of one a week in the mid-1970s. Since the cases were outside Seattle's jurisdiction, there was rarely any reason to pay much attention to them. The fliers were posted as they came in, one on top of another. One from so far south in another state was even less likely to raise any interest.

Much that was later written about these cases would emphasize presumed similarities among the girls; a tendency among them to wear their hair long and parted in the middle was taken as a sign that the hunter was murdering the same girl over and over again. In truth, they were all white, of college age, and most of them were attractive. But they ranged from the worldly-wise to the utterly innocent, alike only in that each one was alone and vulnerable in some way—asleep, distracted, incautious, or upset.

The next victim, the first of two Miss Junes, might not have died if she hadn't been drinking.

Unlike the other girls, Brenda Carol Ball was not a student, and, at age twenty-two, she was the oldest victim to date. Brenda had spent much of the night of May 31, 1974, at the Flame tavern in Burien, a working-class town wedged between Seattle and Sea-Tac Airport to the south. The Flame was a tough, seedy joint set up on cinder blocks and known for the rough character of its patrons. There were fights there, noise complaints, and a report every month or two of a missing person last seen at the Flame.

Around 2:00 A.M. on June 1, closing time, Brenda Ball bid a beery adieu to her fellow patrons and walked out of the Flame in search of a ride. She had talked earlier of hitching to a state park to meet some friends for the weekend.

Brenda could take care of herself. She led an unstructured life that accommodated adventure, and she was largely free of inhibitions. Not until June 17 were the local authorities, the King County police, notified by her friends that Brenda was missing, last seen at the Flame.

Meanwhile, the second Miss June vanished. On page one of the *Seattle Times*'s June 12 editions, under a photograph of President Nixon and Anwar Sadat waving to a crowd of cheering, dusty Cairenes, the story of her disappearance was told:

U.W. COED, 18, DISAPPEARS ON WAY TO SORORITY

Police were seeking information today about an 18-year-old coed who disappeared early yesterday in the University District.

Georgann Hawkins of Lakewood, near Tacoma, last was seen after she left a friend's residence to return to the Kappa Alpha Theta sorority shortly after 1 A.M. yesterday.

The friend said she left via an alley. She told him she was going back to the sorority to study for a final examination.

Several acquaintances reported seeing and speaking with her as she walked back toward the sorority.

But she never arrived and friends became concerned about 3 A.M. When she failed to show up for the final examination, friends began telephoning friends and relatives, according to a sorority supervisor.

"Georgann is an absolutely stable and dependable girl," the supervisor said. "It would not be like her to leave without telling her roommate or her friends."

Then, toward the bottom of the article there came the first tentative public suggestion that these stories about missing girls might somehow be connected. "Police said they were looking for any possible links," the reporter wrote, "between the disappearance of Miss Hawkins and the January 31 disappearance of Lynda Ann Healy, 21, also a U.W. coed."

Georgann Hawkins was a conventionally pretty girl with soft brown hair and an infectious, beaming smile. She was almost exactly the same height and weight as Susan Rancourt. She also had poor eyesight.

She had been a cheerleader at suburban Lakes High School, just south of Tacoma. In her senior year, Georgann won a popularity-cum-beauty contest; she was voted her school's Daffodil Princess, an annual honor bestowed upon girls from several Tacoma-area high schools who preside at the court of the local Daffodil Festival. With the selection went the opportunity to ride with her sister princesses aboard a float in the spring Daffodil Parade through downtown Tacoma.

At the university, she was a B-plus student who somehow found the time and opportunity to be quite tanned by finals week.

The night of June 11, she had gone to an end-of-term party where she drank no more than three beers. Georgann hadn't worn her contacts that night, nor did she bring along her keys. By prior arrangement, she was going to awaken her roommate by throwing pebbles against their room windows.

After midnight, she walked partway home from the party with a girlfriend and then stopped for about a half-hour to chat with her boyfriend at the Beta Theta Pi house. She left by the fraternity's alleyside exit and stopped for maybe five minutes to chat with another Beta brother whose window was open upstairs on this warmish June night. Georgann then had less than 300 feet to walk down a brightly lit alley to her sorority house.

At about the same hour, witnesses later recalled, a tall man wearing what appeared to be a leg cast and using crutches was seen in the vicinity. He had with him a briefcase which he kept fumbling with and dropping. Descriptions offered to the police were very similar to the reports, which came in later, of the stranger with his armload of books who approached Jane Curtis and then Kathleen D'Olivo just before Susan Rancourt disappeared in Ellensburg. He had come full circle back to Seattle's University District.

As Georgann walked along, she peered forward intently, her vision without her lenses as poor as Susan Rancourt's had been that night in April. Along the way, many students' windows were open onto the alley, and at least two groups of people saw Georgann walking down the middle of the alley where the streetlights shone the brightest.

A single person, a fraternity housemother, reported that she heard a high, terrified scream that night, but no one else saw or heard anything. Georgann Hawkins' sleeping roommate didn't hear any sound at all from the darkened area where Georgann was to have stopped and tossed pebbles up. Somewhere in the last thirty or forty feet leading directly up to the back door of the sorority house, a space where the light from the streetlamps was much less intense, Georgann vanished. If she had uttered so much as a sentence, someone probably would have heard her. But no one did. One instant she was there, alive, and then nothing.

The next morning was Captain Herb Swindler's first day as the new head of the homicide squad at the Seattle police. A balding, archetypically gruff cop with thirty years' experience in everything from pounding a beat to busting narcotics traffickers, Swindler was no stranger to multiple homicide; he had worked as many as eighteen different murder cases at one time. Out of the hundreds of homicides he'd investigated over the years, only once, he claims, had he failed to identify the killer. This would be the second time.

He looked over the preliminary report on Georgann Hawkins and shook his head in disbelief. Disbelief, and recognition. Though assigned to another division throughout the preceding months, Herb Swindler had taken a professional interest in the several stories of missing girls. He hadn't seen a pattern—exactly. But he had noted the negative link, the one factor that was consistent in each case: There was no evidence. Now confronted with the Hawkins disappearance, Swindler pondered for a moment and then asked his sergeant for the homicide unit's files on the other missing girls besides Lynda Healy, on which the department already was working. To his surprise, there weren't any other files. Apparently Swindler alone among the Seattle police suspected that a single killer was responsible.

Late in June, Swindler and officers from thirty other regional police jurisdictions in several states gathered in Olympia to discuss their cases. No consensus was reached on whether a pattern was discernible, nor was the conference limited to Lynda Healy, Donna Manson, Susan Rancourt, Kathy Parks, Brenda Ball, and Georgann Hawkins. There were, as usual, dozens of "open" cases of missing persons in Washington and surrounding states. The Seattle area alone listed twenty-nine such cases at the time. Sorting through them, a detective could find what he was looking for, a common thread or no thread at all.

Yet the fact that such a meeting was called was reason enough for the *Seattle Times* and other papers to speculate on their own. Stories linking some of the cases began to appear, all speculative, and all containing the obligatory skeptical quote from an official source.

Cops like Herb Swindler might harbor their private fears, but none of them was articulating these suspicions. It would take another attack, a daylight hunt, to spark the terror.

A rare utterly blue sky greeted Seattleites as they rose on the morning of Sunday, July 14, 1974. The sun, so commonly a stranger, radiated down a luxuriant warmth that loosened limbs and bathed libidos gently. The temperature climbed into the eighties by midday—tropical weather by northwest standards. People lingered abed, dawdled over breakfast, and forwent church and household chores. It was an ideal day to go to the beach.

Swarms of sunbathers, swimmers, and picnickers, an estimated 40,000 of them in all, converged on Lake Sammamish State Park, a gorgeous recreation facility which lies twelve miles to the east of the city by way of U.S. 90, the road to Ellensburg.

That Sunday, Lake Sammamish was a riot to the senses. There was a Seattle police picnic at one end. A local brewery was sponsoring its annual beer party, complete with music and sports contests, including a keg-throwing competition. Water skiers zipped along the shoreline as toddlers gamboled in the shallows. Frisbees whirred through the air. There was the pervasive smell of suntan oil, charcoal, and burnt hamburgers.

For Janice Anne Ott, twenty-three, July 14 began with a trip to the Suds Shop laundromat across the street from her house in Issaquah, about five miles east of Lake Sammamish Park. Striking, with green eyes and reddish-blond hair that fell straight to just above her waist, Jan had been married since December of 1972 to Jim Ott, who in the summer of 1974 was living in southern California. Jan was living with a roommate. There was no particular rift between the Otts—they had chatted amiably by telephone on Saturday night, the thirteenth—but both wife and husband required a lot of breathing room.

As she waited in the laundromat for her clothes to be done, Jan struck up a conversation with the Suds Shop's owner, David McKibben. She told him that she was going to spend the day on the beach at Lake Sam, as the park familiarly was known, and that she worked as a probation officer in Seattle.

When her laundry was dry, the two decided to walk down the street for a cup of coffee. McKibben talked about how he got into the laundry business and about his two little girls. Jan told him that her outlook on life was liberated, that her parents lived in Spokane, that she used to live in Seattle, where she had been burglarized. As a result, she said, she had moved to a smaller, safer community. Jan was friendly, outgoing, and still irritated about the theft. All that she had left was her Volkswagen, her clothes, and her yellow ten-speed bike. McKibben would remember that his new friend wasn't wearing a bra.

After coffee, he headed home and Jan went back to her place to change into her black bikini. Over the swimsuit she put on a pair of Levi's cutoffs and a white blouse that she knotted at her midriff. On her feet were blue and white deck shoes.

Her husband, Jim, later told the police that Jan was a punctual, compulsively organized woman. True to her nature, she left a note on the front door. According to a police report, the note read: "I am at Lake Sammamish sunin' [sic] myself. Jan Ott." Then she climbed aboard her bike and pedaled away.

At noon, about the time that Jan Ott arrived at Lake Sam, Janice Graham, twenty-two, married, and a clerk-typist at the Boeing Company, was standing near the park bandstand. She was waiting to meet her husband and parents. A young man approached her. She guessed he was twenty-four or twenty-five years old. He was wearing a white T-shirt with red trim at the neck and, if Mrs. Graham's memory serves, he had on blue jeans.

He didn't offer his name. He told Janice that he was waiting for some friends who were supposed to help him load his sailboat onto his car. His left arm was in a sling, and he held it tightly against his body. Casually, he explained to her that he had injured it while playing racquetball. Keeping up a steady flow of conversation, he went on to ask if she had ever played the game.

No? Well, you should try it. It's a lot of fun.

With his arm hurting and his friends missing, the man wondered if Janice might help him with the boat. She was willing, and they began to walk toward the parking lot. "This is out of sight!" he exclaimed at one point. "There are so many people!"

According to Mrs. Graham, her acquaintance had curly "sandy blond" hair that he wore short on the sides and longer in the back. She estimated his height at five feet eight or five feet ten, and his weight from 150 to 160 pounds.

When they got to his car—"a newish-looking Volkswagen bug, metallic brown in color"—she saw no boat and no trailer.

"Where is it?" she asked.

"It's at my folks' house," he answered. "It's just up the hill."

"Oh," Janice said. "I really can't go with you, because I have to meet my husband and folks, What time is it?"

He consulted his watch; it was twelve-twenty, he said. Janice was already five minutes late. She had to be going.

"That's okay," he said cheerily. "I should have told you it wasn't in the parking lot. Thanks for bothering."

They walked back toward the park; he repeated his apologies and expressed his gratitude. "He was very polite at all times," Mrs. Graham recounted in her statement to the police. "Very sincere. Easy to talk to. He was real friendly and he had a nice smile."

Janice and the polite stranger parted about halfway back to the bandstand; he continued forward and she turned toward the concession area. Ten minutes or so later, as she stood eating a snow cone in the shade of a concession stand, she saw the fellow again. He was walking toward the parking lot once more. Beside him was a woman that Mrs. Graham couldn't see too well, but she remembered that the woman had a yellow bike with her. It looked like a ten-speed. Janice had two thoughts at that moment. One was that "this guy was a pretty fast worker." Secondly, "I wondered where he was going to put the bike."

Down near the water's edge, Jan Ott had found a good spot for "sunin' " herself. Sylvia Valint, fifteen, and her two high school girlfriends were stretched out next to her, not two feet away.

Sylvia watched the new arrival put down her knapsack, spread a white towel on the sand, peel off her cutoffs and blouse, and sit down. She produced an orange-colored jar and carefully applied cocoa butter from it to her skin.

In a while, maybe half an hour later, Sylvia Valint saw a man come up to her neighbor. From Sylvia's ground-level vantage, he looked to be five feet six or five feet seven, of medium build, and was darkly tanned. His hair appeared to be "blondish brown." It came down to his neck and he parted it on the side. He was clothed in white—white tennis shoes, white socks, white shorts, white T-shirt. His left arm was in a sling. According to Sylvia, a cast extended from his wrist to past his elbow.

"Excuse me," she heard him say, "could you help me put my sailboat onto my car? I can't do it myself because I broke my arm."

To Sylvia Valint's ear, his voice carried "a small English accent, kinda like a fag."

The blonde looked up and eyed her visitor for a moment. "Well," she said, "sit down and let's talk about it. Where's the boat?"

He told her that it was at his parents' house in Issaquah.

"Oh, really," she replied. "I live in Issaquah."

For the next ten minutes they talked back and forth. Plainly audible to the Valint girl were their introductions. The blonde on the towel said her name was Jan. The man called himself "Ted."

Housewife Traci Sharpe, who was sitting with her five children about ten feet from Jan and "Ted," later recalled that the young woman seemed hesitant at first. Mrs. Sharpe couldn't hear as plainly as Sylvia Valint, but she didn't think Jan Ott was buying "Ted's" line.

Yet Jan eventually got up, put on her cutoffs and blouse, and walked off with him; he assured her that he had room for her bike in his car. The witnesses remember "Ted" telling Jan how easy it would be for him to teach her to sail. Jan made him promise to introduce her to his parents.

The witnesses provided a remarkably consistent portrait of a slim, smooth-talking man who could make an unlikely story sound plausible—or at the very least inviting. There were significant differences among them as to his facial features and hairstyle—as if "Ted" were a chameleon who could change his appearance at will. But their descriptions of him matched in the most important detail, the left arm in a sling, and there were no discrepancies as to time.

Imperfect as it is, human memory was to give the police their first solid leads in the case. Of course, by then it was too late for Jan Ott.

And "Ted" wasn't through for the day.

At approximately the same time he was leading Janice Ott away from the park, nineteen-year-old Denise Marie Naslund was sitting with her boyfriend and another couple in a Seattle tavern.

Denise was in a sour mood. She and her boyfriend, Kenny Little, twenty-three, had been partying that weekend—Saturday night they had been out quite late at a card game. Denise had wanted to stay longer, but Kenny insisted they go home. Then they received an early call from Nancy Battema and Bob (also known as "Burrhead") Sargent, who wanted to go to Lake Sam. Denise wasn't up to a day in the sun; she was tired and she wanted to be sure that she was prepared for a Monday exam at her computer-programming school. Denise was serious about not wanting to be a secretary all her life.

Kenny, however, wanted to go, and Denise generally tried to please Kenny. A few days before, she had asked him his favorite color. He said blue, and Denise promptly changed her fingernail polish to that color.

Denise was very close to her mother, Eleanor Rose, who had recently been separated from her second husband. Denise worried about Eleanor's health. On Sunday morning, before she and Kenny left to meet Nancy and Bob, Denise called her mother. She told Eleanor that she really didn't feel like going to the beach, and she also said that if her mom wasn't feeling better by Monday she was personally going to take her to the doctor.

An attractive, dark-eyed girl with long brown hair, Denise was a little vain; she took great care with her appearance and was rewarded with the attention she enjoyed. When she and Nancy went to bars together, Denise often sat at a table by herself so that men would notice her and ask her to dance.

Usually, that was as far as she went with them. "She's not the type that talks a lot," Nancy Battema told the police. "She doesn't seem to be overly impressed by any guy. She wouldn't go out of her way to talk to anybody, nor would she go out of her way to avoid anyone."

Denise made moderate use of drugs. According to her friends, it was rare to find her without a supply of downers. On the way to the park from the tavern in her tan Chevy—a gift from Eleanor—Denise popped four five-milligram Valiums. Her companions each took a number of pills as well.

The beer and Valiums did not immediately take the edge off her mood. She complained that her car wasn't running well. Kenny said he'd fix it. Later on in the day, they snapped at each other over whose responsibility it was to retrieve Kenny's dog when it wandered off.

But Kenny and Denise weren't really fighting. For the most part, she seemed to be enjoying herself. They met some friends, walked around in the crowd for a bit, had a snack at the concession stand, and drank beer from the big ice chest they'd brought along. The four friends also passed around a joint.

Meanwhile, "Ted" had returned. Sindi Seidenbaum, sixteen, recounted the following to the police:

> Approximately 4:00 P.M. I was heading back from the restrooms toward the point where my friends were. I was about 100 yards from the restrooms when a man who was walking towards me said: excuse me young lady could you help me launch my sailboat. I then asked him what he had done to his arm, he stated that he had sprained it and he couldn't find anyone to help him. I told him I was sorry but

couldn't find anyone to help him. I told him I was sorry but I couldn't help him because I had people waiting. The last I saw of him he was walking toward the restrooms. He was about 6′ 0″ or 6′ 2″. I'm not sure how much he weighed but I remember that he was really skinny. I would say that he had a small frame and kind of boney. His hair was salt and pepper colored about 2″ below his ears. It was parted in the middle and bangs over his forehead. It was curly but looked like it had been styled. I think his eyes were either green or blue and he looked bugeyed and set back. His pupils were real small. I would guess this man to be in his 30s. He was clean shaven. It appeared to me that he was nervous. He spoke rapidly and gestured with his hand. His left arm was in a sling and it appeared to be the type a doctor would put on somebody. He was wearing a sort of bleached white boxer swimming suit with elastic for a waist band. His body had a full tan. He had sort of a pointed nose and thin lips.

Next, he approached nineteen-year-old Pat Turner, who had come to the park with her boyfriend Nick. Pat was on her way to the restrooms at about four-fifteen, when he walked up to her with the story about the sailboat. She wasn't feeling well—too much sun—and Pat Turner had no inclination to help strangers with boats. The guy did seem friendly. He was good-looking. But Pat just looked at him as if she didn't understand, then walked off, probably saving her life.

By four, the temperature had pushed into the nineties and Denise Naslund had grown languorous. She told Nancy that she was feeling high, then dozed off for a while in her faded Lee cutoffs and dark blue halter top. Shortly, Kenny fell asleep, too.

Nancy remembered that Denise awoke about four-twenty and they talked for a few minutes. Then, without a word, Denise rose and walked off toward the restrooms. A witness reported seeing Denise in the women's room.

Another said she had seen a girl with long dark hair and wearing a blue halter top laughing with a group of "motorcycle guys." The girl jumped on behind one biker and they turned a couple of circles in the gravel before he drove off toward the parking lot. The girl was shouting, "No I can't! Let me off!" as they sped away.

Kenny awoke a half-hour later to discover Denise gone and he immediately sensed trouble. She didn't have her purse with her;

it was locked in the trunk of her car. Denise would venture nowhere on her own without her cosmetics.

With deepening concern for her whereabouts, Kenny and Bob and Nancy began to search the park. The crowds thinned as twilight approached. Still no Denise. Darkness came. They called for her, asked people if they'd seen her. Nothing.

At eight-thirty, they gave up. Kenny called the police, who told him that a person must be gone twenty-four hours before she's even a candidate for a missing persons investigation. Besides, a relative must make the report.

When Kenny pulled up in Denise's car in front of her mother's house that night, Mrs. Rose ran outside in an instant panic. Kenny was barely able to get the story out before she was back in the house and on the telephone. "I told the police, 'I know Denise would never take off and leave her car,' " Eleanor remembers. "She was so happy when I bought that for her. Or leave her purse. She took too much pride in how she looked. I knew something happened."

The following afternoon, Jan Ott's roommate reported her missing, too, and suddenly the case turned urgent. Divers were dispatched to search the lake bottom for Denise and Jan. Police helicopters crisscrossed above the park and surrounding countryside, using infrared devices to scan for bodies. On the ground, police and volunteers scoured the park searching for clues, anything, and apprehensive about what they might discover. Among the hundreds of items turned in for laboratory analysis were twenty-six pairs of women's underpants picked up throughout the park. But no trace of Denise or Jan was found.

Primary responsibility for investigating the twin disappearances fell to the King County police, who also were handling the Ball case. Captain J.N. (Nick) Mackie headed up the county police investigative unit, but almost from the start—and for several years to come—the point man in the investigation was detective Bob Keppel.

Thirty-one years old, slender and intense, the bespectacled Bob Keppel had handled but a single homicide as a detective in his four years with the county police. All at once, he and his fellow detectives where charged with finding—and stopping— the man who would become the most notorious mass killer in the state's history.

At first, Keppel had discounted the possibility of a single killer stalking the region. He knew of the many similarities between the Hawkins and Rancourt cases. "But," he says, "it was incomprehensible that someone would cross over Snoqualmie Pass, it's such a geographical barrier." Keppel positively did not connect Brenda Ball's disappearance with Hawkins or Rancourt or any of the other cases.

But after talking to Janice Graham, Sylvia Valint, Sindi Seidenbaum, and the rest of the Lake Sammamish witnesses, "Ted's" use of a prop, the sling, seemed certain. Later, it would be pieced together with Lynda Healy's bed with its hospital corners, the speculum used on Mary Adams, and the crutches and leg cast seen on the man with the briefcase the night Georgann Hawkins disappeared.

It was Keppel who, with the help of Alfred Pickles' secretary, reinvestigated the Rancourt case and found Jane Curtis and Kathleen D'Olivo, the Ellensburg co-eds who had encountered the stranger with the finger splint and sling. After interviewing the girls, Keppel had no choice but to concede that "Ted" not only might have abducted Susan Rancourt 120 miles east of Seattle, but that he had gone hunting at least twice in Ellensburg.

The proces then became deductive. If "Ted" killed Healy, Manson, and Rancourt, it was logical that he had taken a victim in May.

Keppel and the other detectives reviewed all the missing-female cases for May, and then eliminated each until they came to Roberta Kathleen Parks. Connecting *her* to "Ted" was even less probable than linking him to Susan Rancourt; she disappeared 260 miles away in another state. But by now, Keppel wasn't going to discount any possibilities when it came to "Ted." Kathy Parks's medical and dental records were officially requested.

Herb Swindler, in charge of the Healy and Hawkins cases, publicly refused to connect them with the Lake Sammamish abductions or any other missing girls, even though he was more certain than ever that "Ted" was a mass killer. The newspapers, however, were undeterred by Swindler's and other officials' efforts not to panic the population. A well-known Seattle psychiatrist was quoted as saying "Ted," if he was a mass killer, probably was "a pretty sick guy who needs to boost his ego by throwing the population into terror."

Failing to find a local cop willing to speculate, reporters interviewed police in distant cities. "You folks have a problem," said a Denver detective after a reporter summarized the several cases to him. "I've never run into anything like that," commented a police sergeant from Phoenix. "Sounds to me like you're dealing with a real nut."

Predictably, such stories and the evident lack of progress in the case spread alarm throughout the population. Nick Mackie held periodic news conferences in which he promised that every lead would be followed. Tacitly conceding that the investigation was going nowhere, he pleaded for anyone who had been at Lake Sam with a camera that day to please bring his film downtown. Thousands of feet of news film and hundreds of snapshots were shown to the witnesses, but none of them recognized "Ted."

With no positive identifications, a series of composite sketches were published, along with the information that "Ted" might drive a Volkswagen and that he spoke with a slight British accent.

Thousands of calls came in to the police, many of them of the crank variety. One man reported seeing Denise Naslund riding Janice Ott's bike in downtown Seattle. Another offered the use of his "body-finding machine." Frightened women reported "Ted" sightings by the hundreds. Men who resembled the composite pictures, or owned a Volkswagen, or were named Ted found it advisable to stay home. In one grimly ironic incident, Lynda Healy's younger sister, Laura, was accosted by a strange man at her job in a FotoMat booth. She called her mother, who dispatched brother Robert to pick her up. The police, who arrived at the scene before Robert, noticed his Volkswagen and that he vaguely resembled one of the "Ted" composites. The police nearly arrested him before Laura could explain that Robert was her brother.

In the absence of any concrete leads as to "Ted's" identity, many northwesterners thought the answer would be found in occultism or Satan worship, creeds that local police say have long found a small but ardent following of practitioners around Seattle. One rumor given broad currency was that "Ted" had been a Jesus freak gone insane after a trip to South America. The theory was that "Ted" believed himself to be the reincarnation of a broken-winged Inca bird god.

Herb Swindler wasn't buying anything so outrageous, but neither was the frustrated investigator above checking out the occult angle. Working quietly and, for the most part, alone, he put together what became File 1004, a dossier on area occultism. In the end, the effort led him no closer to "Ted," but in the absence of anything more substantive to go on, he felt obliged to try.

Swindler took a lot of criticism from the county police and prosecutor's office for his probe into the occult, yet from the perspective of retirement he still defends the interest he took in the subject. "The weirdest thing about these homicides was the lack of any information," he says. "That was really strange. Nobody saw anything. Nobody heard anything. We didn't have a body. The earth just opened up and swallowed the girls down."

At the same time, "this occult stuff was hot and heavy all over. Anything was possible as far as we were concerned. We didn't have anything. The occult sounded as good as anything else we had. In fact, it sounded better because there was such a definite pattern to the known disappearances." Swindler emphasized the word "known."

He also consulted a psychic, Regina Hoffenbrauer, from nearby Kent, Washington. "She scared the hell out of me sometimes," Swindler admits. "She was sorta weird."

Hoffenbrauer spoke with the missing girls' families and handled various items of the girls' belongings. The idea of dealing with a psychic was anathema to Joyce Healy; that she cooperated was a measure of her desperation.

The psychic predicted that "Ted" would kill eleven girls, then move on. That number is very close to the probable count. Most northwest police think that he killed between twelve and eighteen women in the region. Hoffenbrauer told Swindler that several of the bodies would be found east of Seattle, that Georgann Hawkins had been dumped in a riverbed, and that Denise Naslund and Janice Ott lay together on a hillside.

Early in August of 1974, a construction worker sat down for lunch near a road project on U.S. 90 where it passes through Issaquah and begins the vertiginous climb up past North Bend and over Snoqualmie Pass. He found a place to sit on a hillside and opened his lunch pail. Immediately, the stench of putrefying flesh filled his nostrils. He quickly moved away, thinking someone must have poached a deer, or even a black bear, and then left the innards to rot. He thought wrong, but by the time he came forward with his story, potentially valuable evidence had been destroyed.

The summer wore on with no progress in any of the cases. No new disappearances were reported in the press, and the number of newspaper articles fell off. There was little or nothing to report, and Richard Nixon's resignation dominated the front pages. The searches for Denise and Janice were suspended. Labor Day came and went.

Bird-hunting season began. It is the time of year in the northwest when local medical examiners expect reports of grisly discoveries that nearly always turn out to be the remains of elk, bears, deer, dogs, or any of a number of other animals that died over the summer. Sometimes during this "Bone Season" the remains are human, but then they are usually from primitive Indian burial sites.

In early September of 1974, however, the Issaquah hillside that had reeked so in August yielded up a discovery that sent fresh shock waves of terror through the northwest.

September 7, 1974, was the first day of grouse season. Elzie Hammons, thirty-six, loaded his shotgun and drove over to pick up his neighbor, Elza E. Rankin, seventy-one. The hunters headed out in Hammons' jeep for Issaquah and a certain hillside where Elzie had bagged two grouse the previous year. There was good hunting around in there, he told Rankin.

Around ten that morning, Hammons was walking along an abandoned logging road that cut across the slope. The road was overgrown with weeds, and heavy underbrush lined both sides. Moving as slowly and as quietly as possible, Hammons inched forward until an object right in front of him in the roadway made him freeze. His stomach knotted. There, grotesquely splayed across the road, was a skeleton, its yellow-brown bones still connected in most places by desiccated sinews. A few feet away he spotted what was obviously a human skull.

Hammons hustled down the hillside to find his friend Elza Rankin talking with a pair of young target shooters. When Elzie told them of his discovery, they laughed and assured him he had probably found animal remains.

Hammons knew better. "If you don't believe me," he said, "come back with me and I'll show you."

The four returned to the logging road. On the way, one of them caught sight of a long hank of dark hair, almost two feet long. It took just one look at the bones and the doubters were convinced.

They hurried into town and notified the Issaquah police, who in turn called the King County police. By noon, a team led by Bob Keppel had cordoned off the hillside and begun a search of the scene.

News of the discovery made the September 8 newspapers.

They carried initial reports from police indicating that none of the bones discovered in Issaquah belonged to the missing women.

Eleanor Rose, Denise Naslund's mother, heard of the discovery on her car radio and immediately dashed to the scene. As she stood at the bottom of the hill, her fears were allayed by the early news. The cops didn't think Denise was up there in the brush. "We're so very glad, so relieved," she told a reporter.

By the time they had finished, the searchers found twenty-six bones in all, and eight clumps of dark brown and reddish-blond hair strewn over an area about 150 feet across. From the position of the bones, it was evident that the bodies had been dumped farther up the hill, then were dragged down piece by piece into the brush by animals. There were gnaw marks on the bones from coyotes, rodents, and possibly even bears. Among the finds were two spines, a skull, and two lower jawbones. No jewelry or clothes were found.

The police had assuaged Eleanor Rose's worries on the basis of the nearly perfect upper teeth found in the skull. Denise had had a good deal of dental work. But Mrs. Rose's relief was short-lived.

Dr. Daris Swindler, a forensic anthropologist at the University of Washington (and a distant relative of Herb Swindler), took two eternally slow days to make the identifications. From X rays and dental records he concluded that, beyond a doubt, one of the lower jaws belonged to Denise Naslund. He used dental records to identify Janice Ott as well.

But he remembers something else about Janice Ott, a Faustian tableau in his study. The skull he was given was radically elongated, the result of a premature closure of its main cranial suture. "She would never have known about it herself," he says. "It has nothing to do with intelligence. It's just a thing that happens occasionally."

Dr. Swindler cradled the bleached skull in one hand and compared it with Jan Ott's photograph. They matched; an image in life and the substance of death. "It was," he says, "an eerie feeling."

An extra femur, or thighbone, was found at the site, too. It definitely was female, meaning a third girl had been dumped there. Her identity has never been established.

That was about all the police would learn. Janice Ott's bike was never found. It seemed likely that the girls had been killed elsewhere, but no certain cause, or time, of death could be established.

A month later, the remains of two more women were discovered by a deer hunter in rugged countryside between Olympia and the Oregon border. On October 15, 1974, the *Seattle Times* reported that the unidentified skeletons suggested "ominous parallels" with Denise Naslund's and Janice Ott's remains. "The parallels," the paper reported, "include the fact that no traces of clothing were found in either place. In addition, all the bodies apparently were left on the surface of the ground. As in the case of the Issaquah bones, authorities could only guess at a cause of death—probably strangulation. Another similarity is that both areas are a short distance off abandoned roads that can be traveled by vehicles."

Daris Swindler identified just one of the two victims. She was twenty-year-old Carol Valenzuela, and she had vanished from downtown Vancouver, Washington, around noon on a Friday, nineteen days after Naslund and Ott were killed. Carol Valenzuela became Miss August.

The second girl, who has remained unidentified, had long dark hair, was white, stood five feet five to five feet seven, weighed about 125 pounds, and was somewhere between seventeen and twenty-three years old.

All that "Ted" had left for the police was a collection of ravaged bones, hair, and sinew—silent, mocking testimony to the fate of his victims and the helplessness of his would-be captors.

In piteous distress at losing her only daughter, Eleanor Rose asked the King County police if she might have Denise's remains for burial. A compromise was worked out.

A *Seattle Times* reporter was on hand on a characteristically gloomy autumn Saturday when Eleanor, her son Brock, and Denise's father came to Holy Family Catholic Church to hear Father Sean Henighan say the Mass of Christian Burial for Denise. The correspondent noted that several detectives attended the service as well.

Bob Keppel and the other investigators had brought Denise Naslund's remains from a police evidence locker. They sat in the church watching the small group of mourners in the hopes that "Ted," whoever he was, might come to the service.

Father Henighan spoke of the "useless, senseless death that has happened to Denise." He closed by reading a letter she had written to Eleanor after her 1973 graduation from high school. "Dear Mom," Denise wrote, "I can't put into words everything you have done for me. In my life, I've had so much more than some people ever have. I've been very lucky."

The priest blessed the casket and the service was over. Then Keppel and the other officers collected Denise's few bones and tufts of hair from the bier and returned them to the evidence locker downtown. Until the case was officially solved, Denise was police property. She still is.

Winter came to western Washington, and the game hunters left the forests. For the next several months, there would be no more discoveries, and no more reported disappearances.

The northwest newspapers didn't fix on this apparent halt to "Ted's" predations; they continued to treat him as a palpable threat to the area's young women. The level of fear in and around Seattle did not subside.

Yet the police noted the break in "Ted's" pattern. After Carol Valenzuela, there was no Miss September. No Miss October. No Miss November or December. Bob Keppel began to suspect "Ted" had left, just as Herb Swindler's psychic had predicted he would.

Maybe, Keppel thought, "Ted" was a merchant seaman. If so, Seattle and the region were safe again. But so, too, would be "Ted." His identity might never be known.

So 1974 ended and spring approached. The days lengthened and hikers and fishermen ventured out. Another "Bone Season" was about to begin.

On Saturday, March 1, 1975, a call came in to Bob Keppel's office. Two forestry students, he was told, had stumbled onto a skull in the wilds ten miles east of Issaquah, and four miles to the south of U.S. 90. The discovery had been made on the lower slopes of Taylor Mountain, near the town of North Bend.

Keppel gathered up his records, the X rays and dental charts he'd collected and studied since the previous summer, and sped to the scene, a damp, slippery incline covered with brambles, rotting logs, and saplings. All along, he'd been sure that another dumping ground would be found. This time, he hoped, "Ted" might have left some trace of himself, some tangible clue. To date, all Keppel had been able to do was to clean up after his quarry.

Earlier, there had been another find near Taylor Mountain. Herb Swindler's people had turned up some animal bones in an old house. Still working his occult angle, Swindler wondered if they were goat bones, indicative of black rites. Instead, Dr.

Daris Swindler had identified them as the remains of an immature elk.

But a human skull was something different. Keppel saw to it that the entire mountainside around the skull was sealed off, and then sent the bare remains to Seattle for identification. The next morning, the report came back: Brenda Carol Ball, twenty-two, last seen alive at the Flame tavern, had been murdered and dumped on Taylor Mountain. Her skull had been fractured.

For the next eight days, Keppel supervised 200 police and volunteers as they scoured the mountainside inch by inch. Their work was tedious, hideous, heartbreaking.

Keppel himself made the second discovery. The detective was negotiating the steep slope when his feet slipped from beneath him, sending him tumbling down through the tangled underbrush. He landed in a heap, covered in muck and wet leaves. Keppel grunted, stood up and saw before him Death's face, two empty black eye sockets staring frozen on infinity. Death was smiling at him with pretty, expensive teeth; he knew instantly that he'd found Susan Rancourt. He looked more closely and saw that Susan's skull was cracked.

Next came Kathy Parks's skull. The beauty from Oregon State University had been brought 260 miles north and dumped for the animals to eat.

The last to be identified was the first to have been murdered. Joyce and Jim Healy's eldest child, Lynda, the blue-eyed ski-report announcer, was there on Taylor Mountain, too. According to her mother, she was identified on the basis of a single tooth.

The forensic experts who examined the bones could not say with certainty how the girls had died. If the cranial fractures came from human blows, however, some would have required a heavy blunt instrument, such as a tire iron, wielded with incredible fury.

Other factors were more clearly understood. "Ted" had dumped the girls near the roadside after removing all jewelry and clothing. Then the animals had begun their work. Soft, fleshy parts of the bodies were consumed near where they had been left. Then the heads and jaws were torn away and carried back into the brush. Along the way, a hank of hair or a lower jaw might drop off. Farthest away from the road were the skulls, which took the scavengers the longest to penetrate and devour.

Bob Keppel felt he could infer a sequence. The early victims had been brought one by one to Taylor Mountain. The only girl whose remains were not found (or identified) was Donna Gail

Manson. Either she had been taken elsewhere, which seemed unlikely, or some animal had taken her head miles back over the mountain.

In June, "Ted" had apparently abandoned this dumping site and begun using one closer to Seattle—Issaquah. There, resting with Denise Naslund and Janice Ott, was the unidentifiable female, probably that of Georgann Hawkins.

Then, in August, "Ted" began hunting farther south—as far as Vancouver, Washington, on the Oregon border. Here he began his third burial ground. And here was found Miss August, Carol Valenzuela, and her mystery companion in death. She, some police officers felt, had not been a local girl at all, but more probably a hitchhiker, maybe from California, whom "Ted" had chanced upon.

Taylor Mountain was the last "Ted" dumping ground to be found, although others may exist. It established beyond reasonable doubt that he had hunted for months through the northwest, murdering almost at his leisure. What it did not establish was who "Ted" was—and *where* he was, now that the victims had been found.

Bob Keppel had assumed he'd left the area, and Bob Keppel was correct. The previous September, a month after Miss August disappeared, Ted Bundy had moved on to Utah.

# TWO

No ONE noticed that he was different, not like other children. He looked and acted like them. He believed in Santa Claus, hated vegetables, and sometimes imagined ogres and scaly things crouching in his closet waiting for night to fall.

But he was haunted by something else: a fear, a doubt—sometimes only a vague uneasiness—that inhabited his mind with the subtlety of a cat. He felt it for years and years, but he didn't recognize it for what it was until much later. By then this flaw, the rip in his psyche, had become the locus of a cold homicidal rage.

He was born to a prim, modest department store clerk, the eldest of three daughters in the family of a Philadelphia nurseryman. In 1946, fresh out of high school, she was seduced by a rakish veteran of the recent war who hinted to her of an old-money pedigree.

Soon she was pregnant, and Jack Worthington, as he called himself, stopped coming around. Her minister tried to find him. But there was no record of a Jack Worthington at the proper prep school he said he had attended, or at the high-paying job he said he held. Louise Cowell had seen the last of the first man in her life, and she wasn't even sure she knew his real name.

The times were not cordial to women in her predicament, nor was Louise Cowell insulated by family means from the consequences of her misplaced trust. Shamed and used, she braved her way through the first seven months of her term before traveling north to the Elizabeth Lund Home for Unwed Mothers in Burlington, Vermont. On November 24, 1946, she gave birth to her love child. Louise named him Theodore. She had always liked that name.

Just before his fourth birthday, Teddy and his mother left Philadelphia to join her uncle and his family in Tacoma,

Washington. Later, a story attributed to the adult Ted Bundy had it that Louise posed as his older sister, not his mother. This is not so; he always knew her as Mom. However, the little boy was angry and confused about being torn from his grandfather, who doted upon him, and his grandfather's comfortable old house. Teddy didn't know why his last name was briefly changed to Nelson—a temporary measure designed to deter strangers from asking embarrassing questions—or why they had to go live with his great-uncle Jack. He didn't understand why his mother wanted to start a new life.

He also hated Tacoma at first. After Philadelphia, Tacoma seemed raw and impermanent to him—just a jumble of ugly brown and gray buildings on a hillside surrounded by water and mountains. He would outgrow this initial distaste for his new home, but he never got over an innate arrogant disdain for anything he regarded as common. This attitude was linked to how he felt about himself, his self-doubt, and also to his later conviction that life had wronged him.

Jack Cowell was only a few years older than Louise, his niece, and Teddy always called him uncle. A music professor at Tacoma's College of Puget Sound, Uncle Jack was a man of some refinement. His gleaming dark piano, the classical music that filled the house, his air of cultivation, drew Teddy to him. Early on, Teddy decided to pattern himself after Uncle Jack.

Louise went to work as a secretary at the Council of Churches office in downtown Tacoma. There she was befriended by a female coworker who coaxed the tentative newcomer into attending young adult nights at the First Methodist Church. One evening, Louise was introduced to John Culpepper Bundy, known as Johnnie, a soft-spoken North Carolinian who had recently been mustered out of the Navy in nearby Bremerton.

Johnnie's drawl made him seem a little slow, a serious defect as far as Teddy would be concerned. He was unlettered, and his prospects in life were those of a modest southern country boy. With his Navy hitch over, Johnnie had decided to remain in the northwest. He found a job as a cook at a Veterans Administration hospital a few miles south of Tacoma. It turned out to be his life's work.

From the start, Johnnie and Louise saw something special in each other. Johnnie was steady and uncomplicated—the exact opposite of Teddy's errant father—and he fulfilled Louise's first and ultimate requirement by accepting both her and her son. She was also drawn to his mild disposition, although her son Teddy would later learn the consequences of crossing his quiet stepfather.

For Johnnie, Louise was a gentle, God-fearing woman whose history began on the night they met. He didn't ask questions, and beyond the bare facts of her life, Louise did not go into details.

From what Ted could tell us of his boyhood, he seems to have tried to block Johnnie, the interloper, from his mind. Clearly, Johnnie's presence upset him. He remembers staging a scene in a Sears store parking lot and wetting his pants. He conceded to me that this tantrum and others probably were a result of his jealousy over Louise, and his fear that Johnnie's advent would further disrupt his boyhood.

Louise miscarried the summer following her May 1951 marriage to Johnnie. Then a daughter, Linda, was born in the last part of 1952. Here was another confusing mystery for Teddy. He didn't know where babies came from or how they were made. But he knew it had something to do with Johnnie, and he has thought all his life that Louise suffered a great deal at Linda's birth. According to Louise, the pregnancy was uneventful.

Ted told me, without elaborating, that it was around this time that his parents broke him of the habit of crawling into bed with them when he grew frightened in the middle of the night.

The earliest indication of Ted's behavior outside the family comes from his first-grade teacher, Mrs. Oyster. According to Louise, Ted was very fond of Mrs. Oyster. On his report card, the teacher wrote Louise that Teddy grasped the numbers one through twenty, knew the meaning of one hundred, was at ease before the class, and expressed himself well. Ted remembers that he was "unsettled" when Mrs. Oyster left to have a baby and was replaced by a substitute teacher.

However much that affected him, he was definitely upset by his second-grade teacher, a doctrinaire Catholic named Miss Geri. "She was about five feet tall," Ted remembers, "with the shape and menacing attitude of a cannonball about ready to explode." Teddy Bundy, a Protestant, felt Miss Geri discriminated against him; and he vividly recalls the day she broke a ruler over his knuckles for having socked a classmate in the nose during a playground scuffle.

Ted was about seven or eight years old at this point, a not-unusual child from all appearances, and so far only minimally affected by his flaw, the presence of which he only sensed through the uneasiness he often felt. He sometimes escaped into a fantasy about being adopted by Roy Rogers and Dale Evans; a key feature of the fantasy was having his own pony and being rich enough to have anything else he wanted.

His first gesture of defiance was passive; Teddy couldn't yet articulate his hostility, or even recognize it himself, but his acts revealed it. A black family moved onto the block, arousing fears among the whites that their property values were going to be destroyed. Teddy knew that Johnnie was particularly concerned, and that his "dad" was unfavorably disposed toward blacks. So he went out of his way to make friends with one of the black children. "That house," he told me, "was a warm, friendly place, fairly bursting with clouds of pungent odors emerging from the kitchen. Smells that never came from my parents' house and that I just found terribly exotic."

At home, Teddy felt deprived. He was jealous of his cousin John, Uncle Jack's boy, and contemptuous of his own family's modest lifestyle. Ted told me he was mortified by the sensible Ramblers that Johnnie drove, so much so that he recalls being "humiliated" to be seen in them. Likewise, from the time he could first walk and talk, little Teddy always pulled his mother to the most expensive racks in clothing stores. The preoccupation with material possessions would stay with the boy and intensify. Even the little Teddy was deeply class-conscious.

With the birth of another child, Glenn, in February of 1954, the Bundys had outgrown their second house. The following summer, they moved to a roomier tract-development house that would be large enough to accommodate the present family plus the final two arrivals: another daughter, Sandra, in 1956 and a son, Richard, in 1961. This time, Teddy found his new neighborhood decidedly unappealing. The tract had been thrown up in haste and with no eye toward esthetics. It looked to Teddy as if every bit of vegetation had been scraped away, leaving ragged clumps of Scotch broom to invade where graceful firs once stood.

He became close friends with two boys in his new neighborhood, and they would continue to be his nearest pals all the way through high school. One was a gregarious kid named Terry Storwick. Today, Terry is an insurance executive in southern California. The other friend was a roly-poly youngster named Warren Dodge. Warren still lives near the old neighborhood and is manager of a large grocery store.

Terry and Warren found their new friend to be great company, even if he was a little aloof at times—brittle, even. There was also the matter of Teddy's temper. Behind his house in the field of Scotch broom, the boys played guerrilla war games, using as weapons the sword, or spear, fern, which when lopped off a foot or so above the ground made a perfect missile to fling at one another. One afternoon in the heat of combat, Warren caught Teddy just below the eye with the clotty, fibrous root that formed the nose of the fern missile. In an instant, Teddy was on top of Warren, his fist cocked. Terry and the other boys pulled him off before he could hit Warren.

The incident has stayed with Terry Storwick, not because the show of anger was so unusual for an overexcited child, but because the child was Teddy Bundy. "Ted kept himself separate from situations," Terry told me. "So it was something to see him get involved. When he got hit in the eye, he definitely got involved."

Teddy's short fuse got him into other scrapes. At boy scout camp (which he loathed for the discomfort of sweat and overall grittiness), he shoved a plate in fellow scout Jim Rohr's face because Rohr had hatcheted a small tree. Johnnie Bundy, who was an assistant scoutmaster for a time, once misguided the troop in Millersylvania State Park, near Olympia. There was grumbling, little-boy nastiness directed toward Johnnie and taken personally by Teddy.

"He and John Moon got into a kind of scuffle," says Storwick. "Bundy hit him over the head with a stick. It was a very deliberate attack on another person, and the way John Moon described it, he was attacked from behind."

Terry added: "It was really easy to see when Ted got mad. His eyes turned just about black. I suppose that sounds like something out of a cheap novel, but you could see it. He has blue eyes that are kind of flecked with darker colors. When he gets hot, they seem to get less blue and more dark. It didn't have to be a physical affront, either. Someone would say something, and you could see it in his face. The dark flecks seemed to expand."

Like most of her contemporaries, it was Louise Bundy, not Johnnie, who took the most direct hand in raising the family. "We didn't talk a lot about real personal matters," says Ted. "Certainly never about sex or any of those things. My mom has trouble talking on intimate, personal terms. There's this logjam of feeling in her that she doesn't open up and explain.

"We never spoke about her childhood, aside from the fact that she grew up in my grandfather's house with my aunts and my grandma. And that she was extremely successful in high school.

The head of everything! I read her yearbook. She was president of this and president of that, a terribly popular person. Her big disappointment was that she had one B in three years of high school."

Ted reflected for a minute. "And then, I don't know," he went on, "something intervened. I can remember her having some resentment that there was only one scholarship offered in her school, and the richest girl got it. Of course, my mom didn't have enough money to go to school. And she didn't think it was very equitable that the other girl, who had straight A's, got the scholarship. Even years and years later, I detected a strong sorrow in her voice when she told me about it."

His mother's son, Ted always kept himself apart, a device for masking his insecurities. This solitude abetted fantasy, some of it inspired by the late-night radio talk shows he enjoyed listening to. Alone in the dark, he would pretend he was part of a special and secret world. "I'd really get into it," he told me. "As people would be calling in and speaking their minds, I'd be formulating questions as if they were talking to me. It gave me a great deal of comfort to listen to them, and often it didn't make a hell of a lot of difference what they were talking about. Here were people talking, and I was eavesdropping on their conversations."

Ted simply did not want to grow up. Throughout my conversations with him, he would return again and again to recollections of warm, safe places—his grandfather's house, the black family's kitchen, his bedroom and radio. He remembers his grandfather's greenhouse in Philadelphia as such a place; all his life Ted has loved greenhouses. He aches to be enclosed, protected—one reason he would find his prison cells more comforting than confining.

As he matured physically, he developed into a well-coordinated athlete, and a handsome young man. Yet the mental maturity was not there and never would be. Ted was extremely self-conscious and considered himself too skinny to compete with the bigger boys. "I attempted to get on the school basketball team and a couple of baseball teams and I failed," he says. "It was terribly traumatic for me. I just didn't know what to do. I thought it was something personal."

He turned to solitary sports. Terry Storwick remembers that he "really took to skiing. He found the money somehow to buy good equipment. He was pretty serious about it, and he considered himself a pretty good skier."

Ted's costly ski gear was probably stolen, a fact that would have shocked family friends who knew the eldest Bundy boy as a regular churchgoer with his parents, vice-president of the Methodist Youth Fellowship, and a promising teenager interested in a career in law enforcement. Nor could they have imagined that Ted, along with several other boys, had devised a crude ski-lift ticket forgery scheme that involved the careful bleaching and dyeing of the color-coded passes. They were never caught.

Far more ominous, however, were the embitterment and hostility, also unsuspected, that were growing within him.

One day—or so he now insists—Ted was rummaging through some of his parents' papers. He found his birth certificate with "unknown" typed in under "Father's Name." According to a circumspect letter to us from Ted, "it was not an agonizing occasion. I saw it more as an opportunity to make a decision about who I was."

Ted wrote that he took a long walk and came back reconciled to this new knowledge. "It may have gone something like this: 'I am who I am, and what I am I owe to my Mom, Dad, Granddad, and others who raised me.' (Not necessarily profound, but not a bad beginning for a young kid.) Why be concerned about someone I never knew? My Mom loved me enough to give birth to me, care for me and love me. This seemed to be more than enough."

However, a recent book written by his onetime fiancée reports that Ted's cousin John taunted him about his birth. According to her, Ted at first angrily refused to believe his cousin, and would not until John produced Ted's birth certificate. She says that Ted was furious with his mother for leaving him open to such humiliation.

Terry Storwick's unclouded recollections are probably the most reliable. He is the first person with whom Ted shared his knowledge. "Ted never told me how he discovered he was illegitimate," says Terry. "We were in high school and were down at my parents' beach place talking about some personal subject. It might have had to do with how he was arguing with his dad. He just says, 'Of course, you know that's not my real father.'

"It was a bellringer! A lot of things fell into place for me right then and there. I said, 'Well, why is your name Bundy?' He went on to tell me that he'd been born in Philadelphia. Very vague stuff, the rat didn't marry his mother and such.

"I think he was wondering how I was going to think about

him. It seemed to me that this was kind of like being adopted or
something. 'So?' I said. 'There are people who love you now.' I
think I said I thought it was no big deal.

"But he said something to the effect that for him it made a big
difference. This was important to him. It wasn't just something
to be swept under the rug. When I made light of his situation he
said, 'Well, it's not you that's a bastard.' He was bitter when he
said it."

However Ted handled the idea that he was Louise's son by
someone other than Johnnie, it is possible that it was *Ted,* not
Louise, who bore the true resentment for her single mistake, a
hatred at her for committing the impure act that created him. As
far as we know, Ted has never shown *open* resentment or
hostility toward his mother. But following the discovery of his
illegitimacy, Ted's attitude toward Johnnie degenerated into outright defiance.

"Ted's mother loved him very much," Terry Storwick
remembers. "I'm sure that she protected him from Johnnie's
temper. It wasn't that Johnnie was an unreasonable man; I think
his temper was a reaction to Ted's animosity."

The schism between man and boy was expressed in Ted's
sudden refusal to call Johnnie "Dad," after having done so for
years. He began to call Johnnie "Father," then, finally, "John."

"You know, Ted was *way* ahead of Johnnie when it came to
intellectual things," Storwick told me. "He could just talk him
into holes in the ground, leave him no way out but to use his
body. Johnnie is a man of few and simple words, and Ted was
his match by the time he was in the sixth grade. A couple of
times, I thought his dad was going to kill him. The anger was
there, you know.

"Back then, John Bundy was a wiry little sucker, well muscled.
I remember one particular occasion at their lake place. He was
out cutting wood or something. Ted was, I guess, showing off
for me—smart assin'. John took a swing at him and if he
would've hit him he would have laid him flat on his ass. He had
a temper as quick as Ted's."

Ted evidently has compartmentalized the pain of the discover-
ing his illegitimacy, but he does readily acknowledge a contemporary and abrupt halt to his natural social development. "In
junior high everything was fine," Ted told me. "Nothing that I
can recall happened that summer before my sophomore year to
stunt me or otherwise hinder my progress. But I got to high
school and I didn't make any progress."

He sounded genuinely perplexed. "How can I say it?" he asked. "I'm at a loss to describe it even now. Maybe I didn't have the role models at home that could have aided me in school. I don't know. But I felt alienated from my old friends. They just seemed to move on and I didn't. I don't know why and I don't know if there's an explanation. Maybe it's something that was programmed by some kind of genetic thing. In my early schooling, it seemed like there was no problem in learning what the appropriate social behaviors were. It just seemed like I hit a wall in high school."

I asked Ted if he ever talked over these problems with his mother or minister or a school psychologist. "It never crossed my mind," he told me. "I didn't think anything was wrong, necessarily. I wasn't sure what was wrong and what was right. All I knew was that I felt a bit different."

For Terry Storwick, his friend's withdrawal was all the more mysterious for the fact that Ted was so bright and amusing. "He was a lampooner. He had the darts, you know," Storwick recalls. "He was very funny and very much on the mark. To me, he just seemed wonderfully subtle. He could make me laugh with a gesture or one or two words, where I'd need sentences and pictures and diagrams to get the same thing across. I took this to be a token of his intelligence.

"He didn't have the confidence, however, to follow it up. He could have been a really strong influence on a lot of people if he had had the self-confidence to go along with the intellect. It seemed to me that he was just tongue-tied in social situations. It didn't have to be girls; meeting new friends, meeting new people from another school was a difficult thing for him to do."

Even today, Terry can see in his mind's eye Ted "walking down the hall with that half-aggressive, half-hopeful expression. I'm sure he was slighted a lot. At least in my circle of friends, it was important to be popular. We'd be standing in the hallway and someone would come up to me and say, 'Hey, we're going to have a party Friday. Can you come over?' Ted would be standing there and he wouldn't be asked. It wasn't that he was singled out for ridicule, but you have to remember that Ted was a very sensitive person—*very* sensitive."

Ted Bundy had but a single date throughout his three years of high school. As he explained to me, this is an area where he's "particularly dense, or insensitive, not knowing when a woman's interested in me. I've been described as handsome and all this shit, or attractive. I don't believe it. It's a built-in insecurity. I don't believe I'm attractive.''

In high school, he was not afflicted by the aching randiness of most teenaged boys. When his robust buddies talked of their latest scores, real or exaggerated, and compared notes on technique, Ted made a passable show of joining in the discussion, but in truth was mystified by what he heard. He wasn't sure if these guys really were doing what they said they were doing; and even if most of it was callow lies, he had trouble grasping *any* of it. "It kind of went over my head," he told me.

Ted felt at ease in only two environments—the ski slopes and the classroom. "I spoke up in class," he explained. "It's a formalized setting and the ground rules are fairly strict. Your performance is measured by different rules than what happens when everybody's peeling off into little cliques down the hallway.''

Because he was articulate and cultivated an image of serious-mindedness to hide his loneliness, Ted was regarded as a scholar by the other students at Wilson. Yet for all his seeming seriousness of purpose, his grades were only good, not great. He ended high school with just above a B average, good enough to earn him admission to his uncle's school (by now renamed the University of Puget Sound) together with a modest scholarship. Outwardly, conditions seemed ideal for this bright, attractive young man to step forward into the world, to overcome his shyness, and to seize this opportunity. Few people at Wilson High School would have been surprised to hear that he eventually went on to law school and became a rising star in the local Republican firmament.

The closer people felt to Ted, the surer that likelihood seemed. Yet the next thing that many of his boyhood acquaintances would know of the diffident boy with the half-hopeful expression was that the police suspected him of a string of hideous murders.

They'd sort back through their memories, trying to recall something odd or different about him, something *identifiable* in his past that would help explain the tragedy. They couldn't.

Not even his closest friend, Terry Storwick, can bridge what he knew of Ted and what Bundy later became. As we spoke, Terry's eyes teared at times with the pain of fond memories. Aloof though Ted was, the two boys felt a bond, even a debt on Terry's part; Ted once saved Terry's niece, Wendy, from drowning.

"There is no way," Storwick told me, his voice breaking, "that the person I grew up with could have done the things they said he did. And there's no way for me to reconcile the image of the mass murderer and the kid who came running to my back porch when the first snow fell in November, all excited to go skiing. In between those two images, something happened. Definitely, something popped.''

Ted's critical challenge from his teen years onward was the perfection and maintenance of a credible public persona, his mask of sanity. Lacking true adult emotions, he had to put on the look of normalcy while inside him the tumult raged unabated.

He underwent a process of mock acculturation, like an alien life form acquiring appropriate behavior through mimicry and artifice. It was painful and confusing to him, each frequent misstep a stab at the child bewildered by his inability to handle the simplest adult relationships.

"I didn't know what made things tick," Ted told me. "I didn't know what made people want to be friends. I didn't know what made people attractive to one another. I didn't know what underlay social interactions."

His happiest moment during his first year of college came when he bought a '58 Volkswagen bug for $400. The little car meant freedom to Ted. He could get in it and drive and be alone whenever he wanted, a reprise of his early boyhood when he and his collie, Lassie, would disappear out into the trees for hours. Ted loved VW's. He would own two in his life; the second one, a light brown '68, eventually would yield evidence of his victims.

Ted lived at home for his freshman year. "He got along fine, as far as I could tell," his mother remembers. "He got good grades that first year." Louise was not alarmed that her son "never got into the social life of the school at all. He'd come home, study, sleep, and go back to school."

By Ted's account, "my social life was a big zero. I spent a great deal of time with myself. It was a lonely year for me, and it was worse because I didn't have my old neighborhood buddies around."

He declined to join a fraternity and can still recall how cowed he felt in the presence of self-assured, hearty fraternity brothers. Although he was rushed, he wouldn't join because "I didn't feel socially adept enough. I didn't feel I knew how to function with those people. I felt terribly uncomfortable."

Ted only spoke when spoken to, or in class. He made no new friends. For all intents, he was an invisible man that year.

Instinctively, Bundy turned to the classroom as his stage for building an identity. He had found in high school how easy it was to appear scholarly; the ability and willingness to speak up often were enough to set him apart.

But freshman survey courses taken in large, impersonal lecture halls offered scant opportunity to be anything but anonymous and small, the way Ted felt most of the time. He was very disappointed.

Then one day he attended an international affairs lecture on mainland China and immediately was struck with the notion that here was an area where people might take notice of him without threatening him. He didn't think about how much work the subject might entail. Ted saw the Chinese language as exotic, glamorous, a bright cloak in which to wrap himself.

The following autumn, he enrolled as a transfer student at the University of Washington's first-rate Asian studies program in Seattle. As at UPS, he did not see himself measuring up to Fraternity Row, so Ted took a room in a dorm. But he was right about his new major; it did set him apart from the run of the undergraduate population at the huge university. He threw himself into the arcana of ideograms and earned high grades. He acquired a little restaurant Chinese, learned to use chopsticks, and actually made a few friends.

He had made a start at fabricating the public Ted: scholarly, bright, witty, serious-minded, wholesome, and handsome. He developed an air of cool self-assurance, a look that women could not resist. Ted lured females the way a lifeless silk flower can dupe a honey bee. At least twice in his life, the beguilement would endure. With other females, like his first true girlfriend, the spell eventually shattered.

Marjorie Russell† was a co-ed at the University of Washington. A lissome beauty nearly six feet tall, she was wealthy, poised, and worldly. Marjorie was from a class into which Ted previously had only had upward glimpses. Moreover, she knew what she wanted out of life. She was, in short, everything that Ted Bundy was not and wished to become.

He showed her off like a possession to his old friends. Warren Dodge was impressed. "I was kind of surprised that Ted had something like her with him," Dodge remembers. He took her home to meet his mother. "She was very nice," says Louise. "At that time, Ted was very serious about her."

At twenty years of age, Bundy was no more sexually advanced than he'd been in high school when the other boys' talk had gone over his head. Certainly any lust he felt toward Marjorie at this juncture was well hidden. They spent nights together, but he did not make any sexual advances. Ted was content to be boyish and charming, as if introducing carnality to the relationship would somehow taint it.

The summer following his sophomore year he spent down amidst the gum trees and palms and tiled roofs of Stanford University, where he was enrolled in an intensive Chinese language program. He had gone to Stanford mainly to please and impress Marjorie, but it was a mistake.

He was accustomed to being alone, but he was not ready to be alone away from home. Ted missed familiar things. Quickly, he fell behind the other students, and that made it all the harder for him to socialize with them. And there was Marjorie. "I found myself thinking about standards of success that I just didn't seem to be living up to," he told me.

At Stanford, Ted's immaturity was exposed, a particularly hateful experience for him because he had now failed in the one arena—the classroom—that had always been his refuge.

Then Marjorie dropped him. As she later told investigators, what had been his winning boyishness now struck her as puerility. She wearied of his fawning attitude and she was tired of his games. Ted would often sneak up behind her, tap her on her shoulder, and then vanish. That annoyed her. She advised him to grow up.

Ted's brother Glenn recalls that Marjorie "screwed him up for a while. He came home and seemed pretty upset and moody. I'd never seen him like that before. He's always in charge of his emotions."

Louise Bundy remembers something similar. "As I understand it, she told him she couldn't wait around for Ted to have it made. If she found somebody else, she'd go that way. He was pretty hurt by that."

Ted did not understand what had happened to him, why the mask he had been using had failed him. This first tentative foray into the sophisticated world had ended in disaster. It would usher in another period of isolation in which he would brood on his situation, keeping to himself until a better, more workable mask could be fashioned.

The rest of 1967 was, as he remembers, "absolutely the pits for me—the lowest time ever." He gave up on Chinese altogether after having wasted a year in its study. For no better reason than Marjorie having once said that she admired the architect's role played by Albert Finney in the movie *Two for the*

*Road,* Ted applied for the University of Washington's architectural program. The school was filled. So, on the advice of a university counselor, he turned to urban planning—and failed at that, too.

That fall, it was all that he could do to go to class; to concentrate on the material was out of the question. The professors' words meant nothing. His class notes were indecipherable. The university environment had turned hostile, frightening. He developed a phobic dread of encountering Marjorie on campus. By Christmas, he withdrew from school.

He saved a little money, borrowed more, then took off on a flying trip around the country. Ted went to California, to Aspen, Colorado, and back to Philadelphia to visit his grandparents. Dogged by his feelings of worthlessness and failure, he came home to Seattle in the spring of 1968, still unable to face a return to school. He took a small apartment and went to work as a busboy in a hotel dining room as well as a night stocker in a Safeway store.

"I absorbed all this uncertainty," Ted told me, "and all this confusion about why I was doing what I was doing, wondering where I was going, all by myself. Because I'm not the kind of person who socialized a lot, there was no way to let off steam."

Following his return to Seattle, he made a friend named Richard, a sometime thief and drug user whose life at the fringe of society fascinated Ted. At age twenty-one, Ted hadn't been exposed to an outlaw element more sinister than the circle of ski-lift ticket counterfeiters he knew in high school. Now he would encounter the possibility of illicit excitement on a higher plane.

Stealing, especially shoplifting, came naturally to Ted. The unsocialized child within him wanted things—expensive, shiny things such as rich people owned—and Ted had no adult compunctions about acquiring them illegally. Moreover, theft was an adventure, a game, a kind of advanced variation on hide-and-seek, not unlike tapping people on the shoulder and then disappearing.

One night, Ted and Richard sneaked down to a beach near Seattle where landslides had pulled down a cliffside house. They were after anything they could find. "We went down there in the dead of night," Ted told me. "The house was full of shit! I still have some luggage from there. It was really thrilling."

Ted was not a thief in any ordinary sense; he didn't take money and he wouldn't take merchandise for the purpose of selling it. The need was much closer to kleptomania, and it was overpowering. Yet he was never once caught for shoplifting anything, a remarkable fact in light of the number of thefts he made and the way he went about them. Even professional shoplifters, people schooled in the most refined techniques of their trade, customarily have long arrest records.

His first principle was anonymity. Once he decided what he wanted, he would put on his good suit and comb his hair—he wanted to look presentable and forgettable—then he'd down two or three quick beers. "I'd drink just to pump myself up," he told me. "I felt I wouldn't have any inhibitions. I didn't want to be looking over my shoulder and appear nervous. That's important."

He stole a television, a stereo, home furnishings, cookware, clothing, and artwork—things that he wanted to own. Typical of his expeditions was the day he decided he wanted a tree for his apartment. "I walked into the side entrance of this place and went into their greenhouse," he said. "I saw this Benjaminus tree and picked it up. This fucker was eight feet tall, heavy, and a little bulky. But I just walked out the side gate, lifted the thing up and down through the sunroof of the car. There was a good five feet of Benjaminus sticking out of the top as I drove away."

Around the time he was burgling the house on the beach, Ted bumped into an old acquaintance from high school. They talked for a bit on the street corner, then the friend casually mentioned that if Ted was interested he might latch on in some capacity working for Art Fletcher, a black small-town city councilman who then was contending to become the Republican nominee for lieutenant governor. Several mutual acquaintances were already working for Fletcher.

Ted Bundy jumped at the chance. "I just pitched right in," he told me. "Oh, boy! Here we go again! I hadn't had a social life for some time. It just felt good to belong again, to instantly be part of something."

If Ted Bundy the thief inhabited one corner of his personality, then elsewhere there resided Ted Bundy the committed Republican. Ever since high school, when he had delivered a Rockefeller nomination speech at a mock GOP convention, Ted had been drawn to politics. In his senior year, he had joined the re-election effort of a local Republican congressman and had loved the experience.

"The reason I loved politics was because here was something that allowed me to use my talents and assertiveness," he says. "You know, the guy who'd raise his hand in class and speak up.

And the social life came with it. You were accepted. You went out to dinner with people. They *invited* you to dinner.

"I didn't have the money or the tennis-club membership or whatever it takes to really have the inside track. So politics was perfect. You can move among the various strata of society. You can talk to people to whom otherwise you'd have no access."

He immediately quit his jobs and went to work as a full-time Fletcher volunteer. Ted's finances were strained, but it was well worth it to him. It was a time when the bulk of committed, politically conscious young people were part of the peace movement. Ted Bundy, however, was four-square for the Establishment. He had no intention of aligning himself with the outsiders, the dispossessed, or the poor.

That fall, Ted had the great good fortune to be named Art Fletcher's official driver. Had he remained in college, Ted would have been starting his junior year. But he had been so traumatized by Marjorie and his collapse in Chinese that he was still two years away from being able to successfully resume his studies.

He was still a virgin, too, and might have remained so indefinitely if sex had required him to make the first move. However, one night while away from Seattle on campaign business he drank himself into a near stupor at a GOP official's house in eastern Washington. When Ted drank, he often got drunk.

That night, he had to be taken to someone's home to sleep it off. As he remembers the night, he was installed in a downstairs bedroom, only semi-conscious, when the lady of the house gently crawled into bed beside him, stripped him of his clothes, and relieved him of his virginity. His role in the seduction was entirely passive.

Politics is a seasonal business. After Art Fletcher ran a close second in the November election, his driver was thrown back on his own resources. During the campaign, Ted had watched how people get along, and had acquired by rote some of the social skills he could not come by naturally. He had matured into a slim, even-featured young man with clear blue eyes and an ironic smile. He took meticulous care with his appearance and dressed with a casual, studied tweediness. The clothes he couldn't buy he stole.

All the elements of the mask were now coming together, forming a seamless facade. Bundy took a temporary sales job in a Seattle department store, one from which he had shoplifted and where he learned something new about himself—he had a knack for cozening women customers. He could sell them anything.

He saved up some money, sold his '58 VW, and headed once again for Philadelphia. He hoped that he could start school again there, in his grandfather's town, and away from the physical reminders of his days with Marjorie.

He spent the first half of 1969 at Temple University with mixed results. A special urban affairs project was never completed, but he did moderately well in theatrical arts classes. Ted learned a little something about acting and make-up. He also bought a false mustache.

By now he had made yet another realization about himself: his face lacked any single characteristic that stood out above the rest. Like the personality he was creating, his face could be anything he wanted it to be. The mustache, combing his hair differently, gaining or losing a few pounds, growing a beard—all changed his appearance dramatically. He could, when he wished, be as anonymous as he wanted. He had, as one of his judges later observed, "the face of a changeling."

Ted Bundy returned to Seattle in the summer of 1969 and took a room at Ernst and Frieda Rogers' house, one of several University District rooming houses where single people—usually students—could find an inexpensive place to stay.

The Rogerses took an instant liking to him. Ted was polite. He kept his room clean and tidy. He was happy to run Mrs. Rogers to the store or to help Ernst with jobs around the house. He seemed like a gentle person to Frieda. She would remember the time they had coffee together in her kitchen. An outsized fly began to buzz around them. Frieda started to swat it, but Ted jumped up and exclaimed, "Don't kill it!" and chased the fly out the window.

He lived around the corner from the Sandpiper tavern, a college beer joint where he had some success in picking up girls. On the last night of September 1969, he walked into the Sandpiper and sat down at the bar.

Across the crowded dance floor sat Elizabeth Kendall,†* twenty-four, an appealing medical secretary and divorcée out for an evening of fun with a group of her friends. Ted finished a pitcher of beer at the bar before he found the courage to approach her.

As he retells the occasion, Ted walked over to her and asked

---

* "Elizabeth Kendall" wrote an account of her life with Ted Bundy, *The Phantom Prince*, and we have chosen to adopt the same pseudonym for her.

for a dance. "I'm sorry," Liz replied. "I can't dance." On most nights, that would have been enough to send Ted Bundy into a funk. "For my somewhat tentatively developed ego," he explained to me, "it was always a less than pleasant experience for someone to say that they didn't want to dance. I never got over that."

Emboldened by his beer, however, Ted was brave enough to ask one of Liz's friends to dance. She said, "Sure!" and rose. Moments later on the dance floor, Ted noticed Liz now was dancing, too. He flashed her a wolfish smile and said, "Well, you really can't dance, can you?"

Liz reports in her book that she thought he was very charming. According to her account, Ted introduced himself as a law student and said he was working on a book about Vietnam. She didn't necessarily buy the business about the writing project, but Ted was so good-looking and smoothly confident that by the end of the evening, she recalls, "I was already planning the wedding and naming the kids."

She took Ted home with her that night.

Both had drunk a good deal; they slept together clothed. In the morning, her daughter, Joanie,† was up early demanding pop tarts and chocolate. Ted was delighted by the little girl, but Liz made it clear that he should leave, and he did.

But he couldn't get Liz out of his mind. She had struck a chord in Ted. He idealized her as he had Marjorie, but there was also something about Liz, something that he couldn't quite articulate, that made him feel he had known her all his life.

The daughter of a successful Utah doctor, she had gone through an early and painful marriage that left her with a distinct distrust of men. She also had a jealous streak, exacerbated by insecurity and Ted's later philanderings.

Knowing nothing of mature love and respect, he could only seem to be something, or someone. For Liz, he had created the Ted Bundy who wrote books and went to law school. In truth, he was a dropout and working as a legal messenger when they met. Like a child, he couldn't foresee the consequences of his living out this fantasy, just as he could not see how his own babyish behavior had cost him Marjorie.

It wasn't three months after he met Liz that they began to discuss marriage. They took out a license and talked to her relatives about using their home for the ceremony. When he could no longer sustain the charade, Ted stunned Liz by theatrically tearing up their marriage license on the pretext it was too soon and sudden for them to marry. A short while later, he confessed his true station in the world. Liz forgave him.

Liz saw as much of Ted at this time as did anyone. They made love several nights a week, went on day excursions with Joanie, visited his family, telephoned each other constantly. Yet even she did not penetrate the mask. In love with Ted—dazzled by him—she rationalized away his lies and appears to have handled his petty cruelties by responding in kind. When Ted hurt her by ignoring her or made her jealous by seeing other women, she hurt him back. Liz dealt with Ted at his level.

In retrospect, it seems improbable that a woman could be quite so utterly gulled. But she was not alone. His mother detected nothing. The stores from which he stole detected nothing. His Republican friends—the scores of campaign workers and elected officials—detected nothing.

By now, there was more and more for Ted to keep hidden. From what he later told us at the prison, it is certain that by this stage he had a strong appetite for violent pornography. He has conceded to police interrogators that he crept around the University District late at night. Sometimes he stole things from houses. Sometimes he peeped into women's windows.

Also developing within him were cyclical depressions. "It wasn't dictated by the cycle of the moon, or anything else," he told me. "Not mood swings, just changes. It's goddamn hard for me to describe it. All I wanted to do was just lay around, just consume huge volumes of time without doing a thing.

"Even in these periods, however, I'm capable of being genuinely cheerful and gregarious—at least for a limited period of time. I became expert at projecting something very different. That I was very busy. I had a huge part of my life that nobody knew about. It didn't take much effort at all."

Ted felt that, on the surface at least, Liz took the marriage license scene and his lies in stride. When he told her that he was still two years short of an undergraduate degree, she urged him to return to school. Liz gave him a couple hundred dollars to cover tuition and helped launch him into yet another major, psychology.

Ted could offer a number of reasons for choosing psychology, but he conceded to me that the decision "was probably an outgrowth of my confusion about myself." He did feel good about the choice, and beginning with the University of Washington summer term of 1970, he tore into the subject with demonic intensity. Ted did not miss a single question on one final exam. He wrote a paper on schizophrenia that won high praise from his professor. Ted was driven. "It was a marvelous feeling," he told me, "to have purpose and to do *well* at the same time."

The periods of malaise abated for a time, but he couldn't stop his late-night patrols or his impulsive thievery. From May of 1970 until September of 1971, he drove a delivery truck for Ped-Line, a family-owned medical supply company. Once he stole a photograph from a doctor's office and was caught. His boss let him off with a stern lecture. The company didn't know until later that he had been stealing from them, too. Among the things he took was a container of plaster casting material.

Ted's next job was in a work-study program run by the Seattle Crisis Clinic. One night a week, he took calls from the frantic, the lonely, and the suicidal. At least once a month, there would be the high drama of a call from someone who had already taken a lethal dose or slit his wrists. Ted would keep the caller on the line long enough for the number to be traced, then there would be the tense minutes until he could hear the police breaking into the caller's home.

The people he was most sensitive to were women. "I had the best results with women who were lonely and had been abandoned by their husbands or mates," Ted explained to me. "I felt they really hurt the most. They were reaching out because they were alone and really needed someone."

The job was not unlike his boyhood nights alone with the radio. Ted would be the anonymous participant in other people's lives. They couldn't know who he was; he controlled the relationship and created a specious intimacy through his voice.

By the spring of 1972, after seven years and four different majors, Ted Bundy had completed enough course work to earn his degree in psychology. By then, he was sure that he wanted to go to law school, although he was no more certain of what law school would be like than he had been about the Chinese studies. In his mind, he saw an ivy-covered campus where he'd acquire the talents and demeanor of the upward-mobile attorneys he had met in politics. Then three-piece suits, mahogany desks, money, and recognition would follow.

His grades were good enough to qualify Ted for any number of law schools, but despite hundreds of hours of preparation, his Law School Aptitude Test results—a key to admission—were only mediocre. He was particularly upset and embarrassed by his poor showing on the grammar portion of the exam.

Every law school turned him down.

At sea again, he left the Crisis Clinic job in May of 1972 and was hired under a federal grant to work with psychiatric outpatients at Seattle's Harborview Hospital.

He continued to keep his life with Liz carefully sequestered, allowing him to have a brief affair with Cynthia Holt,† a fellow Harborview counselor. According to Cynthia, Ted was often cold and almost abusive with his cases that summer; he was more apt to lecture than to counsel. Ted was further suspected by the hospital staff of calling patients at home at night and making anonymous threats.

Cynthia shares with Liz and Marjorie and a number of other women the unsettling memory that she was willingly, happily intimate with a mass killer who, at the time she knew him, was already half mad and slipping rapidly. She now believes that the forearm he once shoved up against her throat while making love was no accident of overexuberance; Ted could have killed her at that instant.

But the most curious part of their affair—and the aspect that the local police later were most interested in—was the occasional long drives Cynthia took with Ted up through the hills behind Lake Sammamish, the area where many of his victims later were found.

"Ted," she says, "was supposedly looking for an old aunt or some old woman who was family. He said he was trying to find her place. I'll never forget it, because it was my car and my gas and I was not exactly pleased to do this. I kept driving and driving and I kept saying to Ted, 'What does the place look like? At least tell me what the place looks like so I can help look!' There was never any description. We just drove around."

Later, Ted's cousin John told police that he and Ted often hiked in this area. He reluctantly led Bob Keppel to trails they used that ran in and around the Taylor Mountain vicinity. Bundy also visited the area with a political friend, demonstrating what appeared to be a close knowledge of the woods.

Bundy had a personal sense of futility at Harborview, a feeling of inadequacy and helplessness with his patients. He told us that he concluded that the social sciences weren't capable of handling sick people. Psychology had failed him.

To Ted's joy and relief, however, 1972 was an election year; he could take a vacation from himself. He looked up his old friends from the Fletcher campaign and through them was introduced to a number of Republican hierarchs. Soon he was busying himself as a volunteer working for the incumbent GOP governor, Dan Evans.

Vistas reopened. The young women who worked with Ted were captivated by his handsome features, fastidious dress, and correct manners. He flirted with them.

Ted was unfailingly polite to his superiors, and impressed some of the wizened veterans on the governor's staff with his dedication and ready grasp of hardball politics. Ralph Munro, one of Evans' top operatives and later Washington's secretary of state, knew Ted slightly from the 1968 campaign. "He was very friendly, very open," Munro recalled to me. "There were other people in the 1972 campaign that I probably knew better, but I remember him being there and being involved. I thought he was bright, sharp. He had good ideas."

This was the Ted Bundy who'd be remembered to reporters, the absolutely normal young man with no hint of the flaw in his nature. Liz, however, was beginning to see glimpses of the real Ted. Glimpses of the hunchback.

He once threatened to "break your fucking neck" if she ever exposed him for the thief he was. She remembers that late one night he came by to retrieve a crowbar he had left under her radiator. Liz saw something bulging from his pocket and pulled it out; it was a surgical glove.

Another night, she awoke to find Ted examining her body under the bedclothes with a flashlight. Later he tried to talk Liz into anal sex, which she refused in horror to consider. She did allow him to tie her up a few times before they made love. He used her pantyhose, which she noticed he found immediately in her bureau without needing directions.

Still, he could be her warm and caring Theodore, the idealized lover capable of great tenderness. During this period, Liz seems to have been much more concerned about losing Ted to his fancy Republican friends or another woman than she was about the danger signs. Later, they'd terrify her.

After the 1972 election, Ted made a second, successful attempt at law school admission. He prepared an elaborate new packet of materials to support his candidacy (including a letter from Governor Evans and a wordy denunciation of LSAT tests as inadequate measures of his true potential). The ploy worked: Ted was accepted by the University of Utah College of Law for the term beginning in the fall of 1973.

Meanwhile, he went to work at the Seattle Crime Commission,

where he stayed for just a month. He wrote articles for the commission's newsletter, attended its meetings, and aided on pilot studies of white-collar crime and rape prevention.

One day while he was out shopping with Liz, Ted spotted a purse snatcher and ran the man down. He held the suspect until the police arrived. Ted's heroics were duly noted by the *Seattle Times*, the first-ever mention of Ted Bundy in the newspapers.

With help from his political friends, Ted then found a job at the King County Office of Law and Justice Planning. His assignment was to study recidivism among those convicted of minor offenses in King County justice courts. He had access to nearly all pertinent arrest records, rap sheets, and the like. For weeks, he scoured thousands and thousands of arrests, noting with interest how poor the cooperation and coordination were among the various police and judicial jurisdictions.

Ted was amazed to find rap sheets showing arrests that had never resulted in a trial, but neglecting to list convictions for other crimes. There were habitual criminals with two or three dozen arrests shown, but he couldn't figure out from the records what happened to the people. They had just fallen between the cracks.

This was a period akin to his campaign interludes. Ted's hopes and expectations were rising again after the disappointments of the previous summer at Harborview. In May of 1973, he went to work in Olympia for Ross Davis, the new head of the state GOP central committee. Earning what for Ted Bundy was the princely salary of $1,000 a month, he studied cost overruns in the party computer system for Davis, and helped with several other research projects. Those around Ted at the time remember that he looked up to Ross as if he were a big brother or favored uncle.

Ted loved to play with the Davises' two small children. Ross's wife, Sarah, told me that Ted seemed to fit comfortably into their family that summer. "He didn't talk much about himself," she said. "But I didn't feel he was trying to hide anything. He spoke of his mother and family in loving terms."

That summer of 1973, Ted also saw a good deal of Marlin and Sheila Vortman, a law student and his wife who had been active in the 1972 Evans campaign. Like Ross Davis, Marlin was sturdy and purposeful, something of a big brother figure to Ted.

Marlin also knew Ted to be a little quirky. One day, he visited his younger friend and was surprised at the quality of Ted's possessions; they spoke of grander means than Marlin knew Ted to command. Odder still was Ted's explanation that he often came and went from his second-floor room by means of a ladder. He did so, he said, because he didn't want to disturb his fellow roomers.

Marlin persuaded Ted that he, like Vortman, should attend law school at the University of Puget Sound rather than go out of state for his legal training. The newly opened University of Puget Sound law school, he argued, would put Ted in touch with local lawyers and would be a more suitable school for someone with local political ambitions. Ted agreed.

He applied to UPS and was accepted into the night law school. Rather than admitting to the Utah people that he had changed his mind, Ted invented a story for them. He wouldn't be able to attend school in Salt Lake City that autumn, he wrote, because he had been injured in an automobile accident.

Ted almost totally excluded Liz from this part of his life. The Davises didn't know she existed, and she was hostile toward Marlin, whom she correctly guessed had more influence on Ted's decisions and actions than she did. At this time, she was also unaware that her boyfriend felt he had some unfinished business to attend to in California.

In July of 1973, Ted flew to San Francisco to see Marjorie Russell. Although it was Liz whom Ted claimed he loved, Marjorie had remained on his mind for years. He had kept in touch with her from time to time, but now he was ready to confront her again. Happy in his work and fairly bristling with confidence now that his legal education was about to begin, he felt an aura of personal magnetism shimmering about him. He felt that he looked different and acted different.

He *was* different, at least in Marjorie's eyes. She later told the police that she found her erstwhile wishy-washy beau transformed into a Man of Action. He seemed to be in control now.

Once again, Ted was acting out a fantasy. He had tailored his outward appearance to suit Marjorie's expectations, and duped her into believing that he had changed. While he was in the role, *Ted* also believed he had changed.

Back in Seattle, as the summer of 1973 drew to a close, Bundy wound up his work for Ross Davis. One afternoon, he drove his recently acquired '68 Volkswagen bug over to the Davises' house for a visit. Outside in the driveway with Ross, he opened the car's trunk to rummage for something. There was plenty of junk to sort through—Ted Bundy was a pack rat. But as Ross cast an idle glance into the trunk, his eyes picked out a particularly unusual item in the jumble. There, resting in the clutter of tools and rags and other paraphernalia, was a pair of handcuffs.

Unbeknownst to Liz, Marjorie, his family, and his friends, Ted was an immediate and thorough failure in law school. Eight years after he had first been enrolled as a freshman at the University of Puget Sound, Ted expected to return as a graduate student and to find clear-eyed and fastidious young men like himself. What he encountered on orientation day was a motley assortment of aspiring legal scholars who ranged in appearance from the well groomed to the scruffy. And instead of his vision of an ivied citadel—Ted Bundy's idea of what a proper law school should look like—he found a small night school housed temporarily in an anonymous office building in downtown Tacoma. He was appalled.

Ted was unbothered that he had to subsist that autumn on unemployment checks, but the perceived taint of attending a déclassé law school was every bit as demeaning to him in his mid-twenties as Johnnie and Louise's boxy Ramblers were to him as a child. Rigidly fixed on image and emotionally incapable of having much perspective on his circumstances, Ted could not make the best of the situation. In no time, he was hopelessly behind the rest of the class, unable to grasp what his professors were trying to teach him; it was a repeat of his 1967 burnout in Chinese studies. The rest of the fall and winter of 1973 would be a period of unrelieved dolor for him.

By December of 1973, Ted had secretly reapplied to the University of Utah College of Law. He told no one of the decision until the following spring, and the new application to Utah made no mention of his current enrollment at the UPS night law school. Utah accepted Ted once again, but he would not be leaving for Salt Lake City until September of 1974.

In the middle of his year at UPS—when the young girls began to disappear around the region—Ted kept up a convincing show of eager involvement with his studies. He attended classes faithfully until near the end of the spring term, and he applied himself to the material every few weeks when it was his turn to lead his study-group discussion. He wasn't lying to Liz or his mom when he said that he spent much of his time in the law library. What he didn't tell them was that he spent most of his time there daydreaming. Fantasizing.

He was driven ever deeper into himself, into his cyclical and

secret depressions. In his solitude, Ted devised complex rationales for the gaps between his wish to succeed and the reality of
his failure, all the while guarding the secret of his inner turmoil
from the people who thought they were close to him.

He was very good at the deception, all bright-eyed and bushy-
tailed when the occasion demanded. But his tissue of deceits
began to double back on him at Christmastime. Liz had flown to
Utah to be with her family, while Marjorie, ignorant of Liz and
almost everything else to do with Ted, came north for the
holidays.

For a week, she stayed with Ted in the Vortmans' apartment
while Marlin and Sheila were away on vacation in Hawaii.
While the previous summer Ted had even convinced himself that
his life was back on course, now he had to re-create the role of
Changed Man from memory. He succeeded too well; Marjorie
liked what she saw and she wanted to talk marriage. They
discussed it for days—Marjorie in earnest and Ted, under mount-
ing pressure, with the appearance of sincerity. He conned Marjorie again, just as he had repeatedly conned Liz. She flew home
to California thinking that she was engaged to be married.

Ted's well-practiced faculty for compartmentalization was at
work again. He took Marjorie to the airport and kissed her
good-bye. Then he sped in his Volkswagen over to see the other
woman he insisted he loved. Ted found Liz in her kitchen with
an apron on. The tableau was warm, domestic. He remembers
that dinner aromas filled the air that night. Liz smiled up at him
and soon they were making love, the most passionate love they
had ever made.

A month later, as the futile search for Joyce and Jim Healy's
daughter Lynda was being given periodic mention in the Seattle
papers, Ted had his one final confrontation with Marjorie. She
had occupied a segregated section of his mind for seven years,
an ideal woman whose heart he'd won, lost, recaptured, and now
would break. Just as Ted could never fully explain to me his
feelings for Liz, he also never understood his relationship with
Marjorie.

He hadn't exchanged a word with her since their Christmas
betrothal; he had hoped by ignoring the situation to make it go
away. But she telephoned him at his apartment on a Saturday
evening. He had just returned from taking the Law School
Aptitude Test for yet another time and was tucking into a six-
pack of beer when the phone rang.

"Why the hell haven't you written or called!" he remembers

Marjorie yelling. "What kind of way is this for you to treat me?"

Partially anesthetized by the beer, Ted listened serenely to her tirade. He didn't apologize. He didn't explain. He just acted cool. "Don't ever bother to get in touch with me again," she told him.

"Well," Ted recalls replying, "far out, you know."

She hung up and he cracked open another beer. "I felt like the gods had spoken," he told me. "I felt doubly relieved. This meant it was all off my back."

The rest of what we were able to establish about Ted's movements during these months comes principally from his own and police records.

• January 31, the night Lynda Ann Healy was abducted from her basement bedroom, Ted attended his contracts class at UPS in Tacoma. He would have been back in Seattle in the early evening.

• March 12, when Donna Gail Manson left her dorm room at Evergreen State College on her way to a jazz concert and was never seen again, Ted Bundy's dated law school notes indicate that he did not go to school. For the preceding months, these notes show a pattern of regular attendance, but they grow sketchy toward the end of March and stop altogether in early April.

• April 17, the date Susan Rancourt left her dorm advisers' meeting and vanished at Central Washington State College in Ellensburg, a VW similar to Ted's was seen parked at Taylor Mountain, where "Ted's" third dumping ground was discovered.

• May 6, when Kathy Parks disappeared 250 miles south of Seattle in Corvallis, Oregon, Ted filled his VW's gas tank in Seattle and cashed two checks for a total of $20, sufficient money to cover the cost of a 500-mile round trip.

During this period, Ted's gas-credit-card slips reveal that he did an extraordinary amount of driving, far more than would be expected of a money-short law student whose car-pool responsibilities were restricted to a single sixty-mile round trip from Seattle to Tacoma each week.

He chose April to inform Liz that he had decided to transfer to Utah; typically for Ted, he did so in a dramatic scene with tears and hand wringing. He didn't tell Liz that he had arranged the move four months earlier. Ted was also going to need a summer job, so he drove down to Olympia and secured work at the Washington State Department of Emergency Services.

The DES was a catch-all agency. Its duties included coordinating local disaster relief and search and rescue teams. One of its functions was to help in the hunts for Lynda Healy, Donna Manson, and Susan Rancourt. The search for Kathy Parks was Oregon's responsibility. Brenda Ball, Georgann Hawkins, Denise Naslund, and Janice Ott were still alive at this juncture.

But the emphasis at DES in the summer of 1974 was upon a different sort of emergency. The OPEC oil embargo had severely disrupted fuel supplies in Washington. At the time, there was no such thing as a federal or state Energy Department, and so it fell to DES to help bring order out of chaos by allocating the state's dwindling fuel resources.

Ted's arrival at the office in May of 1974 caused the customary stir among the female employees. The males, too, found him charismatic. One who remembers Ted cutting a handsome figure that summer is Larry Diamond. "Frankly," Diamond told me, "he represented what it was that all young males anywhere ever wanted to be. He held that image. I wanted that image, and because of that I was jealous of him. I think half the people in the office were jealous of him. The males—and all of the women—were taken by him, down to the crease in his trousers. If there was any flaw in him it was that he was almost too perfect."

Bundy, who was assigned to work on the DES biennial budget, became something of a mentor to Diamond. He was more familiar than Larry with politics and politicians. He showed Larry how things got done within the state GOP administration. But Bundy didn't share too much of himself, even on subjects as universally popular among men as the curve of a particular woman's leg or her bust dimensions. "He could have damn near any woman he wanted," Diamond recalled. "Most men talk of women in the sense of fantasy. He didn't. It was almost like he compartmentalized them.

"Ted," Diamond continued, "was almost one-dimensional if I think about it. It's like there's a very beautiful storefront that's attractive and lures you in. But when you get inside to see the merchandise, it is sparse to say the least."

A more fateful encounter for Ted Bundy that summer was with Carole Boone, later to become his wife and mother of his child. Carole would one day remake her life for Ted; her subsequent loyalty and devotion to his cause would beggar reason.

In the summer of 1974, she was a lusty-tempered free spirit regarded generally as the most competent staff member at DES.

She is remembered by other DES employees as a sister/mother figure who did her work well but who also was not above starting a rubber-band fight, or leading a circle of her closest co-workers on three-hour liquid lunches in the Voodoo Room at the nearby Bailey Motor Inn. She had the wit and intelligence to do almost anything.

At the time she met Ted Bundy, her personal life was in tatters. A favorite uncle had recently died. She was newly divorced from her second husband. She was trying to raise her son, Jamey, and she was in the midst of a messy affair with "a large, unpleasant man," as she later described him to me.

"I liked Ted immediately," she told me. "We hit it off well. He struck me as being a rather shy person with a lot more going on under the surface than what was on the surface. He certainly was more dignified and restrained than the more certifiable types around the office. He would participate in the silliness partway. But remember, he was a Republican."

According to Carole, Ted made it clear he'd like to date her, but their relationship deepened not into love at first, but into friendship and affection for each other. Part of the attraction was Ted's sensitivity to Carole's emotional problems. "I guess I was closer to him than other people at the agency," she told me.

Carole noticed that from early June onward Ted's health seemed to deteriorate. During three weeks in August, according to her, he lost fifteen pounds. She attributed his poor health to the complex DES budget, which he had to finish before leaving for Utah in September. It hadn't helped that a cleaning woman had thrown out a cardboard box filled with Ted's budget files.

She noticed, too, that Ted was receiving a number of acrimonious calls from Liz. She tried not to eavesdrop on them; just as Ted would politely walk away when she fought by phone with her lover. But Carole could see that the calls from Liz made Ted nervous and cranky.

Ted and Liz had reached another crisis. According to Liz's book, she was waiting for some firm commitment from Ted before he left for Utah. She feared that their relationship would dissolve as Ted established himself in a new town and met new people—especially women.

The previous autumn, she had discovered a bag of women's clothing in his apartment. At other times she had noted the container of plaster Ted had taken from Ped-Line as well as a pair of crutches. Liz had been too embarrassed to say anything.

Then she observed a progressive ebb in his sexual ardor, beginning in the spring of 1974.

Now, his erratic and sometimes bizarre behavior was beginning to frighten her.

On Saturday, the sixth of July, the two of them went river rafting. Liz's book describes the day as peaceful and sunny. They drank a few beers and were drifting along quietly when Bundy suddenly lunged at her and shoved her into the water. She came up stunned and shouted her irritation at him. His unnerving response was not to respond at all; she was looking at a malefic stranger who didn't seem to recognize her. Finally, he said, "It was no big deal. Can't you take a joke?"

Liz chose to bury the incident. The following Saturday, the day before Denise Naslund and Janice Ott were abducted from Lake Sammamish State Park, Liz telephoned Ted at Johnnie and Louise's house in Tacoma. She wanted to know if Ted would be free to see her the next day.

"No, I can't," she remembers him saying. "I have other things to do."

"What other things?" she pressed.

"Just things, Liz," he answered.

As she got ready for church the next morning, Ted arrived unexpectedly and asked Liz her plans for the day. According to her, Ted was eager to know where she was going. She named a small park where, she hoped, he might join her. He didn't.

Late Sunday afternoon—about an hour after Denise Naslund disappeared—Liz returned home to a phone call from Ted; he asked her to have dinner with him and was at her door within ten minutes. Ted said he was starving.

They went to a bowling alley reputed to serve the best hamburgers in Seattle. The burgers were huge. Liz barely finished hers; Ted devoured two and then wanted to go for ice cream. She noticed he had a cold that had worsened since they had talked that morning. He looked tired, too, and was unusually quiet. In response to her questions, he said he'd spent the day cleaning his car and doing chores around the house.

As Terry Storwick had noted years before—and as several witnesses would attest—Ted's eyes gave away much in times of stress. Now Liz saw it, too. She recounts: "As I looked at him across the table, I was struck by how close together his eyes looked. They were a little puffy from his cold, but it was odd that I had never noticed it before."

After dinner they returned to her house, where Ted, in spite of his cold and tiredness, insisted upon taking her ski rack—which they had used to transport his bicycle on the rafting trip—from atop his car and putting it back on Liz's VW. Then he drove home.

Ted's DES work records would later reveal that he missed the Thursday and Friday prior to Sunday the fourteenth, as well as the following Monday and Tuesday. He said he was out sick with the cold that Liz remembers.

Ted Bundy was back at work at the DES office by the time the first composite sketches of the Lake Sammamish "Ted" were published. He took a good deal of kidding from Carole Boone, Larry Diamond, and the others. "Gee, Ted," they would say, "you sure look a lot like that guy. And you do own a Volkswagen."

Mark Adams, Ted's former employer at the medical supply company, saw the composites, too, and remarked to himself how alike they were to Ted Bundy. Adams kept these impressions to himself.

Someone else thought Ted Bundy looked like the composite. He was one of Liz's office friends. As she tells the story, the man handed her the July 22 *Seattle Times* carrying the latest composite drawing. "Don't you think this looks like someone you know?" she recalls him asking, "Doesn't your Ted have a VW?"

Liz tried to laugh, but she went home that night and compared her several snapshots of Ted with the newspaper picture. She noted several similarities—particularly in the jawline and around the eyes—but an equal number of discrepancies. Moreover, published reports indicated that the Lake Sam "Ted" drove a metallic brown VW bug; Ted's was a dull light brown.

Her fears, however, would not subside—a dilemma shared by thousands of women in and around Seattle. Panicked by the latest disclosures from Lake Sam, these women flooded the police with hysterical calls. Acquaintances, strangers, boyfriends, even husbands, were being turned in to the police at the rate of hundreds a day. In the overwhelming majority of cases, these women had far less substantive reason for fear than did Liz Kendall.

At last, she decided to call the special "Ted Hotline" anonymously, but nothing conclusive came of it. After the papers reported that a man using crutches had solicited help with his briefcase in the University District, her thoughts flew to the crutches she had seen in Ted's room. She placed another anonymous call to the police, but wouldn't tell the officer her boyfriend's name. "I can't talk to you over the phone," the policeman said. "You need to come in and fill out a report." Liz hung up.

As the summer wore on, Liz was torn between dread at what Ted might be capable of and apprehension over his coming departure for Utah. There continued to be unsettling experiences, such as the time she discovered a hatchet under the seat of his car, or the afternoon that she secretly searched his room and found an eyeglass case filled with a bewildering assortment of keys. Another time, when she returned from a brief trip to Utah, Ted met her at the airport. "I felt as if I'd been hit in the stomach," she writes. "All his curly hair was gone. It was the shortest haircut I'd ever seen on him, and it changed his appearance dramatically."

Throughout August of 1974, Ted Bundy attacked the DES budget in the haphazard fashion so characteristic of his school work. As his early September departure date approached, he'd bear down for several days, then go flat and do nothing.

His last night in the northwest was spent at the DES office with Liz, and it wasn't until the early hours of the next morning that he at last completed his work.

Ted and Liz drove back up to Seattle, where he hurriedly packed his VW. They breakfasted together and afterward he humored her when she asked him to pose for her camera. Ted was exhausted and Liz was near tears during these final moments. They embraced and kissed, then he jumped in his bug and drove off.

Within days Elzie Hammons, the grouse hunter, stumbled across the desiccated bones and sinews of Denise Naslund and Janice Ott. In a brief news conference, Nick Mackie of the King County police officially acknowledged what the Seattle newspapers had been suggesting for months. "The worst we feared," Mackie told reporters, "is true."

# THREE

THE TERROR began in Utah on October 2, 1974, when sixteen-year-old Nancy Wilcox, a pretty high school cheerleader, disappeared from suburban Holladay, just south of Salt Lake City. She was at first listed by juvenile authorities as a probable runaway; Nancy recently had argued with her parents. She was last reported seen riding in a VW bug. No description was offered for the man driving the Volkswagen. Nothing more is known about the case. Nancy Wilcox is still missing.

She lived in a community near the center of the vast Salt Lake Valley, itself in the geographic heart of what once was called the "Great American Desert." Salt Lake City is a 500-mile drive west from Denver; and it is another 750 miles across the salt flats, through Nevada, and over the High Sierras to San Francisco. Phoenix lies 650 miles to the south. Seattle is 850 miles to the northwest, on the other side of Idaho.

Most of landlocked Utah is hardly inhabited at all; over three-fourths of the state's population lives within fifty miles of Salt Lake City, the capital. Less than 1 percent is black. Less than one in twenty-five is Mexican-American.

Except for its relative aridity and the dominant sociopolitical influence of the Mormon Church, the long valley stretching north and south from Ogden to Provo is not dissimilar to western Washington. To the east rises the Wasatch Front, a wall of purple and white mountains nearly as imposing as Washington's Cascades. It is ski country. And like the lower Cascades, the thousand canyons of the Wasatch are well suited for the disposal of dead girls' bodies.

The cities and towns strung out below the mountains are patriarch Brigham Young's legacy and a monument to his persecuted people's vision and obstinacy. From the capital with its six-spired temple—Mormonism's home—to small towns like

Bountiful, whose names ring with pioneer optimism, the region exults in Christian industry and a deep sense of family. In the main, heterodox views are not encouraged.

Nancy Wilcox's disappearance was duly reported in the local press, as was the case of a second missing girl sixteen days later. She was Melissa Smith, seventeen, the daughter of the town police chief in Midvale, not far from Holladay.

Melissa had light brown hair, hazel eyes, long, carefully tended fingernails, and an often petulant disposition. When she didn't get her own way, she customarily went into a snit.

Friday night, October 18, she was invited to attend a slumber party. But apparently no one had thought to tell Melissa that the party had been postponed or canceled; she called her hostess around 9:00 P.M. and got no answer.

Peeved, Melissa put on a pair of jeans, a flowered blouse, and a heavy blue shirt and walked out of her family's house headed for a pizza restaurant where she had made last-minute arrangements to meet another girlfriend, who was having boy trouble. Melissa listened to her friend's problems, then left the pizzeria, again on foot. She was later reported in a number of teen hangouts in the Midvale and Murray vicinity and was more or less reliably said to have been hitchhiking at one point in the evening.

Her partially frozen, nude, and dirt-caked corpse was discovered ten days later in a Wasatch canyon. Gone were her jeans, blouse, and heavy blue shirt. Still present was one of her blue knee-length stockings. It was tightly bound around her neck.

She was covered with cuts and abrasions, some from blows of the heavy instrument that had been used to fracture her skull, some from her body having been dragged a good distance.

Melissa had been raped and possibly sodomized. A quantity of dirt and twigs was found in her vagina. The lack of blood in her body suggested that she had bled heavily and probably died elsewhere.

Her eye make-up was undisturbed, and none of her fingernails were broken—two indications that she had not fought with her killer. Moreover, the medical examiner thought from the condition of her body that she could have been alive for a week after her disappearance. If so, Melissa might have been a runaway—something she had never done before—the night of her disappearance, or else she was abducted and kept for days, probably unconscious, because there were no signs she had been bound.

Her murder and the lurid details of her discovery stunned the entire state. Bloody, violent homicides were not unknown in Utah, but the nature of this one—the age and sex of the victim, the evidence of what had happened to her, the chill at wondering who could have committed such an outrage—caused immediate alarm.

Three nights later, on Halloween, another girl disappeared.

Laura Aime was a big girl. Nearly six feet tall, she weighed 140 pounds. She was also an incautious and occasionally defiant teenager; her parents couldn't always be certain where Laura was or when they'd see her again.

On Halloween, she attended a house party with several friends in Orem, Utah, about forty miles south of Salt Lake City in Utah County. Some time before midnight, she grew bored and restless and decided to hitch a ride into downtown Orem in search of a pack of cigarettes and perhaps more fun than she was having at the party. Witnesses later provided conflicting and confusing reports of Laura's movements that night, but no one who knew the girl or later recognized her picture remembered seeing Laura Aime much after midnight.

At around 7:00 P.M. on Friday, November 8, Fred and Beth DaRonch's nineteen-year-old daughter Carol parked her maroon Chevrolet Camaro in front of the Sears store at the Fashion Place Mall in Murray, Utah, not far from where Melissa Smith was last seen alive three weeks earlier. Carol had come to the mall to purchase a birthday gift for her cousin.

Just out of high school and recently employed by Mountain Bell Telephone as an operator, Carol came from a strong Mormon family. The slender doe-eyed brunette was respectful toward her elders and had been taught to trust people with authority.

She was also a little naive.

Inside the mall, she was approached by a man who identified himself as Officer Roseland of the Murray police. He asked her for her license plate number and told her that there had been a report of an automobile burglary in the parking lot.

His appearance did little to reinforce his claim. As the DaRonch girl later recollected, the man smelled of liquor, wore patent leather shoes, and had greasy, slicked-back hair. Carol later wavered on whether or not he wore a mustache, the color of his shirt, and the type of jacket he was wearing.

They walked back to her car, with Roseland in front and Carol a couple steps behind him. She kept her eyes cast downward for the most part. When they got to the Camaro, it was clear that her car hadn't been disturbed. She thought that would be the end of it, but no. Now the man said they needed to walk over to the police substation in the mall. Carol hesitantly acquiesced, but she did screw up the nerve to ask him for identification. He flashed her a badge from his wallet.

At the substation (which was, in fact, the back of a laundromat) Roseland tried a door. It wouldn't open. He also mumbled something about a partner and told Carol they better go down to headquarters. If she wasn't alarmed by now, she definitely should have been when the two arrived at the officer's car. It was a ratty, dented Volkswagen bug, a light color, possibly blue, and she noted a lateral tear in the top of the rear seat.

He tried to persuade her to buckle her seat belt, but this time Carol demurred. Were it not for the easy, educated tone of the man's voice and her innate willingness to cooperate with an authority figure, she would have bolted at that instant.

They had left the mall and were heading east, when suddenly Officer Roseland jerked the car over a curb in front of a grade school and lunged for Carol with a pair of handcuffs. She screamed and the two battled each other in the cramped front seat of the bug. He got one cuff on her right wrist, but in the fight he missed her left wrist with the second cuff and managed to lock it instead on her right arm.

Carol's former docility was instantly replaced by animal panic. She clawed at her assailant, ripping her fingernails in the process. Later she thought she remembered a gun and a threat to "blow my head off" if she didn't stop struggling.

The little car rocked with their frantic battle. Somehow she got her door partially open and was halfway out when he pulled a multipronged tire iron out of nowhere and was about to bring it down on her head. With strength born of pure terror, she caught the weapon with her hand just inches before it would have split her skull. At last she gave a furious jerk and broke the man's grip on her arm. She tumbled screaming from the car, not certain if the man would be on top of her in an instant. Crazed with fear, she ran with one shoe off across the road, waving her arms to stop the first car she could. Behind her, the Volkswagen made a screeching U-turn and disappeared.

The night was moonless and misty. Wilbur and Mary Walsh were driving cautiously along the slick streets, their headlights making distended yellow cones in the inky wet air. Suddenly,

Carol DaRonch lurched into view. Wilbur skidded to a stop and the terrified girl threw open Mary's door. At first the Walshes were leery, but Carol's frantic look immediately convinced them that the girl had just encountered something dreadful. Mary later told a court: "When I saw the state this child was in, I realized it couldn't be anything harmful to me. It was harmful to her. I have never seen a human being that frightened in my life. She was trembling and crying and weak, as if she was going to faint. She was in a terrible state."

Wilbur and Mary drove Carol to the nearby police station, where she blurted out a confused tale of her attempted abduction. Meantime, however, another incident was unfolding twenty miles to the north in Bountiful.

That night, the Viewmont High School drama club was presenting *The Redhead* before an audience of 1,500 in the school auditorium. The play was to begin at eight, but the opening curtain was delayed fifteen to twenty minutes. Just before eight, drama teacher Raelynne Shepard, aged twenty-four and attractive, was approached in a hallway by a young man she later described as "very good-looking." Not only was he handsome, she thought, but he was impeccably dressed. She noticed his patent leather shoes.

The first time they met, he simply said, "Hi," and she returned the greeting. About fifteen minutes later, Mrs. Shepard met the handsome stranger again. He told her that she had beautiful eyes, which was true. She asked if he was waiting for someone. "Oh, no," he answered. Just before the play was about to begin, she passed him once more in the hallway. This time he wanted to know if Raelynne knew a Brent Olson. "No," said the drama teacher. "Is he in the orchestra? Does he have a speaking part?"

The man replied that he didn't know, but that it was "no big deal." Raelynne felt his nervousness, and she was also uncomfortable with his steady gaze upon her neck and breasts. She walked back down the hallway toward the dressing rooms, then returned just after the house lights went down. The man was still standing there. "That time he came up and he said that he wanted to know if I would come out in the parking lot and identify a car," Mrs. Shepard said. "I thought that was a little bit strange."

Before intermission, she walked down the hallway once more. "He just stepped out and put his hand on my arm and said, 'I've been watching you go back and forth all night long and I know you have time to come out and identify this car.' He was really forward and he didn't talk to you looking at your eyes. He was staring right at my chest and he commented on my hair, that he liked long hair.''

During the intermission, she saw the man walking outside the auditorium and thought to herself, Well, thank heavens he's gone. He wasn't. Toward the end of the musical, Mrs. Shepard saw the man one more time. She and her husband were seated at the back of the auditorium, three or four rows behind and to the left of Dean and Belva Kent, who had come to the play with their daughter Debra. The man sat down directly across from Mrs. Shepard and her husband, and directly behind the Kents. Raelynne prodded her husband, Jonathan. "That's the guy," she whispered. Jonathan turned to look at the stranger, who looked back and then stood up and left. Raelynne's final impression was that the man looked a little mussed. His shirttail was partially out, and his hair wasn't neatly combed as it was when she first saw him. What is more, the man appeared to be breathing hard.

The only other salient detail Raelynne Shepard recalled was the man's habit of clearing his throat frequently, and each time he did he would softly pat his mustache—as if it were fake and he was afraid it would fall off.

Two other women recalled seeing the man that night. One was sixteen-year-old Katherine Ricks, whom he asked if she knew his brother and if she would come out to the parking lot to help him fix his car. She declined.

The other witness was Debra Kent's locker partner, Tamra Tingey. She saw the man standing at the back of the auditorium, just as Raelynne Shepard had.

Dean and Belva Kent saw none of this. All they remember is that at the intermission their daughter Debra rose and headed for the parking lot. She was going to pick up her brother at a skating rink. Debra Kent was never seen again.

On November 14, the *Deseret News* interviewed Dr. Victor Cline, a University of Utah psychologist. Under the headline "Profile of a Utah Abductor," Cline was quoted as saying that the killer was apt to be a Jekyll and Hyde type. "He may be the most mild-mannered person in the world," Cline said, "yet there is within him this need that drives him to do these things."

Cline further explained that these types of people are "the kind who are known for helping old women across the street in their normal lives. They're extremely difficult to track down."

Of one thing Cline was certain. "I have no doubt this will

happen again,'' he said. "It may be a month or more, but the tension is building inside him. The fact that he has succeeded will feed his compulsion to do it again.''

On Wednesday, November 27, Jim and Shirleen Aime received a call from the police; another body had been discovered in the mountains. They drove to the university medical center in Salt Lake. Jim Aime went alone into the autopsy room. In a moment, his wife heard a short, stabbing wail. When he came out, he told Shirleen not to go in.

# FOUR

## UTAH HIGHWAY PATROL
## INCIDENT REPORT

*Type of Incident:* Attempt to Evade
*Reporting:* Sgt. Robert A Hayward
*Division:* Special Operations

At about 2:30 A.M. on Saturday morning, August 16 [1975], a gray Volkswagen went by me while I was sitting in my patrol car in front of my house. I looked at the license plate and did not recognize it.

About ten minutes later . . . as I was going up Brock Street in Granger, a car took off north bound on Brock Street at a high rate of speed. . . . I was in pursuit . . . at a high rate of speed. We ran the stop sign at Brock and LeMay and again at the entrance to 35th South off of Brock Street. . . . I had the red spotlight on him when he ran the stop sign at Brock and LeMay, but he just went as fast as possible.

. . . I pulled up on him fast, and he pulled over into a gas station. He produced his drivers license which identified him to be Theodore Robert Bundy, 565 1st Avenue, Salt Lake City, Utah, dob 11/24/46. The man was wearing dark pants, a dark turtle neck shirt with long sleeves, and sneakers. He stated that he was lost in the subdivision, but he had been there and again came back in about ten minutes. . . .

I looked in the front seat and there was not a seat on the passenger side, so I looked a little closer and discovered the front seat was lying in the back seat on its side. On the floor were some tools such as a jimmy bar about 14 inches long. . . .

I called for a County car to come over and they sent a Deputy and a Sergeant. They talked to Mr. Bundy and he told them he had been out west to the drive-in theater to see "The Towering

Inferno." We checked at the theater and that movie was not playing, so he just said he was lost.

The deputies looked in the car and asked if there was a gun in it. I said not to my knowledge, but that I had not looked that closely and perhaps we should check further. After that, they came up with a few other items of interest that a person coming from a movie normally would not carry such as an ice pick, a pair of handcuffs, silk stockings with holes cut in for the eyes and nose, and other items that a burglar might carry.

They called for a detective car and Deputy Ondrak came over and took the items into custody. We impounded the car and I took Mr. Bundy to the County Jail and booked him on the charge of "Attempting to Evade a Police Officer." The time of booking was approximately 3:30 A.M.

That Ted was captured so improbably still maddens him. "God damn it," he exploded at the recollection of that night, "it just offends my notion of justice!" He was serious.

'Of course," he added slyly, "we all get lucky. Sometimes I was lucky, and then they got lucky."

"They"—the police—didn't get lucky for a long time. After Mary Adams, who survived, there was Lynda Healy in February of 1974. Then Donna Manson: March. Susan Rancourt: April. Kathy Parks: May. Brenda Ball: June. Georgann Hawkins: June. Denise Naslund and Janice Ott: July.

All were dead or missing before the northwest police even knew of "Ted." Then Carol Valenzuela vanished in August and was found months later beside her unidentifiable sister in death.

Still the authorities had nothing.

When Ted moved on to Utah in the fall of 1974, leaving the northwest in turmoil and its police as confused as ever, he baffled the Salt Lake—area cops by striking at least five times in quick succession, then—apparently—stopping.

In Utah that autumn of 1974, he attacked Nancy Wilcox, Melissa Smith, Laura Aime, Carol DaRonch, and Debra Kent. Then he moved on again.

Ted was lucky, but he was also supremely capable, an almost perfect killing machine who struck with the poise and art of a born predator. His genius was to know when to kill and where to kill, knowledge that was his by instinct and by dint of careful study of his craft.

Counting patrolmen, police detectives, prosecutors and their staffs, private investigators, and volunteer searchers, easily more than 1,000 people had spent over 100,000 hours pursuing him since January of 1974. They had found nothing.

By the time he was caught, two dozen police agencies in four states were looking for him; they had no idea that they all were after the same person.

Even after he was arrested and the probable extent of Ted's predations was known, the police were still stymied. Ted would never be tried for any of these killings.

Nor might he ever have stopped killing had it not been for an uncharacteristic lapse. He was foolhardy the night of his arrest. Bundy may have been lulled by the ease with which he had hunted over the past year and a half. Or he may have been playing a peculiar form of "chicken" with the police—seeing how close he could come to their net and still elude them.

He insists the arrest was a matter of luck, but there is another possibility. Sick, driven by violent urges, unstoppable and unable to stop himself, Ted in effect turned himself in. Before his story was over, he'd be compelled to do so twice again.

Jerry Thompson is a chunky, taciturn cop with a dead-level gaze and an oddly inflected accent that is both clipped and drawling. A detective with the Salt Lake County sheriff's office, he was the one who would make the vital link between the autumn 1974 killings and Ted's chance arrest the following summer.

Nancy Wilcox, the first of Utah's autumn cases, was the sheriff's responsibility from the moment she was no longer presumed to be a runaway. Then Thompson took over the Melissa Smith case at the request of her distraught father, an old friend. Thompson had known Midvale police chief Louis Smith for years and remembered Melissa from the time she was a baby.

At first, the detective was misled to think Nancy and Melissa might be the victims of an unknown killer who the previous July had abducted and murdered Sandra Weaver, an out-of-state hitchhiker who was found nude, dumped in a roadside ditch. It was only a theory; no witnesses and nothing tangible linked the three cases. But like Seattle's Herb Swindler and his occult investigations, it was as good as anything else Thompson had to work on.

The following month, with the assault on Carol DaRonch and the disappearance that same night of high schooler Debra Kent,

Thompson began to compare notes with the Murray police, who were generally disinclined to press too hard on the DaRonch case, and Lieutenant Ira Beal of the Bountiful police, who was certain from the start that Debbie Kent had been taken from the Viewmont High School parking lot.

The two policemen discounted the discrepancies between Carol DaRonch's description of her attacker—slicked-back hair, green pants, liquor on his breath—and the recollections of the witnesses at the Viewmont High School play—handsome, nattily attired. A change of clothes, application of a comb or brush, use of a breath mint or two, and their suspect might easily alter the impression he made.

Thompson and Beal knew that the timing was right; a single killer, frustrated in his attempt to abduct the DaRonch girl in Murray, could have driven north to Bountiful by the time that the good-looking stranger was seen there. Later, a handcuff key was found in the gravel outside the auditorium; it fit the cuffs on Carol DaRonch's arm. Also, at least one resident near the high school reported seeing a VW bug with two people in it leaving the parking lot at high speed that night.

Melissa Smith, Thompson's investigation showed, had walked within a hundred yards of the Fashion Place Mall the night she was taken. It may have been a coincidence that Carol DaRonch was attacked there three weeks later, but Thompson didn't think so.

Then came Laura Aime's autopsy report.

Her frozen, battered corpse was discovered in a canyon several miles east of Orem, in Utah County, where she had last been seen. The medical examiner reported that she had suffered multiple bruises and lacerations around her head and shoulders. They were very similar to the pattern of upper-body injuries noted on Melissa Smith.

There was a deep cut in the back of Laura's head, her jaw was broken, and her skull had been fractured by a blunt instrument (perhaps a tire iron) in nearly the same way as Melissa's. There was evidence of both anal and vaginal violation. And like the Smith girl, Laura Aime was found with one of her stockings knotted tightly around her throat.

Unlike Melissa, Laura was technically drunk at the time of her death. She also had suffered a vaginal puncture wound such as might be made by an ice pick or, as had been the case with Mary Adams many months before in Seattle, a speculum. Finally, there was one reported curiosity: Laura Aime's hair appeared to have been freshly shampooed just before her death. If so, some investigators later felt, the shampooed hair was a clue paralleling Melissa Smith's undisturbed make-up and perfect nails. If Melissa was kept for a time before she was killed, then so might Laura have been. And if they both had been unconscious during captivity, then it was possible that *he* applied Melissa's make-up and *he* washed Laura's hair.

The evidence was not strong enough to confirm such a theory—only to suggest it—but at the very least the autopsies and the rest of what Jerry Thompson knew of the cases convinced him that they were "just about as identical as you're going to get," he told Hugh. "Same type of girl, same situations, same cause of death. I really don't know where else you get everything just the same."

As early as December 3, 1974—six days after Laura Aime was found—Utah County sheriff's sergeant Owen Quarnberg had written to the FBI crime lab in Washington, D.C., concerning the case. "The MO . . . is similar in many respects [to the Smith case]," wrote the sergeant. "The victims in both cases were beaten, sexually assaulted and strangled. Also, many of the wounds were similar in appearance."

So far, Thompson had enjoyed the close cooperation of all police jurisdictions involved with his several cases; no one had been jealous of prerogatives. But now, despite what Sergeant Quarnberg wrote and the obvious investigative opportunities offered by similarities between Smith and Aime, Quarnberg's boss, Utah County sheriff Mack Holley, refused to share information with Thompson. "All I kept getting was a runaround," Thompson explains. "So I basically said, 'The hell with them.' "

Early on, Sheriff Holley was sold on a single suspect in the Aime case, a college student who at the time was suspected of (and later convicted for) the brutal slaying of his girlfriend in a rugged Utah canyon. But Holley's department never developed any evidence of the suspect's culpability for Laura Aime's murder.

A more promising suspect was brought to the attention of Bountiful police lieutenant Ira Beal. Based upon accounts from the several witnesses at Viewmont High School, Beal had put together a description of the stranger who was seen at the play that night. Ten days following Debra Kent's disappearance, Beal received a call from the Park City, Utah, police. "Goddamn," he remembers a Park City cop telling him over the phone, "this guy looks like the guy you're looking for."

The suspect's name was John Badway,† a part-time drug dealer with an arrest record who also happened to drive a Volkswagen that belonged to his girlfriend. At the time, he was working as a waiter in a Park City restaurant.

Beal checked into Badway, found nothing that would exclude him as a suspect, then called Raelynne Shepard, the Viewmont drama teacher who had had the most extensive contact with the stranger the night of Debra Kent's disappearance. Shepard agreed to accompany Beal and a sergeant to Park City. Before they went, Badway's photo was shown to Carol DaRonch, who said he looked something like her attacker, but she couldn't be sure.

On November 25, the two policemen drove Mrs. Shepard to Park City, an old mining town and popular ski resort area east of Salt Lake City. They arrived and sat together in Beal's unmarked car waiting for John Badway to come to work. Shepard had been told nothing but that she would see a possible suspect.

When Badway walked into the restaurant, she turned to Lieutenant Beal. "Is that him?" she asked.

"You tell us," Beal replied.

The two cops and their star witness went into the restaurant to eat. The suspect was their waiter. Throughout the meal, Raelynne eyed Badway closely. He betrayed no sign that he recognized her. When they got back into the car for the return trip to Bountiful, Mrs. Shepard had made up her mind. Badway's voice seemed a little high. He looked to be a couple inches too tall. And she would have liked to see him in a mustache. Like many witnesses before and after her, Mrs. Shepard really wasn't sure who she'd seen. However, she seemed certain: "That's the man I talked to at Viewmont," she said firmly.

Beal and his partner were elated. After a few more days' investigation still failed to exclude Badway, they called him in and braced their suspect with Shepard's identification.

"No, guys," he answered evenly. "I've been to Bountiful, but I'm not involved."

He was asked if he'd take a lie detector test. After consulting with his attorney, Badway agreed to do so. He passed the exam conclusively.

It was a bitter disappointment. The policemen's main witness had proved unreliable, and their hopes for an early resolution to the Kent case melted into despair. They had nothing to go on, and wouldn't have for another eleven months.

\* \* \*

Ted Bundy regards all cops as feckless and dense, bumble-footed bozos who didn't deserve to catch him. He dismisses the idea that anything but bad luck stopped him. Yet luck for so long had been his ally.

He was, for instance, among the first "Teds" reported to the Seattle authorities. An older woman friend from his Crisis Clinic days gave the police his name that summer, as did a professor from the University of Washington and, later, Liz Kendall.

One afternoon in late October of 1974, a friend from Utah told Liz of Melissa Smith's disappearance and death. The case sounded similar to the local killings. Ted, of course, was in Utah. The coincidence was too stark to ignore.

The next day, she called the King County police once more. This time, Liz found the courage to give the police both Ted's name and hers. The detective she talked to informed her that Ted had already been reported to the police and that he had been cleared. Liz immediately felt that finally the matter was closed, but the detective wanted to hear more about Theodore Robert Bundy. Liz at first demurred, then finally agreed to meet with him.

They spent an afternoon talking in his car in the parking lot of a fast-food restaurant, then they went to her house where she gave the detective three photographs of Ted. It was a grueling afternoon for Liz Kendall; the detective pressed her on the most intimate details of her life with Ted.

She heard nothing more from the police for several weeks. Then came a call from the detective. He had shown Ted's picture to their strongest Lake Sam witness, he said. The woman had pulled the photo from a stack of other pictures, then replaced it. The photo of Ted was of someone too old to be "Ted."

"That's hardly a positive I.D.," Liz remembers the detective saying.

She asked what that meant.

"I don't know what it means to you," he said, "but to me it means I'm going to put Ted Bundy in my done-it-twice file and file him away."

More than 3,000 names of possible suspects had been phoned in to the Seattle "Ted Hotline" by the fall of 1974, and it was all that the detectives could do to take down the information, let alone follow it up. In the deluge of tips and hysterical outpourings from frightened women, real police work toward apprehending the killer was a practical impossibility.

Certainly the cops tried. One of Bob Keppel's first moves was to feed the 3,000 names into a computer. Then he added all Washington State Volkswagen owners, the names of all the friends of the victims, names from their address books, class lists of students from each of the missing girls' schools, all mental patients in the state for the previous ten years, known sex offenders, motel lists from the Issaquah area—even the names of the people who had ridden at a horse ranch near Issaquah over the past year.

From this master list, the computer was programmed to print out everyone whose name appeared twice. Hundreds of names came out. When the number of coincidences was raised to four, there were still almost four hundred names—among them, Ted Bundy's. At five coincidences, only twenty-five names appeared. Ted had dropped out. All twenty-five proved to have alibis and were cleared.

The northwest detectives could not recall a stranger or more frustrating case than this one. They had no evidence, and the public pressure to find "Ted" and stop him was intense. In the face of several dead and missing women and no information as to their whereabouts, everyone's imagination ran to extremes. Unspeakable acts, it was said, had been committed on the victims, and the police were withholding details in order not to further panic the population.

There was a rumor that the girls were decapitated. Another story had it that their bones had been boiled. The crimes were thought so heinous that Bob Keppel found shock and horror at them even among the low-lifes and known deviants who routinely come under suspicion when a murderer is loose. Much to Keppel's surprise, "Everyone that we talked to as a suspect was helpful. I mean everybody was always cooperative. Even the best suspects, the murderers we talked to. 'Hey, man, I kill people,' they'd say. 'But I don't kill like that.' "

Given this level of public anxiety, Keppel was careful to avoid public comment on the possibility that "Ted" had disappeared from the region. To speculate in print that he might be gone and then have him strike again would be a final, calamitous blow to public faith in the ability of the police to solve the case.

For a time, the police did not discourage press reports that a number of killings in California might match the local pattern; anything would do to ease the pressure, even for a while. Then, an ex-GI and convicted killer named Harold Carmichael,† forty-seven, became a potential suspect. Maps apparently belonging to Carmichael were said to show scores of inked circles in a trail from the northwest back to Minnesota, where Carmichael was being held on two counts of aggravated sodomy and, said one paper, "taking indecent liberties with a 13-year-old girl." The circles at first were thought to coincide with possible "Ted" burial sites. Carmichael was subsequently cleared of the northwest murders.

Late that autumn, the police did think they had one good lead. An orange Volkswagen was reported to have been seen on several occasions near the Issaquah hillside where Janice Ott and Denise Naslund were discovered in early September. The witness even supplied a license plate number. When one of the Lake Sam witnesses identified the VW owner's license photo as resembling "Ted," the local police moved into action. Finally, they had a good suspect.

A stakeout was begun at his house while other detectives looked into the suspect's background. They established that he had returned from a fishing trip the day before the Lake Sam abductions and he was positively placed in Seattle at the time that Georgann Hawkins disappeared.

After several days of waiting, the police at last apprehended their man. Their euphoria quickly subsided. His hair was long and in pigtails. He looked nothing like "Ted" and nothing like his two-year-old driver's license photo, the one that had been shown to the Lake Sam witness. Moreover, the "Ted" described by the Lake Sam witnesses could not have grown his hair so long in the few months since the crime.

There was an explanation for his presence in Issaquah, too. The man was cultivating his private marijuana patch in the area.

*Luck.*

Even though the Seattle cops were doubtful that Ted was "Ted," the King County police sent Ted Bundy's name, photograph, current whereabouts, a description of his VW, and a précis of Liz's suspicions to Jerry Thompson *before* Carol DaRonch's night with "Officer Roseland." Once again, Ted was among the earliest reported suspects. Under oath, Thompson has sworn that the snapshot was not shown to Carol DaRonch or to any of the other witnesses.

Thompson and Beal soldiered on with their investigation through the end of 1974 and into 1975. Like the northwest police, they were getting nowhere. Moreover, no new victims were reported missing or discovered following the recovery of Laura Aime's body in late November. In a little over a month, there had been two disappearances, two known murders, and an attempted kidnap. Then nothing. If Dr. Cline was right, then the killer was still at work. But where?

The answer was Colorado. In late spring, Thompson took a call from the Pitkin County district attorney's office in Aspen, 390 miles away. On the line was Mike Fisher, chief investigator for the office. Fisher had known of the Utah cases the previous autumn, and now had several problems of his own.

He told Thompson that on January 11, 1975, a twenty-three-year-old nurse from Michigan had arrived in Aspen. Her name was Caryn Campbell. She had come to Colorado with Dr. Raymond Gadowski, a thirty-one-year-old osteopath, and his two children.

Caryn was a pretty and buxom brunette, the sort of woman that men notice. She had lived with Gadowski since the spring of 1974. The doctor and the nurse were in love; she called him "Raymie," he called her "Car" or "Cam," and they were thinking about getting married.

Their proximate reason for being in Aspen was a medical convention, but both Raymond and Caryn were ardent skiers. Plus, the trip gave Gadowski a chance to be away with his kids, and it gave the children and Caryn a chance to get to know one another better. Besides, any excuse will do to escape a Michigan winter.

The four of them took a room with two double beds at the Wildwood Inn in Snowmass, a ski community located about twelve miles from Aspen proper. That night, Raymond, Caryn, and the children were met for dinner by Dr. Allen Rosenthal, another conventioneer and one of Caryn's former boyfriends. Afterward, she bought the current issue of *Viva* magazine, and they all returned to their rooms. Later, as the children slept, Raymie and Car made love.

The next morning, a Sunday, Gadowski rose first to attend a scheduled 8:00 A.M. conference. The meeting bored him, so he returned to the room about an hour later to help Caryn ready the children for a day on the slopes.

They skied most of the day, then Allen Rosenthal joined them again for dinner on Sunday night. They took an upstairs table at a restaurant called the Stewpot. Caryn, whose stomach had been troubling her, ate sparingly. She drank milk with her dinner. By eight that night, they were back in the lobby of the Wildwood Inn.

Allen Rosenthal had a *Playboy* magazine, which he agreed to trade with Caryn for her *Viva*. He left the lobby to fetch it, and Caryn asked Gadowski if he'd mind going to their room for the *Viva*. He declined somewhat brusquely, saying he'd rather sit by the fire with his kids. Caryn turned on her heel in a minor swivet and headed for the elevator. The last report of her that night was from three witnesses who saw her on the way to the room. Caryn's *Viva* was found undisturbed. She never made it to the room.

Thirty-six days later—two weeks before the four dead girls were found on Taylor Mountain in Washington—Caryn Campbell's nude and frozen body was found in a field of snow along a dirt road 2.8 miles from Snowmass. Animals had eaten away much of her face and neck. But Denver coroner Dr. Donald M. Clark established to his satisfaction that Caryn had died from "brain injury due to blunt trauma to the head." Her killer had delivered a vicious blow to her skull. It was uncertain if she had been raped. Judging from the partly digested milk and stew found in her stomach, she had been killed from two to six hours after Dr. Raymond Gadowski refused to retrieve her magazine.

Fisher found it improbable that Caryn Campbell's murderer had himself stayed at the Wildwood Inn. More likely, he felt, she had been approached on her way to her room and lured away from the Wildwood under some ruse. There was too much pedestrian traffic at that hour for someone to have assaulted her and carried her off unseen. The theory made sense, but it didn't bring Fisher any closer to solving the mystery.

He thought he had a break in early March when a chambermaid at the Top of the Village hotel reported that on January 9, 1975, a Manny Treff,† thirty-one, drifter and day laborer, had made untoward advances in the maid's room. The woman, who had discouraged Treff with a left fist to the mouth, told the police that he "had mental problems and was not all there."

Subsequently, Fisher connected Treff with several such incidents. He had cruised the ski resort in his brown station wagon calling, "Here, kitty, kitty," to women. Another maid reported that Treff had tried to fondle her breasts and kept asking when they could "get it on." Variously, the people who remembered him described Treff as "weird," "sick," and "dangerous."

A check on his police record revealed that Manny Treff had been arrested for indecent exposure in Seattle in September of 1974. A telephone conversation with Seattle police detective Ivan Beeson was logged on March 12 by one of Fisher's investigators. "Beeson states," reads the report, "that when suspect Treff was arrested in their case, he was a very violent and dangerous person. . . . Beeson states that in checking their records that they were having one missing girl per month but after subject Treff was incarcerated in Seattle, that the missing girls stopped."

Mike Fisher caught up with Manny Treff at the Roseburg, Oregon, city jail on April 11, 1975.

His fellow inmates at the jail told Fisher that Treff drank his own urine and often laughed spontaneously at nothing. Sometimes he slept under his bunk instead of on it.

He was at first hostile to Fisher and the three investigators who had accompanied him from Aspen. But after he was apprised of the seriousness of Fisher's mission, Treff settled down. Asked if he would submit to a lie detector test, he agreed to—provided the polygraph operator didn't wear a tie.

In all, Treff was given three separate lie detector tests administered by Corporal Donald Cain of the Oregon State Patrol. Cain's conclusion: ". . . this agent is of the opinion that MANNY TREFF apparently is not involved in the murder of KAREN [*sic*] CAMPBELL."

The lie detector results were hardly conclusive; although Treff finally had been responsive and even cooperative, his evident mental imbalance could have invalidated the results. But Fisher had other reasons for doubting Treff's culpability. Once he met the man, he had trouble believing that Treff's characteristically unsubtle approach would have lured a willing Caryn Campbell from the Wildwood Inn.

Then there was the fact that while Treff was in jail two more women had vanished without a trace. On March 15, 1975, ski instructor Julie Cunningham disappeared from Vail, Colorado. She has never been found. On April 6, twenty-five-year-old Denise Oliverson of Grand Junction rode away from her boyfriend's house on her bike. The bike was found under a freeway overpass; she is still officially a missing person.

After telephoning Thompson, Fisher and his investigators drove over to Utah with their Campbell autopsy reports and photos of her body as it was found. Together with Thompson and another Salt Lake City detective, Ben Forbes, the Colorado investigators compared the Campbell case with the Melissa Smith and Laura Aime records.

Fisher later told Hugh, "You couldn't look at those photographs and autopsy slides and read those reports without noting gross similarities. We didn't come back from the meeting saying, 'Okay, we have one man doing all these heinous things.' But we were confident that there was a *high* degree of probability that we all had the same problem."

Manny Treff was cleared of the northwest killings, too—another dead-end lead for the Seattle and King County police.

Under the best of circumstances, these two agencies were wary of each other. Natural allies, they nevertheless maintained a strict division of responsibilities. Neither routinely told the other on what cases they were working or shared information.

With the coming of "Ted" these divisions were exacerbated. The major problem was publicity, and the public terror waxed with the discovery of the bodies on Taylor Mountain, providing fertile conditions for the persistent occult theories of the case to proliferate. An odd-shaped piece of paper was found near the Issaquah hillside, and promptly there was speculation that it was a ceremonial mask. The "mask" turned out to be a wing cover for a model airplane. Many people were convinced that a virulent offshoot of the Charles Manson family had moved to the Seattle area and had begun a new reign of terror led by "Ted."

So taut were people's nerves that an ill-considered official remark could touch off a near panic. Nick Mackie, for instance, was quoted in the press as speculating that "Ted" probably lived somewhere near North Bend and Issaquah, since that was where most of his victims were found.

"A lot of people are scared stiff, especially the younger women," King County deputy D.G. Riser told a reporter from the *Tacoma News Tribune.* A drugstore clerk named Claire Dillman shuddered as she told the paper that "murder was something you read about happening in California or somewhere. Now it's right in our backyards."

Dave Workman, editor of a local weekly, explained that the thought of "Ted" being a neighbor "scares people badly. How are you going to know? You might have passed him in the grocery store, or met him on the street a hundred times."

At the end of the article, Deputy Riser recounted coming upon a North Bend woman in a disabled car quite near the site where

Denise Naslund and Janice Ott were found. As he pulled up, said Riser, the stranded woman ran crying from her car and threw her arms around him. "God I'm glad to see you!" she sobbed in hysteria. "Here I am stranded in Ted's country!"

Such fears among the population did not unite the cops behind the single purpose of catching "Ted"; they put a premium on being the agency that broke the case. Thus, an attempt to merge the Seattle and King County investigations into a single task force operation under Nick Mackie's command was doomed. It lasted for about a month.

"I pulled my guys out of that task force fairly fast," Swindler says. "My sergeant came in to me and said, 'Hey, Captain, we're just not accomplishing anything over there.' When my men complained to their men that they weren't cooperating they were told, 'The lieutenant or the captain says they're afraid you might solve this thing before they do. They told us not to tell you.' "

Whatever their motives, the county police investigators were secretive with their information. It wasn't until 1981 that Herb Swindler learned from us that one of the key Lake Sammamish witnesses was an undercover narcotics agent on the city's payroll.

Herb Swindler retired that summer, ready to take his ease and to pass on the burdens and frustrations of chasing "Ted." He couldn't know how soon the hunt would be over. At the same time, Bob Keppel and the county detectives regrouped. They winnowed down their suspect lists, double-checking each possibility and compiling a new file on the one hundred "Teds" they had not positively cleared. In the end, they ran down every one of them, and each was eliminated finally and absolutely. Every suspect, that is, except one.

Ted Bundy was stoned that night in August, 1975, when he was first arrested in Utah. "I really didn't know what was on my mind," he told me, "or what I wanted to do. I was a little bit fucked up."

He thought he'd cruise State Street, a main north-south thoroughfare in Salt Lake which at that hour might still be full of people and things to do. But he drove south on State Street without stopping. Ted was enjoying his marijuana high and delighted in what the dope was doing to the colors of the night.

Just south of Salt Lake City, he turned onto the interstate and continued south. He still had no particular destination in mind.

Far off to the west, he could see the twinkling lights of the huge Kennecott Company Bingham Canyon copper mine. On an impulse, he headed in that direction.

Short of reaching the vast facility, Ted turned north again until he was about even with the city. He started east and came to suburban Granger. Disoriented by the dope, Bundy soon lost himself in a maze of subdivision streets that seemed to loop and curve endlessly. He stopped to check his map and also took a moment to light another joint. Moments before, he hadn't noticed Sergeant Hayward in his patrol car outside his house.

As Bundy tells it, "All I wanted to do was get home. I started off and it was at that point I saw lights in my rearview mirror. I turned and they turned and all of a sudden I didn't feel right. It didn't look right to me.

"I turned again and it turned and it was clear that the car was following me. I really had no idea why. And so I was just going to try to get away from it. I was very nervous.

"After the first or second turn, I got rid of what little dope was left in the bag and I was headed for what looked like an intersection. The light was red and the car was still following me.

"The guy later said he had his red landing light on, or whatever the fuck it was, but I swear to God he didn't have his goddamn red light on! It just appeared to be a goddamn light-colored car that was tailing me.

"I went through the red light and turned onto what was obviously a main drag. I looked in the mirror as the car was coming around the corner and *then* there was this bright red glow on the side. That's the *first* I saw of that red light. It wasn't flashing. There were no sirens. Nothing. At that point it dawned on me that I had something unusual on my hands."

Ted says that he pulled into a gas station, stopped, and got out of his car. Hayward parked about four feet behind him. Bundy claims that the sergeant was fuming, demanding to know what Ted was doing "in *my* neighborhood" and asking his captive why he didn't try to run "so I can take your head off."

Hayward's vehemence, Ted recalls, was puzzling. "I didn't fully understand it. I mean, there had been no crime committed in the vicinity that night. I wasn't on anybody's hit list at the time, as far as I know. If he lived where he said he lived, it was just coincidence. Certainly, he didn't *lure* me into his neighborhood, and certainly I didn't seek *him* out."

The arrest rattled Ted into a ridiculous alibi, the first and only time he ever offered the police a concrete story of his whereabouts. "I have no idea in the world why I said I'd been to see *Towering Inferno*," he told me. But he put on a smiling, compliant air for the agitated state patrolman and the two other policemen who had answered Hayward's call for assistance. "I'm not sure what I felt," Ted went on. "I thought things were under control, though. I thought I had a bunch of klutzes who were going to fuck me around."

Hayward radioed in Ted's driver's license number and checked the local drive-in. According to Bundy, the three cops kept questioning him about his reasons for being out in the Granger subdivision at that hour, a rapid-fire interrogation that intensified when his movie alibi fell apart. "I thought," he later said, "there might be some time for song and dance. I didn't even get much dance in."

Hayward's initial cursory search of the VW's interior had revealed the dislocated passenger seat and the fourteen-inch "jimmy bar." He decided to call for a detective.

Moments later, Daryle M. Ondrak of the Salt Lake County sheriff's office arrived; and as Ted lounged against the front of Hayward's patrol car, Ondrak and one of the other officers inspected the Volkswagen more thoroughly. Hayward had only shone his flashlight into the car; now Ondrak opened the doors and trunk. In later testimony, the police would say Ted Bundy consented to the search. Ted and his lawyers vigorously argued that he had not.

In any event, Ondrak found the handcuffs (which Ted had forgotten he had in his trunk), the ice pick, a pantyhose mask, a ski mask, several short lengths of rope, and some torn pieces of white sheet. He took the evidence into custody and told Bundy to expect a warrant against him for possession of burglary tools.

Daryle Ondrak pondered his curious suspect over the weekend. The paraphernalia in Ted's car looked anything but innocent. The hour and circumstance of the arrest and the phony alibi made him even more suspicious. What did not add up was the suspect's demeanor and appearance. Polite, friendly, and well-spoken, a law student, Ted hardly seemed the type to be driving around in the early hours with handcuffs and masks.

The following Tuesday, Ondrak sat through the weekly meeting of area detectives in which investigators from several local law enforcement agencies reviewed their cases and exchanged information. Everyone had spoken.

"Is that all?" someone asked.

Ondrak, who had been silent until then, spoke up. "Well," he said, "I don't know if this means anything. But I was involved with a stop this weekend and the guy had a pair of handcuffs in his car among other things." Across the table, Jerry Thompson's attention suddenly was riveted on Ondrak, who went on to explain how Ted was a relaxed and talkative law student and that he drove a Volkswagen.

Thompson's mind raced back to Carol DaRonch. Volkswagen. Handcuffs. Her abductor had seemed educated. It was too good to be true. As he later told Hugh, "The first thing that dawned on me was, 'Hey, I've got a live victim. She's the only hope I have in solving these murders.' "

For Ted Bundy, it now was just a matter of time.

# FIVE

THE *idea* of Ted Bundy preys on the mind. He is his own abstraction, a lethal absurdity masquerading as a man. Nevertheless, there were times at the prison when I was enveloped in the charisma of his madness. He fascinated me like a viper motionless in a crevice; a black, palpable malignancy.

There is a cold, poisonous luster in Bundy's unguarded gaze. I had heard about it before I met him, but I was unprepared for its effect. When his "entity" retreated, a softer blue came into Ted's eyes. His irises cleared and pupils constricted. His expression went from sinister to mild in a moment.

Our interviews were another game to him—a dare. We had to have rules, of course. Ted would talk so long as we agreed that he was only "speculating," in the third person, on the nature of the killer. I could not ask any direct questions. But in fact we weren't playing "let's pretend"; it was "let's pretend to pretend." If I once asked, "How did you do it?" it would spoil the game.

Nor by the rules was I allowed any spontaneous reaction to what Bundy told me. When my gorge rose—as it did often—I'd cover my anger or disgust with a noncommittal "I see" or "Uh-huh." Often he made me literally sick to my stomach, and sometimes it was all I could do to get out of the prison and back to the car before I vomited.

Ted has not openly confessed to the killings, but he also never positively denied them to us, either. It was always his "position" that he was innocent—an arguing point, not a statement of fact. In courtrooms, he has been likewise circumspect. "The person standing before you," he told one jury, "couldn't kill anyone." Ted was compartmentalizing guilt, rationalizing it away. He wasn't responsible for the other person *not* standing before the jurors.

Indicative of the remove he feels from his acts are the euphemisms he employed with me. Murder, for instance, was apt to be called his "inappropriate acting out," and rape, "satisfying that part of himself."

The rigid construct of his mind, the dams and levees and locks with which Ted restrains the flood of reality, are echoed in his tortured locutions. Talking about the killer's need not to succumb wholly to his urges, Ted said, "This person was constantly attempting to be objective and to determine whether or not any of his psychopathological tendencies were being exposed. He was constantly assessing that probability and trying to keep a sense of proportion within himself. Not just for a surface kind of demonstration, but also in the hopes of keeping on an even keel, rationally, normally. Not isolating himself too much from the mainstream. Not simply to preserve conditions under which the malignant part of him could survive, but also sometimes to overcome those desires."

Ted began his story with a preamble of operatic sweep and dimension. Much of it was sociological twaddle, comments on the dissolution of society and the fracturing of the nuclear family, or historical ruminations. It was a picture of the world as he saw it: confusing, threatening, verging toward anomie. The other important ingredient, said Ted, was a flaw, a congenital predisposition, that was exploited by his environment. He wasn't entirely blaming his world for shaping him, but he obviously saw himself as a child of his times.

His first substantive remarks were on the roles of sex and violence in the development of the psychopath. "This condition," he explained, "is not immediately seen by the individual or identified as a serious problem. It sort of manifests itself in an interest concerning sexual behavior, sexual images. It might simply be an attraction such as *Playboy*, or a host of other normal, healthy sexual stimuli that are found in the environment. But this interest, for some unknown reason, becomes geared towards matters of a sexual nature that involve violence. I cannot emphasize enough the gradual development of this. It is not short-term."

He told me that long before there was a need to kill there were juvenile fantasies fed by photos of women in skin magazines, suntan oil advertisements, or jiggly starlets on talk shows. He was transfixed by the sight of women's bodies on provocative display. He told me, too, of the protokiller watching X-rated movies and searching out the more violent police dramas on television. Ted said "this person" would carry home some pornographic book, read it, then shred it in anger, self-disgust, and fear of discovery.

Crime stories fascinated him. He read pulp detective magazines and gradually developed a store of knowledge about criminal techniques—what worked and what didn't. That learning remained incidental to the central thrill of reading about the abuse of female images, but nevertheless he was schooling himself.

"Maybe he focused on pornography as a vicarious way of experiencing what his peers were experiencing in reality," Ted opined, trying to sound reflective. "Then he got sucked into the more sinister doctrines that are implicit in pornography—the use, the abuse, the possession of women as objects."

The "peers" Ted mentioned were the high school boys he had talked of weeks ago, whose lewd conversations had so confused him. He seemed indifferent to the overt parallel between what he'd told me in the first person and what he was revealing to me now.

Bundy explained that "he was not imagining himself actively doing these things, but he found gratification in reading about others so engaged. Eventually, the interest would become so demanding for new material that it could only be catered by what he could find in the so-called dirty book stores.

"In a pornography shop," he said, "you can find a variety of perversions. Anyone that walks into one of these places is not just interested in a Great Dane humping someone or two men engaged in sexual activity. It is just not the way it works."

Clearly Ted was personally familiar with dirty book stores.

"But it does offer variety, and a certain percentage of it is devoted toward literature that explores situations where a man, in the context of sexual encounter, in one way or another engages in some sort of violence toward a woman, or the victim. There are, of course, a whole host of subsituations that could come under that particular heading. Your girlfriend, your wife, a stranger, children—whatever—a whole host of victims are found in this kind of literature. And in this kind of literature, they are treated as victims."

After three days, the first and most important link between us had been forged. Ted was no longer dodging me; he now was going to lead me back along his path to mass murder. He was comfortable behind his veil of fiction. To him, what he'd said already and what he'd soon tell me was not a confession. It couldn't stand the test of admissibility in court, and thus it was outside his definition of guilt. In truth, he was telling me nothing concrete enough to implicate him directly in anything. Yet the narration would be too seamless, the descriptions too detailed and consistent, for this to be anything but the truth. The hunchback had begun to emerge.

I was anything but comfortable. As the spring weeks of 1980 grew progressively hotter and more humid in northern Florida, as the insect population exploded in the swamps and 50,000-foot-high thunderheads rolled across the state each afternoon, I sat sweating in that little room with Ted. He showed very little recognizable emotion and often paid little attention to me—for which I was grateful.

Sometimes I'd take notes simply to avoid having to look at him. They were superfluous; every word was pouring into the tape recorder.

As Ted told it, the preoccupation with sex and violence gave rise to crude fantasies wherein "this person" first began considering himself an actor. This period, I guessed, would have been 1966 or 1967, about the time he first knew Marjorie Russell. The next stage of his psychopathology was about to begin.

"He," Ted told me, "was walking down the street one evening and just totally by chance looked up into the window of a house and saw a woman undressing. He began, with increasing regularity, to canvass, as it were, the community he lived in. He peeped in windows and watched women undress or whatever could be seen during the evening. He approached it almost like a project, throwing himself into it, literally, for years.

"Still, these occasions when he would travel about the neighborhood and search out candidates, places where he could see the things he wanted to see, were dictated by the demands of his normal life. So he wouldn't break a date, or postpone an important event, or rearrange his life in any significant way to accommodate his indulgence in this voyeuristic behavior.

"He gained, at times, a great amount of gratification from it. And became increasingly adept at it, as anyone becomes adept at anything they do over and over and over again."

Voyeurism, Ted explained, helped to satisfy the sick fantasies while keeping the woman—the object—at a safe remove. But the "disordered self" then began to demand a more active type of gratification, something stronger than mere fantasy. Like an addiction, the need for a more powerful experience was coming over him.

This heightened urgency led to clumsy attempts to disable women's cars by pulling the rotor device out of the engine's distributor, and later he deflated their tires. The stratagem was doomed to defeat in a university district where there always seemed to be plenty of guys around to help a woman with car trouble.

I knew that Ted had already confessed his voyeurism to the police, but he hadn't discussed with them this early fantasy. A Peeping Tom is one thing, dreams of kidnap are quite another. Ted's thoughts ran toward forcible control of a woman. Yet typical of his child's pshyche was the playground mood of the fantasy. He didn't yet know what he'd do to a woman if he could disable her car and catch her alone.

"There's not really a strong desire to do this," he said. "But it's like toying around with danger almost. It's kind of a game, sort of like 'Let's see how far it goes.' "

Ted called it a game, the way his stealing had been a game, a flirtation with danger. Still, the habit grew perceptibly more insistent just as Ted had become a bolder and bolder thief over the years. And this "condition," as he called it, like stealing, was abetted by the use of alcohol.

"I think you could make a little more sense out of much of this if you take into account the effect of alcohol," said Bundy. "It's important. It's very important as a trigger. When this person drank a good deal, his inhibitions were significantly diminished. He would find that his urge to engage in voyeuristic behavior on trips to the bookstore would become more prevalent, more urgent. It was as though the dominant personality was sedated. On every occasion when he engaged in such behavior, he was intoxicated."

The "dominant personality" was Ted's term for the public self, the upright law-abider. Had Bundy matured normally, he would have developed a superego, or conscience. Instead, he built a mask of sanity which he confused with a conscience. Lacking this vital component in his psyche, a governor on his impulses, he could not feel guilt or remorse or recognize that he was already very sick. His "dominant personality" was an illusion.

Now, for the first time, I felt Ted's malignant aura. His eyes suddenly darkened and his voice hardened. The constant din of the prison seemed more distant and muffled. He had my undivided attention.

"On one particular evening," Ted said, "when he had been drinking a great deal and as he was passing a bar, he saw a woman leaving the bar and walking up a fairly dark side street. Something seemed to seize him: the urge to do something to that person seized him in a way that he had never been affected before. And it seized him strongly.

"Without a great deal of thought, he searched around for some instrumentality to attack this woman with. He found a piece of two-by-four in a lot and proceeded to follow and track this girl for several blocks.

"There was really no control at this point.

"The situation is novel, because while he may have toyed around with fantasies before, and made several abortive attempts to act out a fantasy, it never had reached the point where actually he was confronted with harming another individual."

Ted was caught up in his narrative, totally heedless of me and the guards who hovered around the interview room. If any of them thought to stop and listen by the door, they would have heard it all. Sometimes I wondered if perhaps that wasn't necessary; maybe the prison authorities were themselves taping our conversations. The suspicion that they did stays with me, although I have no proof or even any good reason to believe that they did. The atmosphere in that room generated many such paranoid notions.

"So he'd gotten ahead of his quarry, this girl," Ted continued, "and was laying in wait for her. But before she reached the point where he was concealed, she turned and went into her house.

"The revelation of the experience and the frenzied desire that seized him really seemed to usher in a new dimension to that part of him that was obsessed with violence and women and sexual activity—a composite kind of thing not terribly well defined but more well defined as time went on. This particular incident spurred him on succeeding evenings to hunt this neighborhood, searching.

"He had, in the months and years previous to this, frequently passed women in alleys, women in dark streets, women alone on any number of occasions when he was making his rounds and looking in windows. But it never occurred to him—ever, at any point—to use this as an opportunity to do anything. It just never occurred to him. For some reason, the sight of that woman under those circumstances on that evening and in the condition he was in sort of signaled a breakthrough. The breaking of the tension. Making a hole in the dam.

"On succeeding evenings, he began to scurry around this same neighborhood, obsessed with the image he had seen. On one particular occasion, he saw a woman park her car and walk up to her door and fumble for her keys. He walked up behind her and struck her with a piece of wood he was carrying. She fell down and began screaming. He panicked and ran.

"What he had done terrified him, purely terrified him. Full of remorse and remonstrating with himself for the suicidal nature of that activity, the ugliness of it all, he quickly sobered up. He was horrified by the recognition that he had the capacity to do such a thing. He was fearful, terribly fearful, that for some reason or another he might be apprehended.

"The effect was for some time to close up the cracks again. For the first time, he sat back and swore to himself that he wouldn't do something like that again, or even anything that would lead to it. He did everything he should have done. He didn't go out at night, and when he was drinking he stayed around friends. For a period of months, the enormity of what he did stuck with him. He watched his behavior, and reinforced the desire to overcome what he had begun to perceive were some problems that were probably more severe than he would have liked to believe they were."

Ted described fear and anxiety at the thought of discovery; there was no mention of remorse at what the attack victim suffered. He made me understand that he felt nothing for his prey. The shock of realizing this helped me keep a distance between us, stopped me from vibrating to the rhythm of his insanity. For the time being, all I had to do was keep silent as he talked.

"It was the deceptive fashion, you might say, in which that psychopathology withdrew into this dormant stage that led the individual to the erroneous belief that he got it out of himself, and this wasn't going to happen again. As a consequence of this new attitude, the individual would throw himself into normal activities with more vigor. Just try to get a second wind. I don't know how to describe it. But he would try to indulge himself in normal activities. Almost as if he was welcoming himself back to a lifestyle, a state of mind, that was without the fear, the terror, and the harm."

Ted turned in his chair and cocked his head to the side. Sweat stood out on his temples and stained the front of his T-shirt. His face was mottled and looked cold to the touch, like the belly of a fish. He began again in a voice tight with tension.

"But slowly, the pressures, tensions, dissatisfactions which, in the very early stages, fueled this thing had an effect. Yet it was more self-sustaining and didn't need as much tension or as much disharmony externally as it did before. It sort of reached a point where this condition would generate its own needs, and wouldn't need that reservoir of tension or stress that it seemed to thrive on before. Gradually, as I say, it would re-emerge.

"This individual would say, 'Well, just one trip to the bookstore. Just once around the neighborhood.' It did this kind of thing. And then, gradually, it would become more and more demanding, as it were.

"However, as he slipped back into his old routine, something did stick with him. That was the incredible danger of allowing himself to fall into spontaneous, unplanned acts of violence. It took six months or so until he was back thinking of alternative means of engaging in similar activity, but not something that would likely result in apprehension or failure of one sort or another.

"Then, on another night, he saw a woman walking home late at night or early in the morning. He followed her home and looked in the window and watched her get ready for bed. He did this on several occasions, for this was a regular kind of thing. Eventually, he created a plan where he would attack her.

"Early one morning, he sneaked in through a door he knew was open and entered the bedroom. Implementing a plan based somewhat on fantasy, based on anything but personal knowledge, he jumped on the woman's bed and attempted to restrain her. All he succeeded in doing was waking her up and causing her to panic and scream. He left very rapidly.

"Then he was seized with the same kind of disgust and repulsion and fear and wonder at why he was allowing himself to attempt such extraordinary violence. But the significance of this particular occasion was that while he stayed off the streets and vowed he'd never do it again and recognized the horror of what he had done and certainly was frightened by what he saw happening, it took him only three months to get over it. In the next incident, he was over it in a month."

We found no official reports of attacks on women such as Ted described, but by our estimates these assaults would have occurred throughout 1973. The first attack on the woman fumbling with her keys might have come in the spring, just before Ted left the King County Office of Law and Justice Planning and went to work in Olympia for the state Republican chairman, Ross Davis.

The "dormant stage," as Ted called it—the time spent in eager social involvement—would coincide with the summer and early fall of 1973, the period when Ted earned the most money he'd ever made, won back Marjorie, and was looking forward to beginning law school.

Then his high expectations were dashed; by mid-autumn of 1973 he was floundering again, the dormancy ended, the "disordered self" reawakened, and there was the abortive assault on the woman in her bed. What else Ted was doing is unknowable, but it was at this time that Liz found a bag of women's clothing in his room.

The next time, Ted said, "it took him only three months to get over it." The re-emergence of the "condition," we think, then coincides with the period of heavy stress following Ted's Christmas week with Marjorie, when he agreed to marry her. Only a few days after New Year's, Mary Adams was assaulted with a speculum in her basement bedroom.

Then, again according to Ted, another attack followed in just a month, or about the time that Lynda Ann Healy vanished from her bedroom.

"What happened was this entity inside him was not capable of being controlled any longer," Ted went on, "at least not for any considerable period of time. It began to try to justify itself, to create rationalizations for what it was doing. Perhaps to satisfy the rational, normal part of the individual. One element that came into play was anger, hostility. But I don't think that was an overriding emotion when he would go out hunting, or however you want to describe it. On most occasions it was a high degree of anticipation, of excitement, or arousal. It was an adventuristic kind of thing.

"He received no pleasure from harming or causing pain to the person he attacked," Bundy insisted. "He received absolutely no gratification. He did everything possible within reason—considering the unreasonableness of the situation—not to torture these individuals, at least not physically. The fantasy that accompanies and generates the anticipation that precedes the crime is always more stimulating than the immediate aftermath of the crime itself. He should have recognized that what really fascinated him was the hunt, the adventure of searching out his victims. And, to a degree, possessing them physically as one would possess a potted plant, a painting, or a Porsche. Owning, as it were, this individual."

I absorbed Ted's revelations as stoically as I could, wondering anxiously from time to time what my endurance limit was. The morning he told me of the thrill of the hunt and the need to "own" a female body, I was so taut that I felt a muscle or ligament tear under my heart. It ached for weeks.

That afternoon, I stopped at a small grocery down the road from the prison. The proprietor, an affable country southerner, knew me as a twice-a-day cigarette and coffee customer. Today I needed aspirin.

"Nice day today," he said as he handed me my change. Then he leaned over the counter. "You okay, son?" he asked. "You look like you just saw a ghost or something."

I managed a weak laugh and then coughed. The muscle tore a little more and felt like a knife in my ribs.

With his descriptions of the first assaults, Ted began to stall me. To this point, he had done almost all the talking. Now, when I prodded him to discuss specific murder cases, he temporized. For several days our conversations went nowhere.

Bundy had obvious legal considerations in mind. If he was *too* specific, *too* detailed, he might trip over what the police call a "key"—a bit of information that is never disclosed to the press and of which only the killer could be aware.

I think he had another reason, too, for the unemotional sketchiness of his answers. While Ted acknowledged that there were an element of conscious hostility, anger, involved in the growth and development of the sickness, he insisted that there was no more rancor in the killings themselves than a hunter might feel when he puts a bullet through an elk's heart. Less perhaps; at least the elk hunter acknowledges that he is killing a live thing. The girls that Ted Bundy talked about had no more flesh-and-blood reality to their killer than a Coppertone billboard. To him, their deaths were consequential only insofar as they placed him in jeopardy of discovery. He often likened the blood lust to a sport, or a hobby. "This is on a different level than this individual would deal with women every day," he explained. "Not in the context of the sexual situation, because that is over here someplace, like collecting stamps. He doesn't retain the taste of glue, so to speak, all day long."

This heartlessness created a welcome hatred in me. It steadied me, and under its influence I was more persistent with him than I might have been. When at last I maneuvered him into discussing Lynda Healy, the first murder, hating Ted made it all the easier to press him as he sought time and again to confuse and evade me.

It was in her case that the police missed the significance of the bloodstains and the potential evidence contained in the semen deposit, as well as any hair or fiber traces the killer might have left. And there were two enduring mysteries: How had he selected her as a victim? (Did he follow her and her friends home from the bar that night?) How had he done it? (Had he slipped into the house before she went to bed?)

"How," I asked Ted, "would it have begun?"

He stiffened. "Well," he answered, "I don't know how the crime was committed, but we can speculate. That's all we can do."

Bundy cleared his throat and looked at me. It wasn't exactly a smile I saw; it was more the look of a boy with a secret, a sly grin. His eyes once again began to darken.

"He had seen the house before," Ted said, "and for one reason or another had been attracted to its occupants. Then one evening, just being in the mood, so to speak, he checked out the house [and] found out the front door was open. He thought about it. What kind of opportunity that offered. And returned to the house later and entered the house and explored it."

"While everybody was asleep?" I asked.

"Yeah."

"Was this some days later?"

"No, that same evening."

"I see," I replied, then thought about the unlocked door. A casual oversight had cost Lynda Healy her life.

"Then," Ted continued, "he went around the house and found a particular bedroom door that he opened—really hit and miss. Not knowing who or what, not looking for any particular individual. And that would be the opportunity. This was late at night. And presumably everyone would be asleep."

"Would he have some sort of knife or club so there would be no noise?"

Ted hesitated. "I really don't know," he finally said. "If he struck the woman she would have probably left a large amount of blood. Or if she was shot there would have been a quantity of blood. If she was stabbed there would also be blood. So it pretty well eliminates the alternatives."

"There was, I believe, a small quantity of blood found on the sheets."

"I suppose you would have to go into the physiology of

strangulation to determine what kind of hemorrhaging was going on.''

This time I hesitated. "How would this person have proceeded from there?" I then asked.

"Well, you can put yourself in that position. You have the young lady in the middle of the night. And we know that at some later time the remains were found somewhere in the Cascades. So, obviously she was transported up there."

I wanted to know how Lynda Healy was taken from her bedroom. "I guess you would have had to dress her?" I ventured.

Ted ignored my use of "you."

"In that kind of situation," he replied mechanically, "a person who was alert enough to be able to dress would not be afraid in terms of struggling or crying out. So it would be unlikely that any attempt was made to clothe the girl."

"Then she was unconscious?"

"Well," he said, as if bored with my density, "walking out under her own power at that hour of the morning would not necessarily be the soundest kind of approach."

"Would she have regained consciousness by the time they reached their destination?"

"Well," he said, "that certainly is a possibility."

I tried another tack. "A mighty curious feature in the bedroom," I said, "was the fact that the bed had been made, but apparently not by Lynda herself, because of the type of fold that was put in the sheet."

Ted shrugged. "It was an attempt to cover up her disappearance."

"Would she be bound with rope or some kind of restraint?"

"[That] would be the way it would be done."

"Would there be words exchanged?"

"I doubt it. He would have gagged the person."

"Where would you guess they'd drive to? Where would be their destination?"

"Someplace that was quiet and private. His home or some secluded area."

"My assumption is that once the abduction had occurred, the person knew what else they were going to do."

"It would depend upon the condition of the girl. It would depend on the traffic. It would depend on a number of things. It would depend on a person's state of mind. How calm or excited or excitable he was under the circumstances."

I was losing patience. "How calm do you think he would be?" I asked.

Evidently my irritation showed. Ted actually responded to the question. "This was one of the first instances that he'd abducted a woman in this fashion. He was extremely nervous, almost frantic, and in a panic trying to attempt anything. There you are, what do you do with the situation?"

"Now having crossed the barrier between contemplation and action. . . ."

"Uh-uh. That barrier had been crossed before. But now it had gone a step or two further. If he was intoxicated just prior to when the crime began, then he would likely regain his senses when he knew that [he had] exposed himself to a great deal of danger."

"Would she be bound and gagged? Unconscious?" I was pushing for more concrete detail. "Would he just throw her in the back seat of his car, or would she be seated next to him?"

Ted wasn't offering any. "He'd probably put her in the back seat of the car and cover her with something."

"Then what?"

"Let's say that he decided to drive to a remote location that he just picked out. Once he had arrived at this point where he didn't have a fear of alarming anyone in the neighborhood with shouts or screams or whatever, [he'd] untie the woman."

"And then what?"

"He would have the girl undress and then, with that part of himself gratified, he found himself in a position where he realized that he couldn't let the girl go. And at that point he would kill her and leave her body where he'd taken her."

"Would he just stab her or whack her on the head or something swift or . . .?"

"We've established the infliction of violence was not something that this individual craved. It would be quick."

"Would there be any conversation between the two of them?"

"There'd be some. Since this girl in front of him represented not a person, but again the image, or something desirable, the last thing we would expect him to want to do would be to personalize this person."

"I see. And there was no confrontation of the fact the victim had to be dispatched, until fairly late?" I was beginning to sound like Ted. I wanted to ask, Had you intended to kill her all along, or didn't you think about it?

Ted considered the question a moment, then spoke. "A certain amount of the need of that malignant condition had been satisfied through the sexual release. . . . That driving force would recede somewhat, allowing the normal individual's mental mechanisms to again begin to take hold, to control the situation, or more so than previously. You'd expect a certain amount of debate, or regret, as it were, that it was faced with a situation. . . .''

''Would there be a period of internal debate? Or would this happen fairly instantaneously?''

''It would vary depending on the strength of the normal self in its responses. For instance, just how the sexual needs have been gratified. It could last a matter of hours. It could last just a few minutes.''

''What would you [say] in this matter?''

''It's impossible to say. Assuming, however, that he drove directly up into the wilds, and assuming a fairly continuous progression of events, it probably would have been a little more than a few hours.''

I asked him about the killer's state of mind in the aftermath of his first murder. Ted was more at ease with this type of question.

''A nominally normal individual,'' he said, ''who has become somewhat subordinate to bizarre desires and abducts a woman and kills her finds himself in a great deal of panic. In the days and weeks following the killing, there would be an undercurrent of anxiety that comes with wondering just what was seen, what was found, what was or was not missed.

''The tension was concentrated principally upon the progress of the police investigation. If nothing of any significance was disclosed in the newspapers, that would be one way the tension was reduced. As far as remorse over the act, that would last for a period of time. But it could all be justified. He would say, 'Well, listen. You fucked up this time, but you're never gonna do it again. So let's just stay together and it won't ever happen again.'

''But this didn't last for very long—a matter of weeks. We go first into a state of semi-dormancy, and then it would sort of regenerate itself. Once it became clear that there was going to be no link made—or that he would not be under suspicion—the only thing which appeared to be relevant was not exposing himself to that kind of risk of harm again. Not thinking about the nature of the act, or the death of the individual herself. The approach is, say, 'Don't ever do it again.' But as time passes, the emphasis is on 'Don't get caught.' ''

It was at this point during our prison interviews that I ceased feeling pity for Bundy. Before, I had pictured him as a victim of his illness. No one, I believed, could have welcomed such a depravity as Ted suffered.

But I was wrong. Without a conscience he wasn't human. His outlook and capacities were repulsive to me. Thenceforward, I could think of his eventual execution with equanimity.

# SIX

Death Row inmates have nothing to look forward to, and therefore little to lose. It is a task in itself for prison authorities to keep them from killing each other, a guard, or themselves.

As a consequence, I couldn't always see Ted when I wanted to. If there had been a prison fight, or if a death warrant had been signed by the governor, the carefully controlled flow of visitors to The Row was further constricted. Sometimes the traffic of attorneys and officials is simply too heavy. Thus it was several days after we discussed Lynda Healy before I saw Ted again.

In the interim, he had reflected on what he'd told me and appeared to have second thoughts about talking further. I brought up Donna Gail Manson and Susan Rancourt, but he wouldn't discuss them. I was forced to backtrack in order to re-establish our connection, to regain the mood.

"Victims," I said. "You indicated that they would be symbols and images. But I'm not really sure. Images of what?"

"Of women!" he exclaimed. "I mean, of the idealized woman. What else can I say?"

"A stereotype?"

"No. They wouldn't be stereotypes necessarily. But they would be reasonable facsimilies to women as a class. A class not of women, per se, but a class that has almost been created through the mythology of women and how they are used as objects."

"Would there be a standard of beauty or attractiveness?" I wondered, thinking of the range in the victims' appearances.

"Everyone," Bundy answered huffily, "has his standards." He said that a distinctly unattractive, overweight, or otherwise unappealing woman wouldn't be a candidate. "The person's criteria," he explained, "would be based upon those standards of attractiveness accepted by his peer group."

Another question had bothered me. Do certain women, as has been suggested, attract their assailants by the way they move or act? I asked Ted if the victims shared some detectable vulnerability.

The answer was no, couched in typically turgid language. "What we're talking about here is just opportunity," he said, "as opposed to more discrete factors that would be exhibited by the person." In other words, the girls simply had been in the wrong place at the wrong time.

Despite the strictness with which visitors are monitored, prison is no obstacle to the convicts' practice of everyday vices. The day after we discussed his standards of beauty, Ted came into the interview room stoned. I took the opportunity to bring up Kathy Parks, who was taken 260 miles from Oregon to Taylor Mountain.

"Why Oregon State?" I began. "Why did he go to Corvallis?"

Ted was in an expansive mood. He felt like talking. "It would be an attempt to commit a crime without it being linked to other crimes," he said.

"Is there a way to distinguish the personality, the characteristics of the personality at that time?"

"Parks disappeared in May, and Ball disappeared on June first, which is just a little less than a month. Georgann Hawkins disappeared on the night of June eleventh, which is just a few days after the Ball disappearance. So we can see by the short period of time that elapsed between the disappearance of Parks and the disappearance of Ball that there would not be a great deal of change in the state of mind of the individual."

Ted's head had begun to loll. His attention strayed to the windows and around the room and then back to me. Keeping him concentrated was like helping a drunk find his car keys.

"How different, Ted, would his approach be from the earlier killings?"

"The M.O.," he slurred, "is somewhat more sophisticated than the one employed in the Healy case. He may have approached her and asked her if she'd like to go to Taylor Mountain!" Bundy laughed. "How about that?" He laughed again. "Just a friendly little get-to-gether up there!"

I wasn't amused. "Would she be walking across campus? Or she'd be sitting in a bar maybe?"

He frowned. "She could have been sitting in a library studying.

She could have been sitting in a cafeteria studying. She was supposed to be depressed and lonely or something.

"She might seek out company just to take her mind off her problem or loneliness—depression. Let's say she was having a snack in the cafeteria and [he] just sat down next to her and began talking, and representing himself to be a student there, and suggested that they go out somewhere to get a bite to eat or to get a drink. Either he was convincing enough or she was depressed enough to accept his invitation. Of course, once she got in his car, then he had her in a position where he wanted her, and could then assume control over her.

"A jog down a local tavern in Corvallis would probably be the farthest he would expect her to accept as a plausible kind of trip."

"Would he be patient enough to go to the tavern?"

"It's unlikely. He wouldn't want to be exposed to a situation where he would be seen in her presence. Certainly no more than necessary."

"If he had been drinking, wouldn't it be evident to her?"

"It's odd that some people are more able to detect the effect of alcohol on people than others. [For] someone who meets a stranger who's under the influence of alcohol, outside of the fact that it might be on his breath, subtle changes in his behavior wouldn't be that evident. We're not talking about some stumbling drunk."

I finally had Ted's attention. "What would transpire once they're in the car?"

"He would not want to confront her in the car and in an area where a struggle could be witnessed by anyone just casually strolling down the street or something. So, once [he] had gained her confidence, then on the way to this tavern they were going to go to, he said that he'd just remembered that he had to pick up the finished copy of his thesis or something from the typist, and then drive out to a remote location." Bundy shut his eyes and sighed. He was smiling.

"I'm interested," I said, "in the mechanics of accosting somebody in a car."

"Oh, oh you are?" He laughed again. "Maybe you want to do it yourself, you know. I don't know about you."

"Could be." I shrugged. "You told me I had it—"

"Yeah," he interrupted. "You have it in you! I mean, I think it's there. Just needs a little, uh, a little development!" Ted was having great fun.

I cleared my throat. "What I'm saying is, What is the most effective way? Pull a gun?"

"Wouldn't need a gun, necessarily. This guy pulls up in a cornfield somewhere, you know, fairly abruptly.

"And this girl. Let's say that as he travels further and further away from a populated area, she probably is becoming uncomfortable. But she still wants to believe in the face validity of the situation her would-be abductor had created for her."

Ted coughed. "And, of course, by the time he pulled up and stopped, there would be virtually nothing she could do about it. In that instance, virtually all that would be necessary would be for the person to get out of the car, ask her to get out of the car, and if a struggle had ensued, he would easily overpower her. And recognizing the disadvantage of the [situation], she would submit to whatever instructions he gave her, out of fear, and out of whatever."

"You say whatever instuctions?"

"At that point he would have to tell her something—to be quiet, to do what he told her to do, et cetera."

"Would [he] typically want the victim to remove her own garments? Or would he prefer to do it himself?"

"I don't know. Let's say that as a result of his voyeuristic activities where he had freqently watched women undress, let's say he had a preference to watch the victims undress."

Ted called the next step the "sexual encounter." He did not describe it, but went on to "speculate" that Kathy Parks was driven alive to Seattle.

I asked if the reason for taking her back alive had to do with the same interim of indecision he had discussed in the Healy case, the time following the rape when the "dominant self" took over and saw that self-protection required that the girl be killed.

"We're not looking at reasons," Ted said testily. "The question you asked was 'Was she alive or was she dead when she was taken from Oregon to Washington?' The reasons why this girl would have been transported that amount of distance while she was still alive is another question entirely."

He calmed down. "And you're right. It certainly could have been a result of that indecision or conflict within the individual. Between the part of him that thought it was necessary to kill his victims, versus the part of him that did not—that found it to be extremely reprehensible, disgusting. The humane, moral, and legal approach to the alternative of killing would be not to kill her at all. Even in comparison to murder, the act of rape is somewhat less severe.

"We're not talking about rational and normal thought processes. A combination of desire to continue that possession in addition to the indecision about murdering her would result in the rather extraordinary act of transporting her that great amount of distance."

"Would you take the precaution of rendering her unconscious?"

Again, he ignored my use of "you." "There certainly wouldn't necessarily be the need for it. We still have to remember that the individual, at least not on a conscious level, has no desire or implements no design with the goal of terrorizing or torturing the person. [And he] ordinarily would not want to inflict any unnecessary violence or pain to the girl. So it wasn't necessary to render her unconscious. He would have had only to tie her up."

"What would you say would go through his mind on the drive to Seattle?"

"You've got this young woman, who's been sexually assaulted, who's tied up in the back of this person's car. If he's going to make a five-hour drive back to the Seattle area, he's gonna be nervous. He's gonna be thinking about what he's going to do."

"How long would it take him to resolve that?"

"In a way he'd probably view the driving time as a luxury, giving him time to think, as opposed to a constant state of agitation and anxiety. And would not really make the final decision until he was back in the Seattle area. When he was really forced to, you know, I mean really forced with facing the fact, 'Well, what are you going to do? You're here now. What are you going to do?' "

"Would there be a second assault on her before she was killed?"

"Well, given the amount of time they would have had to have been together, it's likely."

"Would he need to start drinking again?"

"He may, he could. But the barrier had been bridged, as it were, and the girl was in his possesssion. And it was something he had to deal with, drunk or sober.

"We have to realize that [he] also had his normal obligations to school, to friends and family and work and whatnot. If he had to be at work the next day, he could hardly leave the girl in his house the whole day, without concern that something might happen where she would be discovered."

"What more do you think can be said about the time from the arrival in King County to her arrival on Taylor Mountain?"

"At the Taylor Mountain crime scene?"

"Hmm-mmm." Ted had earlier suggested that Lynda Healy was killed on Taylor Mountain; now he was indicating that Kathy Parks had died there, too. If so, the site wasn't just a dump, as police believed, but a murder scene as well.

Ted was slipping away again. I restated my question, and he mumbled, ". . . whatever it is. With reference to, to, uh, what's her name?"

"I think it's Parks," I said icily.

"Parks. Terrible with names. And faces. Can't remember faces. Uh, you asked me something about going to Taylor Mountain?"

"I asked you what happened from their arrival in King County until when she ended up on Taylor Mountain."

Ted was suddenly very serious. "You asked me to speculate," he said with menace.

"Didn't I say speculate? All right, I asked you to speculate."

Then he laughed. "I've gone through this for hours with other people. Pardon me, but I'll be very meticulous about the wording here. You asked me to describe what happened. I can't tell you what happened. All I can do is just assist you with my educated guesses.

"You know, I'm not trying to put you down. That's not my intention. I'm just, I'm concerned about wording and I'm going to correct the record for that purpose."

"All right. About Taylor Mountain. You did speculate there probably would be another sexual assault before or at the same time she was killed."

"It's a distinct possibility, since they were obviously together for an extended period of time. One would expect that the person became sexually aroused for a second time."

"I'd also guess that if he went through all that trouble, why not—"

"Give it another lick?" Ted asked merrily.

"Yes," I said.

He was laughing again. "But I'm wallowing here. Poor Miss . . . uh, what's her name? Parks? I hope no one ever listens to this. They might think i was approaching a serious situation in a frivolous mood. That's not entirely true."

"All right."

Bundy pulled himself together. "Well, let's just track through.

He's probably tired and very upset, and nervous. Probably the only thing at that point he wants to do is to resolve the situation he finds himself in. And get some rest, or do something. So that before going home, or taking her anywhere else, he just drove directly up to the Taylor Mountain site, without much ado.

"Oh, yeah," he interrupted himself. "There was a lot of conjecture about why all these remains were found in one location. It is rather curious, on the one hand, considering [he] was clearly trying to cover up his crimes."

"Uh-huh."

"Now one of the theories advanced is that the only reason the skulls were found is because the victims had been decapitated."

"Hmm-mmm."

"Well, where did the bodies go, all right? Did they go somewhere else? I think we've discussed that a person that knows even a little bit about law enforcment knows that, in many instances, badly decomposed bodies are identified based on dentition. And so, just merely decapitating the victims wouldn't avoid their later identification.

"Then, what is the explanation for all those skulls and miscellaneous bones being found in the way they were? We'd have to conclude that the bones were found in the condition they were found in because of animal depredation, which is not an unusual thing.

"This might give us one clue as to why this person returned to that site on at least several occasions. Perhaps it was discovered that when a body was left there, and later when the individual would return to check out the situation, [he] would find that it was no longer there. And concluded that the animals in the area were doing, you know, his work for him, as it were. And would continue to go back there simply because he had his own garbage disposal. A whole bunch of little beasties who would, in effect, destroy every last shred of the victim."

"Hmm-mmm."

"With that in mind, we can say that Parks was taken directly to the vicinity where the other bodies were found, and that at that point he killed Parks. Either in the car or he marched her off the road and killed her in a more secluded location."

I bought a quart of scotch that night and tried to eat a cheeseburger; somewhere near dawn, I fell asleep or passed out.

At 9:00 A.M. I was back in the prison. Ted was in a tamer mood. I asked him about Brenda Ball.

Brenda, who disappeared from the Flame tavern on the first day of June 1974, had marked a departure from habit for him. She was not a college girl, and he had stalked her within miles of his first kill, Lynda Healy.

"The Ball case," I offered to Bundy, "didn't seem at all like the ones that came before it."

"He was interested in varying his M.O.," Ted replied, "in such a way as not to fan the flames of community outrage or the intensity of the police investigation. This is why this Ball girl found herself to be the next victim."

"What do you think might have happened that night?" I asked.

Ted repeated that he could only speculate, but he guessed that "he picked her up hitchhiking and they got to talking and she had nothing to do. He would ask her if she wanted to go to a party at his place and take her home. At this point, he would exert an influence on her which would be especially effective if she was under the influence of alcohol."

"He'd take her home?" I asked.

"Sure."

I pictured Ted and Brenda at the Rogerses' rooming house. Did he persuade her to go up the ladder to his window? Or did he maintain a hideout somewhere? "It would seem terribly risky—"

"If you live with someone," Ted explained. "But he had his own house."

"I see. What is going on in his mind on the way to his place?"

"Conversation," Ted said. "To remove himself from the personal aspects of the encounter, the interchange. Chattering and flattering and entertaining, as if seen through a motion picture screen. He would be engaging in the pattern just for the purpose of making the whole encounter seem legitimate—"

"Uh-huh."

"—and to keep her at ease. He didn't want this girl to get second thoughts about going with him to his place. And also, he was afraid if he started thinking about what he was going to do he'd either become more nervous or lose his concentration or in some way betray himself."

"So there's a very delicate balance between being cool and the excitement?"

"Well," Ted observed, "it's a critical balance, not a delicate balance. It became almost like acting a role. It wasn't difficult.

The more an actor acts in a role, the better he becomes at it, the more he is apt to feel comfortable in it, to be able to do things spontaneously. And get better, as it were, in his role.''

"So they go to his place?'' I asked.

"He'd have to explain why there isn't all the activity going on. It was probably not the first time she'd run into that kind of situation. Maybe it was. But in any event, she was somewhat wary of the situation and yet bored enough or intoxicated enough or both to just not really consider it threatening to her. They'd drink until she was exceptionally intoxicated. A dramatic departure from the Healy situation. In part, it is because of design. But in part it is just because of circumstances.''

I asked if the longer the two spoke the more apt she was to emerge as a person and thereby lose her symbolic value.

"Well, drinking has an effect on both parties,'' he explained. "On the one hand, the more intoxicated he became, the more repressed his normal codes of behavior. And the more she drank, the more she would lend herself to stereotypes.''

"How would he proceed?'' I asked, I couldn't be prepared for the response.

"The initial sexual encounter would be more or less a voluntary one, but one which did not wholly gratify the full spectrum of desires that he had intended. And so, after the first sexual encounter, gradually his sexual desire builds back up and joins, as it were, these other, unfulfilled desires, this other need to totally possess her. After she'd passed out, as she lay there somewhere in a state between coma and sleep, he strangled her to death.''

I swallowed hard and forced what I hoped was an even tone into my voice. "It seems to me,'' I said, "that there'd be some kind of logistical problem in getting her out of there.''

Not at all. "There wouldn't be any urgency,'' he answered, "since she was in a place that was private. Ultimately, he'd have to bundle her up in some fashion and take her out to his car when it's late some night.''

I thought with a shudder of the Utah girls, Melissa Smith in her perfect make-up and Laura Aime with her freshly washed hair. How long had Ted played with them?

Ted didn't say how long Brenda Ball was kept.

"What would he do with her?'' I asked.

"Just leave her in the bed,'' said Ted. "Put her in the closet. You know. I mean, no one's coming in.''

\*    \*    \*

There in the prison, insulated from the turmoil and the temptations that had fueled its cold rage when Ted was free, the "disordered self" could express itself in this freak colloquium with its chronicler. At this stage, it often wanted to talk much more than I cared to listen.

We didn't discuss Georgann Hawkins beyond my observation that hers seemed to be the nerviest abduction of all. I asked him if perhaps she did not belong to the rest of the cases. Could it have been a copycat killing?"

Ted allowed that that was a possibility—after all, he was only speculating and anything might be true—but then he addressed this question of consuming boldness. He gave a partial explanation of why such risks were taken in the Hawkins case, and in the twin abductions at Lake Sammamish a month later.

"There were times when he felt almost immune from detection," Bundy said. "Not in a mystical or spiritual sense. He didn't feel like he was invisible or anything like that. But at times he felt that no matter how much he fucked up, nothing could go wrong."

Ted stopped and pondered. "The boldness was probably a result of not being rational," he added. "Of just being moved by a situation, not really thinking it out clearly. Just overcome by that boldness and desire. Only in retrospect would he wonder how he managed to succeed in spite of some of those rash and bold acts."

Here was another stage of the psychopathology, I thought, as he talked on.

"It's clear that the Sammamish incident was either the result of the venting of a great amount of tension, or frustration, that had accumulated over a long period of time. Or," he added, "it was an attempt to indulge in a different M.O."

"Could both factors be at play?" I asked.

"Look at it this way. The individual had contemplated that kind of scheme before, realizing its obvious drawbacks. [He] would not have ordinarily attempted it, but his reluctance to engage in that kind of scheme was erased or otherwise overpowered by the need to seek out another victim. [He] took a great number of risks to carry out this scheme."

"How many days prior to the event would this person have anticipated doing it on that day?"

"Things just [came] together, you know, like the soft spot in a dike. All of a sudden there's that opportunity and that pressure. And the dike breaks."

"That's what you would guess?"

"That's one explanation. That's all I have to say right there."

Ted was warier of talking about Lake Sam than about any other individual case. He would say nothing of the witness identifications, the use of the sling, or how Denise and Janice were approached.

I asked him what happened once the girls had been taken from the park.

"[He] would not be able to drive a great distance without arousing the suspicions of the girls in the car," Bundy said. "And so he would seek a secluded space, a secluded area, within a fairly short driving distance of the Lake Sammamish area."

"Then he'd pull off the side of the road, a dirt road or something like that?"

"Somewhere where there were no cars, no traffic, or whatever."

"What would be the nature of the conversation between the two of them during the drive?"

"[He'd] be acting a role. Talking about the weather, reinforcing the ruse, just chitchat. He had a house somewhere in the area, and took them there, one girl to the house and came back and got the other one. In order to do that, the person had to be very secure that no one would enter the house or disturb it—or that no one else lived there or would be expected to come there.

"That's one hypothesis. The second hypothesis would be that he had killed the first girl and then returned sometime later to search out a second individual."

"Right. So you regard it as unlikely they would have been killed at the spot where they were later found?"

Ted nodded.

"I see," I said, seizing upon this apparent confirmation of a suspicion long held by the police. "The house, would it have been where people were on vacation or something like that? Was he aware this house was empty?"

"That's possible."

"In this instance of the first girl, how does he press ahead with his plan to ensure she does not become a personality to him?"

"I think we discussed before that we'd expect this kind of person would not want to engage in a great deal of serious conversation. We talked about the role playing, the reacting, the kind of dialogue, the pitter-patter used to pacify or otherwise gain the confidence of the person. But once the individual would have her in a spot where he had, you know, security over her, then there would be a minimum amount of conversation which would be, you know, designed to avoid developing some kind of a relationship."

"What would be the method you'd expect him to use to incapacitate her?"

"Fear. I suppose in such circumstances we could expect some sort of fear factor—a knife, a gun, anything to gain the attention of the individual."

"So the weapon is drawn or brandished. Then what?"

"You could tie her up and try to calm her down. It's really hard to say. Once that point had been reached he could sexually assault her, tie her up or whatever."

"Would she be gagged?"

"Well, she might be. If the surroundings he chose were secluded enough, then it wouldn't make any difference."

"How would he kill her?"

"I don't know. Strangle her, stab her, something."

"Did he anticipate getting more than one victim at the start of the day?"

"Well, again, this Lake Sammamish incident would mark an extraordinary departure from the previous crimes attributed to this person. So then, we would probably assume a number of departures.

"In all likelihood, this person knew about the criminal investigation process. If he had been acting more rationally, he would have realized that the disappearance of two girls in this fashion would yield a tremendous amount more interest and activity on the part of the police. So normally he wouldn't want to generate this additional attention."

"But it's obvious he did," I said.

"Yeah," Ted answered, uncomfortably. "It's possible he felt the first one wasn't satisfactory. Or, again, assuming this was an extraordinary departure—he's acting in a less restrained way—we might also expect that whatever desires drove him seemed to be stronger than usual."

"Would this have been the first instance of a double murder?"

"It would probably be."

"Would the M.O. be the same with the second victim?"

With this question he paused. His answer was a marvel of obfuscation. "Since published accounts indicate that a number of women were approached in that same manner that day, and since the first one worked, since he wasn't acting with much restraint, I guess he'd figure a similar approach would also be successful.''

I decided to try shorter questions in hopes of more direct answers. "Would he change clothes?"

"Probably not."

"Would there be any alteration in his appearance?"

"Probably not."

"Would the second woman be taken to the same place as the first?"

"Well, we're figuring this person had fallen into a kind of routine or pattern, and so we'd assume he took her to the same place.''

Ted added: "We can assume that because apparently the bodies were found in close proximity to each other.''

"Would the second victim see the first victim?"

"Oh, yeah, probably. In all probability.''

"Would the other individual still be alive, or not?"

"Well, had he been cautious, he would've probably killed the first individual before leaving to get the second girl. But in this instance, since we've agreed he wasn't acting cautiously, he hadn't killed the first girl when he abducted the second.''

"Would there have been any unique thrill or excitement from having the two of them there together?"

Ted wouldn't answer the question. "In all probability we're talking about an aberration here, a unique circumstance.''

"Would the first victim be conscious?"

"In all probability.''

"What happened when they encountered each other?"

"It seems there would be a little importance attached to the arrival of the second individual. It seems the person would be more acutely interested in her own welfare and well-being.

"I suppose if you took two such individuals and kept them confined for days or months, they would certainly establish a rapport, and be very concerned about each other's welfare. Here there was a good amount of fear and panic—most of us freeze under those circumstances.

"We might surmise that in this case there was little interaction, as such. This individual would not want any interaction, as he did not want interaction on a one-to-one basis.''

"What happens then?"

"He'd follow the same pattern with the second girl as the first.''

"In view of the other girl?"

"In all probability, yes."

I thought that by now I was immune to specific shocks, but I wasn't. According to what Ted had just said, Janice Ott "in all probability" watched him assault Denise Naslund. In what he called an "aberration," a "unique circumstance," the two girls had been alive together at his unknown lair. Hours later, a physically spent Ted was eating hamburgers with Liz Kendall and complaining about his cold.

"After the sexual assault, he has two bound victims," I observed. "What does he do now?"

"Well," came the reply, "by this time his frenzied compulsive activity of that day has run its course. Then he realized the jeopardy he was in. Then the normal self would begin to re-emerge and, realizing the greater danger involved, would suffer panic and begin to think of ways to conceal the acts—or at least his part in them. So, he'd kill the two girls, place them in his car, and take them to a secluded area and leave them."

"Right away?"

"Within a matter of hours."

"Would the killings be quick and as painless as possible? Or—"

"The actual act of killing the victims was just a necessity," he said quickly. "He would not linger or relish the killing, since it was only a means to an end, to avoid detection."

"What would be the emotional aftermath?"

"Well, later in the day this person would be exhausted. After going through what he went through, he wouldn't be in the mood to do much of anything."

"Sleep or eat, huh?"

"Sleep."

Lake Sammamish was the last specific case I discussed with Ted. Before handing responsibility for him over to Hugh, I spent our last interviews exploring some of the features of the "condition."

Ted, for instance, described this psychopathology as an intermittent condition whose demands for gratification would rise and fall according to several factors—principally stress. By way of illustrating that point, I asked him if the killer ever might pick up a girl and not succumb to the urge to murder her.

"We can posit that he was driving down a road one evening," Ted replied, "and saw an attractive, teenaged girl hitchhiking.

He picked her up and they engaged in conversation and, uh, she agreed to go to his house. And they spent the evening.

"She got very, very drunk. They both got drunk. Throughout the evening they engaged in voluntary sexual activity, and throughout the evening he felt himself being tested, debating with himself whether to kill her or to just let the situation run its course normally."

"Would he keep her at arm's length?" I wanted to know.

"Well," Ted said, "not necessarily. He was in one of his reformation periods." Ted laughed. "He'd sworn to himself that he'd never engage in that kind of conduct again. That he wouldn't let himself be carried away like that. But when he was faced with this very attractive girl hitchhiking, it kind of presented a challenge."

I nodded that I was following him.

"He didn't look on it as a challenge," Ted continued, "but as an opportunity; it was sort of an ambiguous situation."

"It seems as if his normal self was responding positively to her," I suggested.

"Uh-huh. That would be fair to say. The sexual activity was very responsive and very energetic."

Bundy paused and looked at the ceiling. "Uh, at certain parts of the evening he felt himself on the edge of taking her life, just, just out of the desire to do so. But the justifications were not there. Nor was that malignant condition that active at that time. It was active, but not at high strength. But when morning came around and they dressed and he took the girl back to the area where she lived, he felt like he'd accomplished something.

"He deluded himself at that point into thinking that he had really conquered those impulses. But within a period of time he discovered that that was an inaccurate conclusion. He didn't recognize then, or perhaps he did not want to recognize, that just a matter of a week or two later he probably would have killed her."

Somewhere, I said to myself, there is an anonymous woman with no idea how lucky she is. How many other anonymous girls are there out in the woods with fractured skulls?

Circumstances, Ted explained, would sometimes force compromise solutions on the killer. He offered an example that reflects the unmanageable power of the compulsion together with the shrewdness with which the hunter would approach his prey.

"In the wake of a particular crime," Bundy said, "he was not in a state of remission. That is, he actively wanted to go out and seek a victim. But he knew that he could not afford to do so without creating an intolerable amount of more public frenzy and panic, as well as police activity.

"But while driving one day, he saw a young girl walking along a deserted area. It was just too good an opportunity to pass up. So he exited his car and approached the girl and shoved her into a bushy field. Without any preparation. Without any planning. Without any disguise. Just an impulsive kind of thing. And then he was faced with the prospect, What should he do with her? He'd have to debate a considerable amount. There had been an illegal act of rape. Yet he refrained from harming her physically and left the scene and returned to his car and drove home. Had it occurred a few weeks later, he wouldn't have acted in the same way. Or a few days later. But he did not want to create a great amount of public furor because it would reduce the opportunity for victims later on and it would increase the possibility of eyewitness reports. And he knew enough about these circumstances that, in all likelihood, it wouldn't be reported. Or if it was reported, nothing much would be done about it. They wouldn't necessarily link it to the other crimes. It would have been a simple act of rape of the type that is fairly common."

Ted went on to say that such an attack, rather than satisfying his desire, would only serve to heighten the killer's need. By this time, anything short of "possession" failed to satisfy him.

The killer maintained a surprising ignorance about the needs of his condition, however. As Ted pointed out, he should have recognized that the hunt was more exciting—and gratifying—to him than the kill. Still, he persisted with certain unrealistic preconceptions such as his mistaken belief that he could somehow root out the homicidal urge on his own.

"As we've discussed before," Bundy told me, "frequently after this individual, uh, committed a murder he would lapse, uh, into a period of sorrow, remorse, et cetera. And for a period of time he would do everything to overcome and otherwise repress the, uh, the overt behavior. Indeed, on one particular occasion he went to extraordinary lengths to do this following a crime, and he felt that he had succeeded, that the abnormal course of conduct had just sort of, uh, extinguished itself .

"But in this instance, the cracks in the facade, as it were, began to appear. He then would attempt to channel the desire within him into a different area, into something which was still, uh, improper, immoral, illegal, but something that was less serious, less severe. Uh, and so he in sort of a, uh, a compromise decided that rather than go out and inflict this mortal injury on someone he would search out a victim in such a way that there would be no possibility of detection and he would not be forced into a position of having to kill. In essence, he compromised into just going out and performing an act of rape, as it were.''

I was staring at Ted. Ted was staring at the tape recorder in his lap, watching the reels turn, collecting his words.

"So he, uh, began to just go out driving around the suburbs, uh, in this city, uh, that he was living in, and one particular evening he's driving down a fairly dark street and saw a girl walking along the street. Okay?''

"Uh-huh."

"Because the area was dark and she was alone, he decided to select her as the victim for this intended act of sexual assault. He parked his car down the street and, uh, then ran up behind the girl. Just as he came up on her they were at a place where there was an orchard, or a number of trees or something. As he came up behind her she heard him. She turned around and he brandished a knife—''

"Uh-huh."

"—and grabbed her by the arm and told her to do what he wanted her to do. You know, to follow him."

"Yeah."

"He pushed her off the sidewalk into this darkened wooded area and, uh, told her to submit and do what he wanted her to do. She began to argue with him and he kept telling her to be quiet. She said she didn't believe he would do anything to her, anyway.''

Ted was keeping his head bowed and turned slightly, so that he stared at the turning tapes from above and to the side. I could see his jaw clench and relax, clench and relax, but he kept on with his story.

"Then he began to try to remove her clothes and she would, uh, continue to struggle in a feeble manner. And also voice verbally her objections to what was going on. And then, uh, the significance now is that his intent with this victim was not to harm her. He thought this was going to be a significant departure; perhaps even a way of deconditioning himself, to climb down that ladder or, uh, I can't think of a good word, de-, de-escalate this level of violence to the point where there would be no violence at all. Even no necessity for that kind of encounter at all.''

"I see.''

"But he found himself with this girl who was struggling and screaming. Uh, not screaming, but let's say just basically arguing with him. There were houses in the vicinity, and he was concerned that somebody might hear. And so, in an attempt to stop her from talking or arguing, he placed his hand over her mouth.

"She stopped and he attempted to remove her clothes and she began to object again. At this point, he was in a state of not just agitation, but something on the order of panic. He was fearing that she would arouse somebody in the vicinity.

"So, not thinking clearly, but still intending not to harm her, let's say he placed his hands around her throat."

"Uh-huh."

"Just to throttle her into unconsciousness so that she wouldn't scream anymore. She stopped struggling and it appeared she was unconscious. But not, in his opinion, to the point where he had killed her."

"Right," I said, my astonishment rising.

"Then let's say he removed her clothes and raped her and put his own clothes back on. At about that point he began to notice that the girl wasn't moving. It appeared, although he wasn't certain, that he'd done what he promised himself he wouldn't do, and he had done it really almost inadvertently.

"Uh, so he took the girl by one of her arms and pulled her over to a darkened corner of this little orchard. And then, in a fit of panic, he fled the scene."

Ted kept his jaw working, but the rest of his body was rigid, frozen at an odd cant, cradling the tape recorder. He seemed to have lost awareness of my presence.

"He got back into his car and drove back to his house, still not knowing if the girl was alive or dead. But once he returned to the house, upon reflection he began to wonder. He didn't know if he'd left anything at the crime scene. He hadn't thought about publicity and physical evidence.

"So he decided to return to the scene and if the body was there to recover it and take it somewhere else where it wouldn't be found."

"Is this the same night?" I asked. The question startled Ted.

"Huh? Oh, yeah. But he faced two problems in returning to the scene. First, prior to the incident he was in a state of intoxication and he didn't know the area that well. So he couldn't remember exactly where it was he had to return, couldn't find his way back, as it were. But let's say after a considerable period of time driving about in the general vicinity, uh, he was able to locate the area. It was getting fairly late about this time.

"Nobody was in the vicinity, so apparently she hadn't gotten up and gone away and the police hadn't returned to the scene. Or she was still there.

"He parked his car at the curb of this small orchard and walked into it and saw that in fact the body was still in the same position he'd left it. So it was clear that the girl was dead."

Ted cleared his throat. "So he carried the body to his car and put it in and covered it. Then he returned to the general area with a flashlight and scoured it to pick up everything that he may have left there—her clothing, et cetera. He placed that in the car and returned to his apartment."

The stress drained from Ted's body and he reached down for a cup of water.

"Did he find everything?" I asked.

Ted saw my little trap and smiled. "I don't know."

# SEVEN

TED'S AUGUST 16, 1975, arrest would have been routine if he hadn't at first fled, then provoked suspicions with his phony alibi. These actions led to the search of the interior of his Volkswagen, where the pantyhose mask and ice pick were found, along with the displaced passenger seat. Had Bundy, who knew the law, insisted upon his rights and forbade a search of the VW, his trunk would not have been opened and the handcuffs would not have been discovered.

Investigator Daryle Ondrak told Ted that night that he intended to pursue a warrant for "possession of burglary tools," an easy charge to beat, especially if the defendant is a young law student with no prior criminal record. Only the incongruity of Ted's demeanor and the suspicious circumstances of the arrest prompted Ondrak to mention the incident, almost in passing, when he attended the next weekly detectives' meeting.

Jerry Thompson alone guessed at a connection between the late-night arrest of a courteous law student and Carol DaRonch's abduction of the previous November. Twice before—in Seattle and then in Salt Lake City—Ted's name had surfaced and disappeared in connection with the killings. Thompson himself had missed one connection when the King County police sent down Liz's photo of Ted. The detective wouldn't make the same error twice.

Still, Thompson was only working a hunch; Ted Bundy was a long-shot suspect. Over the coming weeks, he encountered deep skepticism at his theory.

One doubter was Mack Holley, sheriff of Utah County, who continued to oversee the Laura Aime case. Thompson kept prodding Holley to explore Bundy.

"Jerry!" Thompson remembers Holley lecturing him in exasperation. "Bundy had nothing to do with our case, so forget

137

him. That man didn't do our case. I wish you'd get that through your head!''

Himself struggling with the barely credible notion that Ted Bundy, law student, was a diabolically adroit mass killer, Thompson knew that his chances of demonstrating Ted's culpability rested solely upon Carol DaRonch. There was no description of the man seen in a Volkswagen with Nancy Wilcox. Melissa Smith wasn't seen with anyone, either. Thompson was blocked by Sheriff Holley from pursuing the Aime case, and it wouldn't do the detective much good to show that Bundy had been at the Viewmont High School play in Bountiful. Debra Kent had never been found: without a body, it is difficult to prove that someone has been murdered.

Only Carol DaRonch could link Ted to an indictable offense, and it had been over nine months since the shy girl had encountered "Officer Roseland." She had been shown thousands of mug shots, which had possibly muddied her memory. She was, in police jargon, a "fatigued" witness, who might now be incapable of identifying her attacker.

Before approaching Carol, Thompson wanted to be more certain of what he might have. Ted's mug shot and a photo of the articles found in his car were sent to Bob Keppel in Seattle. Ironically, at the instant Keppel heard from the Utah detective, he and his team were turning to suspect number seven of the top one hundred possible "Teds" they were rechecking. Suspect number seven was Theodore Robert Bundy.

Thompson called Ira Beal in Bountiful, who drove down to Salt Lake City, picked up a copy of the mug shot, and took it back to show it to Raelynne Shepard, the Viewmont drama teacher. "If you put a mustache on this individual," she told Beal, "I'm sure that's probably him."

The identification was heartening, but not at all conclusive. Mrs. Shepard had seemed equally sure about John Badway.

It was Bundy's behavior as much as anything that kept Thompson's attention focused on him as a suspect. By his actions, Ted invited the detective to pursue him, apparently expecting to tease and humiliate the opposition. However, Ted was only an alien student of human emotions, including the appropriate reaction to police inquiries. He didn't realize that he was trapping himself.

Since his arrival in Salt Lake City, Ted had lived in an upstairs apartment—reachable from the outside by a fire escape—in a rooming house situated close to the University of Utah campus.

The living arrangement was nearly identical to the one he'd had at the Rogerses' house in Seattle.

On Thursday, August 21, he was on the first floor refinishing an oak table he had stolen one night from a backyard patio. (He had been appalled that the previous owner had painted the lovely wood a vile shade of green.) Ted looked up from his work and through a window saw Daryle Ondrak striding toward the front door. For a moment, he considered hiding from Ondrak, but thought better of it and went to his upstairs apartment to await the investigator's knock.

At the door, Ondrak presented Bundy with an arrest warrant for possession of burglary tools. "I told you I'd get one," he said simply.

Affecting indifference, Ted changed his clothes and accompanied Ondrak downtown to be fingerprinted, photographed again, and booked. As they drove to the sheriff's office, according to Ted, Ondrak kept saying to him, "You know, I can't figure it out. I mean, you're a nice guy. I just can't figure this out."

Once he had been booked, Ted was placed in a holding cage. Then he was escorted into a small interview room where Thompson's partner, detective Ben Forbes, sat at a table.

It had been decided that Forbes would start Ted off slowly.

"We're basically interested in the things in your car," he told Bundy. "I'd like to know why they were in there."

The question was consistent with the burglary tools charge; Ted sensed no danger. He could have refused to answer any questions and he could have insisted upon having an attorney present. But in his arrogance, he regarded the interview as a game.

Forbes asked about the handcuffs. Ted later was willing to concede to us that he had purchased them from a South Salt Lake City junk shop. But he told the detective that he'd found them at the garbage dump. He kept the cuffs, he went on to explain to a disbelieving Forbes, because he once had to stop someone from stealing a bicycle in Seattle. He had fought with the thief before the police came. Should such an incident occur again, he said, he thought owning a pair of handcuffs would come in handy.

A practiced and agile dissembler with women, Bundy had no such facility when he talked to the police. He had had five days to think of an explanation for the handcuffs, yet he could offer to Forbes only an imbecilic excuse that suggested either that Ted was a fool or, more likely, that he thought Forbes was one. Ted would often insult a questioner's intelligence.

By answering Forbes's questions, Bundy was also locking himself into statements that could later be used against him in court. He'd already been caught in one lie on the night of his arrest. Now he would say things that he'd be forced to stand by in court or else risk a damning inference of guilt by conceding that he'd lied.

Forbes brought up the pantyhose mask. Bundy told the detective that he'd seen a film of mountain climbers who lined their regular ski masks with nylon ones for added protection from cold. He claimed he was simply adapting the idea for Utah's gelid winters when he had evening classes at law school.

I later asked Ted about the mask. He allowed that he'd lied to Forbes, but then probably also lied to me when he went on to say that he'd only worn it once—the night he'd stolen the oak table.

His explanation for the lengths of rope and shreds of sheet found in his car was that they were used to tie together the oars of his rubber raft, a gift to him from Liz. According to Forbes's later written report of the interview, Ted also told him that he regarded the ice pick as "a common household piece of equipment" that had no sinister meaning as far as he was concerned.

At the end of the interview, the detective dropped the other shoe, saying portentously, "My game is homicide." Forbes informed Bundy that he was a suspect in a kidnap and attempted murder case. He didn't mention Carol DaRonch specifically. Caught off guard once again, Ted stupidly agreed to sign a consent form for his apartment to be searched.

A defense psychiatrist would later write of Ted that "in a certain sense, Mr. Bundy is a producer of a play which attempts to show that various authority figures can be manipulated . . . Mr. Bundy does not have the capacity to recognize that the price for this 'thriller' might be his own life."

Ted always underrated the opposition.

After he talked to Forbes, he was walked out to a squad car by a sergeant and a detective; Jerry Thompson was waiting there for him. Bundy was handcuffed and placed in the back seat, then the four men drove out to his rooming house.

On the way to and during the search, Ted's chief concern, he told me, was what the detectives might think of at seeing the amount of expensive merchandise he owned. The apartment was full of stolen goods, from the towering ornamental tree he'd carefully transported from Seattle to the $1,200 Navajo rug he'd boldly taken from a display case in a Salt Lake City hotel lobby.

Thompson did note Ted's luxury, but he was fishing for evidence of something more serious than theft. He glanced in Bundy's closet and saw what he recognized as two or three pairs of patent leather shoes. Carol DaRonch had said her assailant wore patent leather shoes. He didn't ask Ted about them, because he didn't want to tip off his suspect to the object of his search. But Thompson needn't have worried; having his apartment searched was fun, like playing with matches, for Ted.

"Jerry," the detective remembers Ted taunting him, "you do a pretty good job."

"I think I do a *damn* good job," Thompson answered.

"Now you've got a straw," Ted went on with manic delight. "You're trying to fill up a broom. Keep going and one of these days you might make it."

Thompson later told a conference of policemen that Bundy, "would not elaborate any further on this comment."

Thompson found a Colorado road map and a *Colorado Ski County Guide*, '74–'75. They were of only idle interest until, at a question of Thompson's, Ted denied ever having been in Colorado.

Also in the apartment were a brochure from a recreation center in Bountiful, a copy of Ted's June 1975 telephone bill, and a copy of his Chevron gas-credit-card bill. Thompson asked Ted's permission to take the papers back downtown. Bundy consented.

The detective then wanted to photograph Ted's VW, to which Bundy also agreed. In his report dated early September of 1975, Thompson described Ted's VW bug as "white or light gray in color" (Sergeant Hayward had reported it as gray, too) and noted that there was a large tear along the top of the back seat.

A number of evidentiary disputes would grow out of this search and Thompson's later investigative activities. Ted angrily asserts that he has never owned a pair of patent leather shoes. He insists that he never denied to the detective that he'd been to Colorado. But most crucial was the ski brochure. When it was submitted into evidence, an inked X appeared next to the name of the Wildwood Inn where Caryn Campbell disappeared. Bundy steadfastly denies that the mark was his.

Ted would like people to believe that the police manufactured evidence against him. With his own severely impaired capacity to distinguish fact from fiction, he may even have come to believe it himself. Whatever the merit of his protestations, none of this evidence convicted him. The case against him would center on the most serious slip he'd made: letting Carol DaRonch out of his grasp.

After talking to Ted, Jerry Thompson immediately conferred with Mike Fisher in Aspen. He told the Colorado investigator about the ski brochure and Bundy's denial of ever having visited Colorado. After relaying the number of Ted's Chevron gas card, he shared with Fisher his and Ben Forbes's impression that Bundy had something to hide, perhaps a *lot* to hide.

"Well, Jerry," Fisher responded, dubious about Ted Bundy as a suspect, "I'll run the credit card. If the son of a bitch has never been in the state of Colorado, then he shouldn't have been here on January twelfth."

Thompson next turned to his star witness, his *only* witness. On September 1, 1975, he visited Carol DaRonch at the Mountain Bell office where she worked as an operator. First he showed her the Polaroid photos he'd taken of Ted's car on the early evening of August 21. She studied them, noting that the tear in Ted's back seat resembled a tear she had seen in "Officer Roseland's" upholstery. "I believe this could be the Volkswagen," she told Thompson, "but I cannot make a positive identification."

Then Thompson offered her a packet of twenty-seven mug shots, including the one taken of Bundy on August 16. Slowly, Carol sifted through the pictures. When she got to Ted's, she pulled it aside, continued through the rest, and handed them back to Thompson. "I don't see anyone in there that resembles him," she said.

He asked her about Ted's picture, which she still held in her hand. "Oh, here," she replied. "I don't know. I guess it looks something like him."

Carol DaRonch couldn't be more specific than that. "She really just doesn't know," wrote Thompson in his personal notes on the case. "She didn't think she could identify him if she saw him again or not. This is a very poor witness in this detective's opinion, and I don't know if she can identify the individual or if she is scared or what the situation is."

The despairing tone of his report reflected Jerry Thompson's central dilemma. To secure a conviction, Carol DaRonch would have to be able to make an unequivocal identification of her attacker. She would have to do so in court and she would then have to withstand what would undoubtedly be a merciless cross-examination by defense counsel. Thompson clearly doubted that his witness would ever make an identification that was strong enough to stand up in court.

He was wrong.

Just three days later, a new photo was found. It was Ted's December 1974 driver's license picture taken only weeks after "Officer Roseland" attacked Carol. "It was completely dark, different," Jerry Thompson says. "He could have been a black man, it was so much different."

Ira Beal from Bountiful showed her this picture, and this time Carol DaRonch was much surer. She still wasn't positive, but Ted's license photo looked "a lot" like her abductor.

Thompson was halfway home. He now had a tentative photo identification. His next critical step was to give Carol DaRonch a look at Bundy in person.

He waited several weeks to do so. In the interim, a gossamer web began to descend upon Ted. Taken individually, the bits of information turned up by investigators in Washington, Utah, and Colorado were not wholly demonstrative of guilt. Taken together, however, the disparate facts spurred the police toward an astonishing conclusion: There didn't seem to be any way Ted *couldn't* be their man."

On September 8, 1975, an excited Mike Fisher called Jerry Thompson. Ted's credit-card gas purchases placed him in Glenwood Springs, Colorado, some forty miles north of Aspen and the Wildwood Inn, on January 12, the day Caryn Campbell had vanished. The next day, January 13, Ted had bought gas in Green River, Utah, which is on the way from Aspen to Salt Lake City.

And there was more: Bundy bought gas near Vail, Colorado, on March 15, the day Julie Cunningham disappeared from there. Again, on April 6, he had filled up near Grand Junction, the date and place where Denise Oliverson was last seen.

Meanwhile, Bob Keppel in Seattle had turned up an amazing number of coincidences. Ted, it turned out, had once dated Herb Swindler's daughter. Ted's cousin Edna Cowell knew Lynda Healy, and Ted had enrolled in the same psychology class with Lynda. A friend of Ted's used to play racquetball with Donna Manson at Evergreen State College in Olympia. Terry Storwick, Bundy's boyhood friend, attended Central Washington State College in Ellensburg at the same time as Susan Rancourt. Terry and Susan had even jogged together.

As it turned out, the coincidences were only that—fluke connections between suspect and victims. More telling had been

Cynthia Holt's story of searching for Ted's mystery relative in the wilds behind Lake Sam and Issaquah, as well as his cousin John's reluctant recollection of repeated visits with Ted to the same area. A check of his work records at the Washington State Department of Emergency Services revealed his absences before and after the twin abductions at the state park. And Liz Kendall repeated the salient details of her story, which prompted Jerry Thompson and Ira Beal to fly to Seattle on September 18. What she told them dovetailed nicely with the rest of their information.

Later, two of the Lake Sam witnesses positively identified Ted as the man they'd seen with Denise Naslund and Janice Ott. Contrary to some published accounts, these identifications were not tainted by news photos of Ted. Also, the two women approached in Ellensburg by the injured man with the armload of books made tentative identifications of Bundy as the same person.

Ted's employers at Ped-Line, the medical supply company, reported that he'd had access to a wide range of instruments and supplies.

Checking account and gas-credit-card data were compelling, too. While Keppel did not have the nice fits that Mike Fisher found, he could place Bundy in Ellensburg at about the time of Rancourt's disappearance. The day Kathy Parks was taken in Corvallis, Ted bought gas and cashed checks sufficient to cover a 500-mile round trip. Overall, during the period when the girls began to vanish and Ted was supposed to be devoting all his time to his law studies, he was driving a tremendous number of miles.

None of this proved that Ted killed anyone; placing him at Lake Sammamish, for instance, was no more inculpatory than proving he'd been at the Viewmont High School play in Bountiful, Utah, the night Debbie Kent was taken. But it would take deliberate opacity of mind not to infer a pattern.

"Every time we'd get more information, it was on how we couldn't eliminate him," Keppel later told Hugh. "Sure," the detective went on, "we'd love to catch a suspect and charge his ass and put him in jail forever. But we were working *for* him, too. We tried to eliminate the son of a bitch! You *can't* do it! We knew where he ate, where he slept, where he took his shits. But you just couldn't tell where he was on the days those girls disappeared."

Following the Thompson's search of his apartment, Ted posted bail on the burglary tools charge and engaged as counsel John

O'Connell, reputedly the best criminal lawyer in the state. The choice of attorney was telling; for all his bravado and antics, Bundy had begun to consider his peril.

He saw signs of police activity everywhere. A surveillance was begun. Liz, whose allegiances continued to waver, told him that the cops had been to see her. He learned that his law school records were being perused.

Ted responded to the surveillance by trying to turn it into a game. Sometimes he'd photograph his pursuers, sometimes he'd work elaborate ruses to throw them off his tail.

His VW, which detective Thompson had been so interested in, was given a thorough cleaning and renovation. Then he sold it. Ted's stated reason was that he needed the money to pay John O'Connell. He also moved out of his rooming house; the vacated room was never searched.

Bundy joined the Mormon Church that September. He told me that the pressures he was feeling—the police attention, money problems, acrimony with Liz—had deeply unsettled him. He instinctively sought shelter, a desperate retreat from a once again threatening environment, the way he'd hidden himself in his bedroom as a boy, in the classroom as a student, and in politics as a young man.

Joining the Mormon Church offered a practical advantage as well. It wouldn't hurt as a suspect and possible defendant to belong to the most pervasive and powerful institution in the state of Utah.

Around the middle of September, official interest in him suddenly seemed to ease. The surveillance was lifted, and friends stopped reporting contacts from the police.

The interlude (during which Thompson and Forbes were busily reviewing every bit of evidence they had against Ted) lasted until October 1, 1975. That afternoon, Jerry Thompson caught Ted coming out of the shower down the hall from his new room. "We have this subpoena for you to attend this lineup," the detective said, searching Bundy's face for a reaction. Bundy forced a friendly face for the officers and thanked them for coming by. But Jerry Thompson noted that Ted turned chalk-white as he was handed the subpoena.

Much of Bundy's behavior in the weeks following his first arrest makes sense only when viewed through the prism of his psychopathology. Somehow, he was able to sustain the delusion of invulnerability (Bundy still cannot accept the fact that Thompson made a case against him), and he enjoyed taunting the police. But he made several moves suggestive of a cunning criminal intellect, the sort of mind that could plot murder after successful murder.

Outwardly a mild innocent, he hired the best attorney in Utah, disconnected himself from two potential sources of evidence (his room and his car), and switched religions.

And with notification of the lineup, Ted immediately went out and had his hair cut. Aware as anyone of his chameleonlike appearance, he surely knew that his August arrest photos—the ones most likely to have been shown to witnesses—made him look round-faced with bushy medium-length hair. At the lineup, his hair would be much shorter, combed, and parted on the opposite side.

October 2, 1975, dawned bright and brisk in Salt Lake City. Ted selected two sets of clothes for the day; one to wear to the Metropolitan Law Building and one to wear beneath. His plan was to shed the outer garments just before the lineup itself, and then to appear looking as different as possible from the rest of the men in the lineup. He thought such a ploy might invalidate any identification. However, Ted lost his nerve at the last moment and left his second set of clothes at John O'Connell's office.

After a brief appearance before a judge, Ted was taken to a small room to await the lineup while John O'Connell and his partner, Bruce Lubeck, registered objection after objection to the proceedings. Honing their arguments was difficult, inasmuch as they didn't know for sure what witnesses to what crimes would be there to view their client.

In all, seven women had been gathered, but only three of them were actual witnesses: Carol DaRonch, Raelynne Shepard, and Tamra Tingey, Debra Kent's locker partner, who had also seen the stranger at the Viewmont High School play.

Jerry Thompson had two reasons for bringing in his four ringers, who were all county employees. Both Carol DaRonch and Raelynne Shepard had expressed fear at the possibility of Ted or his attorneys recognizing them. Thompson persuaded them they'd be far less conspicuous in a crowded lineup theater. Also, the Law Building press room was close by, and he feared that some enterprising reporter might recognize Carol DaRonch, whom he knew to be easily flustered. One unguarded remark from her and the case could collapse. She was less likely to be seen among six other women.

When Thompson first saw his suspect, Ted's altered appearance stunned him. "When he came out with his new hairdo," says Thompson, "that just blew my mind."

Hastily, the jail inmates who had been selected to stand in the lineup with Ted were repaced with police officers. Now the detective had a fairer lineup, perhaps *too* fair. As the men were called to the stage, Thompson turned to county attorney David Yocom, who was seated beside him. "Friend," he said to Yocom, "we're in a world of shit. Bundy looks exactly like those guys. Our witnesses are going to pull out some of those police officers."

Thompson was wrong again.

The lineup itself took twenty minutes. Each of the eight men was asked to walk the length of the stage, to turn right, left, and backward, and to repeat three phrases read to them by Yocom. In order, the phrases were: "Would you like to come to the station with me?" "Could you come outside and identify a car for me? It'll just take a minute." And, "I'm a police officer; your car has been broken into."

When the lineup concluded, all seven women in the audience, each separated from her neighbor by a police officer, were asked to write down the number of any of the eight men they recognized. Bundy's number was seven.

Ted was taken down to the booking area where seven weeks earlier Sergeant Hayward had first brought him in. Time passed and he began to fidget.

Finally, John O'Connell walked in. "Well, Ted," he said, "this looks like the way it is. You've been identified."

Bundy went numb; he had come to the lineup with every expectation of getting back to class that day. His lawyer went on to say that he still didn't know who had written the number seven on her card (all three witnesses had) or with what the police intended to charge Ted. Moments later, Thompson told them: The charge was kidnap and attempted murder. Bail was set at $100,000.

Bundy stood impassively as Thompson read the charge. Fright and bewilderment blocked his senses. He was now an accused felon; the game was over.

It is hard to say who was most dumbstruck at first, Ted or his family and the people who thought they knew him. No one could believe it.

Ted called his friend Marlin Vortman before he was taken to a cell. He had to leave a message with the attorney's secretary. Vortman then called Johnnie and Louise Bundy and tried to contact Liz. Within minutes of Ted's single telephone call, someone notified the press. The next morning, the *Seattle Post-Intelligencer* bannered the story on the front page: "Ex-Evans Campaign Aide Held in Kidnap." Underneath, a boxed article asked, "Is Utah 'Ted' the Seattle 'Ted'?"

Stewart Elway, an old friend of Ted's from the 1968 lieutenant governor's race, heard of the arrest on his car radio that first afternoon. "I almost went into a ditch," he told me. "I couldn't believe it."

Gwen Grim and Susan Reade, friends from the 1972 campaign, talked until midnight about the news. "It just freaked us out," Gwen recalls. "We thought, Well, how well did we really know him?"

Ralph Munro, the former aide to Governor Evans, learned of the arrest on television, and thought of the bright young man with good ideas. "I just couldn't believe it was Ted," says Munro. "My response was shock."

Larry Diamond, who so admired and envied Ted when they worked together the summer of '74 at the Department of Emergency Services, was told of the arrest by inquiring reporters. "My first impression," Diamond told me, "was 'No, it couldn't be.' It would be like one of us."

Louise Bundy was too stunned by the news to tell the rest of the Bundy children at once. Glenn, who was in his last week of Navy boot camp in San Diego, received a call from his mother, who said that Ted was in trouble, but that she couldn't talk about it. It was a week before Glenn got her letter explaining the situation.

Warren Dodge, who'd seen very little of Ted for years, got home from work at 11:45 P.M. "The news was on," he remembers. "My wife says, 'Sit down. Ted Bundy's been arrested.'

" 'What!' I said. They were just finishing the story on TV and I still didn't understand what was going on. She tried to explain to me what happened. I really couldn't believe it was possible. He was too quiet, too intelligent, too much a nice guy, too much a gentleman to have possibly done anything like that. I was very steadfast in my belief in his innocence for months and months and months."

Not far from where Glenn Bundy was finishing up boot camp, Carole Boone was working in a Vietnamese refugee resettlement camp. She'd been there since May, just after a trip she and two other friends had made from Seattle to visit Ted in Salt Lake.

Carole happened to speak to an old friend in Seattle. "He told me Ted had been arrested and was suspected of murdering all these women in Washington and Utah," she recalls. "Things just kind of went blank. I remember sitting there after we hung up. I remember people coming in and trying to talk to me.

"I don't remember driving home from work that night. I sat practically until dawn in the living room with my little Vietnamese roommates around me, bringing me cups of tea. And a lot of cigarettes. I drank a lot of scotch.

"I do not recall anything else until the next day when I was walking around the camp and feeling the same sort of shock you feel when somebody close to you has died. It's an event so large you can't get hold of it. You can't assimilate it."

Ted's own amazement at the triple identification was genuine. Such was the power of his delusions that the experience was akin to being told the laws of gravity had just been repealed. It made no sense whatever to Ted Bundy that he was suddenly behind bars.

He spent seven weeks in the Salt Lake jail before his bail was reduced from the prohibitive $100,000 to $15,000, which Johnnie and Louise were just able to cover. One obstacle to his release had been the unwillingness of local bondsmen—whose clients are drawn largely from the seamy underside of society—to accept so notorious an alleged mass killer as Ted Bundy. Their fear was that if he got out and committed another murder, they would be held responsible.

The police and Ted's friends feared for *his* safety if he was released; several anonymous death threats were made against Bundy. But for his part, Ted initially was more concerned about his fellow inmates. He cowered in his cell, aware that vows of killing the "baby raper" were circulating throughout the jail.

Outwardly, however, Ted was still the young Republican. He wrote friends that he could not believe what had happened (which was true) and how he looked forward to the system working to correct its error. This was the Ted that they all remembered, the one for whom a "Ted Bundy Defense Fund" was immediately established. Something over $4,000 was raised, and major contributors included Marlin and Sheila Vortman as well as Ralph Munro.

Ted had never in his life enjoyed such recognition and notoriety. Equally mysterious to those who believed him innocent and to those who thought him a mass killer, he gloried in his instant fame, sending letters for publication to newspapers and milking his friends for their sympathy.

In the meantime, he began to adjust to jail life. His fears for his personal safety subsided as he learned which inmates to avoid and which ones to cultivate as friends. Ted discovered in confinement that lack of a conscience and a hatred for the police were social assets. The mask he maintained for the outer world—the one that required such constant attention lest it slip—wasn't necessary on the inside. For practically the first time in his life, Bundy began to relax.

Then came the night of his release, just before Thanksgiving 1975. Suddenly confronted by the world he had always regarded as hostile, Ted was immediately disoriented. He went shopping in a supermarket with Johnnie and Louise that night. All at once, he was taken violently ill. He remembers nausea, heat flashes, fear. The attack lasted for an hour.

The next day, his composure regained, he went to court for a routine hearing to determine if he should be bound over for trial. Illustrative of how his mind works was the copy of Aleksandr Solzhenitsyn's *The Gulag Archipelago* that he carried into the courtroom with him. Ted meant the volume to suggest parallels of oppression and his own martyrdom.

During courtroom breaks that day, Ted mingled with reporters in the hallway. He told them he had been well treated by the jail guards and other county prisoners. "Once you get underneath their exterior," Bundy said, "they're all nice people." To another knot of journalists he announced: "We want everything out in the open. I'd like to see this thing fully aired." Several news accounts described Ted as "pale," "shaky," but "jovial."

"I was trying to project an image," he told me. "I was feeling proud of myself. That's when I started to be pleased about fucking with the press. From then on, it was a lot of fun."

Ted went on with his bizarre posturing. He flew to Seattle and played hide-and-seek with the police there. Friends report him carrying law books on the street and commenting gravely on this important opportunity to participate in the legal system. In restaurants, he was heard to raise his voice in mock outrage at the latest news story about him.

All the while, the police kept up their efforts to link him with the string of homicides that they were now certain Bundy had committed. But with that certainty came an equal measure of doubt that he'd ever be charged with murder. Even the charge of attempted murder in the DaRonch case had been dropped because of insufficient evidence; only the kidnap charge remained. The investigators feared that the estimable John O'Connell would destroy Carol DaRonch on the stand and that Ted Bundy, mass killer, would remain at large.

In November, thirty detectives and prosecutors from Washington, California, Utah, and Colorado met at an Aspen Holiday Inn behind a closed and guarded door. Jerry Thompson, Bob Keppel, and Mike Fisher, the three principal Bundy investigators, gave long presentations recounting what they'd learned to date. Their departments had dug hard, but each had found that the first spate of promising disclosures had led to nothing substantive. Ted's trail was impossible to follow.

The news was generally disheartening, much of it closer to the realm of gossip than evidence. In Seattle, Bob Keppel's team had been told that in junior high school Ted once was found masturbating in the coat room. According to a source, several of Ted's classmates threw water on him.

In Utah, said Thompson, "we're now getting girls who have been out with him and we're all getting the same thing, that he was unusual, he was weird." A neighbor reported that Ted sneaked into her room while she slept and pinched her crotch. Another woman familiar with Bundy said he'd bragged about his sexual success with virgins. Ted, said another acquaintance, liked crude sex jokes of the type that amuse young boys.

Thompson was the only speaker who had actually interviewed Bundy. He recounted his afternoon in Ted's apartment. "You have to shut him up to ask a question," said the detective. "He's always talking." Though not given to hyperbole, he went on to tell the assembly, "He's got eyes on him that you won't forget. I can't really describe them. They're piercing blue."

The information added up to nothing any prosecutor could take to court. Nor had Bundy's gas card, telephone bills, and checking records yielded anything much more positive than what the police had known since September, though Mike Fisher was able to report that Bundy had used two sets of auto license plates on his trips in Colorado.

He had a habit of often—but not always—calling Liz Kendall on the nights that the girls disappeared. His principal checking account purchases seemed to be for food and clothing, particularly socks. He frequently bought gas in small amounts, sometimes putting less than a gallon in his tank.

Based on all these records, the police tentatively decided that Denise Oliverson hadn't been the last of Ted's possible victims. Nancy Baird, a young mother aged twenty-one, had vanished from her job at a Fina gas station some thirty miles from Salt Lake City on July 1, 1975. She was never seen again. There is a complete gap in Ted's records for that day, reason enough for the police to suspect him.

On the other hand, his receipts definitely eliminated him from suspicion in eight murders of women in northern California in 1972 and 1973; nor did Bundy appear to have been involved in two Colorado slayings that took place in the late spring of 1975.

In all, the conference demonstrated that the police knew everything and nothing about Ted Bundy. They were confident enough of what they knew to believe he had killed at least twenty women, and also confident enough to ignore other cases, such as the seventy-two-year-old Salt Lake City rape victim who had identified Bundy as her assailant. But all they had for sure was one frail kidnap indictment. The meeting broke up on a somber tone; for the time being, only Carol DaRonch stood between Ted and freedom.

# EIGHT

UNDER U.S. law, a criminal defendant is entitled not only to be informed of the charges against him, but through a process called discovery the defense may demand of the prosecution any exculpatory evidence that has been collected in the course of its investigation.

As Ted's trial date neared and John O'Connell read over the evidence, he felt with increasing certainty that Thompson and the rest of the police were trammeling his client's rights. Specifically, O'Connell was persuaded that the key evidence, Carol DaRonch's identification of Ted as her abductor, had been coerced.

It was O'Connell's proper role to be indignant on behalf of Bundy, and he is among the best at summoning righteous outrage at the correct moment. Tall and gaunt, O'Connell can bring to mind Jeremiah in a three-piece suit.

So exercised did he become in this case that he once raged to one of the cops that the police should simply shoot Bundy if they were so positive that Ted was a killer. That, he argued loftily, was preferable to stretching the law to gain a conviction.

The attorney was also deeply concerned about the public mood in Utah; picking a jury for a man suspected of murder for hundreds of miles in every direction was going to be trouble. Several weeks before the scheduled February 23, 1976, start of Ted's kidnap trial, O'Connell suggested a bold ploy to Bundy: Why not waive his right to a jury and go with the assigned trial judge, Stewart M. Hanson, Jr?

O'Connell persuaded Ted of the wisdom in waiving a jury with a formidable set of arguments. There was nothing to be done, he pointed out, about the presumed taint on jurors' attitudes after months and months of publicity, innuendo, accusations, and speculation. In most states, a locally infamous trial can be moved to some distant community where the pool of prospective jurors is less likely to have been affected by the uproar. But in Utah, there was no town big enough and distant enough from Salt Lake City to which to move the proceedings. Also, the state's rules under which jurors can be questioned as to their biases allow for no attorney participation. "Voir dire," as it is called, is conducted exclusively by the judge. Bruce Lubeck, O'Connell's associate, told me, "Around here, if you have had pretrial publicity, you're in trouble."

Another consideration was the nature of the state's case. "They had an eyewitness identification," says O'Connell. "Now, eyewitness testimony is lousy testimony. The guy on the street thinks circumstantial evidence is weak, but it is a whole lot more trustworthy than an eyewitness.

"Yet it is the most likely thing for a jury to convict on. Juries like it. So our theory was, Why not go with one juror that we know is intelligent rather than eight or twelve God-only-knows-what?"

The clincher was Hanson's record on the bench. In a state where the line between the rule of law and the tenets of Mormonism can sometimes be blurred, Hanson had built a reputation for unflinching adherence to legal principle. Time after time, he had directed unpopular acquittals on technical grounds in drug cases. Just before Ted's trial, he had presided over another controversial matter. "Hanson had tried the movie *Deep Throat* with a jury," remembers Lubeck. "Around here, that was a pretty heavy deal. He dismissed the case because he felt the city had neglected to prove something. Didn't even give it to the jury. We felt that was an indication that Hanson could stand up to public pressure."

Ted's trial began on Monday morning, February 23, 1976, in room 310 of the old Salt Lake City courthouse. A thin winter light bled through the tall windows behind the impressive darkwood bench at which Judge Hanson presided.

The judge was in large part ignorant of the controversy about Ted's case. He had been away at a judicial gathering in Reno, Nevada, for several weeks during the peak of the publicity, and knew nothing of the several other crimes to which Ted had been linked. Says Hanson: "I was just not really aware of what this case was all about. You may think I was wandering around in a fog, and maybe I was."

He *had* been told that extra security had been arranged for the trial; that explained the beefy, saturnine deputy sheriffs sitting in the otherwise vacant jury box. But as he surveyed his high-ceilinged, red carpeted courtroom, he was astonished to find every seat taken.

Before him were his old law school classmates, John O'Connell and David Yocom, poised for their theatrical and ritualized combat. Next to O'Connell sat his associate, Bruce Lubeck, who recalls: "We were very confident we were going to win. It wasn't so much that we had anything, it was just that they didn't."

The defendant himself came to court in a blue suit that Sheila Vortman had helped him to pick out. He was self-assured and appeared tanned and relaxed after a short skiing vacation he had taken just before the trial.

Ted saw Johnnie and Louise sitting together in numb astonishment at the rear of the courtroom. Their presence made him uncomfortable. The Bundys were staying with Michael Preece, the president of Ted's Mormon ward. Louise especially found Ted's abstemious Mormon friends warm and hospitable in this, her family's hour of need. But she still hadn't gotten over her son's sudden switch in religions. Never would.

Across the aisle from the Bundys sat Debbie Kent's mother, Belva, with her thoughts of her missing daughter. Nearby, Melissa Smith's father, Midvale police chief Louis Smith, sat rigidly, hatred for Bundy evident in his face. At the request of both defense and prosecution, Jerry Thompson had made sure Smith wasn't carrying a weapon into court.

Smith knew by this time that Bundy had gone on a weekend hunting trip with Liz Kendall's father the day after Melissa disappeared. If, as her autopsy suggested, she had not died immediately, then where and in what condition had Ted kept her?

Also discovered by now had been two strands of human hair, one in the trunk of Ted's VW, the other at the base of his gearshift. One of the strands, according to an FBI lab report, was "microscopically indistinguishable" from head hair taken from Caryn Campbell in Colorado. The other was a pubic hair, equally alike to a sample from Chief Smith's daughter. Had there been any more evidence, *anything*, Smith knew that Ted would be on trial for his life that Monday morning.

Toward the back of the courtroom, Judge Hanson's fifteen-year-old daughter caught O'Connell's attention. At the sight of her, he reflected that he and Hanson were the same age, and already his longtime friend had a teenaged daughter. John O'Connell suddenly felt old.

He nudged his client and pointed out the girl. Throughout the trial, Bundy felt the girl's ceaseless gaze. "She sat there *staring* at me," he recalls. "I swear to God! It gave me the willies." Ted felt trapped by her stares, as if the Hanson girl was there to bear mute witness for all the dead women. He also wondered what effect she was having on the man in the black robes.

Stew Hanson was hardly aware that his daughter was in the courtroom. His first concern that morning was to elicit for the record Ted's confirmation that he had waived a jury trial of his own free will. Should he find the defendant guilty, Hanson was not about to have the verdict overturned on a plea that Ted had not understood what he was doing.

> HANSON: Mr. Bundy, was that decision made on your part freely and voluntarily?
> BUNDY: Yes, sir.
> HANSON: With full understanding of the fact that you have a right to a trial by jury in this matter?
> BUNDY: I understand, Your Honor, my right to a trial by jury, and it is my decision, the best decision I could come to, after speaking with my attorneys, that I would waive the jury in this case.

Hanson gave an inward sigh.

With no jury to play to, David Yocom's opening statement was measured and businesslike. The prosecutor confined himself to a retelling of Carol DaRonch's kidnap and Ted's later arrest with that curious bag of equipment in his car. "The state," Yocom concluded, "will request this court in its powers as both judge and jury to find this defendant guilty as charged of aggravated kidnap."

O'Connell followed, with a good deal more force to his remarks. He told his friend the judge that the trial was going to be anticlimactic, "like a Whoozits comedy. There's an awful lot of excitement, but when it comes down to it there's not much there. An awful lot of smoke, but not much fire." He began his assault on Carol DaRonch's credibility as a witness, contending that it would "become apparent that this is a rather immature young lady." O'Connell went on to charge that here was "the most obvious forced identification of anything I have ever seen in my legal career." He characterized Ted as the real victim in the case, and finished with a flourish about the "damn tragedy" of his client to be charged with such a crime. Round one to O'Connell.

Yocom lost no time in getting to the core of his case. He called Carol DaRonch to the stand. "Take your time, Carol," he told her. "Let's go through it slowly. Okay?"

Hanson busied himself with note-taking as he listened to DaRonch's story. In a soft voice, she related how on November 8, 1974, she left her job at Mountain Bell at 6:00 P.M., drove home in her maroon Camaro, then went to the Fashion Place Mall in search of a birthday present. She arrived there at about 7:00 P.M. and remembered meeting her cousin Joanne as well as a friend, Jolynne Turner. Then, as she stood in front of the Waldenbooks store, a man approached her.

> YOCOM: Okay. As best you recall, Carol, what were the first words spoken to you by this man?
> DARONCH: He asked me if I had a car parked in the Sears parking lot.
> YOCOM: Parking lot?
> DARONCH: Yes.
> YOCOM: Is that man present in court today, Carol?
> DARONCH: Yes.
> YOCOM: Where is he seated?
> DARONCH: Right there.
> YOCOM: Will you tell me what he is wearing?
> DARONCH: A blue-gray suit.
> YOCOM: You are referring to the counsel table?
> DARONCH: Yes.
> YOCOM: May the record show the identification of Mr. Bundy?
> O'CONNELL: It may.
> HANSON: It will.

The judge kept scribbling away at his trial notes as Yocom led his witness through the remainder of her story. She testified that she was duped into returning to her car with Ted on the pretext that he was a police officer and that there was a report that someone had attempted to break into her Chevrolet. Upon finding the car locked and undisturbed, "Officer Roseland" led Carol back through the mall to the back of a laundromat, which he said was a police substation. Leery, but still persuaded that he was indeed a policeman, the girl then agreed to drive with him to the Murray police department.

His vehicle, she noted, hardly looked like a police car—a dented, rusty VW bug with a tear along the top of the rear seat. She remembered that it was a light color, white or tan, although on the night of the incident she had told police that the car appeared to be light blue. O'Connell would later bore in on this inconsistency in her testimony, calling it an example of her extreme unreliability as a witness. But Judge Hanson, who owned a tan sedan, took private note of the fact that he himself had been to the Fashion Place Mall after dark, and that under the parking-lot lights his car looked bluish, too.

DaRonch continued her testimony with a description of the attack and her miraculous escape. Then Yocom asked her to recall the limeup.

> YOCOM: Were you able to identify him from your recollection of him on November 8, Carol?
> DARONCH: Yes.
> YOCOM: Did you have any trouble?
> DARONCH: No.
> YOCOM: Did he appear any different then than he did on November 8th?
> DARONCH: Yes.
> YOCOM: In what way?
> DARONCH: He looked more clean-cut. His hair was shorter. He didn't have a mustache.
> YOCOM: Did you notice anything about his appearance that was identical to the way you observed him on November 8th?
> DARONCH: The way he walked.
> YOCOM: Anything else?
> DARONCH: His face.
> YOCOM: Any particular part of his face?
> DARONCH: No.
> YOCHOM: Do you remember any distinctive features, anything about his voice?
> DARONCH: He was polite, sounded like he was well educated by the way he talked.

In all, Carol DaRonch had acquitted herself well on the stand. But the real test would be how she stood up to O'Connell's cross-examination. The advocate began by highlighting several of the inconsistencies in her various reconstructions of the incident.

O'CONNELL: It is your testimony now that you did scratch this man, is that right?

DARONCH: Because all my fingernails were broken.

O'CONNELL: Going to page 38 of the preliminary hearing, do you recall Mr. Yocom asking this question of you: "Do you recall ever scratching him with those fingernails?" And your answer: "No." Do you have an explanation for that?

DARONCH: No.

O'CONNELL: In fact, the officers on November 8th asked you if you remembered if you hurt the man in any way, and you told them no, too, didn't you?

DARONCH: I don't remember.

Ted's lawyer tried to cast doubt on her identification of Bundy.

O'CONNELL: And you say he was wearing a mustache?

DARONCH: Yes.

O'CONNELL: Shortly after the incident you said that you thought it over and decided the man didn't have a mustache, didn't you?

DARONCH: Yes.

O'CONNELL: And sometime later you decided he did, right?

DARONCH: Yes.

O'CONNELL: When did you make that decision?

DARONCH: Right after I decided that he didn't have one.

O'Connell's strategy was to impeach DaRonch's testimony, at the same time demonstrating his contention that the police had forced her into picking out Ted. "You pretty well identify what you think the law-enforcement officers want you to identify, don't you?" O'Connell snarled.

On redirect examination, Yocom shored up his witness.

YOCOM: Did you, when you went to the lineup, know that the man who assaulted you—kidnapped you on November 8th—was going to be there?

DARONCH: No.

YOCOM: Did anyone tell you he was going to be there?

YOCOM: Did you know his name?

DARONCH: No.

YOCOM: Did you know anything about Theodore Bundy on October 2nd at the lineup?

DARONCH: I don't think so.

Then he led her back through the lineup itself

> YOCOM: Seeing Mr. Bundy at the lineup when he first
> walked into the lineup room, what did you associate that
> with, Carol?
> DARONCH: When he first walked in was the way he walked
> on that night.
> YOCOM: What night?
> DARONCH: November 8th.
> YOCOM: Did you know immediately?
> DARONCH: Yes.
> YOCOM: And are you positive today?
> DARONCH: Yes.

Going into the trial, Yocom had seen himself as vulnerable on
two accounts. One, the nearly eleven months between the time
of Carol DaRonch's abduction and her first, tentative identification of Bundy. "That was," he told Hugh, "a prosecution minus,
and a defense plus."

His other concern had been Carol DaRonch herself. "Carol
was very timid," he explained. "She looked down at the floor a
lot. She wouldn't talk directly to you.

"Her inability to express how she felt was her difficulty.
She'd get a question that she knew darn well the answer, but if
she couldn't come up with it really quickly she'd say, 'I don't
know,' or 'I don't remember.' That's horrible for an eyewitness
I.D., especially on cross-examination. I talked to her about it, but
it didn't help much, because she continued to do it."

Her two and a half hours on the stand came to a close at 5:00
P.M. when Hanson adjourned the court for the day. Through her
occasional sobs of confusion and fear had emerged a kind of
gritty defiance to O'Connell's questioning. There had been no
hesitation at all when she identified Ted as her assailant. Yet she
had been vague on key points, and her retelling of the incidents
on the night of November 8 suggested an astonishing naiveté and
blind submissiveness to authority figures. Certainly it was plausible,
many court observers felt, that John O'Connell was right.

But the only view that counted was Judge Hanson's, and
behind his mien of juridical propriety, the judge had formed
some opinions of her testimony. "In spite of what everyone
seems to believe, I thought Carol DaRonch was a very good
witness," he told us. "My feeling was very clear that she was a
strong, positive witness. Very thin, frail girl. And she was up

against someone who is considered one of the finest criminal lawyers in the state. Yet she was really unshakable. Very firm and positive.''

Day two of the trial brought Marlin Vortman to court. Each day, the trusted friend and informal legal adviser took notes on the testimony. Each night, he and Ted would review the day's developments, agreeing generally that the case was going well.

John O'Connell successfully argued to keep one ancillary bit of evidence out of the case. Judge Hanson would not take into his deliberations the fact that Ted Bundy has type O blood, and that type O blood was found on Carol DaRonch's coat collar the Monday following her abduction.

But Yocom pressed ahead Tuesday morning with his police witnesses who reconstructed the odd circumstances of Ted's August 16 arrest. He was allowed to introduce Officer Ondrak's discovery of the handcuffs in Ted's VW trunk. Bitterly contested by the defense as immaterial and illegally obtained, the testimony provided invaluable collateral evidence. It was consistent with guilt.

After the Tuesday afternoon session began, court reporter Ruth Price walked into Hanson's office during a recess. "Did you notice that?" she asked.

"What are you talking about?" Hanson replied.

"Well, he's changed his clothes from what he had on this morning and he's parted his hair on the other side.''

Hanson hadn't noticed, and he wasn't really surprised. After all, this was an eyewitness identification case. "But," he recalls, "as we went through the trial, I did notice some very conscious efforts on his part to change his appearance. His expression would so change his whole appearance that there were some moments that you weren't even sure that you were looking at the same person as you had been half an hour before. Or the day before. Or the morning before.''

Some weeks after the trial, Hanson read Vincent Bugliosi's retelling of the Manson case, *Helter-Skelter*. In it, the former prosecutor tells of how Charles Manson's appearance could change dramatically with his mood. "That was exactly the impression I had of Bundy," says Hanson. "He is really a changeling.''

Yocom next called Jerry Thompson, and began with the detective's search of Ted's apartment.

YOCOM: Now, specifically with regard to the examination of the closet area of his apartment, did you notice any particular shoes located in that area?

> THOMPSON: I noticed shoes which resembled the type that I
> am wearing now, a loafer type, that I assumed—a shiny
> patent leather type. Two or three pairs.

Here was another vital link for the prosecution. O'Connell
would put on witnesses to testify that the Ted Bundy they knew
wouldn't be caught dead in something as tacky as patent leather
shoes. The suggestion that he might own several pairs was
ridiculous—and an affront to the defendant's dignity. Even Liz
Kendall, who could wonder if Ted was a killer, couldn't believe
him capable of wearing patent leather shoes.

Thompson went on to describe the photo spread he had shown
Carol DaRonch on the first of September 1975.

> YOCOM: After she looked at the photographs, what did she
> do with them?
> THOMPSON: She took a picture out of the stack and held it in
> her hand. She went through the rest of the pictures, handed
> me back the stack. She stated. "I don't see anyone in
> there."
> I then asked her how about the photograph that was in her
> hand. She stated something to the effect, "Oh, this one, I
> don't know. Here." And handed it back to me.
> I then asked her why she pulled that photograph out, if
> there was something significant about it. She states, "Yes, I
> believe that looks a lot like the individual, but I'm not
> sure."
> YOCOM: Whose photograph was that?
> THOMPSON: That was Mr. Bundy's.

On cross-examination, O'Connell hoped to demonstrate the
"forced" nature of DaRonch's identification. He asked Thompson about the Polaroid snapshots of Ted's car he had taken with
Ted's blessing on August 21.

> O'CONNELL: Now, on September 1, when you went up to talk
> to Carol DaRonch, you showed her the small photos of the
> automobile?
> THOMPSON: Yes, sir.
> O'CONNELL: And she told you that she definitely remembered
> the tear in the back seat?
> THOMPSON: That resembled the tear, yes, sir.

O'CONNELL: Then you told her that although she had seen a lot of photos, you gave her this packet of photos?

THOMPSON: Yes, sir.

O'CONNELL: And you just said that she went through the process, took Mr. Bundy's photo out and gave you the pack back and said, "The man isn't in there," right?

THOMPSON: Correct.

O'CONNELL: Then you said, "What about this one?" indicating the one she had in her hand?

THOMPSON: Yes.

O'CONNELL: And she said, "I don't know," right?

THOMPSON: Similar to that. "I don't know, it resembles the individual," or—

O'CONNELL: You just testified that she said, "I don't know," and then you asked her again, and at that point she said, "It looks like him."

THOMPSON: Yes.

O'CONNELL: Is that the way it happened?

THOMPSON: That's possible. I don't recall the exact wording with her at that time.

O'CONNELL: All right. Then you testified here just a minute ago that after being asked twice about the photo that was in her hand, she said, "It looks a lot like him."

THOMPSON: Yes.

O'CONNELL: Didn't she say, after your second questioning about Mr. Bundy's photo, after saying, "I don't know," the first time, the second time didn't she really say, "It looks something like him?"

THOMPSON: Similar conversation. I don't recall her exact words.

O'CONNELL: Then she said, after she said it looks something like him, she says, "I really don't know," again, right?

THOMPSON: Something like that.

O'CONNELL: Well, don't you think there's a difference between a witness saying that looks something like him, and that looks a lot like him?

THOMPSON: Yes, I think there's a difference.

O'CONNELL: All right. Well, what you said in your report is, she said, "It looks something like him." You really don't know?

THOMPSON: Yes, sir.

O'CONNELL: And that report was dictated about the time, right?

THOMPSON: It would have been dictated that day, or probably the next day, by me.

Then O'Connell turned to the second photo lineup, the one where detective Beal from Bountiful showed DaRonch Ted's driver's license picture taken in December of 1974.

O'CONNELL: You knew it was improper, didn't you, to show a witness two different pictures of the same individual, to show a witness another picture of an individual after she had made somewhat of an identification, "This looks like him"?
THOMPSON: I figured it was improper to show the same photo, but an entirely different one that looked so much different, I didn't feel there was anything wrong with it.

Hanson had been impressed with O'Connell's spirited questioning. He was not persuaded, however, of the defense's primary contention. By now, he was familiar with the uncanny changes in appearance that would come over Ted in the courtroom, and he noted how different Ted looked in his August mug shot and the driver's license photo taken the December before. "Unless you know who you are looking for," thought Hanson, "it would be very hard to identify him from any of those pictures. She had to have a pretty good image to begin with."

That image was O'Connell's first point of attack after the prosecution rested Wednesday morning. The defense's initial witness was Dr. Elizabeth Loftus, a psychology professor from the University of Washington and an expert on memory. Before she could begin, however, Hanson had to rule on a prosecution objection to the use of an expert. Hanson, the state argued, didn't need any help in evaluating Carol DaRonch's reliability. The judge did not buy their argument. "The Utah Supreme Court and the United States Supreme Court," he noted, "have recognized that eyewitness identification is the most problematical type of testimony that can be offered." Objection overruled.

Loftus testified that the term "unconscious transference" refers "to the mistaken recollection or the confusion of a person seen in one situation as the person who has been seen in a different situation." She illustrated the phenomenon with the story of a railway clerk who identified a sailor as the man who had robbed him, when, in fact, the sailor had previously purchased tickets from the clerk. At the lineup, the sailor's face looked familiar, and the clerk identified him incorrectly as the thief.

Loftus went on about the concepts such as the "retentional interval" in memory, the "forgetting curve," and "cuing." In the latter, she told the court, "the experimenter who has a hypothesis can make his experiment come out to conform to his hypothesis unintentionally." She also reported that experiments have shown that viewing hundreds or thousands of photos, as Carol DaRonch did, can affect memory. And there seems to be no relationship between the confidence of eyewitnesses and the reliability of their identification.

The part of her testimony that most intrigued Hanson had to do with stress. In a move he would not have made had there been a jury, he asked a few questions of his own. First, he wanted to know if being a victim of a crime could affect memory.

"Memory performance is going to be lessened," she answered. The judge pressed her further.

> HANSON: Let's assume you have a time continuum as repre-
> sented by a straight line. At one point in time there is no
> stress whatsoever. As that continuum line proceeds, the
> stress begins to build. The victim begins to suspect that
> [she] might be a victim. At a point further down the line,
> the victim becomes assured of the fact that there is a real
> problem. How would stress in your judgment affect eyewit-
> ness identification under those circumstances? That is, would
> the victim be more likely to be able to identify the perpetrator
> under those circumstances than in a situation where there
> was a sudden violent event like a breaking in through a door
> or a window?
> LOFTUS: My guess is that the sudden event would produce a
> less accurate identification, because the whole experience
> would be while the victim was in an extreme state of stress.

Hanson was intensely interested in the doctor's reply. "Her answers were very revealing," he says. "What she was say-ing was that eyewitness testimony is inherently frail. So I asked her a hypothetical question about a hypothetical situation which happened to fit the evidence in the case. I remember she said that it would be a valid circumstance for a good eyewitness identification."

O'Connell's next witness was Edward M. Barton, the former chief criminal investigator for the Salt Lake County attorney's office. Barton testified as to the quality of evidence that usually was required before he could go to the county attorney to ask that a subject be charged.

O'CONNELL: You wouldn't rely solely on eyewitness identification?
BARTON: Oh, no. No, sir.

Once again, Hanson took it upon himself to question a witness.

HANSON: Would you say that the lineup identifications procedure is or is not a reliable means of identifying a suspect?
BARTON: My personal experience was that it was not the best form of evidence. It was an investigative aid, but it was not the best form.

On Thursday morning, February 26, O'Connell called Ted to the stand. Hanson still didn't know if he believed Carol DaRonch's testimony or not, and a credible performance by the defendant would mean a verdict of innocence. All Ted had to do was come up with a believable story as to just where he was on the night of November 8, 1974.

Later, the consensus was that Ted was a disaster on the witness stand. O'Connell agrees that Ted damaged his own case. "He just didn't seem right. But I never could figure out how he was supposed to act and neither could Ted. If you were hated by nine million people how would you act? No matter what the guy did, it didn't seem right."

Ted's story was that his car broke down the afternoon of November 8, 1974, and that he pushed it into a gas station, where a mechanic helped him to start it. He drove home to his apartment around 5:00 P.M. "Obviously, I can't recall too much past that point," he testified, "except I'm sure I went to my house, and I guess I'd have to say I suppose I had dinner." Later on, Ted remembered, he went out to try to start the car, but couldn't. He was trying to appear innocent, adding, "I'm not going to fool anybody, it's hard to think back ten months, twelve months—sixteen months now." But the candor seemed affected.

The rest of that evening, according to Ted, he probably walked down to Salt Lake's Trolley Square to see a movie, then perhaps he had a beer at the Pub. He knew he was home by eleven-fifty that night, because his telephone records show he called his girlfriend in Seattle at that hour. Specifically, he denied having been at the Fashion Place Mall, or having had any contact with Carol DaRonch.

He fabricated a porous explanation of the handcuffs. "In the early part of 1975, in the course of doing work for my landlord, I took things to the Salt Lake City dump, and I found them in a box of odds and ends there."

O'CONNELL: Why did you take the handcuffs?
BUNDY: I don't know. Why not? They just seemed to be something.

On cross-examination, Yocom reminded Ted that he had told Detective Forbes that in Seattle he had once apprehended a thief and had had to restrain the suspect until the police arrived. Having handcuffs, he felt, might be useful if such a circumstance should ever arise again. In addition to pointing out the discrepancy in Ted's explanations, Yocom wanted to demonstrate the weakness of Ted's initial claim.

YOCOM: Did you ever have a key to those handcuffs?
BUNDY: I don't believe so.
YOCOM: Wouldn't be much value to you in apprehending people without a key, would they?
BUNDY: Well, again, if that was my purpose, as I say, the absence of a key was one of the primary factors in saying they were more of a curiosity than saying something one could use that would have any utility.
YOCOM: But you told Forbes you were going to use them to restrain people, is that right?
BUNDY: Detective Forbes had informed me that his game was homicide. I must tell you that he wanted—
YOCOM: Answer my question rather than editorializing.
BUNDY: Sure. Would you re-ask the question?
YOCOM: You don't remember it?
BUNDY: No, I don't.
YOCUM: You just want to answer the way you want to answer, right?
BUNDY: That's right.

Ted had cobbled up another story to explain why he hadn't admitted to even John O'Connell that he had been smoking marijuana the night of his arrest. "I didn't see any purpose in telling you," he testified. "I was quite embarrassed by it. It's not something you care to admit."

Yocom pounced on that story, pointing out to Ted that as a law student he would know that an admission of having smoked a joint could not be used as evidence against him. Furthermore, possession of marijuana is a simple misdemeanor in Utah, while possession of burglary tools and attempting to elude arrest carry a higher potential penalty. Yocom asked if the arresting officers had questioned Ted.

BUNDY: I was questioned, yes.
YOCOM: And the thrust of their questioning did not go to the question of marijuana use, did it?
BUNDY: It did not, thank God.
YOCOM: Do you remember what you told the officers about the crowbar in the automobile?
BUNDY: I can't remember specifically. I think I may have told them I had been using it that day, shortly before that day. I can't tell you exactly what I said that evening.
YOCOM: A crowbar of this nature is not exactly a tool that you would use with regard to repairing your automobile, would it?
BUNDY: Well, it's a useful tool. What can I say, Dave?

Yocom welcomed Ted's mocking civility, which—like Ted's manner with the police—was backfiring badly. The prosecutor grew more insistent. He questioned Ted about the nature of his car troubles on November 8. Ted explained the trouble was a result of neglect, not the sort of difficulty that crops up suddenly.

YOCOM: How was your car running, say, the two weeks prior to November 8th?
BUNDY: I suppose it was running. A Volkswagen will run.
YOCOM: In fact, you were running the wheels off it, weren't you?
BUNDY: I can't recall.
YOCOM: Didn't you purchase gas on the 25th, 26th, and 28th days—
O'CONNELL: Your Honor, he's going into collateral matters. It's outside the scope.
YOCOM: It's not, Your Honor. He talked about his car not running well. It goes directly to that point.
HANSON: The objection is overruled.

Yocom then asked Ted if he had purchased a total of 22.7 gallons of gas in a four-day period in late October, all within the Bountiful Murray, Utah, area.

> BUNDY: I guess if you added it together properly, that's what it is.
>
> YOCOM: How many miles to the gallon do you get on that car?
>
> BUNDY: Well, when it's not running efficiently, it drops quite low. I can't say during that period. When it's running at peak efficiency, it will run at 28. When it's not running well, it will run down 22, 23, maybe as low as 20 miles per gallon.
>
> YOCOM: So you can tell me generally in your head how many miles you traveled on 23 gallons of gas?
>
> BUNDY: Well, no.
>
> O'CONNELL: I object. This is a math test?
>
> HANSON: The objection is overruled.
>
> YOCOM: Have you computed that yet?
>
> BUNDY: Oh, I'm not really thinking about it, Dave. I thought you made your own conclusion. I'm not here to do mathematical problems.

O'Connell sensed that his client was alienating the court with his sass. He jumped up to shut off Yocom's line of questioning.

> O'CONNEL: May the court take judicial notice of the fact that 20 times 23 is 460?

Yocom agreed to the stipulation.

The highest opinion of Ted's testimony was his own; he gave himself a C-plus, he told me. Says Hanson: "I was really very absorbed by what he was saying. I had no strong feelings about him one way or the other. He was a typical witness who was getting on the stand to give an explanation, or an alibi. He was obviously very articulate. He obviously knew exactly what he was saying. I ended up by not believing him."

Closing arguments were completed at 1:44 P.M. on Friday, and Hanson adjourned the trial to consider his verdict.

For the judge, it would be a long weekend at home in his study sifting through every piece of evidence, reviewing his extensive trial notes, and cataloging his recollections of the trial. Friday night, he took his wife out to dinner. "By Saturday morning, I'd worked myself into such a state that I was really wrought up about it. I didn't leave the house again until Monday morning.''

Ted spent the weekend with Liz Kendall, who flew down from Seattle on Thursday night. He had lured the confused woman back into his orbit. Though Liz would eventually break from him—to be supplanted instantly by Carole Boone—she was, at the time of the trial, ready to believe again that her boyfriend was innocent. They made love for the last time on Sunday afternoon.

Hanson's decision did not come to him in an instant. ''I think I delayed making up my mind for as long as I could,'' he told us. ''It is one thing to have doubts—no one knows anything for certain—but reasonable doubts are another thing. I would say that fairly early on in the weekend reasonable doubts disappeared. Then it was a question of going over and over the material to be sure.''

Hanson called everyone back to court at 1:30 P.M. on Monday, March 1. ''The judge looked like death warmed over when he came in,'' remembered O'Connell. With Ted standing before him, Hanson intoned: ''I find the defendant, Theodore Robert Bundy, guilty of aggravated kidnapping, a first degree felony, as charged.''

**Some of Bundy's innocent victims: (top, l-r) Lynda Healy, Donna Manson, Susan Rancourt; (bottom, l-r) Kathy Parks, Brenda Ball, Georgann Hawkins.**

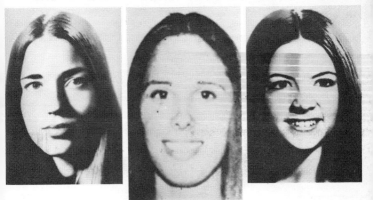

More of the young girls who were victims of Bundy's lethal brutality: (top, l-r) Denise Naslund, Janice Ott, Caryn Campbell; (center, l-r) Laura Aime, Debra Kent, Melissa Smith.

(Bottom) Lisa Levy (l) and Margaret Bowman (r), the two Chi Omega sorority sisters of Florida State University who were mutilated and bludgeoned to death by Bundy

**Bundy's first mug shot, 1975, taken by the Utah authorities.**

**The FBI wanted poster that was circulating shortly before Bundy was arrested in Pensacola, Florida.**

Bundy on his way to the Pitkin County Courthouse in Colorado wearing several layers of clothing in preparation for his escape.

Bundy jumped from a second story courthouse window and escaped into the Colorado mountains for six days before being recaptured.

Florida seventh-grader Kimberly Diane Leach vanished from school only weeks after the sorority killings. Her violated remains were later discovered under an abandoned hog shed.

Carol Da Ronch miraculously survived Bundy's attempted abduction near Salt Lake City, and her testimony later helped send him to prison.

At Bundy's murder trial, Nita Neary testified that Bundy was the man she saw the morning two of her Chi Omega sorority sisters were slain.

Bundy pleading in his own defense during his trial for the slaying of Kimberly Leach. The jury recommended the death penalty.

Carole Boone, convinced of Bundy's innocence, married him while he was standing trial.

Bundy's mother Louise and stepfather John when Bundy received the death penalty for his murder of the two Florida co-eds.

Forensic odontologist, Dr. Richard Souviron, was one of the prosecution's key witnesses as he showed, through a blow-up of Bundy's teeth, that probably only Bundy could have made the bite marks discovered on one of the slain Chi Omega girls.

Richard L. Stephens, a Florida forensic expert, submitted as evidence a pantyhose mask worn during the beating of a ballet dancer the same night as the sorority sisters' murders.

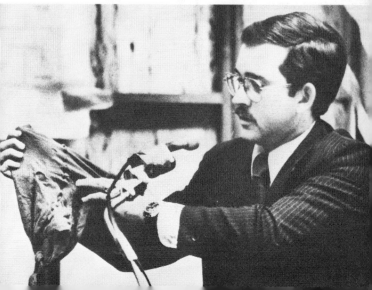

An immaculately groomed, self-confident Bundy believed his courtroom brilliance would win him acquittal.

Mass murderer Theodore Bundy, eventually convicted of three vicious slayings in Florida but suspected in possibly as many as thirty-six other killings.

# NINE

JUDGE HANSON sentenced Ted to a term of one to fifteen years in the Utah State Prison. The punishment was comparatively light; Bundy would be eligible for parole in less than three years.

Once again, after he conquered his initial fright at being in prison, he found the environment almost genial. Ted blossomed as a jailhouse lawyer, exchanging his minimal legal expertise for favors—principally dope. In time, he grew so comfortable with his environment and with himself that he began to forget what he was and the brutal urges he had felt in the outside world. The lack of stress in a simple, elemental existence deceived him into thinking he had rid himself of his homicidal compulsion. But it was only dormant.

In January, just weeks before the trial began, Mike Fisher and Barry Bryant, a prosecutor from Aspen, had met secretly in Salt Lake City civil defense air raid shelter with David Yocom, Jerry Thompson, Bob Keppel, and the prosecutor from Seattle, Phil Killien. Their purpose was to determine if anyone had a strong enough case to indict Bundy for murder. Already concerned about the legal issue of pretrial publicity, they did not want news of such a meeting leaked to the press.

Yocom was loath to prosecute Ted for kidnapping if a murder charge could be brought, but in the four months since Bundy's arrest, Thompson and the rest of the Utah investigators had turned up only a single piece of substantive new evidence against Ted. This was the pubic hair, vacuumed from his impounded VW, that was microscopically indistinguishable from Melissa Smith's. Not enough to indict him.

Bob Keppel and Phil Killien reported that they were no closer to an indictment in Seattle and didn't think they would ever get one, barring a confession from Bundy.

That left Mike Fisher, who had the ski brochure from Ted's apartment, the gas-credit receipts, the hair match between Caryn Campbell and a sample from Ted's car, and, just recently, a witness who might be able to place Ted inside the Wildwood Inn within minutes of Caryn Campbell's disappearance.

While the others waited in Salt Lake, Fisher and Bryant flew to Aspen and presented their evidence to Judge George Lohr, a highly respected jurist known for his regard for defendants' rights. Lohr was unconvinced that Fisher had established probable cause to believe Bundy had murdered Caryn Campbell. He would authorize no indictment or extradition order. Back in the air raid shelter, Fisher reported his disappointment. Bundy would be tried for kidnap only.

But Fisher didn't give up. After the DaRonch trial, the FBI lab reported *another* hair match; they could now link Carol DaRonch to Ted's car. Beyond Fisher's witness, a doctor's wife from California who had tentatively picked Ted's photo as that of the man she saw January 12, 1975, at the Wildwood Inn, a new witness had also come forward to report that she'd seen Bundy hobbling around on crutches in Aspen that spring.

Before going back to Judge Lohr, however, Fisher decided upon a gamble. He wanted to talk to Ted. Perhaps, he hoped, the shock of the conviction had left the suspect vulnerable. Maybe Bundy would make a slip.

Against John O'Connell's advice, Ted agreed to meet with Fisher. And once again Ted thoroughly misjudged his questioner and the effects of his own actions. If he had simply conceded having been to Colorado and then offered an alibi—any alibi— Bundy could have effectively stopped Fisher cold. Instead, he played the same game he had with Ben Forbes, failing to offer credible answers. When, for instance, the investigator asked if Ted recalled having been in Aspen in January of 1975, Bundy replied; "I can't, uh, I can't say for sure, no."

Fisher noticed that Ted was shaking as he spoke. Fisher remembers: "He wouldn't say, 'Well, you know what I did. I had somebody else over there and I didn't want my girlfriend to know.' Or some really plausible story about *why* he was there.

"That would have been an affirmative defense. I mean, the guy could have blown me right out of the state of Utah. I'd have never gone back. He didn't look at the totality of the situation. How he projected himself, how he locked himself in."

Fisher suspected that Judge Lohr hadn't been adequately apprised of the significance of the hair comparison evidence; nor had the jurist yet been told of the Smith and DaRonch matches. The investigator himself was no expert on this type of evidence, so he telephoned William Neil, the FBI lab specialist who had done the Bundy case comparisons. What he received was a short course in the science and an understanding, for the first time, of the significance of his evidence.

Microscopic hair comparison is a less exact but far more exacting science than fingerprint identification. In the latter, it is known that no two people have identical prints. What is more, eight distinct "points of identification" (i.e., whorls, arches, etc.) are recognized. The FBI regards an identification as positive if six out of the eight points are clear enough to match between a known and a questioned print. Today, fingerprint analysis is more or less routine.

With hair, however, an elimination may be done in a moment with the naked eye, or require days of tedious microscopic examination. Even then, the surest an examiner can be of a match is to say that the known and questioned samples are microscopically indistinguishable. That is, it is not *certain* that the samples came from the same person.

Hair analysts look for "points of comparison." Depending upon how these microscopic characteristics are counted, between fifteen and twenty-five of them are generally recognized. So far, they have not been standardized like the universally known eight fingerprint points of identification.

To an examiner, the human hair is analogous to a lead pencil. At the center, corresponding to the graphite core of a pencil, is the medulla, which may be either hollow or filled with a soft protein substance. If the protein is present, it can appear as a continuous thread along the entire length of the hair or, in the wording of the FBI manual, it can be "discontinuous" or "fragmentary."

Surrounding the medulla is the cortex, also made of protein. Among its identifiable features (which may or may not be present in a sample) are irregularly shaped air holes (called "fusi") and tiny granules of pigment.

Each hair is wrapped by a cuticle. Under a microscope, the cuticle reveals scales, often in distinct patterns.

The arrangement of these and other microcharacteristics is random, and their relative abundance and usefulness for purposes of comparison can vary from hair to hair from a single donor and even along a single strand. Known and questioned samples must be viewed under the same microscope at the same power of magnification and under exactly the same light at the same angle. Even then, a sample may be too small for a valid comparison to be made. Often, an analyst can be sure of nothing more than the race of the donor and, possibly, what part of the body the hair came from.

Thus, to find a known and questioned hair sample to be microscopically indistinguishable is to offer evidence powerfully indicative of a common source. In Ted Bundy's case, the discovery of three such close comparisons between hair vacuumed from his car and hair taken from three victims would be a coincidence of mind-boggling rarity.

Mike Fisher spent several hours with William Neil. According to Fisher, Neil told him that in a fifteen-year career he had been asked in maybe 300 to 400 cases to compare known hair samples from multiple victims to questioned samples taken from a single site. Never had Neil been able to match more than one victim.

As Fisher put it to Hugh: "It wasn't like Caryn Campbell, Melissa Smith, and Carol DaRonch were all at the same place at the same time, like maybe some guy's bedroom. DaRonch was at the Fashion Place Mall, Smith was walking down a Midvale street, and Caryn Campbell was in Colorado. She wasn't even *from* Colorado. She was from Michigan, and she'd only been here a day and she's *dead!*

"Think about it! What are the odds of these three young ladies passing through Ted Bundy's car?"

Ted and those who have believed him innocent counter that hair analysis offers at best corroborative evidence; it is not absolute *proof* those girls were in his car. Plus, it has been suggested, the police in their eagerness to build a case could well have planted the hairs in his car.

Against that contention, there is only Jerry Thompson's word (as was also true with the X-marked Colorado ski brochure and the patent leather shoes). However, Carol DaRonch's hair was not submitted with the first samples; Thompson didn't think she could have been in Ted's car long enough to have left such a trace of herself. Only as an afterthought—and too late to be of use at the trial—did he submit a sample of her hair to Neil. Says Mike Fisher: "You don't usually try to frame a guy with evidence you're not going to use."

Armed with Neil's assurance that he could testify to what he'd told him, Fisher went back to Judge Lohr in October 1976 and secured an "information" (a Colorado variant of an indictment) in the Campbell case. Finally, Ted Bundy would be charged with murder.

A month earlier, however, Ted had been alerted to his danger by a premature radio report that announced he was about to be indicted for killing Caryn Campbell. "I would have ridden out the DaRonch thing," Ted told us later, "but a murder beef in Colorado was something different. Fuck that bullshit! I began seriously planning an escape.

"I knew absolutely nothing about the art of escaping," Ted explained. "So, to acquire the necessary information, I began to talk at great length with prisoners I knew had themselves escaped prison in the past. I doubt that I learned anything, except that the fewer people you talk to about such things, the better."

Ted's amateurishness showed in several ways. He couldn't resist a touch of melodrama, so several friends in Seattle received letters in which he alluded to a grim resolution to take matters in his own hands, that he had given up on the criminal justice system. All of these letters were first read by prison censors. The tone of the letters made it obvious that Ted was getting ready to jump, although one impressionable acquaintance in Seattle mistook her letter for a suicide note. She warned his bemused Utah attorneys that their client was contemplating killing himself.

Inside the prison, several informers kept the authorities abreast of Bundy's plans. While working in the prison print shop, he had noticed that several times a week a truck was brought into the prison to pick up goods manufactured by the inmates. Despite previous escape attempts, its cargo area was not always thoroughly searched.

Having chosen his means of escape, Ted patiently collected the material he expected he'd need and secreted these items throughout the print shop. His list of escape essentials included chocolate bars, bags of peanuts, Chap Stick, suntan lotion, a razor and razor blades, and bandages.

On October 19, 1976, the prison officials decided to pull the plug on Ted's travel plans. Work in the print shop was stopped early and the inmates filed back to their cell blocks. As Ted passed through the sally port, or gate, that led into the prison proper, he was stopped and strip-searched. They found nothing, but a half-hour later a team of guards walked onto his cell block and made straight for Bundy. With the entire prison population locked down in the emergency, he was led off to a new cell in maximum security.

Ted Bundy wasn't the only con to cause a stir in the Utah State Prison that fall. An even more notorious inmate, Gary Gilmore, was sent up for the murders of a gas station attendant and a motel clerk and began his quixotic campaign to become the first man executed in the U.S. since 1962. Gilmore underlined his determination to die with two dramatic suicide attempts. Each time, the entire institution was searched; and each time, cherished contraband, from zip guns to dope to tattoo kits, was seized.

As a result of the extra security, Ted saw little chance of breaking out in Utah. But his pending extradition to Colorado—to the laxer security of a county jail—offered him hope of a new escape plan.

Ted and his attorneys fought Fisher's extradition order for a while, even though it was clear that Bundy would ultimately be sent to Colorado to stand trial for murder. Thanksgiving and Christmas 1976 passed. On January 17, 1977, Gary Gilmore was executed by a firing squad at the prison. Ten days later, Mike Fisher arrived to take Ted Bundy to Aspen.

Ted had known all day of January 27, 1977, that he was about to be moved. For security reasons, it had been thought best to transport Bundy at night. He was given a new pair of white coveralls to wear and then was left in his cell with a half-dozen boxloads of his property until late that evening. Ted finally fell asleep, only to be awakened at 2:00 A.M.

He was led, handcuffed, through a thick fog to the rear seat of a four-door Ford sedan. Mike Fisher sat beside him. Two other officers rode in front.

"Someone in the car was wearing cologne," Ted remembers, "the first cologne I'd smelled in months and months and months. I can remember a sudden surge of elation, of almost freedom. I probably hadn't felt so good since some time before I was first arrested.

"I said to myself, 'I've got a chance now. There'll be a chance for something.' "

Ted and his three-man escort arrived in Aspen on the morning of January 28, 1977, after a six-hour drive. For once, Ted had kept his mouth shut; he had spoken only when spoken to from the moment the car left the prison.

After he was formally booked, Fisher took him to a small office. "Well, Ted," he said, "how'd you like to talk to us now? We've got a lot to talk about, don't we, Ted?"

Bundy was even more contemptuous of Fisher than he'd been of Jerry Thompson and Ben Forbes in Utah. He not only thought himself more clever than Fisher, but with all his notoriety he now also saw himself as too important to be in the custody of a small-town detective. "I disliked him," Ted told me. "But at times I felt sorry for him, too. I felt he just did not seem to be equipped to handle the job."

Not that Ted cared what kind of case Fisher could make against him. Bundy had no intention of standing trial for Caryn Campbell's murder.

His first move was to rid himself of his new attorney, public defender Charles Leidner. There had been an immediate personal dislike between the two men from their first meeting back at the Utah State Prison. Ted was upset that Leidner treated him as just another client, and Ted had begun to relish the role of legal expert he'd begun playing among the cons in Utah.

In early March, he petitioned Judge Lohr to be allowed to represent himself in the Campbell case. Citing his Sixth Amendment right to do so, Ted's handwritten motion assured the judge "That the Defendant intends to prepare and present his defense in full accordance with procedural, legal and ethical ground rules [sic] governing the conduct of criminal prosecutions in Colorado." He did concede "pronounced inexperience in certain areas of the criminal law" and asked that a local attorney be named as his advisory counsel.

Lohr tried for weeks to argue Ted out of his position, but was finally obliged to acknowledge that Bundy was manifestly literate and competent, and was petitioning the court voluntarily. Thus, Lohr had scant choice but to grant the motion.

Ted had planned to make his break from the Pitkin County jail, an antique iron box in the basement of the courthouse in Aspen. He calls it "the sorriest jail I've ever seen. The place was filthy, virtually crawling with fungus. The toilet bowl was full of scum. You could walk ten paces across that metal floor and your feet would be black. They wouldn't allow us to have shoes."

Once he settled in, he was even more distressed by the jail's construction and location; it would be as difficult to bust out of as maximum security, he thought. He was further disheartened in April when he was told he'd be moved to the Garfield County jail in Glenwood Springs. A much newer facility, it was reputed to be even more secure than the Aspen lockup.

He was moved on April 17, 1977, the day before Andy Williams' ex-wife, former chorus girl Claudine Longet, checked into the Pitkin County jail to begin serving her one-month sentence for shooting Spider Sabich, her lover. Ted the defendant might have taken heart at Longet's situation. In George Lohr's courtroom, she had been charged with a felony, reckless manslaughter, but had been convicted of a misdemeanor, criminal negligence, and was punished with a thirty-day jail term, two years of probation, and a twenty-five-dollar fine.

But Ted the inmate was unconcerned about his legal prospects, even as pretrial motions began. "The advent of spring gave me an entirely new point of view," Ted told me. "Each time I was transported down to Aspen from Glenwood Springs, I looked anxiously out at the high country to see if the snow had melted yet. I knew I had no chance while the snow was still deep and the weather cold. And as the snow began to melt, I began to look for things around me in Aspen, outside the jail, that I could take advantage of.

"Of course, over the months I'd become well acquainted with all the deputies, very well acquainted with their habits. I knew the layout of the courtroom. I had always done what I was told—a model prisoner—was always very polite and personable.

"Then I began to notice that many of my guardians were now, shall I say, losing interest, not exactly on their toes. Whereas they used to have a contingent of four with me in the courtroom, it dropped to two and sometimes one. Sometimes I was left all alone in the courtroom."

Here was Ted's chance, the one he knew he'd get from the moment he climbed into the back of the Ford sedan for the trip to Aspen. He wouldn't have to risk breaking jail; he'd simply walk out of the courtroom.

"I know this sounds rather unrealistic," he told me, "but if you understand the traffic patterns inside the courthouse you'll see that at certain times of the day there was very little going on, very few people in the halls. I figured that I needed between thirty and forty-five seconds and I could make good my escape."

Ever since he'd known he was going to Aspen, he'd been planning. He stepped up an exercise regimen he'd begun in

Utah; and, he told me, "I got hold of an atlas which had maps of all the states, and I studied the area surrounding Aspen to the point where I thought I'd memorized all the roads, towns, and highway distances.

"Based on a number of factors, I decided that it would be wisest to go toward a place called Crested Butte, then down to Gunnison, Colorado, and south to Durango and then make my way east toward some large city on the east coast. I had no reason for picking this particular way out, except that it just looked good." Ted also fortified himself with health foods as he pored over his maps, trying to burn each trail and landmark into his memory.

As spring came to the Rockies, Ted noticed one more thing about the courtroom routine: on warm days, the room's second-story windows were left open. Why, he figured, should he take the time to walk downstairs when he could just as easily jump? He calculated that a jump would cut the necessary lead time down to fifteen seconds.

Back in his cell, he started jumping off the top bunk in an effort to steel his ankles for the impact of a leap from the courtroom window. He mentally measured the distance from the window to the corner of the courthouse and then to the alley in back and finally to the riverbank where he planned to change clothes.

"Things," he told me, "finally seemed to be coming together. I decided that I'd make the attempt on Tuesday, the seventh of June."

The Thursday prior to his planned escape, he asked to have his hair cut (he wanted to look as different as possible from contemporary photographs of himself) and also asked if he could go to the Glenwood Springs health food store. A pair of plainclothes deputies took Ted on his rounds that day. They neglected to notice that he kept the $5 he got in change from his purchase of peanuts and raisins and vitamins.

The following Tuesday morning, it was with more than his usual care that Ted dressed for court. First, he tucked a bright red bandana into the pocket of his white tennis shorts, then he put a length of string, some matches, and a plastic bag with a supply of vitamins wrapped in tinfoil into the back pocket of his blue-jean cutoffs. He slipped the white shorts on over his underwear, then the cutoffs, then his brown corduroys.

Over his T-shirt went a white long-john top, a yellow and then a

brown turtleneck sweater—and finally a loose wraparound
sweater to hide the bulk of his other garments. Last came a pair
of heavy wollen hiking socks and his leather boots. He slipped
his $5 and a photograph of Liz and her daughter, Joanie, into
an envelope.

Thus attired, Ted fretted for a moment over the food cache
he'd put together. A surprise search such as the one he had been
given at the Utah State Prison would undo all his plans. He
decided to leave the food and also the transistor radio that only
the day before had arrived by mail from his mother in Tacoma.

The deputies who drove Ted down to Aspen that day apparently noticed nothing unusual about their bulkily clad prisoner.
Nor did the officer who met the car and walked with Ted into
Aspen's Victorian courthouse. Inside, he unlocked Ted's handcuffs and chains ("Ted doesn't need the handcuffs today,"
Bundy remembers him saying. "He's not going to try to get
away from us") and delivered his charge to the courtroom.

It was stuffy inside that morning, but nobody remarked about
the defendant sitting at the defense table in a bulky sweater.
Charles Dumas, one of Ted's advisory counsels, didn't; he was
absorbed in his oral argument against the constitutionality of
Colorado's death penalty. The day seemed routine—just the way
Ted had hoped it would be.

At midmorning, Judge Lohr called a recess and the courtroom
quickly emptied. Ted sneaked a quick—but, he hoped, not final—
look at his photo of Liz and Joanie and then casually rose and
walked to the back of the room where the law library was
located. Deputy David Westerlund was watching him from the
open courtroom door.

The meekest zephyr from the open window riffled the files as
Ted picked up one and feigned interest in it. He began to pace
back and forth, closer and closer to the window. Westerlund paid
little attention to him and finally, as was his habit, ambled out
into the hallway for a smoke.

Ted's heart was racing, beating so loudly that he actually
wondered if anyone could hear it. Now was the moment, but as
he looked out the window he saw a female reporter walking
below.

"Damn!" he muttered to himself, and continued pacing.
Westerlund might return at any instant. It seemed like ten minutes to Ted, but it wasn't more than twenty seconds before he
was back in front of the window. This time he knew he had to
jump, no matter who might be down there. He perched on the

ledge, righted himself, and pushed off. The file he had been reading dropped with him and landed under one foot.

Two or three minutes later, a passerby walked into the courthouse with a mystified expression on her face. "Did you know," she said to a deputy downstairs, "that a man just jumped out of the second-floor window and ran off?"

# TEN

Theodore R. Bundy, former Seattleite charged with murder in Colorado, and a suspect in murders of young women in Washington state and Utah, leaped to freedom from the second floor of the Pitkin County courthouse in Apsen, Colo., today.

An extensive manhunt began. About 100 officers and others were hunting him in nearby mountains and throughout the town. Officers speculated he was fleeing in the direction of nearby Smuggler Mountain, which rises just northeast of Aspen.

"I can still feel the jolt of hitting the ground," Ted told me. "I popped up and leaped across the steps in front of the courthouse and then zipped toward the prosecutor's office. Went in back of that and then down to this six-foot-high wire fence. I didn't climb it or anything. I just jumped over it and somersaulted on the other side.

"I ran like crazy down this alleyway in back of Main Street. These two guys in back of a restaurant looked at me kinda strange because I was running full tilt right by 'em! Boom! Boom! Boom! Boom!"

Ted ran another block and ducked down into a gorge where the Roaring Fork River winds through Aspen. There he stripped down to his shorts and long-john top, tied the bandana around his head, and stuffed the rest of his gear into a makeshift pack fashioned from one of the turtlenecks. This he threw over his back, then he casually ambled back up onto a gravel road and made straight for Aspen Mountain. There were cars and people everywhere. No one paid him any attention.

Two hundred yards past the last condominiums at the base of the mountain, Bundy turned right and headed straight up the mountain. "I kept climbing and climbing," he related, "and I finally got to the point where I could look down and see almost the entirety of Aspen. I was really curious. I thought I would hear the siren go off and I'd see red lights flashing all over the place. But it was just *natural*. It was just the natural buzz of activity that you'd expect to hear from that distance."

At first, Judge Lohr's court was too stunned for action. Several people, including deputies, started shouting, "Bundy's gone! Bundy's escaped!" Taken completely by surprise, the courthouse full of lawyers and lawmen was a bedlam of yells and running feet for several minutes before calm was restored.

By then, Ted was halfway up Aspen Mountain. In the midst of the din, Charles Dumas turned to Chuck Leidner at the defense table. "Never," he reportedly remarked, "have I ever had a client show so little faith in my argument."

"At one point, I collapsed," Ted continued. "Just lost my first wind about 500 feet up the mountain. But I had to keep going, going, going. And at some points I had to zip back and forth because it was just too steep, too rocky. There were rock slides that I had to cross, open areas where there were no trees and where I'd be visible to anyone with binoculars looking up the mountain from the town."

He reached the top about 500 yards to the north of the main Aspen Mountain ski lodge. He hopped across a dirt road from grass clump to grass clump, trying to avoid leaving footprints. Once safely over the summit, he rested. He'd covered the approximately four miles from the bottom of the mountain to the top in a little more than an hour.

Ted had hoped that once he had negotiated the shorter southern face of Aspen Mountain he could pick up a trail or roadway that would lead him farther south to Crested Butte. It was a logical enough scheme and one that might have worked had he had any sense of direction at all. As it happened, he ignored at least two dirt roadways on Aspen Mountain's southern slope that would have taken him directly to Crested Butte.

"I wasn't doing much thinking," he remembers. "My mind was dominated by my physical exertion. But I did have these flashes about what was happening in Aspen, or what the judge was thinking. There were also times when it was so peaceful and serene in this forest setting that I had these delusions that no one had missed me. That no one was looking for me. That I was just out there alone. 'I'm not a fugitive. I'm not Ted Bundy.' ''

For the moment at least, Ted could indulge his reverie and forget that he, the hunter, had become the hunted. The police established their roadblocks, began searching Aspen, and decided by consensus that he'd probably headed north; the opposite direction from the one he'd taken. A pack of tracking dogs was summoned and given bits of one of Bundy's sweaters to pick up his scent. What they got was the trail of the female deputy who'd brought the sweater. They promptly led the deputies to her house.

"It was already starting to get dim when I got to the bottom," Ted went on, "and I came upon what apparently had been a campsite. There were some old boards nailed to trees and a couple of dilapidated camp tables. This was about fifty yards from the roadway.

"I put my clothes on again because it was starting to get cool. I began to daydream a little about what was happening. What was my mother thinking? What was Liz thinking? What kind of search was being mounted? It was almost hard for me to grasp the reality of being hunted, because it was so peaceful there. I was faintly amused, too, because I knew that they didn't know where I was."

*The Seattle Post-Intelligencer*

## MOTHER TO BUNDY: GIVE UP

TACOMA—(UPI)—The mother of Theodore Bundy is pleading with him to give up and says she was afraid searchers would shoot first and ask questions later.

Mrs. Louise Bundy, in an interview with Tacoma station KSTW-TV, said she was worried about her son being out in the mountains of Colorado. "But most of all, I'm worried about the people who are out looking for him not using common sense and pulling the trigger first and asking questions later."

Mrs. Bundy said she thought her son's escape from a courthouse in Aspen would hurt his case in Colorado.

"People will think, 'Oh he must be guilty, that's why

he's running.' But I think just all the frustrations piled up and he saw an open window and decided to go. I'm sure by now he's probably sorry he did," said Mrs. Bundy.

Ted went on with his story. "It was just light enough to see when I decided to cross the roadway. I went down another steep decline on the other side. It was maybe twenty-five yards to this riverbed. By this time it was dark. I had no flashlight. No maps. No nothing. Quite frankly, I was just stumbling along the riverbed at this point. I think finally the exertion of the day had started to catch up with me. And it started to get cold."

Bundy had trudged roughly 200 yards up the stream when he noticed the dim silhouette of a log cabin, apparently vacant, off to his left. The prospect of a night's shelter tantalized him, but so, too, did his chances of slipping unnoticed through the night to Crested Butte. He pressed on along the river for a time.

"But I couldn't make any progress there, so I cut up into the forest. I was disoriented and totally lost. I couldn't even make out the outlines of the valley. So I retraced my steps back down to the river and finally to this dirt roadway. I followed it. Immediately the road became rockier and rockier. Then it began to rain. The only thing I could orient myself to was the sound of the river. It was so dark I couldn't even see my feet! The wind picked up. It was getting colder.

"I'd lose the road and find myself up to my knees in grass. I'd have to get down on my hands and knees to retrace my steps. The only way I could tell if I was on the road was the tactile sensation of bare ground and rocks versus grass or whatever else. So I began to crawl. Literally feeling my way along. And soon thereafter I was soaked.

"I was losing it mentally. Going into a state of extreme exhaustion. I just didn't know what I was going to do. I knew I didn't want to travel in the daytime. Yet it seemed clear I couldn't travel at night. I also knew I didn't have it in me physically to go much further. I'd only come maybe two miles, and it must have taken me four hours."

Ted spent the night in misery under a large fir tree. He built a small fire, but it only kept his hands warm. With first light, he took stock of his situation and decided that survival—to say nothing of the success of his escape—depended upon finding shelter fast. His first thought was of the cabin he'd seen along the river the night before.

He found his way back. The cabin was unoccupied, but every

window save one was fitted with three-quarter-inch plywood, bolted on the inside to the window frames, and the one window that wasn't backed with plywood was covered with a heavy wire mesh screen. Days later a caretaker would guess that it took "superhuman strength" to wrench the wire away with bare fingers.

*The Tacoma News Tribune*

## HOUSE-TO-HOUSE CHECK

### SEARCHERS COMB ASPEN FOR BUNDY

ASPEN, Colo.—The search for former Tacoman Theodore Bundy has become a community-wide effort in this Rocky Mountain resort town.

Today, some 100 searchers were combing the area, going from house to house and climbing mountain trails.

Roadblocks remained up around the town, and schools were closed for the day.

About 20 citizens met with law enforcement officials behind the Pitkin County courthouse to organize into teams to comb the green-dotted hills and check vacation homes.

"First, let me say, that unless you are licensed to carry a gun, we want you unarmed," Capt. Dick Wall of the Pitkin County Sheriff's Reserves told the men and women on the lawn.

Said David Harris of Pine Ridge, S.D., a tourist who had volunteered for the search, "I ain't afraid of him—I can take care of myself.

"My friends were scared spitless last night," Harris went on. "They didn't go to sleep until four o'clock. Every time a dog would howl, they'd jump."

Firearms sales were halted in the city. The two main access roads were blocked by police within ten minutes of Bundy's escape.

Although the roadblocks did not turn up Bundy, they did bear fruit—or perhaps grass. A 500-pound haul of marijuana was confiscated by sheriff's deputies.

Ted, meanwhile, was safe in his temporary refuge.

"I cannot describe to you the comfort, serenity, and relief I felt when I walked inside that cabin," he recalls. "I immediately shed all of my clothes.

"It was one of those homey old bona fide log cabins. As I went through the double doors, to the left was a wall full of books. All kinds of neat books by Thoreau and on the flora and fauna of Colorado. Lots of *Sunset* magazines, books on music. No goddamn maps, though."

Ted was too tired even to look for something to eat. He headed straight for the master bedroom, threw off the plastic sheet covering one of the beds, and promptly fell asleep. Around four in the afternoon he awoke famished. "So I headed to the kitchen. I found some stale saltines, a couple boxes of brown sugar, some tins of Polish bacon, stewed tomatoes, ravioli, such things. The larder was *not* well stocked."

Then he recalled the broken window and worried that somebody might see it. On a scrap of paper he wrote, "Tom—Sorry I broke the window while I was putting in the plywood—Amos," and attached it to the plywood pane. It was Wednesday afternoon. A few hours later, Bundy fell asleep again.

*The Seattle Post-Intelligencer*

## BUNDY BECOMES PART OF FOLKLORE

ASPEN, Colo.—Ted Bundy's dramatic escape Tuesday from an antique courthouse here has made him part of the folklore of this summer and winter Rocky Mountain playground.

T-shirts are sprouting out around town with inscriptions about the convicted kidnapper and accused murderer.

One says: "Bundy is in Booth 'D'."

It alludes to a national magazine article that said if you sit in Booth "D" in a certain Aspen disco, you will be served cocaine, the "drug of the elite."

One of Aspen's campy eateries has a "Bundy Burger," open it and discover the meat has fled.

A bar is serving a "Bundy Cocktail"—tequila, rum and two Mexican jumping beans

Revelers at counter-culture meccas or disco-hopping the streets at night yell out slogans such as "Bundy Lives—On a Rocky Mountain High."

Another slogan:

"Bundy's Free—You can bet your Aspen on it."

Hitchhikers have been seen in the area wearing signs: "I'm not Bundy."

The next morning, Thursday, Ted found a long flashlight and a supply of batteries, some Band-Aids, gauze, and wool blankets. These, together with the food, some books, two large garbage bags, and some other items, he stuffed into a plastic-mesh shopping bag he had fashioned into a backpack. For most of the rest of the day he browsed through magazines and monitored the weather. By midafternoon the sun began to shine, and Ted decided he'd strike out again around midnight.

"I went to bed as soon as darkness fell Thursday night. By this time I'd found this .22 Remington automatic. I debated over that rifle for hours. I knew that if they found the cabin and the rifle missing it would make them more nervous. I knew I didn't want the rifle for a shoot-out. But I didn't know if I'd want it for small game or self-protection. I didn't know anything about wild animals or any of that kind of shit."

Bundy at last decided to take the rifle with him. He got up from his nap, looped an Indian belt he'd found around the shopping bag, and glanced at the Timex his mother had given him for Christmas while he was in maximum security at the Utah prison. It read 12:01.

"I was really feeling chipper. I'd had a lot of rest and was fairly well nourished. I also had the flashlight this time. Put some tinfoil over the lens and left just a little slit so I could see the rocks in the roadway. It may have been cold, but I didn't notice it. I had taken this warm coat and gloves from the cabin.

"I headed back down the same roadway I'd taken Tuesday evening and then back early Wednesday morning. I walked along with no problem for four or five miles. Stopped and ate some saltines and drank from the river. I felt like it had it together now."

### *The Seattle Post-Intelligencer*

### FBI ENTERS BUNDY SEARCH

ASPEN, Colo.—The three-day-old manhunt for escaped murder suspect Ted Bundy went nationwide yesterday as the Federal Bureau of Investigation entered the search.

A scaled-down search for Bundy in and around Aspen continued fruitless yesterday. The number of searchers dropped from 150 to about 70.

The searchers' quarry had hiked maybe seven miles south from the cabin when gathering daylight forced him off the trail and up to the cover of the forest. Below him, Ted could see the smoke from campfires on the valley floor, and far in the distance he could make out the form of a lone hiker heading south on the main trail. Had he taken the same route, he would have been to Crested Butte in a matter of hours. But from Ted's vantage point, it seemed impossible for the trail to lead to anything but a dead end at the foot of the mountains ahead.

The only way around them, he reckoned, was to climb higher up the valley side and then pick his way southward along game trails he'd noticed earlier that morning. "My theory was to follow these elk paths, because, for some unknown reason, I figured they'd go up and over and on down to Crested Butte. I reasoned that they wouldn't just go over to this other valley, which was right next door. I don't know. I don't know a thing about goddamn elk. I mean, I was tryin' to *think* like an *elk.*"

About all that could be said for Bundy's plan was that it would allow him to travel by day. At around noon he struck out again.

He negotiated a zigzag traverse of the steep valley slope. Afraid of heights since his boyhood, he grew ever more frightened the farther up he went.

It was nearly five o'clock Friday afternoon when he began his final, painful push to the top. If nightfall had found him exposed to the weather at that altitude, he faced a threat to his well-being that was far more immediate than recapture by the police.

Sheer will and the fugitive's desperation drove Ted to the top, at last. Yet agony's reward was to be the taste of ashes. There, in the distance, rose the Maroon Bells, a formation of reddish stone monoliths that even the most casual visitor to Aspen would recognize. Ted's midday detour had taken him in almost exactly the opposite direction from Crested Butte.

"I didn't cry, but I knew I'd made a serious, *serious* error. This was no joke.

"But mistake or not, I knew I had to get down about a thousand feet to the tree line. I almost skied down. My legs took a great deal of punishment. I got to the bottom with very little daylight left."

*The Tacoma News Tribune*

BUNDY MAY HAVE JOINED THRONG "ESCAPING"
IN ASPEN

ASPEN, Colo.—People come here to escape.

It is not hard to get lost in Aspen, even on Main St., right outside the Pitkin County courthouse, as Bundy apparently did.

His only handicap would be lack of money. Lucy Moreno of the Garfield County Jail said yesterday that Bundy had no cash.

If Bundy is outside, he will also have to deal with the weather and the rough terrain.

From the air, it is easy to see that a man could hide himself in this rugged country—but also that it might be hard to survive for long.

"At first light I packed up my gear and began moving down. There was no water in this area. No streams. No springs, no nothing. There was a river floor, maybe a thousand feet below me. This was Saturday morning and I really hadn't slept since Wednesday night. I knew I'd fucked up. Blown my wad."

Bundy's scheme, a desperate one, was to make his way back north to the cabin. His left knee began to trouble him; it, and the lack of forest cover, forced him to stop in a glade south of Aspen, where he waited for nightfall. Ted was ravenous and on the edge of delirium.

He discarded the rifle and with darkness began to move again. Hobbling, sometimes dragging his useless left leg, he picked his way along a circuitous route back through the town to an old stone church he knew stood at the intersection of a road that would lead him to the cabin.

"Now it's a race against time. It's about four in the morning, and I knew that first light would be around five-thirty. I had five miles to cover, and I could *barely* walk. Still carrying this pack full of all this nonsense.

"No more detours. I just had to go for it. Right up the road, you know. I walked and walked and walked, looking over my shoulder for cars, expecting one to appear at any moment. I didn't know if I was going to run into a roadblock or people just lyin' around waiting, looking out their front windows for Ted Bundy to pass by. I was in such a mental state that I actually began to hallucinate, seeing things like cars parked off in the distance. I was pushing myself to the *absolute* limit.

"Then I could see the cabin, about a quarter of a mile in the distance. Rather than approaching it directly, I went off into this thick foliage on the right side of the road and set down my pack.

Then I slowly approached the cabin, very, very cautiously. Stealthily. Of course, the thought had crossed my mind that someone may have discovered it had been broken into. Still, I just felt, 'Gee! Finally I made it!'

"I crouched and crawled toward the back side of the cabin, just along the ridge of the embankment looking down into the creek. There's a lot of loose, dry soil there, and I'd left a lot of footprints. I figured it would be the first place to look to see if anyone else had been there."

What Ted found were hundreds of boot prints, only a few of them his. First, the Maroon Bells, now this. "It would be hard for me to describe the sheer and utter panic I felt when I saw those prints."

A caretaker had discovered Ted's break-in the previous morning. Fingerprints had confirmed that Bundy was the burglar. Now, Sunday, the plan was to put dogs on his trail with first light. Not a half-hour after Ted had returned from his night-long hike and found the footprints, the first helicopter carrying tracking hounds descended. The fugitive was lying no more than 200 yards away.

"I couldn't figure out what was happening," Ted remembers. "I didn't know if I'd been spotted. I was tired and confused, so I decided to just sit there and wait and see.

"Just about then, I heard these twigs snapping in the brush on the mountain just below me. Ever so slowly and lightly. I just *froze*. I'd been reaching the point of not caring anymore, but then the old juices started flowing again. I knew I didn't want to be recaptured.

"I tried to figure out how I'd beat a retreat, because the sounds were coming from several different directions and they were advancing up the hill, towards me. Stealthily as I could, I sneaked up the hill and down a ravine. I heard some more snaps off to my right. I looked. And there were a half-dozen mule deer. Then I saw some more. They were all grazing up the hill toward me."

The double shock of the helicopter and the encounter with the deer acted upon Ted like a jolt of amphetamines. In an instant the left leg felt fine. He could even run and climb on it. His weariness evaporated. His mind cleared.

"I came up with a plan. I figured that they knew I'd been at the cabin and that they'd track me south, up the valley. They wouldn't think I was dumb enough to take the route I'd actually taken, so I thought I had 'em bamboozled. Maybe they'd taken down the roadblocks and I could find an easy way out of Aspen.

"I started traversing back down the valley, toward Aspen. I finally reached the point where I'd crossed into the valley on the first day. I found an old roadway almost obscured by grass and followed it north to a point maybe two miles below the cabin. This is broad daylight, getting pretty close to noon. I was flirting with danger, and the thought occurred to me that I was getting a bit too brazen. Just then, I looked down the road and a very tall man with a huge red beard and long red hair rounded the corner. He immediately stopped and pulled from a huge holster an *enormous* pistol. It was a .44. He pointed it right at me and said, 'Hey you! Get down here!'

"I said, 'Oh, hey! Hi!'' Waved my stick at him. 'How ya doin'? What's goin' on?'

"He says, 'Get down here!' He's pointin' this full-fledged .44 at me. He says, 'We're lookin' for Bundy.'

"I say, 'You're lookin' for who?'

"He says, 'Bundy. This guy's escaped and it's dangerous for you to be up here.'

"I say, 'For God's sake! I didn't know that.'

"He says, 'Now, who are you again?'

"I'd given him a name and this whole business about being a dentist. He's still not convinced. And he's pointing this gun at me.

"I said, 'I've got a wife and kids. Please don't point that gun at me.'

"He says, 'Oh, okay. But you shouldn't be on my land. We're lookin' for this guy and he's dangerous and you shouldn't be up here. I'm tellin' ya to get your tail off my property and back down the road the way you came.'

"So I started slowly down the road. Stopping every once in a while and picking a flower. Out of the corner of my eye, I could see him walk on, then turn around and begin to walk toward me, behind me, maybe three hundred yards back. Well, I didn't pick up my pace. I'd walk maybe ten yards off the road and pick a couple more flowers. By this time, I had a genuine bouquet. I didn't want to appear to be in any hurry."

The encounter with the bearded rancher had given Ted confidence. For the rest of the afternoon he half sauntered on down toward Aspen, thinking that maybe no one would recognize him, because Aspen seemed the last place they'd expect to find him. By nightfall, he'd made it to a main road at the city limits.

"When there was a break in the traffic, I dashed across the

road and onto this golf course. Then, without warning, my leg went boink! It just went on me. So I'm playing Chester from *Gunsmoke* on the golf course. My plan had been to reach the railhead of an old railroad track that ended somewhere near the outskirts of Aspen. I didn't know exactly where, but I knew it went all the way down the valley to Glenwood Springs. I thought I'd just stick along this track and walk my way out.

"By now, my leg was gone and I knew I was going to have a hell of a time. I was totally disoriented. I started to hallucinate again. Then, almost without warning, I got to the end of the golf course and tumbled down into a ravine. I don't know how long I lay there, probably about three hours. For the longest time I didn't know where I was. I couldn't get up. I couldn't make myself get up. I really had lost it there."

Around eleven that night Ted pulled himself out of the ravine and stumbled out in search of a bicycle. In his pain and delirium, he had hoped that his left leg could hold up to pedaling. It didn't.

"There were a couple bicycles on the porch of this house. I picked one up and just started motorin' along. There were cars passing me. I've got this growth of beard, wearin' funny-lookin' clothes. And I'm pedaling around midnight on this bicycle that is obviously too small for me.

"My leg couldn't take it. So I pulled up at the bottom of this long descent. I'd gone about a mile and a half. And I said, 'Fuck it. I'm going to get a car. This bicycle thing isn't going to make it. It's too cold.'

"I ditched the bike and started looking for cars. My first choice was going to be a Volkswagen. I tried three cars and then came to a house with three vehicles in front of it. One was a 1966 Cadillac and, lo and behold, there were keys in it. I said, 'Lord almighty! Here we are!'

"I hopped in and cranked it up. It was beautiful. Turned on the stereo and backed out. Then I thought, which way shall I go? The roadblocks might still be up down valley. Why don't I try heading up to the pass?

"So I drove out to the main road, crossed a bridge or two, and went right into Aspen. I drove right down Main Street. Stopped at the stoplight almost in front of the courthouse I'd jumped out of six days before. I continued on a couple more miles when I saw a blinking amber light ahead. I wasn't thinking really clearly, but it flashed on me that this might be a roadblock."

As Ted would soon learn, there was no roadblock on the pass.

Had he continued on, he could have made it to the top, where the road was partially blocked by a landslide. Bundy could have abandoned the Cadillac there and, if his leg held, made his way out of the area to freedom.

But he was now about to call attention to himself in a manner similar to his arrest by Sergeant Hayward in Granger. The hour was even about the same.

Bundy turned his stolen car around and drove back toward Aspen. At the same moment, two deputies were racing in the opposite direction to the scene of a reported rape. Ahead of them, they saw the Cadillac, its headlights dimmed, weaving back and forth in the oncoming lane. It was an invitation to investigate.

"The moment they passed me they switched on their lights and made a quick U-turn," Ted says. "They zoomed right up in back of me."

Bundy would never concede that he probably engineered his own recapture. Instead, at this point in his story he turned to a mocking depiction of his captors. Ted Bundy, raconteur, recalls the scene as a highly comic one.

"I pulled the old Cadillac over. I'm composed enough to say, 'Okay, it's time to be Joe Cool again.' And up walks my good friend from the jail, Gene Flatt.

"He walks up and says, 'You all right, mister?' He looked right at me.

"Now I'm wearin' a pair of glasses I'd found in the car and this old seaman's hat and the coat. I'm lookin' pretty scruffy. I say, 'Yeah, I'm all right.'

"He says, 'Well, I thought you were having a little bit of trouble driving here. Can I see your identification, please?'

"I say, 'Okay, just a second. I'll look for it.' All I'm doing is buying time, now, on the outside chance he'll let me go.

"So I'm fishin' around in the glove compartment and Gene gets jumpy. He says, 'Out! Now!' And he's got his *fuckin'* gun out. He's pointing it at me. 'Out of the car *now!*'

"The female deputy with him was Maureen Higgins. A redhead. Good-looking girl and a nice person. she says, 'Just wait a minute, Gene. He's looking for his I.D.'

" 'Out!'

"So I say, 'Okay,' and I get out of the car. He's looking at me. Shining his flashlight in my eyes. Trying to determine if I'm drunk or not. Then Gene starts to get suspicious. He's still got his Colt Python out and he's wiggling it at me. I'm too tired to care anymore. But I thought, Aw shit. What a way to go.

"He calls to Maureen. 'Come over here. Who does this look like?'

"She says, 'I don't know, Gene. Who does it look like?'

"He says, 'Maureen, this looks like Ted Bundy.'

"Now this is Gene Flatt, who for seventy days as a Pitkin County deputy served me my breakfast every morning. Constantly there. Took me to court on a dozen different occasions. So much for eyewitness identifications.

"Now I'm not sayin' a word. I've dummied up. Then he says, 'Okay, take off your glasses.'

"Took off my glasses. He shines the light in my eyes. He says, 'Maureen, I don't know. But he *still* looks like Ted Bundy.'

"She says, 'Well, why don't you call Sergeant Davis and ask him to come up here? He knows what he looks like.' "

Sergeant Davis, the imposing, physically powerful jailer who had intimidated Bundy since he first arrived in Aspen, drove out to the scene of the arrest and quickly announced that it was indeed Ted Bundy they'd arrested.

According to Ted, the roadside scene took on the air of a block party as more and more officers arrived. Passersby would shout, "Hey, what's goin' on?" and the cops would answer back, "We think we've got Bundy." They searched him and found half a pound of sugar, half a dozen vitamin pills still wrapped in his tinfoil, his $5, and the photo of Liz and Joanie. Not until he was back in the Pitkin County jail did Ted finally admit his identity.

It was 2:00 A.M. Monday, June 13, when Ted was hauled back to jail. He had covered almost fifty miles on foot during his 133 hours as a fugitive. And he'd lost thirty pounds.

*The Tacoma News Tribune*

BUNDY'S "RUN" MOTIVE MULLED

ASPEN, Colo.—The most discussed—and so far unanswered—question surrounding the escape of Ted Bundy was: "Why did he do it?"

Last Wednesday, the day after Bundy leaped from the second-floor window of the Pitkin County courthouse, most observers were dumbfounded.

Not only would escape add psychological credence to the

charges against him, but it also would result in sure prison time for him, regardless of the outcome of the other cases.

So, why?

Sgt. Don Davis of the county sheriff's department asked Bundy that question when he interrogated the 30-year-old former Tacoman after his capture at 2 A.M. yesterday.

Davis, 6-foot-4 and 225 pounds, smiled when he related what Bundy had told him.

"He said it was just too nice a day to stay inside," Davis said.

Back in custody that night, Ted was only too happy to tell Davis of his adventures in the wild and to wolf down the sandwiches and coffee the sergeant offered him. He would not, however, talk to Mike Fisher, who came down to the jail the moment he heard of Bundy's recapture. Toward dawn, Ted was returned to a basement lockup, where he rummaged through the garbage in search of more food. Then he stretched out on a bunk and began plotting his next escape.

At first glance, the pending case against Ted looked strong. But Mike Fisher's case was disintegrating. That spring, the prosecution lost its one witness who could place Bundy at the Wildwood Inn; in court she identified not Ted but a deputy sheriff as the man most resembling the person she'd encountered the night of Caryn Campbell's disappearance.

Fisher and Milt Blakey, the state attorney in charge of the prosecution, had hoped to bolster their case by introducing evidence gathered in Utah. Under the legal doctrine of "similar transactions," they endeavored to show "a common plan, scheme, or design."

Judge Lohr, however, consistently ruled against the admissibility of evidence from the Smith and Aime cases. Without them and the DaRonch conviction, prosecutor Blakey had only the marked ski brochure, the gas slips placing Ted in Colorado on January 12, 1975, the fact that he used two sets of license plates, and the discovery in Ted's VW of a head hair microscopically indistinguishable from that of Caryn Campbell.

"The judge," Mike Fisher later told Hugh, "dealt us just some terrible blows! At best we had an even shot."

A more rational defendant might have seen that he stood a good chance of acquittal, and that beating the murder charge in

Colorado would have dissuaded other prosecutors. In fact, with as little as a year and a half to serve in the DaRonch case, had Ted persevered he would have been a free man.

But Bundy had had a taste of freedom, during which—as he later indicated to police in Florida—he'd felt none of his violent compulsions. "Ted"—the tortured, driven murderer—seemed to have vanished after fifteen months behind bars. And with him, as far as Bundy was concerned, had gone the reality of his acts.

Bundy had reinvented himself. The new man bore no connection to the legal machinery "Ted's" crimes had set in motion. So entirely had Bundy dissociated that the prospects of acquittal and parole had no meaning for him. The new Ted would arrange for freedom on his own terms.

Bundy spent six months plotting his next escape. Unconcerned with the course or outcome of the legal proceedings, he nevertheless used his status as his own attorney to wheedle several special dispensations from Judge Lohr.

Ted was given a telephone credit card, with which he ran up huge monthly bills; most of the calls were placed to friends and reporters. He filed motion after motion with the court, covering everything from the appointment of a defense investigator to requests for office supplies. He even took on an active role in the courtroom, going so far in November as to personally cross-examine Carol DaRonch at a hearing to determine if she'd be allowed to testify against him.

When Bundy learned that Liz Kendall was now contemplating marriage to another man, he immediately set about to replace her. In late June of 1977, he began cultivating Carole Boone.

He wrote her long letters, poking fun at the uproar that his escape caused and asking for health food shipments because, as he wrote in June, "they are really starving me down here."

At the time, Ted was making similar requests of all his friends. He typed up tables, listing the kinds of health foods he would ask each to send, and sometimes specifying individual brand names within generic health food categories.

Carole was pleased to help out, and she began to send him what he called his "Care packages" on a routine basis. He began calling her, too. The more in need of a friend Ted seemed, the more of a friend Carole seemed willing to become.

Over the months, his letters to Carole grew more effusive. He rhapsodized over the health food treats she sent or mentioned the fine progress he was making on all legal fronts. "Dear Carole" became "Beloved Boone" by July, "Oh My Boone" in August, and "Tender Apparition of Loveliness" in September.

In early December 1977 she came to visit Ted at the Glenwood Springs jail. Carole had never been in a jail before, and she found the place as dispiriting as anyone does the first time a cold steel door clangs shut behind them.

She remembers passing through three such doors on her way in to see Ted for the first time since her trip to Salt Lake City in May of 1975. She knew that her uneasiness showed plainly, and she hoped that Ted wouldn't mistake it for anything more than what it was—just jitters. From his letters, she expected to find him looking drawn and undernourished; food had become a constant preoccupation of his, and the jail diet, as he described it, sounded ghastly, inhumane. When she saw him, he actually looked far fitter than she had imagined, although the wear and strain of his life was etched into his face. "I was shocked," she told me, "to see him in a cell, to see that loss of movement, of freedom. It is hard to describe except that in some strange way he was as far away, as far removed, as a person can be. Exiled in the midst."

At first, the jail authorities would only allow them to speak through the small wire-mesh window in Ted's cell door. "Ted," Carole remembers, "had a lot of trouble meeting my eyes at first. He was really happy to see me and I was really happy to see him. But he was very edgy."

Inside the cell, Carole could see Ted's two-tier bunk, his files and books and typewriter, and on the gray-painted floor there was a worn pink spot where Ted pivoted when he paced. Carole also noted a hole in his cell ceiling, but she didn't say anything about it.

The two friends were later allowed to spend several long hours together; Carole remembers the sheriff saying it was a crime that no one ever came to see Ted and how the case against Bundy was ridiculous. According to her, Ted was the best-liked prisoner in the place. She was struck by his compassion for other inmates who were in far less trouble than he. That was the Ted she remembered from the summer at the Department of Emergency Services in Olympia.

Already, her belief in his total innocence was firm; it never would be shaken. She ached at seeing this once vital, warm, and intelligent young man locked away for crimes he could not have committed. "It wasn't so much the goodness of his character," she told me, "although I've always felt that Ted was a good person. One of the reasons that I feel so confident about my conclusions is that they're strictly mine. I've always broken this down case by case, and formed opinions on each one individually. Not on the basis of Ted's character or sweet nature or cute ways.''

By the time Carole reluctantly left the jail and returned to Seattle, a permanent bond surpassing friendship, tinged with motherly love and bordering on devotion, had been formed. Her later implacable advocacy would reach a single-minded intensity commonly associated with mid-Eastern extremists, perfervid revivalists, and the dark paranoia of conspiracy theorists everywhere. Such has been Ted's hold on her.

Following Ted's jump from the courtroom in June, security around him had been tightened. But alone in his cell, he had hit upon a new plan that took advantage of lax jail management.

The hole Carole had seen in his ceiling was a narrow aperture exposed when Ted sawed through the sloppy welds holding a metal plate over an old light fixture. He accomplished the cutting with hacksaw blades provided by a friend from the Pitkin County jail, who also, Ted says, anted up a $500 escape fund.

He had to shed several pounds of weight to squeeze through the small hole, through which he could clamber around in the crawl space above the jail. Repeatedly, a snitch had reported hearing Bundy moving around above the cell block at night, but nothing was done.

The months passed and a trial date was set. Ted was in no hurry to bolt, but his schedule was pushed ahead in December, ironically when he won yet another round in court. Two days before Christmas, Judge Lohr granted a defense motion for a change of venue; agreeing, in effect, with Ted's contention that massive pretrial publicity had tainted the pool of prospective jurors living in and around Aspen. To Ted's dismay, Lohr decided to move the trial more than 125 miles to Colorado Springs.

"You're sentencing me to death!" Bundy pled in court, pointing a finger at the judge. Ted argued that guilty verdicts and death penalties were as routine as the winter snow in conservative Colorado Springs, but his true worry was that such a distant venue would mean that he'd be moved from Glenwood Springs and his cell with the hole in its ceiling.

It was time to go.

On December 30, 1977, after the evening meal was served at

the Garfield County jail, Ted Bundy put on a pair of blue jeans, a turtleneck, a red quilted down vest, a billed University of Texas Longhorn football cap, and a pair of blue sneakers. It was a quiet Friday night in the jail. The trusties were watching television, and the head jailer had gone to a movie with his wife. Ted Bundy took a deep breath and then made an agile leap for the escape hole. In a second, he was up and gone.

# ELEVEN

THAT NIGHT, Ted felt he was escaping *toward* as well as away from something. After nearly two years behind bars, he believed himself free of the "entity." The delusion prevented Bundy from anticipating the abyss that awaited him outside the walls of his cell. His latent, inchoate fury would soon wax unchecked like a tumor and in its fullness demand a final blood prize, its tribute. But at that moment Ted had no presentiment of what he was about to do.

As he slipped up through the ceiling of his cell, he glanced below him to his cot, where he'd arranged books and clothes to resemble his sleeping form beneath a blanket. For several days before the escape, he had refused breakfast and stayed in bed, feigning sleep. The next morning, Saturday, December 31, 1977, it would appear that Bundy was asleep again. Not until noon would his escape be discovered.

In the dark crawl space, he noticed a shaft of light coming from the chief jailer's linen closet. It was only noticeable that night because the jailer and his wife had left the closet door open when they left to go to the movies.

Ted pondered this piece of luck for a moment, wondering if maybe this was a trap and there was a deputy with a shotgun waiting for him to climb down. If so—he shrugged—that would be that. He headed for the light and in a matter of seconds had slipped unnoticed out through the jailer's front door into the cold Colorado night.

Ted delights in recalling his first hours of freedom. Danger and adventure were everywhere, while within him an ineffable power made everything possible.

"It's an incomparable feeling," he told me. "And I've often said to myself, 'Why can't I feel like this all the time? Why are these incredibly elated feelings so few and far between? When I feel so personally in control of what's happening around me.' It sounds vague, obviously, but whatever it is, it's real!

"I felt that way that night. I had that feeling that everything was just going my way! The stars were right. How can I explain it? I mean, *nothing* went wrong."

It was 7:30 P.M. or so when Bundy walked out of the jail, and for nearly four hours he tramped the streets of Glenwood Springs looking for a car to steal. His foremost requirement was that the vehicle have keys in it; Ted had no idea how to hot-wire an ignition.

About an hour into his search, he found an old jalopy with keys, but it didn't have snow tires. He decided to look some more, then came back in discouragement only to find the car's owner had driven it away. "Like I said, it was one of those nights," Ted explained. "If I would have taken that one, it would have been reported right away."

Finally, he found a derelict MG with no heater, no second gear, and very little gas. "But I was goin' for it!"

He started the car up, drove it down a side street by the police station, over a bridge, and into a gas station where he filled the tank and headed for the freeway. It was snowing and the flakes were coming thicker with each minute.

"I got this thing into first gear, and then to third," he went on. "Vroom! Vroom! Vroom! Then I couldn't get it out of third! And there's this incline, right? Cars all over the place. Trucks and buses standing sideways. And people putting chains on.

"I just popped this thing and floored it. I'm zooming around, weaving around. Like it's a slalom course. There were state patrolmen all over the place, flares and everything! I didn't even slow down! I knew that if I stopped in this little fucker on that hill, I'd never get moving again."

The snowstorm had become a full blizzard before Bundy had traveled twenty-five miles in his stolen MG. By then, he could only get the transmission into first gear, from which it refused to budge. "Finally," he told me, "it just went phewwwwwwww. It wouldn't move."

The roadway was totally obscured by the snow, and the temperature was dropping. Ted began to wonder if his great escape would end ignominiously with him frozen in a snowdrift in the middle of nowhere. In fact, for several days following his escape, his family, friends, and many of the police guessed that that had been his fate. Or that, hoping to make it to Denver, he had sneaked aboard a freight car and died of exposure en route.

But this was still Ted's night. Along came a soldier in a Mazda who helped push the MG off to one side. Bundy told him that he had to get to Denver fast because his wife was about to have a baby. The GI was happy for the company on such a night; he would drive Ted there.

They followed a snowplow to Vail, arriving sometime after one in the morning. The mountain pass on the other side of Vail, however, was closed to all but those vehicles equipped with chains. Ted's new friend didn't have any.

This was a serious problem. He had to get out of Colorado before his empty bed was discovered; Bundy certainly didn't want to be snowbound in Vail with his picture on every TV set. He asked around a Holiday Inn for a ride over the pass, but no one was going to attempt it that night. Then, in yet another stroke of luck, a Trailways bus pulled in. Next stop: Denver.

"Sorry buddy," Ted told his soldier friend, "I gotta get movin'." Early that morning, the bus pulled into Denver and Ted, whose high had not subsided, treated three fellow passengers to a cab ride to the airport. With five minutes to spare, he made the 8:55 A.M. TWA flight to Chicago. He settled into his seat, tucked his Bell Telephone plastic carrying bag underneath him, ordered a scotch and soda, and leaned back to enjoy the flight.

The escape was another page-one Bundy story throughout the west, and it provoked a round of angry editorial comment from Seattle to Aspen. The *Deseret News* in Salt Lake City lambasted the "cavalier attitude" of Bundy's jailers, and called for an investigation. "A lot of people," opined the *Seattle Times,* "especially families with ties to victims of crimes for which Bundy was being investigated, are furious over what was plainly an astonishing boner. We'd say that they are fully entitled to their anger." Just as upset as the editorial writers was Mike Fisher, who had complained for months that the security in Glenwood Springs was poor.

Bundy had a seventeen-hour head start. An order was issued to set up roadblocks, but according to Fisher, none were ever established. Prosecutor Milt Blakey coodinated a blanket watch on all Colorado public transportation terminals. The police correctly surmised that Ted would head for Denver's Stapleton airport, but they were several hours late in establishing their surveillance.

It was several days before the police determined how Ted had managed to get away from Glenwood Springs. The abandoned MG was found with its windows rolled down, buried under a mountain of snow at the side of U.S. 70. The snowplow operator who bumped into it with his machine had angrily reported the find to local authorities.

When he learned where his car had been found, its young owner was amazed and oddly delighted; Bundy probably had stolen the poorest excuse for transportation in all of Glenwood Springs. "I can't believe it!" the excited owner told Fisher. "I wouldn't even drive that thing around town."

From Chicago, Ted had originally intended to head for Columbus, Ohio, and the sprawling campus of Ohio State University. He reasoned that he was most familiar with university settings and would have his best chance of appearing inconspicuous among students and professors. However, he didn't want to take a bus and there was no direct train service to Columbus from Chicago. So Ted boarded the Amtrack Twilight Limited for Detroit. He planned to get off in Ann Arbor, home of the University of Michigan.

Bundy arrived in frigid Ann Arbor just before midnight on Saturday, New Year's Eve. Colorado was one day and a whole world behind him now; he felt safe. He met a drunk reveler on the street and managed to coax from the woozy celebrant directions to the local YMCA. There, he paid $12 for his first night's lodging, gave the night clerk a phony name, and explained that he'd come to Ann Arbor to see his brother, who unfortunately appeared to be out for the night. Upstairs on the third floor, Ted could watch the massive snowstorm that had nearly trapped him in Vail now descend in the night upon lower Michigan. He sat quietly in his room enjoying the silent snowfall.

The next day, January 1, 1978, the story of his escape made the first editions of the Seattle papers. Louise Bundy once again was distraught, wondering if her son would be shot down by some trigger-happy deputy or, worse, was already dead. Similar fears were with Carole Boone, who was preparing to leave for a winter holiday in Jamaica. When the police contacted her, she told them everything she knew, which was next to nothing, and she resented the implication in their voices that she was somehow involved. Also in Seattle, Liz Kendall had been told of Ted's escape. She doubted that he'd head for home, but nevertheless she was afraid. If Ted was a killer, what would she do if he came to her? To ease her anxiety, a police car was assigned to cruise her street periodically, and Liz nailed up the windows in the basement.

In Ann Arbor, Bundy treated himself that Sunday to a long, long shower; it had been nearly two years since he'd experienced the small luxury of having both a hot and a cold water tap to control and he savored it. Walking back to his room, he chanced to hear the tail end of a news report on someone's transistor radio. The announcer was saying that kidnapper and suspected mass murderer Theodore Robert Bundy had escaped from a jail cell in Colorado. "It really floored me," Ted told me. "I wasn't worried, because it was clear from the report that they didn't know where the hell I was. But I was surprised that I'd be news in this part of Michigan." Actually, he shouldn't have been surprised. Caryn Campbell and Ray Gadowski had lived in the Detroit suburb of Farmington, just thirty-five miles from Ann Arbor.

Ted had grown a full beard and let his hair grow long as part of his escape plan. This shaggy appearance, he reasoned, would be the one described in the first police bulletins. On Sunday, he shaved the beard, but left on a mustache. On Tuesday of that week, he also had his hair cut short. He now bore scant resemblance to the Ted of the Friday before.

Bundy once told me how much he'd enjoyed and empathized with *King Rat,* James Clavell's saga of a Japanese prisoner of war camp in which the protagonist, King Rat, is an American Army sergeant who not only adjusts to the filth and degradation of prison camp life, but actually flourishes. With liberation, however, King Rat reverts into a loser, now vilified and scorned by his fellow inmates who'd paid him obeisance just days before.

In a rare moment of candor, Ted conceded that "I might be like that." He was referring to the period following his arrival in Ann Arbor. Inch by inch, the cosmic confidence began to erode. "I sort of reverted to type," Ted explained. "I felt overwhelmed by things. I felt out of control. I felt I couldn't manipulate the environment around me. I failed miserably."

The first unmistakable sign came on Monday, January 2, 1978, when he wandered into a college bar to watch his alma mater, the University of Washington, play the University of Michigan Wolverines in the Rose Bowl. Passing himself off as a medical student, Ted cheered lustily for the Washington Huskies, calling attention to himself in a Wolverine bar, and drank himself into a stupor by half time.

Bundy drank only beer and only for the hour or so it takes to play a half of college football. But the alcohol had a powerful effect. He spent the second half of the game retching in the men's room and barely stumbled out the door before the bartender could make good on a threat to call the police to have Ted removed from the men's room's single toilet.

"I scared myself," Ted told me.

With the episode in the bar came the recurrence of psychic deterioration. Bewilderment and then anger that he hadn't experienced for years began to build. Ted saw the threat as external to him; in his word, he could not "manipulate" a hostile environment. His thoughts at this point would not be on the inevitable consequence of a reawakened "entity," the gathering compulsion to kill, but more likely on the possibility that he wouldn't be able to keep his secret hidden. Fearful of exposure, he instinctively tried to run from it.

His official story has been that Ann Arbor was too cold and that the student housing market was too tight for him to stay much longer. He had already spent half of his $500. He sneaked out of the YMCA without settling his bill and walked over to the university library, where he perused college catalogs in search of a campus somewhere to the south. His plan, only partially worked out, was to make for the Gulf Coast, where he intended to look for work in boatyards. He couldn't find a suitable school on the water, so he chose one near the coast, Florida State University in Tallahassee.

He spent much of Tuesday, January 3, walking around Ann Arbor in the snow, looking as he had in Glenwood Springs for an untended car with keys in it. Ted couldn't find a thing. He ate a despondent dinner at a McDonald's, then slipped into the sanctuary of a Methodist church, where he slept through the night.

Wednesday morning by seven he was out searching for cars again. He looked all day through supermarket parking lots, car dealerships, repair shops. Not until around five that afternoon did he find his car, a gray sedan of Japanese manufacture. He spotted it parked in a darkened area by a repair shop. The keys were in the glove compartment. The car carried Arizona plates.

Even though he had a map, Ted got lost trying to get out of Ann Arbor that night. He was very tired and had to be especially careful not to speed lest a state patrolman stop him. With only two pauses to sleep in the stolen sedan, he made it straight south to Atlanta by Friday morning.

North of the city, Ted went into a sporting goods store and stole a blue sleeping bag. Then he spent two hours carefully wiping his fingerprints from the car's interior. Satisfied that he'd erased every trace of himself, he drove the car into a slum area and parked it with the keys left in the ignition. The auto has never been recovered.

This was to be Ted's last rational act as a fugitive determined to remain at large. Cunning—and luck—had brought him far from Colorado, and he had left no trail. But his psychopathology, which he seemed to experience as a series of plateaus, was now back upon him. He had lost control.

After abandoning the car, he made his way to Atlanta's Omni Center, where he took in a movie *(The Sting)* and then waited for a bus south to Tallahassee.

It was there in the Omni, an anonymous stranger, watching the crowds come and go, that Ted Bundy capitulated. "All of a sudden," he told me, "I just felt smaller and smaller and smaller. And more insecure, too. And more alone. Bit by bit by bit, I felt something drain out of me. I felt it slip away from me like in the old movies where you see the ghost lift out of the body lying on the ground.

"And by the time I got off the bus in Tallahassee, things just didn't seem right. From the time I first set foot on Tennessee Street, I kept saying to myself, 'I gotta leave here.' "

A series of winter storm systems was about to turn northern Florida cold, wet, and windy for the next several weeks; that day a heavy calm preceding them had settled over Tallahassee. It was warm and muggy. The early-morning sun hung in the sky like a rotting lemon.

The warmth was welcome to Ted after the chills of Colorado and Michigan, but there was a kind of fulsomeness to the thick air and the look of the city itself that depressed him further. He found the campus of Florida State University and was disappointed at its appearance. "It looked like a large old junior college surrounded by a vast slum," he recalled. Several times that first day Ted thought of getting on another bus, perhaps for Gainesville, farther south and east, where the University of Florida is located.

But that would cost $20 of the $160 he had left. Bundy reluctantly decided he'd better stay. Emotionally, he was incapable of going any further. The decision to stay and the subsequent sudden lack of care in his actions are consistent with an unconscious need to return to confinement as well as the purely destructive dictates of the illness, whose power now eclipsed Ted's ability to control it.

He stashed his stolen sleeping bag and extra clothing in a locker at the student bookstore, then bought a local paper and began searching for a place to stay. His funk deepened as he trudged around the periphery of the university looking at rooms that were beyond his means and wondering how dismal rabbit warrens could fetch such high prices. During the nearly two years he had spent behind bars, Ted had been immune to—and largely ignorant of—the effects of inflation.

Late on Saturday, January 7, he returned to a rooming house he'd checked out and rejected earlier in the day. The Oaks was a ramshackle affair situated on the edge of the campus, not far from the Chi Omega sorority house. When he first had come by, assistant manager Larry Wingfield, aged twenty-one, had told him that a room would cost $80 a month, paid in advance, together with a $100 security deposit. Bundy had told Wingfield that he'd be back later with the money, but when he returned he asked if he could put just $100 down and then make up the difference on the first of February. Wingfield agreed, and rented the room to the man he knew as Chris M. Hagen, late of Ann Arbor, Michigan. Bundy had made up the alias on the spot.

For the next five weeks, room twelve on the second floor of 409 College Avenue, Tallahassee, Florida, would be home for Ted Bundy, aka Chris Hagen. For his money, he got what he described to me as "this filthy, filthy room" furnished with a single bed, a chair, a Formica-topped table, and a rickety chest of drawers. The rooming house was a dark masonry structure and shaded by a huge oak tree. Hence its name, the Oaks. Ted thought the place was eerie.

According to their later statements to the police, Chris Hagen's fellow renters saw and heard little of him. Larry Wingfield remembered that Hagen borrowed his vacuum cleaner several times. Was there anything unusual about him? the police asked. "I don't know," Wingfield replied. "Maybe it was the look in his eyes, or whatever. But he did seem basically different. I couldn't really tell you anything further than that."

An Asian-American student lived across the hall. He recalled a couple of brief conversations with Hagen and that Chris had borrowed an exercise device. Anything else? No, he said, except that Hagen had once given him a cookie.

Tina Hopkins, nineteen, also lived on the second floor. "I just know that he was quiet, he was real quiet," she told the police.

One night—she couldn't remember which—"he just seemed real nervous. He turned his head away from us a lot. His way of talking was just real strange. It just seemed real eerie to me. It was real late, you know, like four in the morning."

One of the renters at the Oaks thought Ted was an accountant; most of them assumed he was a graduate student. Few remember ever hearing his last name, or much about his background. Some noticed that he drank a lot. They all agreed that he jogged a great deal, kept very late hours, and was very polite. Once in a while, he was seen in glasses.

Ted, or Chris, raised few suspicions among those who lived at the Oaks, and he might have stayed on there indefinitely in anonymity had he been able to control himself. That power had deserted him in Atlanta.

Bundy waited until Tuesday, January 10, to walk to the FSU student employment office, where he learned of a laborer's job at a consruction site two or three miles away. He walked to the site and talked to the foreman, who told Ted that the job was still open; all he needed was to produce some identification and he'd go to work.

That was the hitch. Ted didn't know what part of town to go to—or what sort of people to ask—for false or stolen papers. He had no street smarts. What he did was steal a student identification card from a countertop in the FSU registrar's office. The printed description of the card's owner, a Kenneth Misner, matched Bundy's fairly well, but it would be weeks before he could send away for and receive back a duplicate copy of Misner's birth certificate. Meantime, he would be a non-person for whom the slightest misstep—a jaywalking ticket, for instance, or any contact with the police—could mean recapture.

Ted was a rookie at this, and he was no longer thinking clearly. He took the calculated risk of stealing a bicycle for transportation. That was easy enough; he'd done it a number of times before in his life. But then he turned needlessly bold on Tuesday night when he broke into two parked cars. One was a 1971 Toyota from which he stole a new Panasonic TV, a Sony transistor radio, and a Smith-Corona typewriter. Another fugitive would have fenced the stolen goods. Ted kept them. His other target was a 1976 Mustang. From it he took a golf umbrella and a notebook.

Each theft increased his chances of being caught, but Bundy could not seem to help himself. When his money ran out, he began shoplifting in supermarkets. He'd walk into a store and fill his pack, also stolen, with jars of peanut butter, sardines, any small item easily palmed and tucked away.

Bundy knew that he should be off the streets by sundown, but he was driven to roam Tallahassee until very late. Sometimes, he'd make it home by dark, but after a few hours of TV—and several beers—he'd slip into dark clothes and head out prowling.

According to him, on Saturday, January 14, 1978, fifteen days after his escape from Colorado and four days after the FBI had entered the hunt for him, he stole some chicken and potato salad from the deli section of a supermarket, and then pedaled his new red bike over to a schoolyard, where he ate a solitary picnic. His knee, he told me was acting up again. He thought that he might have injured it permanently during his first escape attempt.

He claims that he can't recall his actions for the rest of Saturday and early Sunday, although Ted has said he's "pretty sure" he spent the night alone in his room.

Others recall the events of the bloody night much differently.

The Chi Omega sorority house, an architecturally nondescript split-level structure, stands next to FSU's main gate on West Jefferson Street. Up and down West Jefferson are several similar sorority and fraternity houses, interspersed with small shops and college night spots. Pedestrian and vehicular traffic is often heavy in front of the Chi O house, but an abundance of shade trees and azalea bushes in the neighborhood lends the sorority a peaceful, manorial look. There are many shadows.

Next door to Chi Omega stands Sherrod's, in 1978 a new disco bar popular with Tallahassee's large college population in general, and specifically favored for its convenience by the Chi O sisters.

Terri Murphy, a Chi O, worked as a waitress in Sherrod's. The night of the fourteenth, she later told a county sheriff's investigator, Terri served a drink to a lone male she described as wearing a dark-colored turtleneck and blue jeans, who acted "overly polite" in her estimation. She guessed that he was in his early thirties, somewhat old for the Sherrod's crowd, which was usually between the late teens and early twenties. According to the investigator's subsequent report, Murphy was shown a photographic lineup and "then stated that the man in photograph number five (Theodore Robert Bundy) looked like the man that she had seen."

At about ten-thirty, Connie Hastings, twenty, Mary Anne Picano, twenty, Anna Inglett, twenty, and two other girls arrived at Sherrod's. They left their car in the parking lot behind the Chi Omega house.

Connie Hastings later told Ted's jury in Miami that Sherrod's was "right crowded." As she recalled, she didn't drink anything that night; she was preoccupied from the start by the man she saw standing on the staircase, arms folded, "kinda scanning the dance floor." He was dressed in dark clothes, and appeared to Hastings to be wearing other garments beneath them.

"The reason I thought he was unusual," she went on, "was because he was scanning, scanning all the girls, just looking around. He caught my eye several times. It was a stare that kinda bothered me. I felt very uncomfortable with it."

In court, Connie Hastings identified Ted as the man she saw in Sherrod's that night. On cross-examination, Ted's attorney Margaret Good tried to mitigate the identification by inquiring if it wasn't usual for men to stare at girls in bars. Hastings agreed, but "it was like a cold stare. It was strange, no expression on his face. You know, a lot of times when you go out if a guy looks like he's interested in you he will smile at you, acknowledge you, not stare at you."

Good then sought to suggest that Hastings' recall had been tainted by the several Bundy photos she had seen in the *Tallahassee Democrat.* To the contrary, the girl replied, she didn't connect the pictures with the man she'd seen. "They looked like totally different people," she said.

It was the contemporary mug shot she was shown, photograph number five in the lineup, that she had identified. Particularly, she recognized "his eyes and that stare."

Her friend Mary Anne Picano, dark-haired and exceptionally pretty, also saw the man, whom she too later identified as having "the same expression and same eyes" as mug shot number five.

"The first impression," Picano told the court, "was a really strange impression. I looked at him and saw him looking at me and I turned around and tried to ignore him. A few minutes later, he came and asked me if I would like to dance."

Mary Anne remembered replying, "Well, not really," and tried to use the drink in her hand as an excuse not to dance. The man was not to be deterred; he said he'd put her drink with his and be right back. Dreading the experience, Mary Anne turned to her friend Anna Inglett. "I said, 'Anna, look at this guy I'm getting ready to dance with. He looks like an ex-con.'"

The prosecutor then asked her if she'd looked very hard at the man. "While I was dancing with him, barely," she replied. "I mean, when we first started dancing, he tried to make small talk. . . . And I just kept concentrating on not looking at him. I had a really scared feeling inside. I was looking over at Connie and I was looking at my feet. I was looking everywhere but at him. I was trying to avoid him. I just had a feeling inside.''

After a single dance, Connie collected her friends and all five hurriedly left together. They'd been at the disco no more than a half hour. Soon after they left, Carla Jean Black, a social worker recently graduated from SU, arrived at Sherrod's with her friend Valerie Stone. She encountered a "sort of strange-looking person" with an "unnerving stare" whom she also later identified as Ted Bundy. He had watched her for at least twenty minutes, Black testified, and even followed her to the ladies' room.

Outside of Sherrod's at about midnight, Tom Trice and a male friend were trying to decide if they wanted to ante up the disco's cover charge, or to go drink elsewhere on their limited funds.

As they debated, Trice noted a silent figure sitting alone on a bench in the subfreezing night. The stranger was wearing a dark knit cap, light-colored pants, and a Navy pea coat. Trice thought that he saw a mustache, too.

A group of girls emerged from Sherrod's; Trice and his friend made a clumsy joking pass at them. "Sort of a 'Wow!' '' he told an investigator. "We knew they weren't going to waste their time on us.''

As he and his friend flirted with the departing girls, Trice heard the man on the bench mumble something guttural and inaudible. "Other than that,'' Trice reported, "he actually was looking straight down. But he was looking kinda just spaced out. . . . The guy wasn't extremely friendly.''

A short while later, and in the same neighborhood, Cheryl Rafferty parked her car, locked it, and began to walk home to her dormitory. All of a sudden, a stranger stepped out of the bushes. "Ms. Rafferty,'' read the report prepared by an FSU security officer, "stated that the subject startled her by the rapid manner in which he approached her and that she initially had walked quickly away from him. When the subject quickened his pace to match hers she ran the remaining distance to Reynolds Hall. At that point, the subject began running and was last seen running down [a] bicycle path. Ms. Rafferty stated that the subject was approx. 5' 10", 160 lbs., medium build, and that he was wearing khaki colored pants, a dark solid-color knit cap and a dark blue Navy watch jacket ('P' coat). Ms. Rafferty is unable to say, positively, that Bundy is the same subject who chased her. She does, however, believe that the possibility exists.''

Sherrod's closed shortly after 2:00 A.M. Pi Kappa Alpha brothers Greg Lowder and Scott Corwin left the disco, drove around for fifteen to forty-five minutes, then parked their car and walked back to their fraternity house near the Chi Omega house.

On the way, they were approached by a man Lowder later described as being five feet nine inches tall, with a ''scraggly'' beard and brown mustache. He wore a dark knit cap, beige or khaki pants, and a navy-blue coat. The man asked for directions to the Holiday Inn.

When Lowder was shown the photographic lineup, he selected photograph number five, Theodore Robert Bundy.

Chi Omega roommates Karen Chandler and Kathy Kleiner were both in bed and ready for sleep in their second-floor room, number eight, by about midnight. Kathy had eaten dinner with her fiancé that night. Karen had driven home to fix dinner for her mother, who was down with the flu. Their conscious recollections of that night cease at around 12:30 A.M.

Across the hall in room number four lived Lisa Levy, a freshman from St. Petersburg majoring in fashion merchandising, and her roommate, Debra O'Brien.

Saturday afternoon, Lisa had left her job at a local clothing store and headed back for the sorority house, hoping that the cold weather would bring snow. It didn't.

About nine-thirty or maybe a little later, the fashion-conscious young co-ed put on her beige ensemble—cordinated blouse, skirt, and wool blazer—and then walked over to Sherrod's with her roommate, Debra, and another Chi O sister, Melanie Nelson.

Debra O'Brien last saw Lisa alive about an hour later when Debra and a male friend left Sherrod's. Melanie Nelson stayed at the disco until closing time. But Sherrod's bored Lisa. When no one in the house wanted to go try Big Daddy's or Byron's, two other popular college bars in the area, Lisa decided to call the night a fizzle. She was back in the sorority recreation room watching television in her jeans and a gray sweatshirt by 11:30 P.M. at the latest.

Before she went to bed, Lisa made plans to attend church the next day with one of her friends in the house, Helen Haynes. She hadn't yet told her family, but she had converted from Judaism to Christianity and now kept a Bible and a small necklace with a crucifix by her bedside. On her door, she had put up two inspirational posters. One read: "Faith is the substance of things hoped for, the evidence of things not seen." The other poster read: "No goal is too high if we climb with care and confidence."

Lisa Levy went to sleep for the last time in her life around 1:30 A.M.

Next door to Karen Chandler and Kathy Kleiner lived Margaret Bowman, who shared room number nine with Kim Weeks. Kim was away for the weekend.

The night of the fourteenth, Margaret had a date with Doug Johnson, a Phi Delta Theta brother from Houston, Texas. They went to a fraternity party. Margaret drove. As 2:00 A.M. approached Doug tried to coax his date into staying out a little later than was usual for her. She demurred, and dropped him off at his fraternity house before driving back to the Chi O house.

She was changing for bed when Melaine Nelson came home. Melanie had returned from Sherrod's with Leslie Waddell, another Chi O sister, and a young man. When the trio reached the sliding glass door that opened into the downstairs rec room, they found it ajar. In cold weather, the door's combination lock sometimes did not catch properly. Melanie made sure that it was secure before going upstairs.

Leslie Waddell and her friend were hungry, and she asked Margaret Bowman if she'd like to go out for a hamburger. No, she said, but she'd be happy to give Leslie the use of her car. Margaret then continued to undress, chatting the while with Melanie and recounting her evening with Doug, which she said had been fun.

As they spoke, Nancy Dowdy came home; she was in bed in room number three—across the hall from Karen Chandler and Kathy Kleiner and next door to Lisa Levy—by 2:30 A.M. At 2:40 A.M. Terri Murphy returned from her job at Sherrod's. Like Nancy Dowdy, she found the combination lock secure on the sliding glass door.

Five minutes later, Melanie Nelson said a final good night to Margaret Bowman and to Kim Wasniewski, from room number ten, who had risen to go to the bathroom. None of the women noticed anything unusual.

At 3:00 A.M., Carol Johnston came in the sliding glass door; this time it was open. Carol was also surprised to find the upstairs hall lights off. That was odd. Before retiring to room number two (across the hall from Margaret Bowman), Carol went to the bathroom, where, because of the hour, she didn't close the door. She later remembered hearing a doorknob click while she was in the bathroom. Carol's digital clock read 3:14 when she returned to her room and turned out the lights.

Had Nita Neary come home earlier—or much later—that night, the horror might have gone undiscovered until morning. But it wasn't until shortly after 3:00 A.M. that Nita, who was Nancy Dowdy's roommate in number three, kissed her date good night at the back door.

Nita noticed, in passing, that the door was unlocked. And just as she walked into the rec room, she heard a definite thump. She thought it might have been her date tripping outside. But when she peered out, he was gone.

Someone had left a number of lights on downstairs, so Nita walked through the rec room, the living room, and into the foyer turning them off. Then she heard running footsteps above her in the upstairs hallway. She guessed that the noise she made coming in and walking around had awakened one of her sisters.

Standing in the foyer about sixteen feet from the sorority's tall double front doors, she heard the footfalls coming down the carpeted staircase to her left. Then she saw the man; he was crouched low by the front doors. His left hand was on the door handle. In his right hand, which was nearer her, she could see what looked like a club, wrapped in some sort of dark material.

He was wearing a dark knit cap, pulled low, almost to his eyebrows. He had on light-colored pants and a dark coat that appeared to be cut about mid-thigh. She estimated that the club was three feet long.

Nita Neary only saw the man's profile. He appeared to be a white male, early twenties, about five feet eight, weighing maybe 150 pounds. She distinctly remembered his long straight nose in profile, and his thin lips. In an instant, he was out the door with his club and gone.

Nita's first move was to run upstairs to her room, number three, and to awaken Nancy Dowdy. She told Nancy what she had seen, and the two decided to go back downstairs to check the locks. Everything was secure. The house was utterly quiet.

It was possible, they knew, that one of the Chi O girls had sneaked a boy into her room. If so, they wouldn't want to make trouble. But what use was there for a three-foot club on a late-night tryst?

They decided to awaken the house president, Jacqueline McGill, who was asleep in room number one. Jackie McGill's roommate, Susan Denton, remained asleep while the president listened in the hallway to Nita Neary's story.

It took Nita only a couple of seconds to tell McGill what she had seen, and there was little time for discussion before the door to room eight opened and out staggered Karen Chandler, bent at the waist, and apparently headed for the bathroom. At first glance, she looked as if she might be drunk; but the three girls called to her, and when she turned they saw that her face was a bloody mess. She was gurgling incoherently through the blood.

Nita Neary, whose roommate of the previous year had been assaulted on campus by a man with a beard, exploded in panic and ran in the opposite direction from Chandler, whom Nancy Dowdy already was leading into her own room, number three. Neary's screams of "Get up! Get up!" awakened Carla Griffin and Susie Appleby in room eleven. Twenty minutes earlier, Susie Appleby had gone to the bathroom and heard nothing unusual. Now they saw Karen Chandler with Nancy Dowdy and ran for a washcloth.

Dowdy had already telephoned the police. Now Nita Neary woke up Mary Carol Verlander in number twelve and told her to call the authorities as well. By then, Jackie McGill had gone into number eight and found Karen Chandler's roommate, Kathy Kleiner, sitting cross-legged on her bed, blood pouring from her mouth, rocking back and forth and moaning. It sounded as if she were calling for her parents.

Carol Johnston, whose digital clock had read 3:14 when she went to bed, was awakened by the noise at 3:19 by her clock. She got up, saw McGill, Neary, and Dowdy in the hallway, went back to her room, number two, and shook Helen Haynes awake. "Karen and Kathy," Carol told Helen, "have been slightly mutilated."

Karen and Kathy's room was spattered and smeared with their blood; even the ceiling was dotted with red drops that had sprayed up from their attacker's thrashing club.

Chandler's jaw, right arm and one finger were broken. Her skull had been fractured, as had the orbit of her right eye and both her cheekbones. Terrible gashes and abrasions from the club covered her head and face.

Kleiner, too, had suffered a broken jaw as well as several deep cuts and contusions. As she sat in her bed in shock and terror, she could hear her sorority sisters sobbing, "Oh, my God! Help her! Help her!" Kathy couldn't make out much without her glasses, but she could see her own blood on the walls. After she was carried from the room and rushed to Tallahassee Memorial Hospital with Karen, several of Kathy Kleiner's teeth were found in her red-soaked bedclothes.

Both girls had been bludgeoned in their sleep and neither could offer a description of her attacker. Something told Karen Chandler that the man was young, but she couldn't say what it was or why she had that feeling. Later Kathy Kleiner, her jaw wired shut and her pain eased by tranquilizers and opiates, would recollect the sound of plants rustling in the room that night, as if they had been stirred by some rapid movement. That was all.

According to police logs, the first officers on the scene arrived at the Chi Omega house at 3:23 A.M. Nita Neary gave them the description of the man she saw in the doorway and a BOLO (for "Be on the Lookout") was instantly radioed to every cop in the vicinity.

Ambulances, squad cars, detectives' vehicles, and later a hearse all converged on the sorority house. Sirens, flashing lights, and crackling police radios created a tumult, while upstairs in the house the cops and emergency medical teams had to deal with nearly forty terrified co-eds who by now were milling around in their nightgowns, clinging to one another, screaming, crying, or huddling together in corners, staring quietly at the guns and uniforms.

Gently, Officer Henry Newkirk of the Tallahassee police department began to shepherd the girls into number two, Helen Haynes and Carol Johnston's room. Ray Crew, also from the Tallahassee police, undertook a room-by-room search accompanied by house mother Mary Crenshaw.

Crew opened the door to number four and found Lisa Levy lying on her stomach in bed, a sheet pulled up to her head. He called her name; Lisa didn't stir.

The policeman flipped on the light switch and noted the clothing strewn about the floor. He crossed the room and cautiously rolled the silent girl over onto her back. When he saw the twisted neck and the unseeing eyes, he shouted for the emergency medical technicians.

Emergency medic Don Allen left his partner, Amelia Roberts, in number eight with Chandler and Kleiner and dashed into number four, where he found Lisa Levy in complete cardiac arrest. Roberts then joined him. Lisa was placed on her back on the floor. First mouth-to-mouth resuscitation was tried, then an air tube was placed in her throat and oxygen pumped to her lifeless lungs. The emergency medical teams started two intravenous tubes in her arm and hooked up their cardiac monitor. It remained flat.

They could see the swelling around her jaw, and Amelia Roberts noticed what she at first took to be a puncture wound, as if from a bullet, at the nipple of Lisa's right breast. They rolled her over in search of an exit wound, but saw none.

She wasn't bleeding that the medics saw, but their examination did not extend below Lisa's chest. The vivid human bite mark on her left buttock and the extensive injuries to her rectum and vagina weren't discovered until the autopsy later that morning. It would be several days before an aerosol bottle covered with viscera, blood, and matted hair was retrieved from the floor of the room.

Lisa was DOA at Tallahassee Memorial.

For a grim instant, the police thought Melanie Nelson was dead, too. She had to be shouted awake in number fourteen. Melanie groggily stepped out into the hallway and toward number two, where Henry Newkirk was gathering the girls and beginning to question them. Where, she asked Newkirk, was Margaret Bowman? Someone should check room number nine.

From Newkirk's report:

> This writer entered room #9 and immediately closed the door behind me once I observed blood on a pillow. Ms Bowman was lying on the bed in the southwest corner of the room with her head and feet pointing in the south-north direction, respectively. The bedspread was covering Ms. Bowman's entire body with the exception of her head—which was tilted to the right lying on her pillow. (Her face was facing the west wall.) This writer pulled back the cover (bedspread) and observed Ms. Bowman had been strangled with a pair of nylon pantyhose. Her legs were bent outward slightly and spread open. (Note: Ms. Bowman was lying on her stomach.) Her right arm was extended down her side and her left arm was bent with her elbow facing east and her left hand resting on her back. Both palms of the hands were turned upwards. This writer turned Ms. Bowman over onto her right side to check for a heartbeat or pulse and discovered neither. This writer looked at Ms. Bowman's head and observed where Ms. Bowman had received a crushing blow to her right forehead coupled with what appeared to be two puncture wounds in the same vicinity. Massive bleeding occurred from both the forehead and right ear, with clotting occurring in the right ear. Additionally Ms. Bowman's neck appeared to be disjointed leading this writer to believe there was a possible neck fracture. Ms. Bowman's body was

relatively warm to the touch and her eyes were glassy with pupils dilated. . . . There was no evidence of a struggle either on the bed or in the room. The room was not ransacked and at this writing nothing was known to be missing.

Margaret Bowman was the last of the victims at the Chi O house that night. As her body was being taken to the walk-in refrigerator at the city morgue, the surviving sorority sisters were each interviewed and fingerprinted. Many of the girls then placed frantic calls to family and friends. For the next several days, those who could do so would be sleeping anywhere but upstairs at Chi Omega.

Karen Chandler and Kathy Kleiner underwent emergency surgery for their injuries. They would survive.

It would later be ascertained that of the four victims, only Lisa Levy had been sexually assaulted—although Margaret Bowman's underpants had been torn from her with such violence that a burn mark was visible on her thigh.

A piece of chewing gum was found in Lisa Levy's hair, and was preserved for tests. But the single most crucial bit of evidence from the autopsies was the double bite mark on Lisa's buttock. At the morgue, the mark was photographed next to a ruler for scale and then the section of tissue containing it was excised and placed in an aqueous solution.

Bundy refused us any substantive description of that night at Chi Omega—either in the first person or as part of his "speculations." He did once boast to Hugh that "I'm the only one that can do it. The only one." But absent what Bundy himself *could* offer and wouldn't, enough is known to piece together the following reconstruction: He started drinking heavily that first week in Tallahassee—his neighbors at the Oaks remember seeing Ted repeatedly drunk—thus further undermining his stability and dampening his inhibitions. Meanwhile, the newly liberated homicidal side of his nature was feeding upon Ted's insecurity and confusion. Two years of latency had only made the need to kill and possess that much stronger, less controllable, more demanding. It crested in a great wave of fury on Saturday night.

Ted probably left the Oaks that night in two or more sets of clothes. Annie Hastings had noticed it at Sherrod's. The police in Utah suspect that is how Ted had been able to appear so different to Carol DeRonch in Murray than he did to the women who saw him in Bountiful at the school play. Wearing multiple sets of clothes was a key to his first escape. We also know from Bundy that he planned on wearing two sets of clothes to his lineup in October of 1975.

On January 14, 1978, he appears also to have taken three sets of women's pantyhose with him. He had stolen them from their owner or owners, because each, when found, showed signs of wear and laundering. He neatly cut the right leg from one pair and looped the left leg back through to form a ligature. He left this pair around Margaret Bowman's neck. A second pair, altered identically, he dropped in Bowman's room. They were found in Margaret's roommate's bed. He used the third set as a mask.

He began hunting at Sherrod's, where it is possible that he first began to think of the Chi Omega house and its forty unprotected women. Ted might have met one or more of the many Chi O's who were at Sherrod's that night. Terri Murphy served him a drink. Lisa Levy was there, too.

Evidence that the Chi O house was, in fact, a last-minute target, comes from Cheryl Rafferty, whom he chased near Reynolds Hall two hours earlier. Drunk, agitated by all the girls he had seen at Sherrod's, frustrated by his failed approach to Rafferty, and now deprived of potential victims by the closing of Sherrod's, the late hour, and the bitter cold, Ted then thought of the Holiday Inn, where a bar or restaurant might still be open. He asked directions sometime between 2:30 A.M. and 3:00 A.M. from Greg Lowder and Scott Corwin, whom he approached on the street very near the Chi Omega house.

Dubious about the hunting at the Holiday Inn (and perhaps uneasy about being seen there by potential witnesses), Bundy may have looked up at the Chi Omega sorority house and been struck with a plan.

From oak bark found in the victims' three rooms and leading to them from the downstairs sliding door, his choice of weapon and point of entry seem clear. It is not so obvious why he decided to wrap the club in cloth, although he may have been thinking to muffle it.

He would know to use the back door by watching the returning Chi O sisters park their cars in the rear of the building and then walk over to it. There was a good deal of traffic in and out of the door between two and three that morning. Gripped as he was by an animal need, Ted probably did not enter the house and then wait for any length of time before heading upstairs. He may have come in just before Carol Johnston did at three, and had probably completed his first attack when she heard the doorknob click while in the bathroom.

That first victim was probably Lisa Levy, whose autopsy indicated that she was already dead, or dying, when Bundy bit her. Then he slipped across the hall and entered Karen Chandler and Kathy Kleiner's room. Blood type O, Lisa Levy's type, was found mixed with their type A blood on the walls and ceiling of the room. Margaret Bowman, then, would have been his last victim.

Maybe it was all the movement in and out of the two upstairs bathrooms that startled him, or it could have been Nita Neary stirring below, but Ted broke off his brief, furious slaughter and decided to flee.

He was not, however, done for the night.

At about 3:30 A.M. Yomi Segun was driving down Jefferson Street near the Chi Omega house when he saw a white male in light brown pants, a blue coat, and a dark knit cap walking rapidly along. The man had brown hair and a pointed nose. He was carrying something in his left hand and held the object close to his left leg. According to the police report:

> When asked what drew his attention to the man, Mr. Segun states that he appeared to be drunk, and it was suspicious that he was concealing the object by his left side. Mr. Segun states that he slowed down, and took a second look at the subject and got a good look at his face. Mr. Segun states that in his mind, he is positive that the subject is Theodore Bundy whose photographs he recognized in the newspapers. Mr. Segun also stated that he cannot be 100% sure, but sure enough that he is satisfied that they are one and the same.

At about four-fifteen that morning, Debbie Ciccarelli, twenty, was awakened by a staccato of thumps coming through the wall of her apartment on Dunwoody Street, less than three blocks from the Chi Omega sorority house. Debbie listened for a minute, then awakened her roommate, Nancy Young. Nancy's bed was positioned next to the thin wall separating their half of the house from that of Cheryl Thomas, twenty-one, a serious-minded and utterly devoted dance student from Virginia. Cheryl's bed abutted the other side of the wall.

It was possible, the girls thought, that Cheryl and a friend were spending the night together, although that was not Cheryl's habit. The roommates spoke for a bit, then listened again and heard nothing. Then they could make out the sound of footsteps next door.

They decided to call Debbie's boyfriend and to ask him what they should do. Debbie dialed him twice on their bedroom telephone, both times reaching the wrong number. She got out of bed, walked to the adjacent living room, where she consulted a directory, and then came back to bed to call her boyfriend again. This time she reached him. His advice: Check on Cheryl personally, or call her.

Debbie and Nancy were afraid, so they called. Through the wall, they could hear the telephone ring six times before they hung up. Then they heard moans and what they thought was the sound of someone moving Cheryl's kitchen table. Debbie and Nancy dialed 911.

Three minutes later, a contingent of Tallahassee police appeared. They found the front door to Cheryl's apartment was locked and secure. So was the rear entrance, although later in the back yard they'd find a set of keys that would open her back door. The keys suggested that the attack was not random.

At that moment, the presumed point of entry was a kitchen window with its screen removed. The police saw what they took to be telltale signs of the window having been forced. Inside, the kitchen table rested beside the window and a potted plant was later found broken beneath it.

The officers were about to force the window themselves when Ciccarelli and Young appeared at the front of the house with a key to Cheryl's door.

Once inside it, the police could see through the living room and into Cheryl's bedroom, where they found her bloodied and semi-conscious in her bed. No weapon was found, but near the bed was a pair of Sears Clingalon pantyhose fashioned into a mask with nickel-size eye holes cut into it.

Though Cheryl was not sexually assaulted, subsequent laboratory tests revealed a large semen stain on her blood-soaked bedspread. Thomas was described in the police reports as dimly conscious that night; she remembers nothing from the time she fell asleep until after her arrival at the hospital. But though she does not recollect the attack, she'll carry its reminders for the rest of her life.

As in the attacks on Margaret Bowman, Lisa Levy, Karen Chandler, and Kathy Kleiner, Cheryl Thomas' jaw was smashed by several blows from the killer's club. The jaw would eventually heal, but Cheryl is permanently deaf in one ear, and she has suffered a partial loss of balance. Dancing, which until the early morning of January 15, 1978, had been her life and her future, is no longer possible.

About four-thirty that morning, Sigma Chi brother Orley Sorrell was stopped and questioned on the street by a sheriff's deputy. He was told of the Chi O murders at that time. Sorrell, who was returning to the fraternity house from an early breakfast, continued home.

When he got to Sigma Chi, which is located one block from the Oaks, Sorrell stood on the front porch waiting for friends to pick him up for a day's hunting expedition. Standing there in the cold, he saw a figure dressed in light pants, "a Navy pullover thing," and what Sorrell called a dark "snow cap."

He didn't think the man saw him. Instead, the man dashed down the street and hid in some bushes as if he thought he was being followed. Then he jumped up and ran as far as the 400 block on College Avenue. The last Sorrell saw of the stranger was nearly in front of the Oaks. Sorrell later told the police that he couldn't swear to it in court, but he was "pretty sure" the man he saw was Ted Bundy.

At about this time, Oaks resident Henry Polumbo and his buddy Rusty Gage were returning to the rooming house together. Polumbo played in a band. After his performance that night at the Villanova Lounge, he had picked up Rusty and some beer and the two had gone to Rusty's house, where they drank and listened to music.

Polumbo told a grand jury that he and Gage were horsing around, clowning, that morning as they approached the Oaks. He remembered looking up as they reached the cement stairs in front and found Chris Hagen standing motionless at the bottom of the steps. Polumbo and Gage greeted Chris, but Hagen said nothing.

"He was in complete silence," Polumbo told the grand jurors who were considering an indictment against Ted. "He wasn't doing anything. He was just standing there."

# TWELVE

IT HAD BEEN nearly three and a half years since Dr. Daris Swindler, the forensic anthropologist from the University of Washington, had examined the remains of Denise Naslund, Janice Ott, and the nameless third victim found on the Issaquah hillside. Those murders had never been far from his mind, not with the indelible memory of cradling Jan Ott's peculiarly elongated skull in one hand while he compared it with the photograph of her that he held in his other.

On Sunday morning, January 15, 1978, Swindler awoke in Tallahassee, Florida. He and his wife, Cathy, were on their way to a Caribbean vacation and had stopped in the Florida capital to visit a favored ex-student, then teaching at FSU.

When they heard the gruesome news of the Chi Omega slaughter that morning, Cathy Swindler felt "this shudder of recognition." She remembered the horror of 1974 in Seattle. Their host also recalled the "Ted" killings and his former professor's involvement with the case. "What are you doing?" he asked jocularly. "Bringing more dead girls along with you from Seattle?"

Swindler laughed uneasily.

The next day, a combined wire service story headlined "2 Co-eds Slain, 3 Beaten by Florida Night Stalker" ran in the *Seattle Times*. Paul Henderson, a *Times* reporter who had covered the early days of the "Ted" story, clipped the article and handed it to fellow reporter Richard Larsen, who had also covered the story and who knew Bundy personally. Attached was a typewritten note: "Dick: Shades of Lynda Healy (basement abduction where the roommates did not awake), Georgann Hawkins (which took a lot of balls), and the Sammamish victims (where one was not enough). This guy appears to be in Bundy's class . . . a sorority row rapist. Do you think Ted could find happiness in Florida?"

Across town, county police detective Bob Keppell, still in charge of the "Ted" investigations and still no closer to indicting the now-fugitive Ted Bundy, read the news account and experienced his own shudder of recognition. Keppell called Tallahassee and gave the local police Ted's name, description, and a brief history of his background. Keppell thought it distinctly possible that Bundy would try to find happiness in Florida.

Mike Fisher heard about the killings in Washington, D.C., where he was attending a thirteen-week FBI course in criminology. Fisher consulted with prosecutor Milt Blakey in Colorado, who then forwarded to Florida a package of materials on Ted, including what was known or supposed about Bundy's modus operandi.

Despite the brutality of the attacks and the death toll, most of America was at first only dimly aware of what had happened early Sunday morning in northern Florida. Sunday's news was dominated by Super Bowl XII in New Orleans, won 27–10 by Dallas over Denver. Elsewhere across the country, the Reverend Martin Luther King's birthday was observed and millions of people mourned the recent passing of Hubert Humphrey, who lay in state under the Capitol rotunda in Washington, D.C.

On Monday, *The New York Times* ran a brief story on an inside page headlined "2 Killed, 2 Beaten in Florida Sorority House." The *Washington Post* printed its story of the murder on page A-3 as part of a national news roundup.

Yet in Tallahassee, the murders had the impact of an earthquake or hurricane. Ammunition sales and locksmiths' business spurted as boyfriends, husbands, fathers, and brothers loaded their weapons and warned their women to stay indoors. In churches throughout the city, ministers had planned sermons around Dr. King's anniversary. Instead, they dwelt upon the power of faith to help their stricken parishioners cope with the tragedy.

Suddenly, there was a jackal in their midst. What the *Tallahassee Democrat* would call "the shadow of murder" hung over the FSU campus. A widely reproduced news photo showed a frightened Chi Omega sister in a cowl-necked sweater peering out from behind a sorority house window, clutching the curtain. Fear and confusion seemed to overwhelm her.

All day, a team of FSU campus officials led by Claudia Grace, assistant director of activities, visited the houses along Sorority Row. At the Pi Beta Phi house, reported the *Democrat*, Grace told the girls, "We're here because we want to tell you the facts, and we want to put the fear of the Lord in you."

She sternly advised that no one should walk anywhere alone at any time of day or night. "We have a deranged murderer on our hands," she continued. "We don't know where he is, why he is doing it, what he will do next."

Ted Bundy couldn't know what he'd do next either; the Chi Omega attack was not the work of the sly hunter he once had been. The psychopathology was now ascendant within him, an overt presence not content with periodic arousal and gratification. Hours after the slaughter, Bundy was practically boasting about what he'd done.

"We were all sitting around discussing what had happened," Oaks resident Henry Polumbo later told the grand jury. "That's all we had to talk about." According to Polumbo, Chris Hagen walked into his room in the midst of the excited discussion. "I was giving my view," Polumbo testified. "I thought it was someone who had done it and stayed in town."

Chris Hagen had disagreed. "He automatically jumped in," Polumbo remembered, "and said he thought it was somebody very professional and that he had done it before. He also said it was kind of smart how the guy used a weapon that couldn't be traced. It sorta struck me funny because I hadn't heard that over the radio or anything."

Polumbo's friend Rusty Gage told the grand jurors that Chris Hagen was "just one of those people who cast weird vibes at you. . . . He usually wanted to tell us how great he was. He wanted people to acknowledge that he was a great person. Apparently, no one ever had."

Several days after the murders, Gage testified, he again discussed the case with Hagen. This time, Chris loftily explained to Rusty how truly stupid the police were and how a criminal could get away with anything if he knew a little about the law. "I know myself," Gage quoted him, "that I could get away with any crime I wanted to—even murder if I really wanted to— because I know how to get around the law."

Bundy had previously disciplined and regulated his homicidal urges; now he embraced them. Judging from his remarks to his fellow roomers at the Oaks, he swelled with self-importance at the terror he had wrought, and the familiar indications that the police had no idea who they were looking for.

Even before he set himself loose on the sleeping co-eds, Bundy appears to have become entirely a creature of his needs. And while he probably did not intend such obvious carnage (Ted wouldn't have had headlines in his mind when he entered the sorority house), suddenly this self-acknowledged fake and loser had a city in his thrall. He achieved a lunatic apotheosis. From now on, he would behave in a manner consistent with how he viewed himself—beyond mortal law and in accord with the separate reality of his madness. Only when he felt spent, consumed by what he was and what he'd done, would he arrange once again for the security of confinement.

One mark of these final days was his total recklessness; Bundy acted as if nothing could touch him. He also regressed, behaving more and more like a child and abandoning the mask of sanity for outright predation as manifest as that of a rabid wolf. He and the "entity" had fused.

On January 12, the evidence would later show, Bundy had plucked the ignition keys from a white Dodge delivery van parked at the FSU campus media center. He had copies made, then returned the originals several days later. The mysterious disappearance and reappearance of the keys were duly reported to the campus police, but there was no reason to associate the incident with the Chi Omega killings three days later.

Also on the twelfth, Ted stole Florida license plate number 13-D-1130 from teenager Randy Ragans' 1972 VW camper. Ragans, who did not report the stolen tag, lived directly behind Cheryl Thomas' Dunwoody Street apartment.

On Saturday, January 21, Bundy pedaled over to the Publix supermarket in Tallahassee's Northwood Mall, where he stole Mrs. Mark Labadie's purse from her grocery cart. In it, he found $20, Mrs. Labadie's Georgia driver's license, and her husband's credit cards.

Ted was initially interested only in the cash; he threw the purse and the rest of its contents in a dumpster. Later, however, he retrieved the purse. It had occurred to him that he might make use of a credit card.

An escapee bent on staying at large would never have stolen and used credit cards. For one thing, Ted now would create a trail, evidence of his whereabouts. For another, theft and use of credit cards represents a double risk of exposure—and capture—plus a double felony charge.

What is more, Bundy's only previous experience with credit cards had been with his Chevron gas card, the one whose receipts had provided Mike Fisher with his first break in the Campbell case. As he knew, the slips had sparked the investigation that led to his extradition.

Ted also needed cash, not credit, if he intended to remain free.

Far more simply and at far less risk to himself he could have robbed a liquor store or held up a gas station. But not Ted. That Saturday night, Mark Labadie's Visa card paid for a $12 dinner at a restaurant called the Deli.

For the first few days following the theft, Bundy confined most of his purchases to meals at the Holiday Inn. Later, several waitresses would remember him because he was a low tipper. "Strictly a tenpercenter," one of them sniffed to the police.

On Saturday, January 28, Ted started outfitting himself in earnest. The full extent of his shopping spree has never been established; he used so many cards so many times in so many places all across northern Florida that many purchases were lost or otherwise never recorded in the later charges against him. Perhaps out of habit or need—or maybe just to vary the routine—he also continued shoplifting.

On the twenty-eighth, he charged at least $150 worth of goods and clothing—mostly tennis gear and socks—in five stores. On Wednesday, February 1, he again used Labadie's card to buy more socks and two shirts.

On Friday of that week, he went to the FSU library, where he rifled co-ed Kathy Evans' purse. Using her father's Master Charge that afternoon and the next day, Ted acquired a pair of shoes, a belt, underwear, luggage, a new pipe, lighter, and tobacco, as well as washcloths, towels, sheets, and, again, more socks. Total purchases came to more than $260.

This passion for socks—all told Ted charged more than thirty pairs—is symptomatic of the foot fetishism Bundy willingly concedes; Ted thinks it's funny, an amusing little quirk. Psychiatrists, on the other hand, recognize such fetishism as common among people suffering from severe sexual disorientation. When the condition is pathological, a morbid fascination with female genitalia is also observed.

After stealing Kathy Evans' Master Charge on Friday, Ted reappeared at Sherrod's, where he stole wallets or purses from four young women. He seemed unconcerned at the possibility of being recognized. The next night, he was in Big Daddy's Lounge and lifted at least one other woman's wallet.

Sometime on Saturday or Sunday, he used his duplicate keys to the white Dodge van to steal it from the FSU media center parking lot. He then affixed Randy Ragans' licence plate—13-D-11300—to the stolen van. On Monday, February 6, he charged about $60 more—shirts, slacks, pajamas, and a blanket—then loaded up the van and headed east toward Jacksonville. On the way out of town, he indulged his sweet tooth with $8.58 worth of pastries and cookies that he charged at the Tasty Pastry Shop.

If Ted had departed Florida then, it is highly unlikely that he would ever have been charged. But a cold lust for blood sport welled within him as he drove the white van east from Tallahassee. Bundy was hunting again.

About a hundred miles east of Tallahassee, just north of Lake City, along Interstate 10, Martha Jean Stephens pumped gas between 11:00 A.M. and noon on Tuesday, February 7, 1978, for a nervous young man in a gray jogging suit. He had a mustache. She remembered him as "visibly shaken" with "scary blue eyes." He used William R. Evans' Gulf credit card and bought 7.4 gallons of gas at 61.9¢ per gallon. The license number on his white van was 13-D-11300.

No more than three hours later and about seventy-five miles farther east, in Jacksonville, on the east coast of Florida, the same license plate number was recorded by another Gulf station attendant. This time, the man bought 8.4 gallons at 60.9¢ per gallon. The attendant, Milton Johnson, vaguely recalled a "celebrity name tag" on his customer's coat. It was different from the name on the man's credit card.

Later on Tuesday night, W.R. Evans' Master Charge card was used to pay for a meal at the Holiday Inn in Orange Park, just south of Jacksonville. Between 10:00 P.M. and 11:00 P.M., the meal was served by waitress Maria Smith at station four. She paid no attention to the diner, except to wonder idly at the size of the meal at such a late hour. He ate a shrimp cocktail from the salad bar, a steak (medium rare) and lobster combination plate, and blueberry pie with ice cream for desert. The dinner came to $13.76, including tax and tip. With the meal came all the beer he could drink.

Customers Robert and Carol Burgeois of St. Petersburg saw the lone individual at station four. Mrs. Burgeois couldn't remember much about him except that he "possibly wore glasses" and was "weird-looking." Her husband thought the man was "bombed."

"W. R. Evans" then appeared at the Holiday Inn on Stockton Street in Jacksonville and was checked into room number 134 shortly after midnight. He left the next morning without stopping at the front desk.

Sometime between that Tuesday and Friday, the tenth, a disheveled young man bought a Buck brand hunting knife with a ten-inch blade from John Farhat, proprietor of the Green Acres Sporting Goods store in Jacksonville. In court, John Farhat identified Ted Bundy as the man who bought the knife.

Early on Wednesday, February 8, Mark Labadie's Gulf card was used to buy 4.5 gallons of gas and a road map in Jacksonville.

A chill drizzle was falling that afternoon as fourteen-year-old Leslie Parmenter, daughter of a Jacksonville police detective, left J. E. B. Stuart Junior High School and walked across the street to the K-Mart parking lot. She was going to meet her brother Danny, twenty, who had reluctantly agreed to give his little sister a ride home in his truck.

As the Parmenters later testified in court, a man in a white van, license plate number 13-D-11300, drove up in front of Leslie and approached her. He was wearing glasses. According to her testimony, "he was dark-haired, messy-haired, sloppily dressed. He had a couple days' growth of beard and a mustache. He had on an overjacket and he had on a badge that said, 'Fire Department, Richard Burton.' It was plastic, like a plastic badge with a white tag inside of it."

Leslie told the court that the man was "real fidgety, digging in his pockets like he didn't know what he was going to say next or anything, like he was unsure of himself." His speech was confused. He told the girl that someone had pointed her out to him, asked her if she went to school across the street, and if she was headed for the K-Mart.

She hardly had time to answer—or to figure out just what it was that the agitated man wanted—before her brother Danny pulled up in his truck.

Next, as Danny Parmenter testified, "I stuck my head out of the window . . . and asked my sister what he wanted and . . . she said she didn't know and I told her to walk around to my side of the truck.

"I asked the man, 'Whatta you want?' and he started going back to the van. So I got out of the truck . . . and I went up to the man and asked him again what he wanted . . . He was acting very nervous and he started rolling up his window while I was still askin' him what he wanted.

"He said, 'I just asked her a question and she told me she couldn't answer it,' or something like that. And he rolled up his window in the van and started to drive off."

Brother and sister tried to follow the white van, but lost it in the afternoon traffic. They carefully noted its license number and the fact that the van was very dirty. There were dirt marks on its sides, indicating that the vehicle had been driven through underbrush.

Danny and Leslie drove straight home. Since their father was out of town that day, they called a detective they knew, described the incident, and gave the policeman the license number.

At 8:44 P.M., Ted Bundy checked into the Lake City Holiday Inn and was given room number 443. Two desk clerks remembered that the man who used Ralf Miller's Visa card appeared drunk. William Dal Scongers told the police that the guest was "scrubby" and "he had slurred speech."

Pearlie Mae Walker, a maid, saw him in the lobby that night, and remembered his "funny eyes." When she saw him later, he appeared to have composed himself somewhat. His hair was combed, at least. Ted bought dinner at the Holiday Inn using one person's credit card, and then bought drinks using another one.

As his mental state continued to deteriorate—a process he aided and abetted by drinking heavily—Bundy appears to have undergone a steep regression, a plummet back to the time in his preadolescence when all further emotional maturity was arrested.

The first indication of this was his approach on Wednesday afternoon to Leslie Parmenter in the Jacksonville parking lot. Only fourteen, Leslie was younger by years than any of Ted's previous targets. Danny Parmenter foiled Bundy's impulse, but that would only intensify the degenerate fantasy and push Ted toward his ultimate outrage the following day.

Killer child was about to become child killer.

On Thursday morning, February 9, 1978, Ted left the Lake City Holiday Inn through a slanting rain. Again, he didn't bother to check out.

About then, twelve-year-old Kimberly Diane Leach, a happy child just poised on the brink of young womanhood, was being driven by her mother, Frieda, to Lake City Junior High School, where Kim was a seventh-grader. The girl's mind that morning was upon the upcoming school Valentine dance and the new dress she'd wear.

Before school started, she was seen at several points on campus, gossiping with girlfriends. Kim apparently did not notice as did other people that a lone man in a white van was even then slowly circling the school.

She went to her first period class, gym, only to be told moments later that she'd left her denim purse in her homeroom, Mr. Bishop's class. Rather than simply forwarding the purse by way of Kim's friend Tandy Bonner, Mr. Bishop dispatched Bonner with a note for Kim to come back herself for the purse.

As many as a dozen white vans of varying descriptions were later reported near the school that morning, but no one would ever be able to say for certain in court that Ted Bundy was in any of the trucks. He was identified—tentatively—as the man seen hours later driving west in a white van, weaving and lurching down the road. The only thing that is known for certain from the witnesses, is that Kim Leach headed back to the gym through the morning rain after picking up her purse. She was never seen alive again.

A search for Kim was begun that afternoon after her mother reported her missing. When she wasn't found immediately, her parents and the citizens of Lake City began to feel presentiments of horror.

By late afternoon, Ted Bundy had returned to Tallahassee and abandoned the van. If he had taken the same precautions in leaving it as he had with the sedan he abandoned in Atlanta a month earlier, the vehicle would not have been recovered and the most telling evidence against him would never have surfaced. He did remove the stolen license plate, but he didn't discard or destroy it.

Bundy was now well beyond reason. Previously, he had told himself he'd leave Tallahassee as soon as Kenneth Misner's duplicate birth certificate arrived in the mail. It was there upon his return from Lake City, as were several dunning notes from Oaks manager Larry Wingfield. Ted's February rent was over a week late.

With no reason to stay any longer, and plenty of reasons to leave, a rational Ted Bundy would have left the state immediately—and probably still could have escaped detection if he had. Instead, Bundy could not stir himself for three days.

He did steal a green Toyota on Friday, February 10, and told himself he'd leave no later than eleven that night for Houston, Texas. Instead, Bundy took a girl from the Oaks to dinner and then went back to the rooming house to watch *The Rockford Files* on his stolen television set with her.

It was after 1:00 A.M. before he had gotten his cache of stolen goods organized and had brought the Toyota to the vicinity of the Oaks. He was just about to lock the car when Leon County sheriff's deputy Keith Dawes pulled up behind him.

Dawes asked Ted for identification, which Bundy could not

produce. Then the deputy noticed license plate 13-D-11300 resting on the front floorboards of the Toyota.

"Where do you live?" he asked Bundy.

Ted replied, "College Avenue."

At first, Dawes had only been curious about the man and the car. But the lack of identification and the license plate made him suspicious. He walked back to the patrol car to run a check on the Toyota and the license plate. As he was doing so, Ted took foot across the street, darted behind an apartment building, and then leaped over the fence into the back yard of the Oaks.

He lay trembling for several moments in a bramble, listening for sounds of pursuit. When he heard nothing, he stumbled across the darkened yard and scurried up the fire escape to his room. In his room, he turned the light out and sat in the dark, heart thumping.

The next morning, Saturday, Bundy put on a tennis outfit and walked over to discuss his rent arrears with Larry Wingfield's supervisor, Robert Fulford. He told the manager that he was getting some money from his mother in Michigan, and even placed a fake long-distance call to Ann Arbor for Fulford's benefit. In the midst of his act, Ted looked down at a bowl on the table in front of him. In it, he saw a police investigator's business card.

The circle was drawing tighter around Bundy, yet he could not stir himself. He dallied through Saturday, riding his bike, playing racquetball. For all he knew, the police could be waiting for him when he returned to his room.

Finally, on Sunday, February 12, he pulled himself together and went out in search of a car. His first find was a teenager's heavily modified and souped-up VW, which Ted stole and then abandoned after driving it around for a while. He didn't think the vehicle would hold up on a long drive.

Just after 10:00 P.M., Ted spotted a 1972 orange VW bug parked on the street and noted in gratitude that the owner had left the keys in it. Bundy still loved Volkswagens. This would be the last one he'd ever drive.

He hurried back to the Oaks, where he stuffed his belongings into the car, thoroughly wiped his room (including the ceiling) for fingerprints, and then headed west. The drive through the night was nerve-racking. Bundy was physically and mentally drained by his most recent hunt, his encounter with Kim Leach, and the strain of fighting back the chaos within him. He had only barely been able to find a car and get out of town.

Now he discovered that whenever his speed exceeded fifty mph, one of the rear wheels would shake the entire car, forcing him to slow down. At the same time, road construction forced him off the interstate and onto the two-lane Highway 90 at several points. Whenever he passed through a small town, Ted risked a speed trap or a spontaneous arrest by some bored or overzealous local cop. A number of times that night his exhaustion overcame him and he pulled into rest stops for fitful naps.

Near dawn on Monday, Bundy had driven the crippled VW 154 miles to Crestview, Florida, and was only thirty-five miles from Pensacola, near the Alabama border. By now, he knew that the VW was probably listed as hot and he should be trading it for another car. But he didn't.

Instead, in Crestview, he pulled into a garage. The mechanic told him he'd have to replace the tire. None the right size was on hand at the station. Holding on to the slenderest thread of stability, Ted drove to the local Holiday Inn for breakfast. He attempted to pay for the meal with one of his credit cards, but by now most of them had been reported. An alert waitress checked the one Bundy handed her, found that it was stolen, and then literally chased him out of the restaurant and into his car, which, bad tire or not, Ted gunned away from the restaurant.

Several miles away, he turned down a dirt road and parked the VW on an incline. Ted decided that he'd wait for dark before moving on. He didn't know that he'd blundered onto a restricted area of Eglin Air Force Base.

Soon after he stopped, he began to hear the intermittent beat of helicopter blades above him, and the roar of jet aircraft engines in the distance. He deduced that he was on some sort of military reservation, but he couldn't be sure that the helicopters up there weren't looking for him. The periodic din kept him on edge throughout the day.

At first dark, Ted tried to back the overloaded VW up the hill. Instantly, it slewed and wallowed in the soft earth beneath it. Bundy was stuck.

For the next three hours or more, he clawed and dug frantically beneath the car, trying to move it the sixty feet he needed to get back on the road. He shoved everything he could find under the rear wheels—including, at one point, the rear seat—but nothing worked. In the dark, with much of his clothing and many other items now strewn in the dirt, Ted glumly found his backpack and started hitchhiking back to the interstate.

After a couple of miles on foot, an airman in civilian clothes picked him up and drove him the rest of the way. He asked Ted a lot of questions about why he was out there alone. The airman left him off at a cluster of gas stations near the interstate and drove on. Bundy luckily found an obliging attendant who agreed to take him back to the car and to help him push it back up to the road. Before saying his thank yous and motoring off west again, Ted was told how lucky he was that the military police hadn't arrested him. The gas jockey said it happened to his friends all the time.

In Pensacola, Bundy found a motel and fished out an American gas card to pay for his room. The woman at the desk gave him the wrong key, and when he returned to the lobby he saw her on the telephone, his registration card before her.

"I just phoned in the credit card and they say it is stolen," she told him evenly. She didn't seem at all upset.

Ted tried to look surprised. "Well," he replied, "it was missing but we found it." He told her that he would go out to his car for cash, and then drove off. He spent Monday night, the thirteenth, trying to sleep upright in the VW.

Bundy's last day of freedom began at six-thirty the following morning, when he achily awoke, ate breakfast, and then with no particular objective in mind drove out to the Pensacola airport.

Around 9:00 A.M., he pulled into a community college near the airport and used its men's locker room to shower, shave, and change his clothes. He then drove to a laundromat and washed all of his clothing, including his thirty pairs of socks. The remainder of the daylight hours he spent at the beach.

Ted Bundy ate a large and early dinner that night; he noted ruefully that many of his fellow patrons at the restaurant were couples out celebrating Valentine's Day. It upset him. He drank heavily.

At a shopping mall he purchased more clothing and socks. Then he found a bar where he intended to steal more purses and wallets.

By now, Ted's agility was seriously impaired. A waitress saw him dipping into a girl's wallet. Before he knew it, Bundy was surrounded by a half-dozen angry-looking bouncers. They took him to a back room, where, when their backs were turned, he quickly stashed his wad of stolen credit cards on a shelf behind him.

The bouncers questioned Ted closely about his reasons for being there. They brought in the woman whose purse he had been seen rifling. She told the bouncers that nothing was missing.

They told Bundy to leave. He accepted his $1 cover charge back, made a deft grab for his credit cards, and did as he was told.

By now it was getting late. At the wheel of the VW, Ted was still drunk and once again disoriented. Four times in the past four days he'd nearly been caught, yet somehow he was still free. As if by instinct, he lurched onto the freeway and then off again and into an industrial area where he was soon lost. Creeping along the deserted streets in the dark, calling attention to himself as he had twice before late at night, Bundy checked his rearview mirror and saw a police car.

# THIRTEEN

Case 75-29267

The date is 2/21/78. The time is 1520 hours. This will be an interview with Elizabeth Kendall. Those present at the interview [include] Major Nick Mackie and Detective Robert Keppell.

KEPPELL: Are you aware that his interview is being taped?

E.K.: Yes.

KEPPEL: Is it taped with your approval?

E.K.: Yes.

KEPPEL: Okay. Would you begin on February 16, '78 about 5:00 on Thursday and describe a telephone call that you received from Ted Bundy?

E.K.: Yes. It was 5:00 P.M. on Thursday.

KEPPEL: Okay.

E.K.: And he called collect and my daughter accepted the charges. I told him that he shouldn't be calling me that my phone had a tap on it and he said he was in custody. I asked him "where?" and he said: "Florida." And later in the conversation, he said, he repeated over and over again, that this was really going to be bad when it broke, that it wasn't going to break until tomorrow morning in the press but it was going to be really ugly. I asked him if he was referring to the murders of some sorority girls in Florida. And he said that he wouldn't talk about it. And I told him that I had asked an FBI agent about those murders up here 'cause I was concerned about them. And he didn't want to talk about it. And, ah, then in the conversation he told me that he wished we could sit down and talk about . . . things, without anyone listening—about why he was the way he is, and I said: "Are you telling me that you're sick?" And he was

237

very defensive, and he told me to back off, and what he was referring to was how come he had hurt me so many times. . . . We talked for about an hour . . . and then he was going to hang up and call his mother and call back, and when he called back we didn't accept charges and then we took the phone off the hook. Then the next Saturday morning at 2:00 he called again, collect, and he said he wanted to talk about what we'd been talking about in the first phone call. And I said: "You mean about being sick?" And he said: "Yes." Then he said that he was going to try to clear things up in a way that he could be back in Washington close to his family. . . . I can't remember exactly how he got into talking about . . . the crimes. . . . He told me that he was sick and that he was consumed by something that he didn't understand and that ah, that he just couldn't contain it. . . .

KEPPEL: Did he mention why he couldn't contain it?

E.K.: Well, he said that he tried, he said that it took so much of his time, and that's why he wasn't doing well in law school. . . . He said that he was preoccupied with this force. . . . I asked him if I somehow had played a part in what had happened, and he said that no, for years before he even met me he'd been fighting the same sickness and that when it broke we just happened to be together. Ah, he mentioned an incident about following a sorority girl, ah, he didn't do anything that night. But that's how it was, that he was out late at night and he would follow people. . . . He'd try not to but he just did it anyway.

KEPPEL: Did he mention anything to do with sorority girls at the University of Washington?

E.K.: Well, this incident did take place on campus. . . . Ah, he did talk about Lake Sammamish. . . . He started by saying that he was sick, and he said: "I don't have a split personality, and I don't have blackouts." He said: "I remember everything that I've done." And he mentioned the day, July 14 . . . and he said that it wasn't that he'd forgotten what he'd done that day or that he couldn't remember, but just said that it was over.

KEPPEL: The incident was over?

E.K.: Yes, that's the implication I got.

KEPPEL: Did he mention the incident specifically?

E.K.: Yes. . . . He said: "The day of Lake Sammamish."

KEPPEL: Did he specifically say that he had done something to some women that day?

E.K.: No. No. I knew what he was talking about and he knew that I knew it. . . . Ah, he said that he would answer any questions that he could, and I asked him about the night that Brenda Ball disappeared because he'd been with me and my family and he'd left early in the evening and then the next day was late to my daughter's baptism and I asked him if that's where he'd been, and he mumbled something . . . and then he said: "It's pretty scary, isn't it?" And I said: "Yeah."

Liz told Keppel that she asked Ted if he'd ever tried to kill her and, according to her, Ted said that one time he did. Bundy insisted to us that Liz misunderstood him, but she related to Keppel:

He told me that he'd been really trying hard to control this sickness and that he'd been staying off the streets and trying to be normal and that it just happened that I was there when he felt it coming on and that he wanted to kill me that night.

She thought it was the autumn of 1973 and that Ted's alleged method had been to stop up her chimney, place towels around the bottom of the door, and then to leave. Liz awoke gasping and threw up a window for air.

She continued:

. . . and I believe he said that during '71 and '72 and '73 it was taking up more of his time. . . .

Ah, I mentioned that there was a phone call that he made to me from Salt Lake City when a woman down there was abducted and it was late at night and I've always thought well, he couldn't be out abducting women because I'd talked to him on the phone that night and I asked if he didn't sometimes call me or come over to touch base with reality after he'd done some of these things, and he said: "That's a pretty good guess."

Keppel asked Liz if Ted had given her any other specifics.

No. Well . . . I asked him specifically about the Florida murders. And he told me that he didn't want to talk about them, but then . . . he said that he felt like he had a disease like alcoholism or something like alcoholics that couldn't take another drink, and he told me it was just something that he couldn't be around and he knew it now. And I asked what that was and he said: "Don't make me say it."

Bundy had spent almost two days in custody and was near total emotional collapse at the time he called Liz with his oblique confession. Even though he had engineered his own recapture and welcomed the relief of sanctuary inside his cell, he also dreaded the prospect of exposure and accusation for his crimes. Ted would do anything not to stand helpless before the world.

One measure of his mood was his exchange with Pensacola police officer David Lew while being driven to the police station the night of his arrest. So broken was Bundy that he twice asked Officer Lee if he'd let Ted try to run, and then shoot him dead. Drunk and defeated, Bundy was instead taken to a cell, where he passed out.

Three hours later, Norm Chapman, a burly city detective, awoke Bundy and took him upstairs to be interviewed. The affable, drawling southerner, large enough to be mistaken for a retired professional linebacker, had himself been summoned to the jail well before his 7:00 A.M. shift was to start. Bundy's stolen VW and the paraphernalia in it would not have justified the call, but the twenty-one credit cards found in his possession as well as the several identity cards belonging to FSU co-eds did. All of northern Florida was still keenly anxious about the Chi Omega murders; any suspect arrested who could be linked with Tallahassee was immediately given special attention.

Chapman's first interview with Ted was brief. Bundy told him that his name was Kenneth Misner and little more. The detective sent him back to his cell and then called Tallahassee, where he was put in touch with police department detective Don Patchen. Chapman ran down what he knew about his suspect and then hung up. Shortly thereafter, Kenneth Misner himself called Chapman from Tallahassee to emphatically insist that *he* was Misner, not the man in the Pensacola jail.

Discovery of the alias was enough to bring Don Patchen and Leon County sheriff's detective Stephen Bodiford on the run to talk to this mystery suspect. As they sped toward Pensacola, Chapman again awoke Ted and confronted him with the news. Bundy still could not bring himself to admit he was Bundy.

"Well, my name's John Doe," he told Chapman. "John R. Doe." The detective sent him back to his cell once again.

When Patchen and Bodiford arrived later that day, they conferred immediately with Chapman. None of the three lawmen knew quite what to make of John R. Doe except to notice the obvious: The prisoner, whoever he was, was in a state of exhaustion. It was impossible to get any answers out of him, so they decided to give him a night's sleep before questioning him further.

Meantime, Ted had been taken once again from his cell and brought to the jail's booking area for fingerprinting. On hand were assistant state attorney Ronald Johnson and Isaac Koran, an attorney from the local public defender's office. Koran had automatically been notified that he might have a new client at the jail.

Koran watched Johnson on one side of the fingerprinting table and the bedraggled John R. Doe on the other. Despite "Doe's" condition and his baggy jail-issue overalls, Koran marked his polite manner and the note of cultivation in his voice. He compared the mystery suspect with the suited state attorney. "I was kinda wondering," Koran later told Hugh, "what could have happened that this person's on one side of the counter and this guy's on the other."

At seven the following morning, February 16, Chapman, Patchen, and Bodiford had Bundy brought to Chapman's office. In a tape-recorded interview, Ted still refused to give his name. He did, however, admit to stealing the orange VW.

He was then arraigned on charges including grand larceny and possession of stolen property. The judge refused to set bail until "John R. Doe" revealed his true identity.

With him again that day was Isaac Koran. Several things had begun to bother Koran. First, his mystery client had been kept in the city jail and was not transferred, as was usual, to the county lockup. Koran knew "Doe" was talking to the police, and he knew that the interviewers included Don Patchen, and Steve Bodiford from Tallahassee. At the arraignment, he was surprised to see state attorney Curtis Golden in court. Golden would not take a personal interest in a routine larceny case.

Earlier, Koran's client had placed a call to Atlanta, where he tried to reach Millard Farmer, a controversial attorney whom Bundy had once written from Colorado, hoping to interest him in the Caryn Campbell case. After "Doe" was returned to his cell, Koran called Farmer himself. It was then that he learned Ted's real name and began to understand all the suspicious activity. Farmer, Koran realized, involved himself almost exclusively with capital cases. Bundy, Farmer, Tallahassee; they added up to Chi Omega. Koran reached for the telephone again.

He called Michael Minerva, the Tallahassee public defender, for whom he had once worked. He knew Minerva might be assigned the case. "Mike," he said, "there's something going on here that you might want to know about. They've got a guy here that they think might be involved with Chi Omega. Millard Farmer's involved. I don't know if you'll get involved, but I wanted you to know what's going on."

The two public defenders were most concerned about Bundy's conversations with the police investigators. Ted had looked "uptight, very shaky" to Koran; if he was a murder suspect, he might be blurting all sorts of incriminating details to the police.

Minerva, for his part, did not want to inherit a client whose rights had not been zealously guarded. After listening intently to Koran and asking a few questions, he quietly warned his counterpart: "Don't fuck this up, Koran."

It was decided that someone from the Pensacola public defender's office should stick with Bundy as continuously as possible. But unbeknownst to Koran and the rest, Ted was even then formulating his own private agenda.

He feared a trial and public condemnation and so he hoped, as he mentioned to Liz in his second call to her, that he could bargain information for institutionalization. His psychopathology, of course, precluded a full confession, but in his desperate emotional state and continuing inability to evaluate his circumstances rationally, Ted would flirt with self-incrimination. Plus, he appears to have needed to talk; not out of guilt or as a gesture of atonement, but to share before an appreciative audience the enormity of what he was and what he had done.

Bundy kept his intentions hidden that Thursday night when, after consulting with his attorneys, he finally gave the police his true name. In exchange, he was granted access to the telephone in Chapman's office and a promise that news of his recapture would not be released until 9:00 A.M. on the seventeenth. His first call was to Liz Kendall.

Ted was on the telephone for two hours that Thursday night. During that time, his fingerprints were matched with a set provided by the local FBI office. He was Ted Bundy all right, and the police learned that he had just been placed on the bureau's Ten Most Wanted List.

Some one or more of the several people he called from Chapman's office also notified the Seattle police and press that Ted Bundy was back in custody. The telephones at the Pensacola police station started jangling first with inquiries from Seattle and then from cities throughout the west. The name Ted Bundy had meant nothing to Chapman, Patchen, and Bodiford; but they soon learned what manner of celebrity they had caught.

The three detectives took dozens of calls and soon were lost in a sea of Bundy stories, mixed-up versions of his days in Washington, Utah, and Colorado. They couldn't begin to organize and assimilate the deluge of names, dates, suspected victims, suggested M.O.'s, and the rest of the confused and startling information that engulfed them.

When he was finished with his calls, Bundy was returned to his cell, where, at his request, he met with Michael Moody, a Catholic priest. Neither Bundy nor Moody will divulge the content of their conversation, although Ted later told me he was surprised when the priest counseled him not to talk to the police. Despite this advice and his attorneys' best efforts to keep Bundy away from the interviewers, Ted had sent word to Chapman that he wished to meet with them. Shortly after midnight, the Pensacola detective brought Bundy back to his office.

Later there would be criticism from several quarters over the way Chapman, Patchen, and Bodiford handled Bundy. There were too many of them (no more than two interrogators generally are used in such situations), the detectives talked too much, sometimes interrupting Bundy, and they were far too gentle with him. Bundy himself was surprised that they didn't ask tougher questions.

Ted set a confessional tone to the talks, leading the three lawmen to believe him on the brink of a full, outright confession. He asked their help "to break these barriers down" so he could talk, and to keep the public defenders away from him. Around his attorneys, he said, a "defense Ted" would emerge and suppress the part of him that wanted to explain what had happened. "I want you to understand me," he told them. "So you can understand my problem."

Bruce Lubeck, who helped defend Bundy in the DaRonch case in Utah, recognizes in these statements the Ted he knew. "Ted's a showman," Lubeck says. "It's clear he knew he was in a lot of trouble down there, and he was doing what I would call pimping. Seeing what they would go for. What sort of bargaining position, if any, he could have."

Two hours into the interrogation, Bundy asked that the tape recorder be turned off. The detectives readily agreed, confident that their surreptitious bug would pick up everything. They'd discover later that it had malfunctioned.

Bundy rambled on through the night, admitting to his voyeurism, a taste for pornography, and discussing what he called "my problem." It was a bravura performance, complete with tears, and managed in such a way that by ten o'clock the following morning the detectives were sure beyond any doubt that they had the Chi Omega killer. What they didn't have was anything that amounted to a legal confession. The single time all three bore down on Ted was when they asked point-blank if he'd killed the girls in Tallahassee. "The evidence is there," Bundy responded. "Look for it."

This was the first of five long sessions Bundy held with the police in Pensacola and then in Tallahassee. Initially, their interest was focused solely upon the Chi Omega case, but by Friday, after Ted's public defenders angrily broke up the first marathon interrogation, the police discovered Bundy's link to Kimberly Diane Leach. The key was the white Dodge van stolen from the FSU media center.

It was found on a Tallahassee street on Monday, February 13, the same day that Ted had spent in the woods at Eglin Air Force Base. Four days earlier, Steve Bodiford had received a call from Lester Parmenter in Jacksonville, who related how his daughter Leslie had been approached in a parking lot on Wednesday, the eighth. Parmenter relayed his children's description of the man and his white Dodge van with the license plate number 13-D-11300. He also told Bodiford that the license had been traced to Randy Ragans in Tallahassee.

On Monday morning, Bodiford learned of deputy Keith Dawes's encounter on the preceding Friday night. Dawes had recovered 13-D-11300 from a stolen green Toyota. His suspect had fled.

Bodiford, who was still ignorant of Ted Bundy's presence in Florida and had not made a connection between Kim Leach's disappearance on Thursday the ninth and Chi Omega or the Parmenter girl, then began a check for white vans stolen in the vicinity. Routine police work.

Around four-thirty that Monday afternoon, he was informed of the recovery of the FSU media center van; the only white van, it turned out, to have been reported missing in Tallahassee since the first of the year. Working with FSU's chief investigator, Clarence Hooker, Bodiford determined that the van had been missing from the fourth or fifth of February until the thirteenth and that its thief had put about 750 miles on the vehicle. It could easily have been driven to Jacksonville and back. The van was impounded and then processed by the Florida Department of Law Enforcement crime lab in Tallahassee.

Two days later, Bodiford was off to Pensacola with Don Patchen on what he thought was an altogether separate piece of police business—the interrogation of Chi Omega suspect "John R. Doe." But once there he was informed that Bundy's stolen credit cards placed the suspect in Jacksonville at the time of Leslie Parmenter's encounter with "Richard Burton" and also put Bundy in Lake City the next day when Kim Leach disappeared.

Bodiford thought of Keith Dawes and sent three polaroid snaps of Bundy from Pensacola to Tallahassee. Deputy Dawes positively identified Ted as the suspect with the 13-D-11300 license plate. Suddenly, Bodiford realized what he had; not only was Bundy now a prime suspect in the Leach case, too, but by serendipity the detective had secured a vitally important source of evidence. Kim Leach, he knew, had probably been in the van.

Still, the Florida police hoped such evidence wouldn't be necessary; they wanted a confession. From what he had told them the first night in Pensacola, it appeared as if Ted really could be brought to the point of telling all. But appearance, as always with Ted, was deceiving. Bundy was only too happy to keep talking to them even though his effort to "pimp," as Bruce Lubeck put it, a deal had been rejected by the police. Ted recognized that he commanded attention, even a kind of awe, from the interrogators. In this respect, he was as much captor as captive. That idea excited him.

Many months later, Steve Bodiford recounted the tone and content of these interviews in a deposition taken by Mike Minerva. The Tallahassee public defender asked if the lawmen ever specifically questioned Bundy about committing violence.

BODIFORD: We'd talk about what we'd refer to as a problem. You know, "you have a problem. You do this and this." Generally, it was my impression and the impression of the other investigators, and I feel that it was Ted's impression, that when we said "problem," I meant killing people.

But did I come right out and say, "Look, did you commit those murders in Washington that they say you committed?" No, I never asked him like that.

Minerva endeavored to exploit the fact that Bundy had been vague and that he was never actually confronted about his murders except in the Chi Omega case. Bodiford tried to explain the ways in which Bundy would put his various revelations.

> BODIFORD: We talked one night about his car, for example. He said the front seat was either loose or out of it, the right front of his Volkswagen.
> "Well, why?"
> "Well, I can carry things easier that way."
> "You mean you can carry bodies easier that way?"
> And he said, "Well, let's just say I can carry cargo better that way."
> Now we asked him, "That cargo you carried, was it sometimes—was it damaged?"
> And he said, "Sometimes it was damaged and sometimes it wasn't."

Bodiford testified that Bundy was shown Florida's "Mentally Disordered Sex Offender" statute, under which he might avoid the electric chair and be given help. Bundy told the detectives such a law didn't apply to him. Also—and contrary to several published reports—Bodiford recollected no time when Ted offered any number of victims for which he might be responsible. Ted did tell the three policemen that he feared Florida's electric chair.

The lawmen tried on several occasions to guide Bundy toward a discussion of Kimberly Leach. She had been missing for eight days when she first became a suspect in her disappearance. Police were certain that he had killed her, and Bundy, the three detectives later related, did nothing to dissuade them from that view. Once again, he indirectly implicated himself, describing Kim's fate as "horrible" and adding a warning that they "wouldn't want to see her."

But ultimately these statements were as insubstantive as anything else Ted had said about his "problem"; and they were of no help in what became, in the weeks ahead, the detectives' most pressing concern—locating Kimberly's remains. That she was dead, they now knew for a certainty. But despite the ample circumstantial evidence pointing to Bundy as her slayer, the police knew that in court, where it counted, they would have trouble demonstrating that she was dead without a body.

It took them another seven weeks.

Every day, teams of state troopers and volunteers fanned out to search thousands of acres of the north Florida underbrush, sinkholes, and dense pine stands. One day, a pair of women's underpants with a dark-brownish stain resembling blood were found. They were rushed to the lab for analysis. The searchers waited for hours for the results. And then the call came. The stain, said the technician, was from baked beans.

The break in the case came April 6, 1978, when crime lab analyst George D. Barrow in Tallahassee called FDLE special agent J. O. Jackson in Lake City. Barrow had a thought. He had compared a pile of cigarette butts found together with a $5 bill in a wooded area roughly thirty miles west of Lake City with cigarette butts left—presumably by Ted—in the white Dodge van. They weren't the same brand and neither sample yielded fingerprints or serological evidence. But to Barrow, there seemed to be a striking similarity in the way they apparently had been smoked and stubbed out. Why not, he suggested, search that area again?

The next day, a team of state troopers headed by First Sergeant Talmadge Pace returned to the general area where the butts and the $5 were found. They searched through the morning, quadrant by quadrant, then broke for a dusty roadside lunch. They'd found nothing.

In the afternoon, the searchers concentrated on the dense brush around a massive sinkhole. Reachable from the entrance to Suwannee River State Park by means of a dirt access road, the location was just north of State Highway 90. It was separated from the road and a large cleared area by a low wire fence.

It was a perfect spot for a murder. Old oaks covered in moss stood brooding over the scene. Crows and buzzards flapped up through the tangle of saplings and underbrush. Nearby, a local meat packer had for years dumped the butchered remains of pigs and chickens in the woods, attracting the birds and ground-dwelling scavengers. Bleached bones were scattered everywhere.

Pace led his team along the wire fence, each searcher responsible for a single patch of ground. At around 1:00 P.M., one of the troopers made out an old hog shed, abandoned and dilapidated. Under it, he saw what looked like a shoe, then a foot. He called to Pace. Fifty-seven days after her disappearance Kim Leach had been found.

    . . . after initial photography of the intact hogshed and the parts of the body that were visible from the outside, the roof of the hogshed and the wall that it was leaning onto were removed and further photography and examination of the body were performed. The body was resting on its left side with the left thigh and knee drawn up close and the right leg resting on the left thigh with the hip and knee joints at approximately right angles. The left arm was stretched out straight and resting underneath the left thin parallel to the long axis of the torso and protruding underneath both thighs being parallel to the right lower leg. The abdomen and chest were resting as follows: the abdomen partially resting on its left and left posterier aspects, and the chest and upper shoulder area being flat on the back. The right arm was stretched straight up with a slight bend in the elbow joint going past and slightly encircling the head. The head was resting on its right side facing the upper right arm and being immediately adjacent to it. The only clothing item on the body was a stained, off-white appearing body shirt with a short turtle neck and long sleeves . . . The body was subsequently transported to the Medical Examiner's Office and further examination revealed that the entire intact area of the body skin surfaces was mummified (parchment-like skin). The skin of the right side of the face and scalp . . . was absent and completely skeletonized. The remaining scalp, including the left ear and the skin of the left face, was mummified and intact showing intact orbital openings, nostrils, and an oral opening. . . . The skin of the entire neck area, anterior and posterior, was absent. This skin loss extended into the upper chest area to approximately the level of the sternoclavicular joint. The edges of this skin defect were rounded and weathered, hence no determination of the exact nature of this injury can be made. . . . There was a large area of missing skin and internal organs starting at the pubic mound 3″ below the navel and proceeding through the inguinal regions, bilaterally, the inner thighs, and up to the level of the coccyx. . . .

*Diagnoses*
(1) Homicidal violence, neck region, type undetermined
(2) Sexual battery, vaginal and anal regions, type determined

*Opinion*
Kimberly Diane Leach died of homicidal violence to the neck region, type undetermined. The manner of death is homicide.

Peter Lipkovic, M.D.
Chief Medical Examiner.

Lipkovic's diagnoses and opinion would be vigorously disputed by a defense expert. Such skin loss in the neck and groin area, he contended, was common in bodies where animal predation has occurred. Decomposition, too, would account for massive tissue losses in these parts of the body.

Yet several factors argue for Lipkovic's conclusions. Specifically, the positioning of her body, especially her arms and legs, is consistent with the girl having been crouched on all fours, then allowed to slump forward. The guess—and it is only a guess—is that Ted brutally slit Kim's throat from above and behind her. The massive injury to her pelvic region—if it is an injury—could have occurred before, during, or after her murder.

Steve Bodiford, whose patient police work in the days immediately following Kim Leach's disappearance had helped secure the vital white Dodge van as evidence, could only read Dr. Lipkovic's report and reflect on the nature of the man the state would later prove was responsible for Kim's death. Bodiford, together with Chapman and Patchen, had pleaded with Bundy to tell them where the Leach girl was. Mistakenly, they had tried to appeal on a human level.

As Bodiford would relate in his deposition with Mike Minerva, "He was sitting kind of slumped in a chair, you know, kind of sitting next to a desk with his arm on it, kind of leaning over. There was a pack of cigarettes on the desk, an empty pack. . . . We were talking to him and trying to really impress him that he should, you know, ease these people's minds. . . . He raised up in the chair and grabbed the pack of cigarettes and crumpled them and threw them on the floor and said, 'But I'm the most cold-hearted son of a bitch you'll ever meet.' "

# FOURTEEN

FROM A rational point of view, Ted Bundy's legal situation was bleak. Once Kim Leach's body was found in April of 1978, it was only a matter of time before he'd be charged with her murder along with the Chi Omega homicides. But even before the capital indictments were handed up in July of 1978, the outlook for Bundy was hopeless. The state of Utah wanted him back to serve his kidnap sentence. Colorado wished to extradite and try him for the Campbell murder as well as his two jailbreaks. The local felony warrants alone—some sixty were filed in Tallahassee and Pensacola in the days immediately following his recapture—carried hundreds of years in potential prison sentences for crimes ranging from auto theft to fraud.

Yet Bundy's ability to appreciate his peril—and his own mental deterioration—was limited to preconscious recognition that he was afraid to be free again. Ted had sustained considerable psychic damage while out in the world, enough to trigger near total dissociation from the terrible crimes he'd committed. The result, in the coming months, was a delusion of invincibility that made Ted behave as if none of his legal difficulties existed, because, for him, they didn't. He felt no guilt and he'd long since ceased to acknowledge society's right to judge him.

These disturbed mental processes did not go unnoticed by those around Ted. In the midst of the nightmare of trying to provide him an adequate defense, public defender Mike Minerva retained a psychiatrist to help judge the viability of an insanity defense. Minerva's choice was the eminent Dr. Emanuel Tanay, a professor at Wayne State University in Detroit and an expert on the insanity defense. Before talking to Ted—who had reluctantly acceded to the interview, warning his attorney that "there's no way Tanay's going to find me insane"—the psychiatrist examined the entire Bundy file, from Sergeant Hayward's Utah arrest report to the autopsies done on the Florida victims.

> Mr. Bundy has an incapacity to recognize the significance of evidence held against him [he later wrote]. . . . It would be simplistic to characterize this as merely lying inasmuch as he acts as if his perception of the significance of evidence was real. He makes decisions based upon these distorted perceptions of reality. Furthermore, he maintains an attitude and mood consistent with his perception of reality, namely, he is neither concerned nor distressed in an appropriate manner by the charges facing him.
>
> The interactions of Mr. Bundy with the police and the whole criminal justice system have been discussed at length with him and his attorneys. It is my opinion, based upon a variety of data, that his dealings with the criminal justice system are dominated by psychopathology. . . .
>
> Transcripts of the many hours of his conversations with police officers constitute a variety of "confession." When this is pointed out to him by me, he does not dispute my inference, he merely provides a different explanation. Whatever the explanation, the consequences of the verbal games which Mr. Bundy played with investigators were counterproductive to his defense and occurred against the advice of his counsel. Mr. Bundy confessed the crimes charged against him while maintaining his innocence. . . . This behavior was not, in my opinion, the result of rational reflection and decision making process but a manifestation of the psychiatric illness from which Mr. Bundy suffers. . . .
>
> I have discussed with Mr. Bundy his appraisal of the evidence held against him. It is his view that the case against him is weak or even frivolous. This judgment of Mr. Bundy's is considered to be inaccurate by his defense counsel and, most likely, represents a manifestation of his illness. In view of the fact that on conviction he faces the death sentence, the acceptance of an offer of a life sentence in exchange for a guilty plea is a consideration. This possibility seems precluded by Mr. Bundy's view that the prosecution's case against him is weak. This is at least his explanation why he is unwilling to consider this particular approach. It is my impression that a major factor is his deep-seated need to have a trial, which he views as an opportunity to confront and confound various authority

figures. In this last category I include, for his purpose, not only judges and prosecutors but also his defense attorneys.

In other words, the only reality Ted now acknowledged was the sense of power he derived from being at the center of things, the focus of national attention. And out of the "need" Dr. Tanay identified was born yet another Ted Bundy—an impostor who flourished in the new role of All-America boy. In the coming months, millions of people would know him not for the faintly wormy psychopath he was, but rather as the handsome young courtroom dazzler who defended himself on television.

The image of brilliance owes much to the newspeople who fostered it. Ted made very good copy. But it was wholly his creation, a final public incarnation as master of his own elaborate melodrama.

In truth, he became as monomaniacal as any twelve-year-old who suddenly finds the world at his feet. Willful and often petulant, Bundy plotted and lied, demanded fealty from his attorneys, staged tantrums when he didn't get his way, and fell into a deep narcissistic love with his fabricated self.

Ted rejected, accepted, then rejected again the appointment of Mike Minerva's team of public defenders to represent him. For many months, he acted *pro se*, officially his own attorney, and maintained that the only other lawyer of sufficient stature to defend him was Millard Farmer. The Atlanta attorney—who earlier had not taken the Campbell case when Bundy sought him out—was now eager to represent Ted. However, his petitions to do so were repeatedly denied by the state on the grounds that a Georgia contempt citation against Farmer made him ineligible to practice in Florida.

The attorneys who finally did represent Bundy learned early on that his burgeoning mania made prudent legal moves impossible. Ted would not confess, of course, which prevented them from pursuing an insanity defense. Bundy insisted that he was innocent and demanded that he be defended on that basis. As Tanay noted, so complete was his compartmentalization of guilt that he could not accept that the state had a case against him. And even after he was convicted in court, Ted was able to stand before a judge and deny the legitimacy of the verdict.

He began his orchestration of events within a week of his return to Tallahassee. Carole Boone had been writing and calling almost daily. Her letters were chatty, witty, newsy, but they also had a cautious tone. Carole had been badgered by the FBI while Ted was at large, and it appears she was bothered by the Chi Omega connection. She wrote Ted that the truth, no matter how awful, should be known.

Bundy's first written reply, dated February 28, 1978, ignored Carole's final admonition and instead railed about the FBI, calling them "Fornicators, Bastards and Imposters," a suggestive choice of epithets. He touched Carole with a description of his pitiable cell conditions and the cockroaches with which, he claimed, he shared his food, then quoted a soul-stirring bromide from Richard Bach about triumphing over adversity. The letter closed, "I love you Boone. I need you. More than ever."

Bundy was not the first inmate to learn how powerfully affecting such bathos can be to certain people; many prisoners use similar appeals to coax money and gifts from sympathetic outsiders. Carole once again took up Ted's cause and put aside—forever— all doubts as to his innocence. Soon, she was writing to "Angelbuns," "Sweet Theodore," "Dearest Bunzo," "Darling Bunnykins." In return came letters to "Darling Boone," "Precious Fleshpot," "Tender Peachblossom," and "My Beloved Quintessential Quark."

In time, Ted would make more and more use of Carole Boone, but for now there was action to be attended to on other fronts. Leon County Sheriff Ken Katsaris at first would permit no newsmen near Ted; while, as Bundy suspected, the sheriff's office was the source of damning innuendo that was finding its way onto television and into print.

Ted boiled at the negative stories and began countering them with his own public relations campaign. "I have killed no one," he wrote in a three-page letter smuggled out of the Leon County jail to a *Rocky Mountain News* reporter from Denver. "Outside of a few minor thefts, I have done nothing wrong." He added: "What the media reports now is completely one-sided, nothing but accusation and insinuation—spoon-fed by investigative authorities."

In April, Ted wrote his first attorney, John O'Connell, in Salt Lake City. He told the lawyer that he was representing himself again—"my 'pro se' act," he called it—and explained that being his own lawyer gave him peace of mind. "It also," he added, "gives me things like phone calls, a typewriter, law books, and other considerations which foaming-at-the-mouth, blood-thirsty, escape-prone monsters don't receive."

Ted realized these objectives and more. When Katsaris balked at a court-order improvement in Ted's cell lighting, his exercise regimen, and other "considerations," Bundy named the sheriff as one of several co-defendants in a $300,000 civil suit. It cost Katsaris $7,000 of his own money to defend himself. Katsaris later acknowledged to Hugh Ted's amazing ability to flourish in adversity. (Just like King Rat.) "I mean," said the sheriff, "he got Special! Special! Special! Special!"

Bundy also enjoyed playing lawyer again. That spring, he was convinced that Nita Neary's identification of the man with the club at the Chi Omega door would be the pivot of the prosecution's case. He wrote the public defenders a letter ordering them to go to Neary's parents' home in Indiana and to conduct a surprise interview. Bundy gave them 115 questions to ask the witness.

When at Mike Minerva's direction, Neary was forewarned of the interview, Ted exploded in anger at the "deviations" from his plan. "It was not pursued—not properly," he wrote to Farmer. "And this has disappointed me."

When murder indictments were handed up in July 1978, Bundy began issuing periodic "Statements to the Media" in which he complained of "the unfairness of it all" and compared his treatment to that of Soviet dissidents.

He tangled repeatedly with Judge John A. Rudd, who continued to refuse to allow Millard Farmer to represent Bundy. Rudd, a crusty, no-nonsense jurist, ruled again and again against Farmer, referring to the contempt citation against Farmer as among the reasons he felt the attorney would be a "disruptive influence" in court and therefore not in Ted's best interests.

Farmer fought back, going to federal court for relief, but he finally lost his bid to represent Ted. Bundy's vindication, such as it was, came later in the year when the Florida supreme court ordered Rudd to disqualify himself as per a defense motion that Rudd had shown bias against the defendant.

An autumn trial date for the Chi Omega case was set, but it wasn't until the summer of 1979 that the case was at last brought to court. At first, the delays were due to the *pro se* defendant. Sooner or later, Ted knew, he would have to allow Mike Minerva to represent him. But before Ted ceded titular control of his defense, he was driven to gratify his warped ego by demonstrating again and again his control over people.

A favored tool in this game was the deposition, in which witnesses are questioned prior to trial on the facts to which they are prepared to attest. Not only did Ted call scores of policemen and lab technicians to be interviewed by him at the jail, he also demanded to see the surviving Chi Omega sisters.

The authorities had no recourse but to comply. One by one, the girls were brought before him and forced, under Bundy's questioning, to relive the bloody early hours of January 15, 1978. Even Karen Chandler, who had survived physical assault by Bundy, now had to submit to his will.

Finally, in early 1979, Bundy accepted Mike Minerva as his counsel. Sometime in March, Minerva visited Ted in the Leon County jail. According to Ted, Minerva announced that he had just finished reviewing Bundy's statements to Chapman, Patchen, and Bodiford. "He felt the statements were devastating," Bundy later told me "and there was no way we could keep them out of court. He didn't see how we could win the case."

Still, according to Ted, Minerva then told him that Larry Simpson would trade a life sentence for a confession if it could be arranged soon; once the strength of the prosecution's case was revealed in upcoming hearings, the state attorney would be under irresistible pressure to press on to trial. Bundy absolutely refused to consider a confession and was enraged, as he told me, when Minerva said, "I wouldn't advise a client to do this unless I thought he was culpable."

Ted at that moment marked his attorney for revenge. By being frank with Bundy in an effort to save his life, Minerva had threatened him. As Dr. Tanay had noted, guilt, to Ted, was an abstraction to be debated in court according to the rules. Bundy insisted that the people on his side also think that way, and no deviations would be brooked.

Nothing further was said about the matter until May of 1979 on the weekend that the state of Florida put John Spenkelink to death at the state prison. The day before the electrocution, Ted received a visit from Millard Farmer.

Both Farmer and Mike Minerva refused comment to us on their dealings with Bundy and each other, but from what Ted told us it appears that the Atlanta attorney had come to Florida to try to maneuver Bundy into saving his own life. Farmer would expend a great amount of effort in this cause, more than most busy attorneys would devote to a case they don't represent. That he did so suggests extralegal motivation, perhaps even guilt at having failed once to help Ted in Colorado. Maybe someone could have perceived Bundy's condition then, had it diagnosed and dealt with, and thus prevented the later Florida killings.

Farmer chose for his visit a time when Ted might be in mind

of his own mortality, and he presented his plan in a way that suggests a shrewd appreciation for Bundy's psychopathology.

"Ted," Bundy remembered Farmer saying to him in his cell, "I don't like the way the prosecution against you is shaping up. You're not getting any play. You're not disturbing their pace."

This was bald flattery, an appeal to Ted's conceit as an attorney. And to Ted, it ratified what he had been saying about his defense. Ever since Minerva had told Bundy he thought him guilty, Ted had sniped at the public defender, calling his methods too circumspect, uninspired.

Farmer, says Bundy, then brought up the plea-bargain agreement again. This time, however, it was presented as a ploy, a calculated move in the continuing legal game. As Ted tells the story, Farmer argued that playing with the deal would lull the prosecution. Sometime later, the case against him in disarray, Bundy could suddenly come to court and claim the confession had been signed under duress and *then* demand to be tried.

Later that afternoon, Minerva himself came to Ted's cell. "Is what Millard told me true?" he asked.

"Yes," Ted answered, thinking himself part of a plot. "I want you to explore the possibility of a plea bargain."

Apparently persuaded that his plan had a chance, Farmer flew to Seattle, where first Carole Boone and then Louise Bundy were enlisted in support of the plea bargain. Farmer convinced them both that the issue of guilt or innocence notwithstanding. Ted would be convicted and sentenced to execution unless he agreed to the plea bargain.

The attorney moved rapidly. In a matter of days, Ted was told that Simpson and Bob Dekle (who was in charge of the Leach prosecution) had agreed to accept the deal. The victims' families had endorsed it. And the two assigned judges, Edward Cowart and Wallace Jopling, were ready to sit in joint session to hear the plea.

"Suddenly," Ted told me, "it dawned on me that Millard had gotten his foot in the door in some devious way to put me in a position of accepting a plea bargain. I felt like he was conceding that I was guilty. And if you look at the cases he takes, that's essentially what he does, just avoids the death penalty. I didn't consider myself in that category."

Bundy began plotting his revenge for being drawn into the plea-bargain scheme. However, his enmity was directed not at Millard Farmer, but at Mike Minerva—who very possibly was unaware of what Farmer was doing. Bundy, the arch manipulator, could forgive and even appreciate a clever maneuver. More important, Farmer hadn't made the mistake of telling Ted he thought he was guilty. That was Minerva's sin in Ted's eyes, and now the public defender would be made to pay for his apostasy.

He allowed the subterfuge to continue. Carole and Louise flew down to be near him and to encourage him to go through with the deal. According to both Carole and Ted as well as a guard in the jail, the two took advantage on at least one visit together to consummate their relationship.

Joe Aloi, chief investigator on Mike Minerva's staff, was present at the jail through much of the tense time leading up to Bundy's scheduled appearance before Cowart and Jopling. "You woulda loved it!" he says. "Carole Boone was runnin' in, beggin' Bundy. His mother was begging him. Bundy was eating it up."

Ted denies it, but Joe Aloi also insists that Bundy was popping pills the morning he was due in court. "About an hour before," says Aloi, "Ted was really ripped, trashed."

Drugged or not, Bundy's mind that morning was upon vengeance against his attorney. Sitting in the holding cell, "I began to derive satisfaction," Ted later told me, "from the fact that I was going to stand up and slap these people in the face for what they were doing to me."

Ken Katsaris was accused of packing the courtroom that day, telling every law-enforcement officer and interested attorney to come watch Bundy confess. Katsaris denies having done so, but somehow word did get out that Ted was about to cop a plea. The room was jammed.

"I couldn't believe the masses of people who were hanging around," Vic Africano, the lawyer who would later represent Ted in the Leach case, told me. Africano remembers seeing Katsaris "walking around like a peacock."

Ted walked in carrying the confessions in one hand and a motion to dismiss his attorneys in the other. He stood up in court, looked around the room at the hushed crowd waiting to hear him confess, and then proceeded, as he described to me, to "skewer" Mike Minerva. He charged that the public defender was unprepared, overwhelmed by the state's case, guilty along with the rest of his attorneys of "serious mental errors," unconscionably convinced that Ted was guilty, and possessed of a 'defeatist posture."

Mike Minerva was stung. A thorough, highly ethical, and

sensitive defense attorney, his reputation was being attacked in open court before his colleagues and peers.

"Your Honor," Ted went on, glorying in the spotlight—and confirming Tanay's diagnosis—"it is not simply my point of view that I'm not receiving effectiveness of counsel. It is my position that my counsel, one, believe that I'm guilty; two, that they have told me they see no way of presenting an effective defense, and in no uncertain terms they have told me that; and three, that they see no way of avoiding conviction.

"Now, Your Honor, if this doesn't raise itself to the level of ineffectiveness of counsel, I don't know what does."

A brief recess was called. Back in the holding cell Millard Farmer gave Bundy a tired look. "Well, Ted," said Farmer, "we really gave it a try here. I've got no hard feelings, but I've only got so much time and I'm going to spend it on people who want to live."

In court, Simpson, Dekle, and the rest of the prosecutors silently signaled the defense table that the plea bargain was off; they weren't about to give Ted the legal issue of attorney incompetency in some later bid to invalidate the confessions.

Later that afternoon, Judge Cowart found no merit in Ted's assertions, but allowed Minerva to withdraw from the case.

By then, Carole Boone had boarded a plane back to Seattle. She had believed that only a plea bargain would save Ted's life, and she left Tallahassee as upset as anyone at Bundy's courtroom show. Still firm in her faith in him, Carole nevertheless seemed dismayed at this act of revenge. "Poops," she wrote him on the flight home, "check to see if you're part of the problem."

Though he was officially separated from the defense, Mike Minerva made a final vain effort to save Bundy from himself. He requested and was granted a hearing to determine if Bundy was competent to stand trial. But without Ted's cooperation, such a move was doomed, no matter how persuasive the evidence of his incompetency might be.

It was a brief hearing. Dr. Tanay told the court that he believed Bundy "does suffer from a mental disorder."

Judge Cowart asked if Ted could be expected to listen to an attorney. "On the question of willingness," Tanay replied, "I'm of the opinion that Mr. Bundy's behavior in most instances is beyond his control."

Prosecution psychiatrist Dr. Hervey Cleckley, co-author of

*The Three Faces of Eve* and this country's leading authority on psychopaths, generally agreed with Tanay's diagnosis.

But Ted Bundy would have none of it. He insisted that he was sane and innocent and demanded that his case be tried. Judge Cowart felt obliged to find him competent to do so. Bundy had gotten what he wanted. Unconcerned with the outcome of the trial or the real-world consequence of forcing his own prosecution, Ted only saw his one big chance to be somebody. On June 12, 1979, the judge granted a change of venue motion and set the trial date at June 25, in Miami.

# FIFTEEN

*The Miami Herald,* June 25, 1979
NATION'S EYES ON BUNDY

Theodore Robert Bundy, a native of Vermont, a resident of Washington, a convict of Utah, an escapee of Colorado, a prisoner of Florida, is now perhaps the most famous criminal defendant in America.

At 9:00 A.M. today in Courtroom 4-1 of the Metropolitan Justice Building in Miami, Theodore Robert Bundy goes on trial.

Ted selected earth tones for his opening appearance in court that Monday: a brown-and-white-striped sports jacket, tan shirt and slacks, brown tie, brown shoes. The look was spiffy but subdued, appropriate to his arrogated role as head of the defense team.

But behind the facade, Bundy's mind was hopelessly fractured. Like an obsessed actor who becomes the part he plays, Ted denied the substance of everything but his celebrity. He knew that nowhere else was there an alleged mass killer of his stature or one, as he saw it, who had the charisma to turn a murder trial into a vehicle for showcasing his considerable talents.

This was a Bundy far different from the bumptious young Republican of 1968 who had come to Miami as an anonymous gofer at the GOP National Convention. There as a reward for his volunteer services in Seattle, he had seen at the fountain of fame Nelson Rockefeller (Ted's candidate), Richard Nixon, the winner, and New York mayor John Lindsay, who actually shook his hand. Eleven years later, *Ted Bundy* was now the main attraction.

The press arrangements for the trial were elaborate. According to an ABC News official, the special satellite feed set up for the televised trial was transmitted to one of the largest pools of subscribing affiliates that the network had ever put together.

A public TV half-hour daily digest of trial highlights (entitled "The State of Florida vs. Theodore Robert Bundy," and broadcast with the warning "May not be suitable viewing for children") was beamed to Washington State, Utah, and Colorado and to many of the major metropolitan television markets.

Two years earlier, when Ted had sent a lengthy polemic in support of the *pro se* defense to *Time* magazine, they had declined to publish it. Now *Time* carried an article about him, as did *Newsweek*. The wire services provided trial coverage on an hourly basis, and scores of other news-gathering organizations assigned their ablest reporters to stay with the trial as long as it lasted.

On hand to share the spotlight was Carole Boone; her picture appeared in the *Washington Post* and several other papers. She granted interviews and offered certain selected reporters controlled access to her "Bunny."

Carole acted as Ted's advocate and acolyte, her part in their *folie à deux*. The association had elevated Carole from obscurity and conferred upon her a mantle of derived authority. She was jealous of these prerogatives and suspicious of anyone who tried to get too close to Ted. As far as Carole could manage it, she and Bundy now thought and acted as one.

One of the people familiar with her at the time was Chuck Doud, a *Tacoma News Tribune* editor whom Boone cultivated for advice on Ted's behalf. Carole consulted Doud before she agreed to endorse Millard Farmer's plea-bargain deal.

I later asked Doud what sort of person he thought Carole was to have devoted herself so utterly to Bundy. He answered that he thought she was part "prison groupie" and partly motivated by boredom in her life. "She really rebels against dullness," said Doud. Also, "she likes causes, and Bundy is a cause."

Carole called her open support of Bundy "going public"; previously, she had agreed to discuss him with reporters only if her name wasn't used. The decision cost Carole her job in state government and meant that she arrived in Miami nearly broke, with her teenaged son Jamey to look after while she saw to Ted's demands as well.

It was an onerous time for her, living on the largesse of reporters who bought her meals and even paid for her room. The charity was repaid, in part, with "exclusive" stories about Ted, stories that Carole hoped would depict Bundy more favorably.

She complained in print and on television that even Ted's good looks and amiability were twisted against him in the media, making innocent, wholesome qualities seem somehow sinister. She argued law, personality, and facts of the case to reporters, impressing many of them with her encyclopedic command of detail.

Her first principle was Ted's innocence, and she reacted with increasing bitterness when, as the trial went on, she saw her naive hopes of acquittal dwindle away. She blamed nearly everyone but Ted for this, particularly his attorneys. But she was most vituperative toward the press. "The people who covered Ted," she told me, "were a bunch of drunkards and people who'd rather do crossword puzzles than watch what was going on. I was really shocked to learn how a story works. I always assumed that reporters did their own work. But a mistake early on about Ted or one of the victims kept getting repeated over and over again. I didn't realize that once a story gets written other reporters rip it off and embellish it with new errors as events occur. I feel that Ted's story has been grossly misreported and misinvestigated."

Carole's lame rationalizations for Bundy's problems ran parallel to his own; as time passed she seemed ever more strongly influenced by his thinking. According to Carole, it was "unfair" to expect Ted to offer verifiable alibis. She awaits "irrefutable physical evidence" of Bundy's guilt—such as a photograph of Ted killing one of his victims—before she'll abandon her trust in him. Never mind that every rational—and legal—standard of guilt had been met, "There is no i.p.e. to date," she says. "And unless (not until) such a thing happens or unless Ted tells me that he has killed, I stand on my rock."

Actually, it was Ted's rock that Carole occupied, the core "truth" of guiltlessness that he could never abandon. Measured against it, the prospect of going to the electric chair meant little to Bundy. He refused even to acknowledge that such an outcome to the trial was possible, or that anyone could hold Theodore Bundy responsible for acts whose reality he denied.

Representing Ted in Miami were Margaret Good, a twenty-nine-year-old appellate specialist who had never tried a felony case; Lynn Thompson, thirty, a quiet, methodical lawyer who until just before the trial had assumed his involvement would be restricted to legal research; and Ed Harvey, twenty-nine, who for a time was head of the team. Harvey would ask to be excused before the trial's end.

Into their midst came Bob Haggard, a local attorney, whose help was urged upon them by Joe Aloi and Emil Spielman, a psychologist retained by the defense to help them with jury selection. Thirty-four years old, blond and boyish-looking, Bob Haggard had one commodity sorely lacking among the defense team: experience.

Not modest about his abilities, Haggard was soon giving directions. That brought him into direct conflict with Ted, and chaos ensued. From the sidelines, a dismayed Vic Africano, Ted's attorney in the upcoming Leach trial, looked on. "Haggard," Vic recalls, "ran into a personality conflict with the client, and that caused the client to want to take over even more. With Ted being somewhat of a manipulator, playing one person off against the other, it was a total disaster."

Ted's intention was plain from the first day, when he rose in court to be the first member of the defense to speak for the defense. It was Bundy's pleasure that the trial be postponed for one day; he wanted more time to prepare. "What in the world," he asked Judge Cowart, "can I add to a defense I don't know anything about?"

He also wanted perquisites—a different desk and better lighting in his cell, access to the jail law library—which the judge granted. But Cowart, a jowly ex-cop with a shrewd judicial mind, wasn't going to allow Ted to dictate the tempo of the trial. He denied the motion for more time.

Bundy was peeved; he had grown accustomed to getting his own way. Several days later, he violated the judge's gag order when he grandly explained to a knot of reporters that *he* was in charge of jury selection. "The final decision on all jurors is up to me," Ted said. "That is the way it should be."

The quotes appeared in the next morning's papers, and a furious Cowart ordered that thenceforward the defendant would be returned to a holding cell during each recess. The punishment was not unlike a stern father ordering his fractious child to stand in the corner.

Jury selection required five days of mind-numbing voir dire, the repetitive questioning of eighty jury candidates by judge, defense, and prosecution, before twelve were chosen and three alternate jurors seated. Because the panel would be sequestered for several weeks, one prospective juror was allowed to leave after he explained that his wife had sustained a shoulder injury; he was needed each night to unfasten her bra for her. Another man, divorced, was excused to be at home with his children. His alcoholic ex-wife, he conceded, lived with him, too. But she wasn't dependable. Still another candidate, a young woman, was dismissed after she volunteered to the court that looking at Ted Bundy scared her.

At times, Ted seemed to be as bored as everyone else with the interminable questioning, although he huddled constantly with Haggard, Good, Harvey, Thompson, and their jury expert, Dr. Spielman, who prepared a series of profiles to aid in their decision making. "You've got so many cooks," Judge Coward drawled at one point, "I hope someone's stirring the broth."

On Friday night, June 29, Ted's twelve jurors—seven men (four black, three white) and five women (three black, one white, one Hispanic)—were sworn and sequestered. They ranged in occupation from a Texaco engineer to a maid.

Juror number seven, Robert Burns Corbett, who installed awnings for a living, said being sequestered would be tolerable. "My wife likes to run me out of the house every once in a while," he explained.

Floy C. Mitchell, fifty-two, a widow, said her hobbies included reading the Bible and watching television. She liked soap operas.

Juror number eight, Vernon Swindle, was a gasoline station pump repairman. He'd been to a murder trial before, his cousin's.

The Texaco engineer, Rudolph E. Treml, eventually was elected jury foreman. A specialist in fluid dynamics, his major reading included *Platt's Oilgram* and *The Wall Street Journal*.

The last juror seated was James L. Bennett, a forty-three-year-old truck driver, who, like everyone else in the jury pool, had been asked if he knew anything about the case. "You'd have to almost be in Siberia not to know about it," he answered.

Once the jury was impaneled, Judge Cowart turned his attention to evidentiary issues. Over the next week, the avuncular judge, fond of quoting the Bible and adding "Bless your heart" to his obiter dicta from the bench, would rule on just how much of the state's case would be heard by the jury.

Prosecutor Larry Simpson and his assistant, Dan McKeever, won two important rounds and lost another. Nita Neary would be allowed to describe her encounter with the intruder at the Chi Omega door, and Dr. Richard Souviron, a forensic odontologist and the state's most important forensic expert witness, would testify on the bite marks. However, Ted's statements to detectives Chapman, Patchen, and Bodiford, so highly indicative of guilt, were ruled inadmissible because of several tape malfunctions.

"That," growled McKeever to a reporter, "is a disaster with a capital D!" Both prosecutors knew that their eyewitnesses alone would not be sufficient to convict Bundy; much now would come down to the successful presentation of the complex forensic evidence.

Another disappointment came when Judge Cowart refused to allow the jury to hear that a pantyhose mask similar to the one found in Cheryl Thomas' apartment had been recovered three years earlier from Ted's VW by the Utah police. Cowart ruled that the "probative value" of the Utah mask did not outweigh its "prejudicial concept." McKeever was miffed, again. "People," he said, "just don't carry pantyhose masks around with them."

But despite their setbacks, Simpson and McKeever went to trial with a number of qualitative advantages. As they began presenting their case, they were working with a jury sensitized by seventeen months of publicity since the sorority house murders. The men and women selected to judge Ted Bundy might honestly tell the court their verdict would be based upon the evidence, but the overwhelming bulk of what they had been exposed to in the media was suggestive of guilt. Never was Ted Bundy mentioned except in connection with murder and mayhem.

Then there was the nature of the crimes, which powerfully affected the jury. They were shown, in the words of defense attorney Margaret Good, "indescribably gruesome" color photographs of the crime scenes, of Margaret Bowman's battered head, of Lisa Levy's torn nipple, the bite mark on her buttock, her bludgeoned face. The savagery sickened the jury; one woman nearly vomited at the sight of the evidence.

Also marked into evidence were piles of bloodstained clothing and bedding, the pantyhose ligature from around Margaret Bowman's neck, and the pantyhose mask found in Cheryl Thomas' apartment. The jurors were shown the Clairol bottle used to sodomize Lisa Levy.

Karen Chandler and Kathy Kleiner testified to the injuries they received. Cheryl Thomas limped into court. "I had five skull fractures and multiple contusions in my head," she testified. "The eighth nerve was damaged and I lost the hearing of my left ear and equilibrium. And I had a broken jaw and my left shoulder was pulled out of joint."

Perhaps the prosecution's greatest courtroom asset was the

defendant himself. "I would anticipate," Dr. Tanay had written months before, "that in the unlikely event that the prosecution's case against him should weaken, he would through his behavior bolster the prosecution's case. I have much less doubt about Mr. Bundy's capacity to assist prosecution than his ability to assist his own counsel."

Ted was lost to reality. Bundy felt, in the *Miami Herald*'s phrase, the eyes of the nation upon him. Each day in court, the television cameraman and a still photographer trained their lenses on the defense table, capturing Ted's every move. Each night in the jail, Bundy could watch himself on television. Each morning, he could read about himself in the papers.

Carole Boone sat behind him in court, eyeing Ted with adoration. His groupies stared, too. Some sent him lewdly suggestive notes or asked for his autograph. Others were content to sit for a full day in court, happy if just once he would look their way.

This was heady stuff. Bundy preened for the audience and exploited their fascination with him. Before the jury began hearing evidence, he went so far as to act as defendant, attorney, and witness in the battle to exclude the Utah pantyhose mask from the trial.

These were silly and harmless indulgences. But Bundy also insisted upon representing himself before the jury once the trial was under way. Since it was decided that he was not going to testify in front of them—Larry Simpson would have gleefully exploited Ted's lack of alibi—the appearances as his own attorney raised questions among the jurors. Why, they wondered, if Bundy was innocent and so well-spoken, didn't he simply tell them what he was doing that night?

Also damaging to the defense were the content and thrust of Ted's questioning. He ragged Pensacola officer David Lee over the policeman's alleged brutality toward him rather than concentrating on the prosecution contention that his own behavior that night was consistent with guilty knowledge of crimes.

On the day that the prosecution saturated the jurors with the blood and gore of the crimes, Bundy cross-examined Officer Ray Crew. Slowly and always eliciting detail, Ted led Crew back through the awful night, searing the crimes' bloody aftermath into the jurors' minds. Ted made sure everyone had an enduring impression of the brutal handiwork.

These appearances as his own attorney grew less frequent as the trial wore on. Ted continued to join each bench conference with Judge Cowart and he did not lose his zest for courtroom spectacle. But he was beginning to buckle.

Rigid as Ted's mental apparatus was, it was also brittle. The first cracks had appeared even before the trial when Bundy discovered his Miami jailers intended to treat him no better than their 700 other prisoners. Ted felt put upon. His resentment intensified when the judge began removing him from the courtroom during recesses.

Bundy's paranoia worked on him. He was sure that his attorneys were keeping secrets from him, and he soon believed that Judge Cowart was part of a conspiracy to break him. As his sense of control began to slip, he grew angrier and more afraid.

Late one night, eleven days into the trial, he petulantly flung an orange from his cell and broke the light bulb in the hallway. He then stuffed toilet paper in his keyhole and refused to budge the next morning when the guards came to wake him. The uncontrollable child in him was throwing a tantrum.

After presenting their eyewitnesses, including Nita Neary, who could not be certain that Bundy was the man she saw at the door but whose identification was nevertheless strong enough not to be damaged under cross-examination from Bob Haggard, Simpson and McKeever went on to the pivotal physical evidence. As Larry Simpson later told Hugh, Bundy's prosecution "was nothing less than a tribute to the progress we've made in forensic science. Without the physical evidence and the laboratory work that was done, we wouldn't have made it to first base."

The first important exhibit was the pantyhose mask found at Cheryl Thomas' apartment. In it, testified Florida Department of Law Enforcement analyst Pat Lasko, were two hairs "microscopically similar" to Ted's. When questioned by the defense, the technician conceded that since she had not examined head hairs from every person on earth, she couldn't say absolutely that the two she found on the mask were from Bundy. But within the range of certainty that hair analysis allows, she was firm: "Either those hairs came from Mr. Bundy," she testified, "or from someone else whose hair is exactly like his who happened to have been at the Dunwoody apartment."

More critical were the human tooth wounds discovered on Lisa Levy's buttock. Bite-mark experts—forensic odontologists—know that human teeth exhibit individual characteristics nearly as unique as fingerprints and usually simpler to analyze than hair samples. Under the right conditions, a forensic odontologist can say "within a reasonable degree of dental certainty" whether or not a specific set of teeth was responsible for a bite wound.

Only rarely do scientists rely upon an excised wound itself to make these comparisons; the pliant tissue is inevitably distorted in removal or in preservation. They much prefer to use—as they did in the Levy case—a well-focused color photo of the undisturbed wound taken soon after the attack. In this instance, the doctors were also aided by a ruler placed next to the wound in the picture. The ruler made it possible to create an exact-scale reproduction of the wound. Moreover, since the true color of the ruler was known, they could use that standard (a known color value) to establish the amount of tissue discoloration associated with each tooth imprint. This, in turn, told the scientists that the wounds had been inflicted within minutes of Lisa's death.

Larry Simpson's first expert, Dr. Richard Souviron of Miami, testified that Lisa Levy had been bitten twice. This was another analytical aid. With two so-called rings of marks to work with, each mark could be double-checked.

Souviron used for illustration the picture of the wound and a huge color photograph of Bundy's mouth with the lips retracted and Ted's incisors, canines, bicuspids, and molars glinting horribly out from red gums in the camera's strobe light. Several jurors squirmed at the sight.

The doctor pointed out to them the one row of bruises Ted left the first time he bit her, then the second "ring" of bottom tooth marks left as he dropped his lower jaw, pivoted slightly with his upper teeth still clamped down, and bit her again. Three short scratches were also visible. Souviron said that they were consistent with three of Bundy's upper teeth being pulled along her skin as he opened his mouth, turned his head, and bit her again.

Even before Souviron and the state's other expert, Dr. Lowell Levine, then a consultant to the New York City medical examiner's office, had examined their wax and stone impressions of Ted's teeth, they looked at the wound photograph and saw the marks from what obviously were human incisors, canines, and a premolar. The incisors interested them most.

A person with perfect lower teeth would have left four rectangular marks, all in a row. Whoever bit Lisa Levy, they could see, had "bumps" on his two lower incisors, while the two outer teeth were beveled, producing knife-edged marks. They were also slanted.

When the scientists looked at their casts of Bundy's teeth, all these individual characteristics—and more—were obvious. "It is a practical impossibility," Dr. Levine later told me, "to find any other set of teeth that could have made those marks."

In court, each expert was asked by Larry Simpson if he had an opinion—"within a reasonable degree of dental certainty"—as to who bit Lisa Levy. Neither hesitated to name Theodore Robert Bundy.

Late in the trial, Ted would try to introduce photographic evidence supporting his claim that one of his *top* teeth (one of the three that would have left the scrapes) had been chipped in jail between the time of the murder and the day that Souviron took his impressions.

Cowart disallowed these pictures, which in any case would not have affected Souviron's and Levine's conclusions. Their matches had been made on the basis of Ted's bottom teeth.

After two weeks of testimony from forty-nine prosecution witnesses, Larry Simpson rested his case on July 19, 1979. Then it was the demoralized defense team's turn. Most of what they presented to the jury was put together in a hurried and slapdash manner, a reflection of the constant turmoil Ted was creating and a sign, too, of their inexperience.

They felt they had one hope in a piece of physical evidence that they argued positively excluded their client from at least one of the assaults. The disputed specimen was the semen stain found in Cheryl Thomas's bedding.

The stain had been tested at the FDLE lab by serologist Dr. Richard Stephens. The scientists had looked for indications of the stain donor's blood type; about four out of five people naturally secrete their blood-type antigens A, B, AB, or O into other body fluids such as sweat, mucus, and semen. In the presence of the proper substance, these antigens will clot in a test tube, thus indicating blood type.

Ted Bundy is a type-O secretor, meaning, to the defense, that if it was his semen (or his chewing gum in Lisa Levy's hair) then Stephens should have gotten an O-positive blood-type result. The gum yielded nothing, and his tests of the semen stain were officially "inconclusive." That, argued the defense, was consistent with the donor being a non-secretor and therefore someone other than Ted Bundy.

The defense's own technical expert, technician Michael Grubb of the Institute of Forensic Science in Oakland, California, was brought to Miami, where Ted provided him with a sample of his semen. Grubb testified that his analysis showed Ted was an

O-type secretor, and that Stephens' tests should have been positive if, in fact, Ted had left the stain. Grubb did not personally test the questioned sample.

But "inconclusive," as Stephens later explained to Hugh, is a fairly common result in the lab and meant just what it said: it wasn't a result that excluded anyone. Almost 60 percent of all such stains examined in the FDLE lab in that period yielded "inconclusive" results on donors' blood types. Sometimes the test worked; sometimes it didn't.

Dr. Grubb's testimony did not have its intended effect of planting doubt in the jury's mind. Few of the panel seemed to grasp the subtleties of conclusive versus inconclusive results in the secretor tests. And since the state had not argued that the stain came from Bundy, they saw little reason for the defense arguing so strenuously that it hadn't.

Nor could Dr. Dwayne DeVore, the defense's expert in forensic odontology, offer much in refutation of the damaging Souviron and Levine testimony. DeVore, a professor at the University of Maryland, disputed Sourviron on the uniqueness of Bundy's twisted teeth; he said such a pattern was fairly common.

The prosecution case had come across far stronger than Bundy had anticipated. He was satisfied that guilt had not been demonstrated, but he saw, from his rock, that the charade he'd orchestrated might in fact conclude with a conviction. It confirmed his belief that life was unfair.

Inside him, a guilty verdict could be ignored as meaningless, and furthermore he could rationalize the expected decision as a terrible mistake, the fault of someone else. The blame, he decided, would go to his attorneys.

Bundy complained to Judge Cowart that his attorneys were excluding him from important decisions, such as the choice of Bob Haggard to deliver the defense's final argument. To that, Ted said, he was "unalterably opposed."

Cowart had blessed Ted's heart several times, allowing Bundy to carry on in court—outside the jury's presence—and then smoothly protecting the trial record from appeal points with encomia for the defense team. But now he seemed out of patience with Ted's antics.

"This court," he answered irritably, "is finding clearly and unequivocally you've had the most counsel I've ever seen any defendant in the state of Florida have! I'm not going to hear any more nonsensical information about competency or incompetency of counsel.''

But Bundy's carping continued; and Cowart, concerned that Ted was trying to salt the trial transcript with potential points for appeal, got a few points of his own on the record. "This dancing around and putting innuendos on the record is not satisfactory,'' he said. Then he called Ted's bluff. "You have a Sixth Amendment right to represent yourself. And if you want to do so, the court is not going to deprive you of it.''

Ted didn't have to fire Bob Haggard; the volunteer attorney quit and soon was to be found available for interviews in the ninth-floor media center. Ed Harvey wanted to leave, but Judge Cowart wouldn't let him. Harvey at that time suggested that Ted be given another competency hearing. With his defense now totally in disarray, Ted contemplated delivering the closing argument himself. But he was too far gone, and he knew it.

The inexperienced Margaret Good spoke for him on the last day.

The case went to the jury on Tuesday afternoon, July 24, 2:57 P.M. Carole Boone, now furious with the press, the judge, the prosecution, and the defense, spent most of the afternoon with Louise Bundy, who had arrived for the end of the trial.

Ted's mother was grateful for Carole's support and pleased that her son had so lively and articulate a champion. But Mrs. Bundy's natural reserve tempered her enthusiasm for Carole. The heat of Boone's attachment to Ted made Louise uneasy.

Bundy's exhausted attorneys—sure as anyone of the verdict— retired to the nearby Holiday Inn to await the inevitable. Ted himself found access to a telephone and told reporters he felt a hung jury was probable. Bundy clung to a belief that James Bennett, the truck driver on the panel, was sympathetic to the defense. He also was heartened by reports that laughter had been heard coming from the jury room; laughing juries, it is said, do not convict.

Carole's son, Jamey, was even more optimistic. He had been told by his mother that once all the nonsense was over, he and she would live somewhere with Ted.

Around 9:00 P.M., Carole and Louise were sitting in the courtroom, not thirty feet from Ted, waiting for Judge Cowart to send the jury back to their hotel for the night. Jamey arrived and sat down by them.

Louise was edgy. "It's so late!" she said to Carole. "Why doesn't the judge send them home?"

Just then the court bailiff, Mr. Watson, came into the courtroom and announced that the jury had reached a verdict.

"It's too soon! It's too soon!" Louise Bundy gasped.

Carole held her hand.

The twelve jurors filed in, their eyes averted from Ted, who stood up to hear their verdict. Louise, her back absolutely straight, inched forward in her seat.

She watched her son sag for an instant as court clerk Shirley Lewis began to read the verdicts. "Guilty," Lewis said, seven times.

Louise Bundy could not absorb this. The boy she'd suckled, her love child, the issue of her one unrestrained moment in life, was being adjudged in court an archfiend who had ripped and torn, bludgeoned, mutilated, *murdered* young women.

Louise was silent and still. But down the row from her and Carole and Jamey sat three girls who looked like co-eds. With the second "guilty" from the court clerk, each began making excited clapping motions with her hands. And each—ever so slightly—was bouncing in her seat.

The courtroom emptied quickly. Ted was taken to a jail conference room, where he spoke by telephone with Carole and began to call reporters. He told Richard Larsen of the *Seattle Times* that he was surprised at the jury's decision and the speed with which they made it. "I just read them all wrong," he said. "We thought we had some holdouts in there." He seemed calm over the phone.

Louise left the courtroom, only to face a battery of cameras and reporters. Her shock by then had been replaced by anger and determination. "This isn't it!" she told them defiantly. "We are by no means finished!" With tears in her eyes, she went on: "The family is devastated, but we will stick by him because we know he is innocent."

Most of the jurors later declined comment to the press, but Vernon Swindle, the gas pump repairman, told the *Miami Herald* that he had been persuaded of Ted's guilt by the mass of circumstantial evidence. He also felt that the defense presentation was "dragged out and boring."

James Bennett, the truck driver Ted thought was on his side, told the newspaper that Bundy seemed "incapable of emotion." The bitemark evidence convinced Bennett that Ted was a murderer, Bennett said.

From his quoted remarks, Bennett also appears to have thought Ted was stupid, or at the very least a fool. "We wondered," he explained, "that if a guy made bite marks like that, wouldn't he take the trouble to alter his mouth? I mean, I would have knocked all my teeth out before they caught me." If Ted had done so, he surely would have avoided conviction.

Rudolph Treml, the Texaco engineer who was elected jury foreman, told the *Herald* that five votes were needed before the jurors were unanimous on guilt. He remembered his first impression of Ted.

"Here was this guy in a Madison Avenue suit with his shoes shined," said Treml, "and who looked just like me. I couldn't do such a horrible thing. How could he have?"

In the end, "there were some things that didn't quite piece together." However, he went on, "everything just kept building. It couldn't be just so much coincidence."

There was no doubt that Ted would be given death for his crimes; only the ritual of the so-called penalty phase of the trial remained before sentencing.

Carol DaRonch, now married, came as a witness in the penalty phase, as did detective Jerry Thompson, from Salt Lake City, and detective Mike Fisher, from Aspen. Ted's attorneys did not care to have DaRonch testify and agreed, in lieu of testimony, to a negotiated statement that was read to the court. Thompson produced a copy of Ted's kidnap conviction, and Fisher was used to establish that Bundy was supposed to be on trial in Colorado on the night of the Chi Omega killings.

Against these "aggravating" circumstances, the defense's major weapon was Louise Bundy. "Now settle down, mother," Judge Cowart gently told her as Louise began in a faltering voice. "Don't be nervous, okay?"

Sadness and fear ringed with righteousness colored her testimony as Ted's mother told the jury that he was "my pride and joy, our relationship was always very special." Speaking from her heart, Louise called the death penalty "the most primitive and barbaric thing that a human being can impose on another." She added: "I don't think the state of Florida is above the laws of God."

The jurors were touched, but were reminded by Larry Simpson that no mother had been there to plead for Margaret Bowman or Lisa Levy when they were killed. It took them one hour and forty minutes and three ballots to decide that Ted Bundy deserved electrocution.

Judge Cowart sentenced Ted on Tuesday, July 31, 1979. After reviewing for the court the bloody details of the murders, Cowart characterized them in the language of the statute under which the death penalty is imposed in Florida.

"This court," he said somberly, "finds that the killings were indeed heinous, atrocious, and cruel in that they were extremely wicked, shockingly evil, vile, and the product of a design to inflict a high degree of pain and with utter indifference to human life."

Ted himself then spoke for half an hour. He criticized the press and spoke of his "massive disappointment" that the jurors hadn't deliberated longer. As he went on, he grew less and less coherent.

"In a way," Ted said, occasionally stuttering, trying and failing to hold back his tears, "this is my opening statement. What we have seen here is just the first round, uh, the second round, uh, an early round after the first battle."

His thoughts were running together. Ted pleaded and argued at the same time. About the victims' families, he said, "I don't think it's hypocritical of me, God knows, to say that I sympathize with them to the best I can." He called the Chi Omega killings "without mercy, vicious, cruel, and unfeeling."

It was an eerie speech, Ted's mad scene. Out of control—out of his mind—Ted stood trembling before Judge Cowart and a hushed courtroom.

"I will tell the court that I am not really able to accept the verdict," he said. *Not really able to accept the verdict* "because all the verdict found in part was that these crimes had been committed. They erred in finding who committed them."

Here was the twisted logic of the psychopath in statements as strange and unnerving as any ever uttered in a courtroom.

"And," Ted continued, "as a consequence I cannot accept the sentence, even though one will be imposed, even though I recognize the lawful way in which the court will impose it, because it is not a sentence to me." *It is not a sentence to me,* "it is a sentence to someone else who is not standing here today."

Ted's speech rambled on and ended. "So I will be tortured for and suffer for and receive the pain for that act," he said, "but I will not share the burden and the guilt. That's all I have."

As clearly as he could, Ted had revealed to the court—and the world—the nature of his condition. He denied the legitimacy of the proceedings, the verdict, and the impending sentence. In front of a huge national audience, he declared himself as the only reality, a non-contingent being beyond mortal judgment.

Edward D. Cowart was unimpressed. "Mr. Bundy," he said when Ted was done, "the court is going to sentence the person found guilty of the offense. Your name, sir, was in the verdict form." With that, he condemned Bundy to electrocution and then gaveled the trial to a close.

# SIXTEEN

It required several weeks of what Ted calls his "healing process" to restore him to calm. It was a withdrawn, chrysalid phase he'd undergone first in the Utah and Colorado lockups, and then in Tallahassee's Leon County jail. Each time reality blitzed his frail defenses—at the Utah trial, during his second escape when he went helter-skelter, and then in Miami in front of the cameras—Bundy retreated to metamorphose. Each time, a new-model Ted would then emerge, another mad abstraction further detached from the real world.

On Death Row at Florida State Prison, the reinvented Bundy blocked all thoughts of Old Sparky behind the door two cells down from his. He began to deny the future as effectively as he rejected the past. His main occupation was adjusting to life on The Row and conditioning himself against the threat of his next and last trial, for the murder of Kimberly Leach.

Bundy initially was housed on Q Wing at the prison, otherwise known as the "Bug" Wing. It was home not only to Death Row prisoners, but as Ted wrote in an early letter to Carole, Q Wing contained "the uncontrollable and the insane from all around the institution." Bundy, who didn't think of himself as sick at all, didn't understand why he'd been put there.

He met pederasts, sodomites, pyromaniacs, infanticides, parricides, and every imaginable type in between. He met, as he wrote to Boone, "the infamous 'shit-eater' whose grotesque fetish is closely followed by the 'shit-buyer' who purchases the stuff from other inmates and smears it all over his body." In such surroundings, Ted's degenerate urges lost much of their singularity. He was just one of the bugs.

It did take Bundy a while to convince his fellow Death Row inmates that he was not "a rich, naive college boy, someone who people can run games on.'' Everyone tried to borrow money, sell him watches, share his dope, take things from him.

His strategy was first to cause trouble, the mark of a "stand-up con.'' Ted refused to take down posters Louise had sent him, and he spit at the guard who ordered him to do so. Result: A "Disciplinary Report'' and thirty-day loss of privileges.

Another time, Ted later told me, "some guy came up to the gate down the hall from my cell. He sounded like an officer. He said, 'Is Bundy down there?' And the trusty says, 'Yeah.' And the guy says, 'Well, is Bundy a sissy?'

"I doubt that I can duplicate the string of red-hot expletives that came out of my mouth. It was something like *'You dog mutherfuckin' punk bring your fat ass down here I'll show you who's a sissy I'll turn you out you mutherfucker I'll leave you on the floor dyin' in your own blood I'll slit you right open mutherfucker!'* ''

Ted smiled at the recollection. "Or words to that effect,'' he said.

Bundy found also that the savagery of his crimes helped to establish him on The Row. There, he encouraged people to think him guilty. "I know a lot of guys wonder what I might do if pushed far enough,'' he explained to me.

He enjoyed frightening visitors to Death Row as well. "I had this one man who put his arm around a woman and escorted her past my cell,'' Bundy recalled to Hugh. "She was just scared to *death!*

"Other people have this fascination, too. They stand and look at me. I can look in my television and see their reflections. They all cluster around in big groups; not one at a time, but four or five at once. Then I turn around and they scatter!''

Although Ted momentarily disappeared from the six o'clock news and the front pages, his national following did not diminish. The Ted he'd created for the cameras continued to receive heavy fan mail from all parts of the country.

Miss R.A. in Colorado wrote: "I used to date a man in Aspen who told me in gory detail about killing girls, and you're not a bit like him. I can tell from your nice face that you're a 'good guy'; woman's intuition.''

From Washington State, Mr. R.H. opined: "I think you are a Political Prisoner and President Carter should look her [*sic*] in this country about human writes [*sic*] instead of Screaming about the Russians and the Argentines.''

Mental patients contacted Bundy continually. "I hope you

make parole or [are] released cause I know your [*sic*] not a murderer; You've been good to me,'' Wrote Miss L.W. "If you get out of that place come see me.''

Another group intensely interested in Ted were Christian fundamentalists. One woman advised, "Surely Ted you must have a HORRIBLE evil spirit inside you. One of Satan's imps for sure. It's HIGH TIME, Ted, to repent of these sins and ask God's forgiveness.'' Still another assured Bundy that "while God hates your sins He still loves you. . . . God has a plan for your life.''

The strangest correspondents of all were Bundy's groupies. Some exhibited a mothering instinct gone seriously awry, while others apparently lived in an appalling fantasy world that required an unattainable object of devotion.

Most worshipful was a woman named Janet, who began writing Bundy in the summer of 1979. He returned a single letter after going to Death Row, enough response from her hero to inspire Janet for months. In September, she wrote him, "I got the letter you sent me and read it again. I kissed it all over and held it to me. I don't mind telling you I am crying. I just don't see how I can stand it anymore. I love you so very much, Ted.''

Janet sent him photographs of her and begged for pictures back. Her letters poured in. "I adore you and I just can't stand not hearing from you,'' she wrote. "It's absolutely tearing me apart. You are so precious to me. I want you so much I can almost taste it. What I wouldn't give to have an hour alone with you. I would show you in every way how much I love you. There's nothing I wouldn't do.''

Janet, who was married, was jealous of Carole. "I guess I should not be writing to you until I get a letter from you letting me know just where I stand,'' she told him. Janet was willing to overlook Carole, even though "you can't imagine how bad it hurts me and still is tearing my insides out.''

By now Ted was disabused of the notion that he could make a trial into his own stage; his prior incarnation had created the furor in Miami that nearly undid him. The experience had been too painful.

His attitude toward the Leach trial, scheduled for Orlando in early January of 1980, was to ignore it as best he could. "Orlando must be a non-event,'' he wrote Carole in December. He was determined not "to sustain the physical and mental abuse of this trial.''

He did consult with his new attorney, Vic Africano, and

offered a few minor suggestions for the defense. But Bundy disengaged himself and stuck to a typical and wholly unrealistic argument. While he conceded that he'd probably be convicted again, he maintained that guilt could not be demonstrated. "They just can't prove it!" he told Africano over and over.

Africano, a New Jersey native, had taken his law degree at the same time as Mike Minerva at the University of Florida in Gainesville. The attorney settled in north-central Florida several years ago with his wife, Betty, daughter of one of the First Families of Live Oak (population 6,732), a farming center about thirty miles west of Lake City. Africano is well liked among the town's thick-shouldered and square-fingered farmers; he fits in at the alligator roasts, the raucous neighborly bar at the Live Oak Elks' Club, or on the golf links, where the talk is of horses, crop prices, hunting, and local politics. His friends in the local gentry are good-natured and likable. They'll laughingly call themselves "ig'nert hick rednecks," but at the same time will eye a stranger to see if he agrees. Africano doesn't; despite the incongruous Roman profile and his traces of eastern urbanity, Africano is at home with his neighbors.

Nevertheless, accepting Ted Bundy as a client brought certain potential risks. There had been rumblings in the community that Bundy deserved a bullet, not a trial. Defending him would not make Africano popular.

Not that the attorney had any hope of winning the case. "We knew going in," he told me, "that nothing short of someone stepping forward and confessing was going to secure an acquittal, and even that would still leave people with a lot of doubt."

I asked him if he ever considered putting Ted on the stand.

'We did discuss it," he answered. "I think Ted suggested it. He said, 'Well, what if I get on the stand and say such-and-such?' I said, 'What else are you going to say if you get on the stand? You just can't say A without going from B to Z. Before you decide that you might want to take the stand, you better be prepared to tell me where you were from February 3, 1978, to February 13, 1978, each and every minute of that time to my satisfaction. Then you'll get on the stand.'

"He said, 'Well, let me talk it over with Carole and I'll let you know tomorrow.'

"We decided that it wouldn't be wise for him to testify."

Africano considered an innovative insanity defense, one that he felt might work despite Ted's insistence that he was innocent. "I think," he explained, "that it is legally possible to plead in the alternative—that is, not guilty and then not guilty by reason of insanity—and still have the defendant remain silent.

"My argument to the jury would have been that Ted Bundy does not admit his guilt, he says he's innocent. But even if you don't believe him, the unrefuted psychiatric testimony is that if he did commit this crime and he also committed the Chi Omega crimes, he had to be crazy at the time he did it."

Africano tried out the idea on Dr. Emanuel Tanay, who, Africano says, "was confident that this was a correct analysis," but "said in his experience that it would not be very arguable in a court of law." Tanay cautioned Africano that the state could find psychiatrists who'd disagree and that he, as an expert witness for the defense, would be in the tenuous position of testifying before a jury that he thought Ted was insane without Bundy having admitted he was a killer.

"We all know," said Africano, "that certain things exist, but whether or not they're going to carry any water in a court of law is rather difficult."

Thus at trial, assisted by Lynn Thompson, who was on loan from Mike Minerva's office in Tallahassee, and investigator Don Kennedy, who ordinarily worked for the Lake City public defender, Africano would present a defense that argued the state's case had not been proven "beyond and to the exclusion of every reasonable doubt." This strategy, matching Ted's thinking, was a poor choice, but it was the only one open to Africano.

His opposite number, assistant state attorney Bob Dekle, had problems of his own, but none which seriously jeopardized his chances of convicting Ted.

Dekle is an easy man to underestimate. In the courtroom he appears graceless, a shambling country boy in baggy brown suits, squeaky shoes, and given to arguing legal points on the grounds that "it just ain't right, Your Honor." Outside court, he often boasts he can spit tobacco juice twenty feet and more.

But Dekle is no rube. Of an evening, the assistant state attorney might dip into Homer or Herodotus in the original Greek, or pass his time working on a translation of the New Testament. As often as not, a bit of Shakespeare finds its way into his legal briefs.

He devoted a tremendous amount of effort to the Leach case, from the moment the little girl was first reported missing. Perhaps because the prosecutor himself had recently become a father and could empathize with Frieda and Tom Leach's ordeal, he took a direct role in organizing the search for their daughter and was on hand to absorb the dreadful shock of her discovery.

Dekle, like Larry Simpson and Mike Fisher before him, worked hard to introduce "similar transactions" as evidence of Bundy's common scheme or design. He reinterviewed the Kent case witnesses, Raelynne Shepard, Katherine Ricks, and Tamra Tingey, Debra Kent's locker partner. He went so far as to have them hypnotized and constructed a chart that showed coincidences of location, weather, victim descriptions, and modus operandi.

It was an impressive effort, but most of it went for naught. Africano lodged several objections to the chart, the most telling of which was that the analysis ignored the Chi Omega cases, the sole murder convictions against Bundy. Judge Wallace Jopling ruled that only Leslie Parmenter—close in age and geographic proximity to Kim Leach at the moment of her disappearance— could describe her encounter with "Richard Burton, Fire Department" on the day preceding Kimberly's abduction.

Dekle also lost on the admissibility of Ted's statements to the police. The jury would hear no tapes and no testimony on what Bundy said to Chapman, Patchen, or Bodiford.

But Dekle's prosecution of Bundy would not turn on these issues. Even more than Larry Simpson he benefited from Bundy's notoriety; a poll showed that Ted's name recognition in Orange County around Orlando was 98 percent, about the same as President Carter's.

There was nothing Vic Africano could do about the possibility of pretrial publicity tainting jurors. He did mount an effective attack on Dekle's eyewitnesses, assuming they would be critical to the jury. If their credibility was impeached, then the circumstantial evidence placing Bundy in Lake City on the day of Kim Leach's disappearance became less important.

Yet all the while, Bob Dekle knew that the eyewitnesses and the credit-card slips and even Leslie Parmenter were of secondary value to the state. He would ably demonstrate that it was the physical evidence, the white Dodge van, that tied Ted Bundy to Kimberly Diane Leach beyond a reasonable doubt.

Bundy was brought to court on January 7, 1980. He sat down at the defense table next to Vic Africano and Lynn Thompson and began to write. As jury selection began, Bundy hardly looked up.

"I'm getting writer's cramp," he scribbled, "which is a small price to pay for missing the proceedings. I just looked up and heard some guy with moon-crater cheeks say that he had formed an opinion of my guilt, but that he would put it aside. Now Africano is questioning the man. His personal opinion is that Mr. Bundy is guilty. Blah. It's just entertainment. I will feel and act like an interested bystander. None of this has anything to do with me.''

Several reporters, veterans of Ted's Miami trial, noted the change in him. Not only did Bundy appear uninterested, but he was physically transformed as well. In Miami, Ted had been a slender and agile 160 pounds as he moved around the front of the court. Now, thirty pounds heavier, he barely fit into his trousers. Bundy thought the added weight flattered him, but it did not. He looked fleshy.

Jury selection, which Judge Jopling called "the grinding process," went on for two weeks and set a Florida record for the time required to find a panel. Over 130 prospective jurors were called.

In the early going, Bundy was able to maintain his calm. From time to time, he'd survey the audience, smiling at Carole Boone in the front row and flashing grins at his groupies. Janet the letter writer came and stared at him. Pale, with severely pulled-back hair, Janet sat smoldering for Ted. She apparently meant what she said in her love letters.

"Dear Carole," Ted wrote one day, "please do not sit in the same row with Janet. When I look over toward you, there she sits contemplating me with her mad eyes like a deranged seagull studying a clam. I can feel her spreading hot sauce on me already."

Carole, who by now had moved to Florida permanently to be near Ted, came to the trial to help him insulate himself from the proceedings. Each morning, she would prepare and package elaborate lunches for him, then deliver them to the jail before the start of the day's proceedings. Unbeknownst to Vic Africano, these lunches often contained hidden caches of Valium or vodka mixed into cans of fruit juice.

Off and on throughout the trial, before his attorneys and the bailiffs caught on to Carole's smuggling operation and stopped it, Bundy would get loaded. One day, he popped eighty milligrams of Valium and barely made it back to his cell after court before he passed out. Another time, when Ted and defense investigator Don Kennedy were together alone in an office just off the courtroom, Kennedy couldn't help noticing Bundy had been drinking.

"He wasn't stumbling drunk," Kennedy later told Hugh, "but his speech was slurred and his eyes were watery and red. He started ramblin' on in a real low voice, 'I like to go out and have a good time like anyone else. I'm not a bad guy! I like to have a few drinks.'

"It was sorta eerie bein' in there with him. The way he was talkin' and the way he was lookin' at me. It was like he wanted to grab hold of you and just strangle you."

Carole had provided the vodka—at Bundy's demand—in the hope that it would help keep him sedated. To the contrary, Ted's drinking in the early part of the trial probably made him more vulnerable to stress.

Into the second week of voir dire he was still able to joke that the best way to minimize the inequities of jury selection was to hold consecutive trials on a best-of-seven basis like the World Series. The first team to win four trials gets the verdict.

But toward the end of the second week, Bundy began to slip. On Friday morning, January 18, he tried to walk out of court. "I'm leaving!" he announced. "This is a game and I won't be a party to this kind of Waterloo!" He scuffled briefly with a bailiff, and returned to court a half-hour later.

The scene was not spontaneous; Ted did it primarily for consumption back on Death Row, where his new friends would applaud the defiance. But another explosion that day had not been planned. By late afternoon, the last member of his seven-woman, five-man all-white jury was seated. He was an *Orlando Sentinel Star* employee named Pat Walski, who conceded a negative impression of Bundy, but told the judge that he could put it aside.

Ted lost control, banged on the defense table with his fist, and then harangued Judge Jopling about the prosecutors. "Look at what they are doing!" he shouted. "They want people who bring their prejudice to court and you are playing that game!"

Ted turned ashen. When Vic Africano announced he would accept the jury "with reservations," Bundy interjected, "I'm not accepting it! I can't accept it!"

He tried to leave the court but was quickly surrounded by three bailiffs. So he turned his rage on Jerry Blair, Bob Dekle's boss, who was part of the prosecution team. Blair had argued that Bundy was required to be in court for the impaneling of the jury. "Try to make me stay!" Bundy yelled, taking a couple of steps in Blair's direction. "You want a circus? I'll make a circus! I'll rain on your parade, Jack!"

And Ted's outbursts weren't the only source of tension in the courtroom. The long hours of voir dire began to wear down the attorneys as well and exacerbated a personal enmity between Africano and Dekle. During jury selection, Africano needled the prosecution constantly by referring to the death penalty as "the final insult." Flustered, Dekle would argue, "It just ain't *right*, Your Honor!" In a session in chambers, Dekle called Africano a "self-righteous ass" and drew a rebuke from Judge Jopling.

At another point in the trial, Africano sent Don Kennedy to the prosecutors in search of a document. Kennedy approached Lynn Register, the prosecutors' legal researcher, and asked Register for the paper.

"From now on," Register growled at him, "it's going to be all asses and elbows."

Kennedy shrugged. "Well," he said, "I guess that makes us the elbows."

Bob Dekle opened the state's case on Monday, January 21; and the defense, emotionally and physically fatigued by the jury selection process, at first took heart. "No one really deluded themselves that we had a shot," Africano later told me. "But it was 'Could you fucking possibly believe we *might* have?' "

His excitement was aroused by the state's three eyewitnesses. One was a seventy-three-year-old crossing guard who remembered seeing a white van near Lake City Junior High on the morning of February 9, 1978, the day Kim Leach disappeared. Clinch Edenfield testified that Ted was the man he'd seen in the van, but could offer no other details. On cross-examination, Lynn Thompson established that Edenfield hadn't identified Ted until he saw him on television and that Edenfield remembered the day as sunny while, in fact, it had been windy and wet. Thompson also reminded Edenfield that during a deposition he'd told the attorney that he knew he'd picked the right man because an FBI agent winked at him when he picked the right picture in a photo lineup.

Jacqueline Moore, a Lake City houswife, testifed to an encounter with a white van that day on Highway 90 between Lake City and Live Oak to the west. With her maid, Beulah, beside her in the car, Mrs. Moore had seen the van swerving down the highway headed west. The man inside was bobbing his head in a strange manner (as if, suggested the prosecution, he was contending with a struggling victim). The last she saw of him he was taking a sharp right turn that leads in a long loop to the road near where Kim Leach's body was found.

The problem with Mrs. Moore's testimony was that she had not been able to identify Ted as the man for nearly two years, but had seen his outbreak in court on television the preceding Friday and finally recognized him from his profile. Jopling ruled her testimony inadmissible.

The last of the three important eyewitnesses was C.L. (Andy) Andersen, a paramedic who remembered driving home from work on the morning of February 9, 1978, and being stopped on Duval Street in front of the junior high. Three cars in front of him, he testified, a man who "strongly resembled" Ted was leading a distraught-looking girl from the schoolyard to his white van parked in a traffic lane.

Vic Africano had felt this identification was the key to Dekle's case. Andersen's testimony, he believed, was the most positive link between Ted and Kim Leach. He managed to discredit the testimony somewhat when he established that Andersen had waited six months before coming forward—and then only after seeing Ted on television.

He was later able to successfully attack the two hypnotic sessions used in an effort to improve Andersen's recall. It was never suggested that Andy Andersen was lying on the stand, only that his recollection was faulty and unduly influenced by the hypnotists. But the greatest flaw in what he recalled witnessing was the location of the van.

If Andersen was right, Ted would have parked the van in the street's only west-bound lane in the middle of the morning rush hour and left it backing up traffic while he roamed the school-yard looking for a victim. The idea was hardly credible.

In contrast to Africano's cautious optimism as the prosecution case began was Ted's growing irritation with the proceedings and with himself. He controlled it fairly well in court, with the exception of the morning John Farhat testified.

Farhat, proprietor of the Green Acres Sporting Goods store in Jacksonville, was shown a photo of two price tags, stuck together, that had been found in the FSU media center van. One said "$24" and the one stuck atop it said "$26." The only item, Farhat testified, that had gone up from $24 to $26 was a Buck hunting knife with a ten-inch blade.

When originally shown a photo lineup, Farhat had picked a

garage mechanic from Live Oak as the man most similar to the one who'd bought the knife. But in court, he picked out Bundy.

"That's a damn lie!" Ted yelled. "A damn lie!"

Jopling called the attorneys to the bench.

"I think the defendant might make [another] outburst," Dekle told the judge.

"Your Honor," Africano answered, "I don't know what to tell him. I will admonish him to be quiet."

Ted settled down again, but he was close to the edge.

"I told Vic I'm coming unglued," Ted reported to Carole on the phone that night. "I just can't keep it together anymore. I'm sorry. I'm just starting to lose it. I was strong as long as I can be.

"I don't know what these guys expect of me. Not only to just go through jury selection and listen to all that rot, but then listening to witness after witness after witness Lie! Lie! Lie! I'm fed up with it! I need some goddamn special attention! I *demand* it!"

Bundy was able—but barely—to keep his demons at bay for most of the rest of the trial. He experienced severe physical discomfort, numbness in his limbs, vertigo, deep muscle and joint aches, and heart palpitations. And his attention span contracted to a maximum of a few minutes. Clearly, Ted was expending huge amounts of energy just to keep from blowing apart.

Meantime, Bob Dekle moved relentlessly toward his master stroke. Dr. Peter Lipkovic, who had performed the autopsy on Kim Leach was called to the stand. His expert testimony was limited to the opinion that "homicidal violence to the neck region" was the cause of death. There would be no discussion of her body's peculiar position, or informal speculation from Lipkovic as to his opinion that Kim was raped and murdered with a knife.

But the jury—just like the twelve in Miami—was shown color photos of the crime scene, vivid slides of the hog shed and partial views of the body that provoked shudders throughout the courtroom. With the lights dimmed, no one could catch Bundy's expression as he watched the slides glow on the screen. But in the back of the court a man alone was seen with his coat in his lap. He smelled of liquor and made low noises to himself. Under his dark coat, he was fidgeting with something.

Bob Dekle administered the coup de grace on Tuesday, January 29, the final day of the prosecution's case.

Earlier, the jury had heard from Dr. Richard Stephens, the

FDLE serologist who had made the "inconclusive" test of the semen stain found in Cheryl Thomas' bedding. In Orlando, Stephens testified that stains of blood type B—Kim Leach's blood type—had been found in the seat of her jeans and toward the rear of the FSU media center's white van. Moreover, his test of the van stains had been, in her term, "indicative" of a specific blood protein also known to be in the Leach girl's blood.

In her underpants, found next to her body, there was a semen stain. This time, Stephens' results were unequivocal: An O-blood-type secretor had deposited the semen. Regarded together with the blood found in her jeans, the semen seemed to indicate that Kim Leach had been attacked and reclothed before her body was stripped again. However, rapists often wipe themselves with articles of their victims' clothing after assaulting them. Thus it was unclear what might have been done to the girl in the van or elsewhere before she was killed.

Dekle had established that the media center's white Dodge van was missing from February 5 until February 13, 1978. According to its odometer, it had been driven about 750 miles. Ted, it was shown, had been in Jacksonville the day Leslie Parmenter was approached, and in Lake City the day Kimberly Leach disappeared. Deputy Keith Dawes testified that he saw Ted in Tallahassee at the stolen green Toyota with Florida license tag 13-D-11300, the same license number reported by the Parmenters as being on the white van "Richard Burton" drove.

But Dekle had one further problem; he needed to link Bundy more directly to the media center van. No hairs matching Ted's (or Kim Leach's) had been found in the van, and it had been wiped clean of fingerprints.

The crucial tie came with the fiber evidence.

Mary Lynn Hinson, a microanalyst at the FDLE lab, first testified that a shoe print found inside the van *could* have come from a pair of Ted's sneakers, and that a shoe print discovered on the rear bumper *could* have been made by one of his loafers.

She went on to explain fiber analysis, which is similar to hair analysis in that only class characteristics can be ascertained by testing. It is almost always impossible to say that a questioned fiber had to come from a specific source unless that source is unique in all the world. But working from color, size, shape, texture and what is known about the chemical properties of a fiber, an analyst can make a highly educated guess as to the probability that two articles have been in contact with each other or a third item. The more instances in which a match can be made, the higher the probability.

Then Hinson explained that she had examined a rug from the van together with Kim Leach's jeans, purse, bra, socks, coat, football jersey—all found near her body—and the white turtleneck Kim wore at the moment of her death. From all the clothes found in the stolen orange Volkswagen, her tests led her to concentrate on a torn burgundy shirt and a blue sports coat.

Using a complicated chart for illustration, the analyst testified that she found four colors of polypropylene were used to make the van's rug. Three of these color fibers were clinging to Kim Leach's jeans, three to her purse, two to her bra, one to her jersey, and all four to her socks.

Fibers similar to the blue and white cotton of her jeans and denim purse were found in the van. Also recovered from the van were red, green, yellow, and orange cotton fibers that matched the decorative stitching on the purse. The other matches were of white acrylic from her socks, modacrylic from the fake fur of her coat collar, nylon from her jersey, and another type of acrylic fiber from her turtleneck.

Polyester and wool fibers similar to those used to make Ted's blue sports coat (and bearing the same distinctive "nubbing" caused by heat treatment of the fabric) were found in Kim Leach's socks, her jeans, and in the van. One type of polyester and one type of cotton identical to that of the burgundy shirt were also found in her socks. Finally, matching red cotton and red acrylic fibers—source unknown—were found on the shirt and in the van.

"Do you," asked Dekle, "have an opinion whether the clothing of Theodore Robert Bundy, the clothing of Kimberly Leach, and the interior of that white van came into contact?"

Hinson, like all FDLE analysts, was a schooled and experienced witness. She had been taught to address the jury when she answered a question, and to keep her responses short and to the point.

"Yes I do," she said, turning mechanically to the jury box. "I would say that it is very probable they were in physical contact."

"Very probable" seemed to leave some room for defense rebuttal. But the defense fiber expert told Ted's attorneys that he had never seen so many cross comparisons. Hinson's testimony had been literally fatal to Ted.

The trial was over before the defense began. Africano completed his dismantling of Andy Andersen's testimony, but there was nothing to be done about the physical evidence except to contest Lipkovic's conclusion that Kim Leach had been killed by trauma to the neck.

There was a spirited debate waged over the rate at which a body might decompose over eight weeks given variables of temperature and humidity. The life cycle of the common blowfly was discussed, and opinions were offered as to how quickly such-and-such an animal might attack dead flesh and where the carrion eaters would start. None of the dispute seemed to have much impact on the jury.

Ted was convicted on Thursday, February 7, 1980. No one was surprised. As the jurors filed into court, Ted stood up and said in a loud stage whisper to Africano, "The one thing I like about this is that at least there's no suspense." The penalty phase was set to be heard on Saturday, February 9, the third anniversary of Kim Leach's disappearance.

All that was left to Ted was his final speech to the jury, in which he compared himself to Barabbas—much to the jurors' confusion—and then fell into tears.

He did, however, pull one last headline-grabbing stunt that confounded the court and earned him a round of applause from his friends back on Death Row, who watched it all on television. On February 9, Ted and Carole got married.

They had begun their campaign to be wed the day after Mary Lynn Hinson testified. Both Carole and Ted that day wrote individual letters to the Reverend Jerry J. Jordan, the Orange County jail chaplain, explaining why he should bless their union.

"We are both approaching marriage . . . only after obtaining a profound knowledge of each other," Ted wrote. Further down he said, "For my part, I find her devotion to me awesome . . . and her love for me soothing and inspiring."

Carole was far less effusive. She wrote the Reverend Jordan that "Ted is a major figure in my son's life; he takes a great deal of interest in Jamey and provides him with guidance and advice that a teenage boy needs."

She added: "Formalizing our relationship will be comforting to the three of us and is something that Ted and I have wanted for a long time."

Several days later, their marriage request was denied. According to the formal notification, the jail felt marriage to Carole was "not in the inmate's best interest."

Ted seemed willing to let the marriage talk go at that. He reminded Carole that he was under two death sentences and was about to be handed a third. But Carole Boone was not to be deterred; she argued, among other things, that she had torn up her life for Ted and the least he could do was lend some legitimacy to their relationship.

Clearly, the jail personnel were going to have to be circumvented, and Ted's attorneys wanted no part in the matter. While she waited for a solution to these two dilemmas, Carole went ahead and obtained a marriage license and had her blood tested. Bailiffs tried to prevent a doctor from taking Ted's blood, but Ted successfully argued to Judge Jopling that he had a right to see the doctor, a defense consultant.

Managing the ceremony itself was far trickier. Carole couldn't find a minister who'd perform the rite, and Don Kennedy, a notary public (empowered, in Florida, to wed people), was under orders from Africano not to do it.

The ideas of them marrying by telephone, by mail, and by proxy were considered and then discarded. It was essential to get Carole, Ted, and a sympathetic notary public all in the same room at the same time. A plan came to Carole. The only room where she and Ted could be together was the courtroom. Why not get married there?

The plan quickly took shape. On Saturday, during the penalty phase, Ted would act as his own attorney. He could call Carole as a character witness. While she was on the stand, under oath, and in front of the judge, jurors, attorneys, and spectators— hundreds of wedding witnesses—Ted would lead her through a series of questions about her feelings for him. At last, she would say something like, "I love and respect you so much that I want to marry you." Ted would answer, "And I want to marry you," and that, according to Florida law, was all that was needed. A friendly notary public would be found to sit in the audience.

Bundy was enchanted by the plan. However, he nearly botched it.

Ted put on a new bow tie, khaki slacks, and a pair of argyle socks (he loved the socks) for his wedding day. Carole borrowed a black knit top from a woman she'd befriended. Under it, she wore her white blouse.

The court was nearly full. At 10:13 A.M., Ted stood up and announced, "The defendant calls Carole Boone." A little gasp went up from the audience.

On the stand, she wasted little time getting to her point. But

Ted started referring to himself as the defendant, so Carole first said, "I want to marry him."

Bundy grew more confused and asked Carole if *he* wanted to marry *her*.

At last he got it right. "Do you want to marry me?"

"Yes."

"I want to marry you."

The exchange of vows might have gone unnoticed had Bundy done it right. But the third time, everyone in the courtroom figured out what was happening. Jerry Blair sneered and called it "a Valentine saga."

Africano seemed amused. *He* couldn't be blamed for what had gone on, although once Ted sat down, his attorney told him he ought to go back and exchange vows properly. Ted did, and the two were—finally—married. By most counts, they did it four times.

Then the jury retired and came back with a death penalty recommendation. They had deliberated ten minutes. Three days later, on Tuesday, February 12, Judge Jopling condemned Ted to the electric chair for the murder of Kimberly Leach.

# SEVENTEEN

BUNDY NOW saw the end of his life in the near distance before him, but he could contemplate his last days with unfeigned equanimity. His was a contentment not unlike that of a retired suburban squire: Ted belonged to an exclusive club and even wore the uniform of his distinction—the apricot T-shirt of the Death Row con. He felt sheltered, accepted for the first time in his life. Ted was especially proud that the black inmates on The Row allowed him to play basketball with them once a week. "One of the guys complimented me," he wrote Carole, "saying that whites aren't supposed to be able to play basketball. So it was clear to him that I had to have some nigger in me."

Carole Boone, Mrs. Ted Bundy, took a house in Gainesville, about forty miles southwest of the prison. Once a week, on Saturday or Sunday, Carole and Jamey drove to the prison, where they could sit with Ted, Jamey's stepfather, in the "visiting park," a large room supplied with bolted-down tables and chairs arranged like a cafeteria. Under the eye of an armed guard, Ted and Carole and the rest of the Death Row inmates and their families met and talked in the open room. Touching was permitted and, from time to time, intercourse was possible behind a water cooler, in the restroom, or sometimes at the tables. In time, Carole gave birth to a girl, and Ted proudly showed pictures of the child to his friends.

While Bundy was still smoking dope, Carole brought it to him in her vagina, using smooth round containers she purchased at a drugstore. This method, employed commonly throughout the U.S. prison system, worked well enough until the day Carole was forced to use child-proof aspirin bottles to transport the marijuana. Bundy, as usual, took the dope back to his cell in his rectum, but was two days in extracting the irregular-shaped bottles.

*      *      *

It was this Ted-in-retirement whom I began interviewing at the prison that spring of 1980, three weeks after the close of the Leach trial. Hugh and I had first been approached on Bundy's behalf a full year earlier and had agreed, in the late summer of 1979, to undertake the proposed book based upon Ted's guarantees of total cooperation.

We decided that Hugh would take responsibility for reinvestigating the cases against Bundy while I would interview Ted himself. I was to conduct conversations, not interrogations. Showing Ted patience and appreciation, my role was to listen and listen and listen. Then Hugh would focus exclusively on the concrete issues of guilt and innocence, and would confront Bundy in a decidedly unsympathetic way. We were trying, in effect, a variation on the time-honored tactic of good guy-bad guy interviewing.

Hugh's first job, the re-examination of Bundy's enormously complex story, was made even more difficult by Carole Boone. She told us her Bunny could not be guilty, no matter what the evidence showed, and prepared lengthy memos arguing for alternative suspects—a long list of misfits and psychotics whose names she culled from the police reports. Heading the list of society's detritus, the "types" who always surface when sensational crimes are committed, was Manny Treff, the troubled drifter whom Mike Fisher investigated in connection with the Caryn Campbell case and eventually cleared.

By the time I began interviewing Ted, Hugh had already eliminated most of these alternative suspects as he retraced the loops and oxbows of Bundy's serpentine course through Washington, Oregon, Utah, and Colorado. Any possibility that Ted was telling the truth when he claimed utter innocence had vanished entirely.

For his part, Bundy made it clear that he didn't expect us to believe him innocent. Months before the start of the Leach trial, he wrote us a letter from Death Row in which he outlined *his* agenda. The letter contained a list of ten suggestions.

"I don't care what you write," he began, "just so you get it right and just so it sells." Nowhere in the letter did Bundy mention his pleas of innocence except to note that there are "those who wish to accept them unconditionally and to the exclusion of all guilt evidence." These people, Ted wrote, were his solace. "As long as I have strong supporters," he explained, "I have all I can ask for."

Bundy urged us to emphasize the mystery surrounding him; he specifically urged us not to search for evidence that he was guiltless as he claimed. "The facts to prove unequivocally that I'm innocent are not there," he informed us.

In all, Bundy's ten points added up to a revealing self-portrait. He was confident that *his* definition of innocence—the absence of Carole's "irrefutable physical evidence"—was secure against anything we might find. He said, "There is no true answer, only controversy." Unlike Carole, who believed that somewhere, somehow proof of Ted's innocence must exist, Bundy knew it did not, *said* it did not, and argued that we should not go in search of it.

Such a mind is a challenge to comprehend, let alone deal with. Nothing Ted wrote sorted with our expectations, and very little of it was rationally consistent. But Bundy beckoned us—and unwittingly pulled himself—toward the "true answer." He ended the letter with a tease, a line similar to the "pimping" he'd tried with detectives Chapman, Patchen and Bodiford. "I may not have all the answers," he wrote, "but I have all the ones which count."

We had no doubt that Bundy was right about that; certainly no one else seemed to have the faintest idea of who he was. His friends and family had given us generally benign recollections of Ted, while the psychiatrists argued he was mentally ill. The press depicted him as a four-square Republican, when the police knew him as a skilled killer. His attorneys had dealt with a mercurial client too unstrung, at times, to make sense to them at any level. It was a monstrous puzzle; precocious Methodist youngsters from good families simply do not become mass killers for no reason at all. We knew that the answer had to come from Ted, if we could pry it out.

I found him operating on low wattage after the Leach trial, listless and withdrawn from its strains as well as from the effects of the dope he was consuming. Bundy didn't feel defeated, however. Quite the contrary. After his languor lifted somewhat, he told me of his contentment.

"Anybody matures, I'm sure," he said, "no matter where they are. But so many times in these past couple of years I felt like I was looking down from a mountain and seeing so many things I never saw before. I feel much more confident about myself. It's really marvelous! I feel not powerful, but in control of things."

I couldn't then fathom what Ted was saying; his serenity in the face of three death sentences perplexed me. I was also annoyed, as we spoke, with his effrontery at pledging his full cooperation in a project that should, if he wasn't lying, prove him innocent, then rambling off into the ether whenever I tried to discuss substantive issues.

I tried not to betray my irritation; it would be Hugh's later responsibility to attack Ted for his ludicrous denials of guilt. I was there to listen and perhaps to devise some way of eliciting the truth from Bundy.

At first, I reminded Ted of what he'd written, that he had the answers that counted. If so, I said, what then of the Leach case? Was that Ted who approached Leslie Parmenter?

"No." He was lying.

"What about Deputy Dawes and the license tag identification?" Ted belched. "Well, I don't know."

"Are you saying that is manufactured evidence?"

"Manufactured or something," he answered. "I'm not sure. I stopped asking those questions a long time ago."

His implacability was unassailable. Bundy would not confess, and I had no leverage with him. If he wouldn't talk to save his life, then no number of threats, cajolery, or tricks from me were going to pry the truth from him. I told Bundy that if he felt what he had to say was controversial he was wrong; he was serving up very weak tea.

A period of indecision ensued. We continued to talk, but I was less and less interested in hearing his fond recollections of Liz Kendall or how he once hunted frogs with his dog Lassie. Whenever he could, Bundy maneuvered the conversations to talk of his life before he reached puberty.

That, at last, gave me the idea. Bundy *was* still a child—a killer child—an emotionally twisted preadolescent contained in the body of a man. A look at his life revealed a consistent pattern of puerility. The press's favorite adjective for Ted, "boyish," took on an apt irony.

It was then I chanced the offer for this child to "speculate" on what had happened. There was nothing to lose anyway, except perhaps my own stability. The subsequent encounters with the "entity" within him were a severe test of that mental balance.

Many months later, Hugh and I took several of the tape recordings we had made with Bundy talking in the third person and played them for Dr. Al Carlisle, a clinical psychologist on the medical staff at the Utah State Prison. Carlisle knew Bundy from his stay there when Ted underwent a court-ordered ninety-day diagnostic evaluation.

We were curious to see if our lay diagnosis of Bundy's condition was clinically sound. We explained the interview protocol to Dr. Carlisle, but we did not share our theory of arrested development.

Before listening to the tapes, Carlisle offered us some background on what he had learned in the course of working with sex offenders at the prison.

"You are going to get one of three things with sex offenders," Carlisle explained. "First, you have the male who starts playing around sexually when he's very young with sisters or a cousin or out playing house with girls. Often, there will be some homosexual tendencies. They begin to blossom by the time he enters his teens.

"Ted didn't say anything or [imply] anything or show anything that made me think that there was something there."

The second variety, said Carlisle, is "a very chronic, inadequate sex offender who's generally so inadequate that it's just obvious; not the Ted Bundy type."

The Ted Bundy type, Carlisle suggested, is a boy "who has been hurt by girls but he also doesn't feel that he can relate very well. He hasn't had very many good experiences in school. Doesn't have too many friends. Some inadequacy. He feels inferior and he wants to date. He wants to have a close, loving relationship with a girl. He feels he can't. He feels he's not going to be accepted. It all begins to come out in the teens. You don't find a lot of evidence of this going back into his childhood."

We talked to Carlisle about Ted's fascination with spying, his habit of sneaking up on girls and scaring them, his hide-and-seek games with the police. "It's uncommon for most killers," Carlisle said, "because most killers are not as bright as Ted. But with him it fits very well, and it fits in with his compartmentalization too. If a person is going to be a good spy, he has to be very calculating, very cold. They have to keep their behavior on an even keel. They can't show anything through their emotions or they give themselves away."

Carlisle does not believe that Bundy has a split personality. "I think, though," he explained, "there's another way of looking at it that can confuse people. When this type of personality is hunting, he shifts into a new personality. Now, in a real split personality syndrome, there are two personalities, but they do not know each other. In Ted's case, it would be much like a person playing a role on stage. They'll go out and live a part, feel a part, talk a part; their voice even conforms to the role they're playing.''

Much of what Carlisle had to say was interchangeable with Ted's third-person description of the killer. Then came his indirect ratification of our theory. After he listened to Ted on the tape recordings—particularly Bundy's re-creation of the murder in the orchard—the psychologist said that Ted's expressed desire to ''possess'' a lifeless or unconscious female was highly unusual for rapists. ''With so many of these guys,'' he said, ''if the body is not moving, or the victim is not aware of what's going on, he doesn't feel in control. She has to be awake.'' But for Ted, ''it's childlike. I can picture a nine-, ten-, or eleven-year-old doing it that way. The adult personality likes to have his victim show him that she knows he's in control.''

Yet Ted's depersonalization of his victims and his comments on the thrill of the hunt are also very typical of many rapists and killers. ''Most of our rapists do not see the woman at the time they are raping,'' he explained. ''In fact, when she goes to court, many guys do not recognize her. Some guys say, 'Good heavens! Did I rape her?' The victims are objects.

''For somebody who likes to stalk a victim, the major part is the plan. That's what is so exciting to them. That plan and the hunt combined are *extremely* exciting to them. The person is anticipating. There is a feeling of power. 'If I'm hunting *them*, then I have to be better. I have to be smarter. I'm very cunning.' The old detective, cops-and-robbers type of thing. The spy.''

I had taken a gentle hand with Bundy, playing a variation on the theme of Trilby enraptured by Svengali. Ted enjoyed the relationship; I didn't.

After weeks of quietly listening to his weird tale, hearing from his point of view the repellent murders and rapes, I was happy to give Bundy over to Hugh. Now Ted would feel the heat.

We realized that outside the courtroom no one but Mike Minerva had ever confronted Bundy with his guilt; it was Bundy's sick genius to deter even the police from bearding him. We decided to give it a try, for Hugh to pound away at Ted until something gave. There would be no deliberate confession, we knew, but perhaps sufficient stress could drive Ted out of his shell and force an open confrontation with his guilt.

In time, Ted did crack, or rather shatter, under the pressure. The crisis led to another and final metamorphosis in which Ted Bundy barred and locked the last doors, divorcing himself totally from the world. The process was horrible and fascinating to watch.

Hugh started Ted out slowly, taking him back over every case and patiently asking if Bundy cared to offer any exculpatory information. Although it was understood between them that Ted *was* a killer—he'd explained in his "speculations"—Hugh fixed on the illogic of Bundy's official position of innocence. Each of their encounters tore away a bit more of Ted's facade. He had conceded so much to me in the third person that his denials of complicity sounded more hollow than ever. Even Ted, for all his compartmentalization, had trouble talking in the third person about "posession" while in the first person swearing he'd never hurt a soul.

With me, he had been able to stand apart from his acts, but Hugh was doggedly literal with Ted. "When you stick an instrument up a person's vagina," he observed, "that is not normal sexual gratification."

Bundy angrily conceded the act was insane. "We're not talking about *normal* sexual gratification!" he hissed. "We're not talking about *normal* anything. Okay? Certainly it's abnormal."

The stress began to tell. Hugh's insistence on reality challenged Ted's tautly woven web of rationalization; he felt fear again. Hugh mentioned electrocution and Bundy agreed that perhaps it wasn't too late to explore some deal with the governor. In his developing turmoil, he later denied interest in such a deal; then, after hearing his own voice on the tape recorder endorse it, he nervously stammered, "Then I reject it now."

Bundy grew desperate to rid himself of Hugh; and appealed to me, through Carole, to replace his tormentor. He was caught in such a tangle of patent contradictions and gibberish that anything he said—short of a confession—only sank him further into the quagmire of his own creation.

Inevitably, the strain precipitated another emotional collapse. We saw it coming and were not surprised when, in March of 1981, Ted declared he no longer wanted to continue the interviews. What Bundy had to say to Hugh in their last meeting made it clear that he had leapt one final time from reality.

"My position on my innocence, while not widely believed, has been certainly well known, and my stubbornness has been well known to you," he said calmly that day. "It should have been known to you prior to the time you came into this thing. Maybe you succumbed to the same things these police succumbed to. Hoping, you know, that he'll come through."

"I thought," Hugh told him, "you came close two or three times. And I thought that talking about it perhaps would be a great burden off your mind."

"A burden?" Ted asked. "I carry no burden, except being in prison."

There it was again. "You can compartmentalize better than anyone I've ever known!" Hugh said.

"It's not a matter of, well . . ." Bundy paused for a moment. "It *may* have been a matter of compartmentalization, which is *not* the process by any means.

"I've learned to live absolutely and completely and totally in the *here* and *now*. I don't worry, think, or concern myself with the past or, for that matter, with the future except only to the extent necessary.

"That, in itself, is not pathological. If you study, as I have been studying to some extensive degree, Oriental philosophy— Buddhism, Taoism, and spiritual-physical traditions of the East— they are much in tune with the way I have become. I find that the pressures on me have actually permitted me to enter into a period of growth."

"I don't understand," Hugh said, wondering where Bundy was leading.

"Well," Ted replied, "whatever I've done in the past—you know, the emotions of omissions or commissions—doesn't bother me. Try to touch the past! Try to deal with the past. It's not *real*. It's just a dream."

"You say the past is not real," Hugh said, "and yet you tell us that you remember everything you've done. So why the hell don't you talk about it? Get it all out and get it done?"

Deliberately, Hugh was asking the impossible of Ted. The saner the suggestion, the more insane would be Bundy's response. Hugh was making Ted reveal just how crazy he'd become.

"I remember as you might remember a Humphrey Bogart movie," Ted answered. "When it's over, you don't talk about it all the time."

"Going to a movie," Hugh told him, "isn't exactly like killing people, Ted. Now God damn it! You're straining reality again."

Ted skipped lightly over the remark. "We're always straining reality every day," he said. "I don't know what to say to you except to tell you that I view things a lot differently. Prison has helped me because it forces me and everyone else to live in the here and now. Only I do so differently.

"Some people in prison try to escape from being right here, right now. They do it with drugs or they do it with any number of cute devices. But I've been able to use that tremendous gift of *living* right now, to see everything where it is—as much as I can—right now. It's to my advantage. I used to live each day at a time just to protect myself. Now I live each day and each moment to try to expand myself. It may not make sense to you, but—"

Here Hugh interrupted after being momentarily dumbstruck that Ted was now calling his disease a tremendous gift. "Actually, it doesn't make sense to me," he told Ted.

"Well," Bundy explained, "a lot of people, most people, are encumbered with a kind of mechanism that is called guilt. As I understand it, guilt is a mechanism. To a degree, I've certainly experienced it, but much less so now than ever when I was on the streets or even two years ago."

"What do you mean, less?"

"I mean I don't feel guilty for anything. I feel less guilty now than I've felt in any time of my life. It's not that I've forgotten anything or else closed down part of my mind, or compartmentalized; I compartmentalize less now than I ever have.

"It's just *done*. It's back *there* in the mists. I say mists because I don't think anyone actually touches the past the way they can touch the present, or the future.

"Guilt. It's this mechanism we use to control people. It's an illusion. It's a kind of social control mechanism and it's very unhealthy. It does terrible things to our bodies.

"I guess," he went on, "I'm in the enviable position of not having to deal with guilt. There's just no reason for it. I don't think I need to feel guilty anymore, because I try to do what's right, right *now*. And that's it!

"Now, some people," he conceded, "could listen to what I just said and say, 'See, he's a sociopath,' or whatever term they use. 'He doesn't feel any guilt. Oh, how terrible! He doesn't feel any guilt. Ha!'

"I feel sorry for people who feel guilt. I feel sorry for people who are drug addicts, or who are *criminals*. I feel sorry for business executives who have to lust after money and power. I feel sorry for a lot of people who have to do things that hurt them. But I don't feel sorry for anyone who doesn't feel guilt, because the guilt doesn't solve anything, *really*. It hurts you."

Ted then confirmed what we already knew. "I'll be serious with you right now," he said. "I would not trade where I am, in this year, right now, for a new shot at my old existence. It would be too painful.''

The next moment he startled Hugh by thanking him for all the long sessions in which he kept forcing Bundy back into his past and asking for explanations. ''It started to put me on the path to where I am now. Just thinking about this business was so *terrible*, so *horrible*,'' he said. ''You really jarred me a couple of times, knocked me back from where I *thought* I was to where you thought I ought to be. I don't recall exactly when it happened, but while I was facing all this from you—which wasn't easy for any given session—I slowly began to understand what I had to do next, how I had to restructure my life. I'm in a lot better shape now.''

Ted had been forced to see what he had done without the barriers of rationalization. With that, the fantasy dissolved, ''possession'' became, for a time, what it really was—murder. *Real people* had actually died at his hands. Rather than pretend any longer that they hadn't, Bundy shut the whole thing off and turned resolutely to the *here and now*.

The conversation was nearly at an end. Ted observed that his and many other Death Row inmates' executions seemed more certain than ever with the election of a conservative President and a mood of vengeance developing in the country toward criminals.

''Does that worry you a lot?'' Hugh asked.

''Does it worry me? No. I don't sit around and worry about it. If it's going to happen, it's going to happen. I've always had the death penalty. It's just a matter of knowing *when* you're going to die. I've come to terms with *that* threat. I mean, I'm going to die. What will worrying change? Worrying won't change things one iota.''

''It would make you not enjoy your remaining days,'' Hugh said, not knowing exactly what was appropriate to say at that point.

''Sure,'' Ted answered as they rose to leave the interview room. ''Or to take advantage of them. That's precisely what I'd like to do.''

The din of the clanging steel gates came up, as if on cue, as Hugh put away his notebook and reached over to shut off the tape recorder for the final time. The last sound was a shuffling noise.

From Hugh's notes of later that day:

After the interview, we stood in front of The Colonel's Office as I waited for an escort back out of the prison. I shook Ted's hand (he was in handcuffs) and I thought he had tried to grasp my hand as strongly as he could. But his grip didn't have any life in it. He grinned but said nothing when he saw me staring at his hands.

Then a sergeant led Ted to the yellow holding cage, and then held the gate open for me to leave the prison for the last time. I didn't look back.

# Epilogue

TED BUNDY'S wearying saga of waste, failure, and death had one villain and no heroes. All systems failed. Nothing was redeemed. There was but a single bleak truth to be learned. Nobody is safe.

Ted was truly invisible. His family and friends didn't suspect. His lovers were unaware. The police couldn't catch him. The doctors didn't diagnose him until it was far too late. And the courts only stopped Bundy after Bundy decided to stop himself.

The people who knew Ted best in his youth—his mother and his close friend Terry—noticed nothing alarming. Shy boys such as he aren't rare, nor is it uncommon for self-conscious teenagers to compensate for social deficiencies by concentrating on the classroom. The outward manifestations of Ted's developing madness were slight and indistinct.

Marjorie Russell later saw his immaturity and soon tired of it. But she didn't sense the fraud. She would not have believed the violent fantasies he probably already entertained at the time they first met. Seven years later, she thought she'd found a new, adult Ted whom she very much wanted to marry. By then, the real Bundy had begun to stalk his victims.

His political friends detected not a trace of psychopathology in the bright young man with good ideas. Ted was perfectly credible as the handsome and hard-working Republican campaign staffer. The girls adored him and his superiors, the starchy elders of the GOP, could compare Ted with their own sons and only wish they'd raised a boy like that.

Then there was Liz Kendall, who loved Ted through the years he slid imperceptibly from sexual disorientation to homicidal insanity. By her account, Liz was blinded by his smile, the gentle, intelligent way Ted often acted with her, and her enduring fear of losing him to another woman.

Liz was the first to suspect Ted was disturbed, but only after she had seen a great many concrete indications of her lover's dark side. Despite the thefts, the weapons, the medical supply equipment, the odd hours, Ted's several sexual quirks—even an attempt on her life—Liz was apt to question her own mind as often as she feared that Ted was indeed a killer. As late as the time following his first conviction for kidnap, Liz Kendall was blaming herself for what happened to Ted and believed him innocent.

Once Ted began to prey on society, he became the responsibility of the police, who also failed; they were as helpless to stop "Ted" as those around him had been to recognize the most feared killer in northwest history. While the dedication and determination of detectives like Bob Keppel and Herb Swindler in Seattle, and later Jerry Thompson in Utah, Mike Fisher in Colorado, and Steve Bodiford and the rest in Florida were laudable, the police did not "solve" the case. Bundy wasn't tracked down; he engineered his own arrests. When he was at large, nothing that any policeman did averted a single death.

There was nothing these police *could* do, or would be able to do if another psychopath like Ted began a new string of murders. The harrowing truth is that society, especially a free society, is essentially defenseless against the intelligent, dedicated killer. From sleeping co-eds to savvy barflies—hippies, prudes, daddies' girls, and children—no daughter was protected from Ted.

Even after apprehending Bundy, the police continued to be frustrated in their attempts to tie him to the crimes they were positive he'd committed. Bob Keppel established Ted's whereabouts down to the hour in many instances, but he couldn't demonstrate anything of legal substance. Jerry Thompson and Ira Beal in Utah might have secured a murder indictment in the Debra Kent case, but they couldn't find the high school girl's body. As it was, the successful prosecution for Carol DaRonch's kidnap was due as much to Ted's performance on the stand as it was to the evidence presented. After the trial, prosecutor David Yocom was asked when he knew he'd won the case. "When the judge announced the verdict," he said.

Ted, of course, did not serve out his sentence for kidnapping Carol DaRonch and he was never tried in Colorado for killing Caryn Campbell. He spent about as much time in jail as he wanted to, and then chose his moment to leave. But even had he not exercised that option, it was entirely possible he would have beaten the Campbell indictment and then been released on parole within eighteen months.

Nor did the authorities in Florida finally *bring* him to justice; here again, it was Bundy who delivered himself up for capture and conviction. If he had wanted to, he could have fled the state and escaped detection, just as he might have escaped conviction later if he'd properly disposed of the white Dodge van and altered his bottom teeth.

And the psychiatric experts failed; their insights were interesting and valuable, but only as a retrospective view, the way an autopsy is useful in reconstructing the course and cause of death.

The hope in so vulnerable a world is for a diagnostic test of homicidal insanity, some clinical means for identifying the aberrant mind as other lethal diseases are found. Yet so far, a reliable measure of a person's future potential to kill remains well beyond the art or science of modern psychology and psychiatry. In the instance of the psychopath, unless a doctor is aware that he is interviewing one he cannot diagnose the condition.

The first such expert to examine Bundy was Dr. Gary Jorgensen, a University of Utah clinical psychologist. He was retained by John O'Connell prior to the DaRonch kidnap trial to determine, if he could, whether Ted suffered from a psychopathology. The doctor spent two hours with Bundy and administered six tests, including a Rorschach and the Minnesota Multiphasic Personality Inventory exam.

For diagnostic purposes, Jorgensen was obliged to accept Bundy's insistence that he was innocent. In his report, he concluded Ted was a "normal person."

The next inquiry into Bundy's mental health was ordered by Judge Stewart Hanson following his guilty verdict. It was a ninety-day evaluation undertaken by the staff at the Utah State Prison.

The tests were extensive. Bundy was shown inkblots again and sketches. He was given several objective tests, asked to draw pictures, and interviewed by staff doctors—including Al Carlisle—for over fifty hours. Ted's skull was X-rayed (a small benign tumor was discovered in a left frontal sinus), and a brain scan was negative. Electroencephalograms were "completely unremarkable," and the doctors found "no evidence of organic brain disease" or intellectual impairment.

But this time the examiners knew (or could assume) that their subject was capable of violence toward women; Ted had, after all, been convicted of kidnap. Thus, Dr. Van O. Austin, the prison psychiatrist found some problems. Bundy "does have some features of the anti-social personality," Austin wrote in his report, "such as a lack of guilt feelings, callousness, and a very pronounced tendency to compartmentalize and methodically rationalize his behaviour. . . . At times he has lived a lonely, somewhat withdrawn, seclusive existence which is consistent with, but not diagnostic of, a schizoid personality."

The prison doctors might have uncovered Bundy's entire psychopathology had he cooperated with their examinations. But Ted continued to insist he hadn't hurt anybody, which naturally prevented him from discussing *why* he had attacked Carol DaRonch.

Three years later and just before Bundy was to be tried in Miami for the Chi Omega murders, Dr. Emanuel Tanay interviewed him for the defense and diagnosed his illness. By then, the medical information was of potential concrete value only to the attorneys and the courts whose job it was to find "justice" for Ted. All of the women were already dead.

Tanay reported to Mike Minerva that the brutality of the Chi Omega murders indicated that "the possibility of mental derangement at the time of the acts would be a definite consideration." Translation: If Ted did it, he probably was insane within the definition of the law.

Who is crazy, and who isn't?

Legally, Ted Bundy was presumed to have been sane at the times of the killings because he would not allow the issue of his sanity to be joined in court. A public airing of the nature of Ted's illness was a far greater threat to him than the ritual of a criminal trial.

That he is insane—and certainly was at the time of the murders—raises questions as to the "justice" he received. Tanay had pointed up the defense attorney's dilemma in representing psychopaths. He wrote that their psychopathology "is not easily recognized because they do not provide symptoms easily recognized by a lay person or even a psychiatrist. [They] arouse, understandably, a great deal of hostility and there is, therefore, a tendency to view them more as bad than sick. Furthermore, they themselves deny that they suffer from an illness."

By contrast, there is John W. Hinckley, Jr., diagnosed by several doctors as schizophrenic, whom a jury found not guilty by reason of insanity for shooting President Reagan. It is difficult to see how John Hinckley is any crazier than Ted Bundy, but that was the "just" decision.

In effect, Ted was sentenced in absentia, and therefore dodged personal responsibility for his atrocities. He also denied society any edification. In the course of three criminal prosecutions, much was learned about what he did, but very little emerged about who he was and why he did it. Unlike John Hinckley, Bundy protected that information—his only avenue to expiation—with his life.

The death sentences were no tribute to the courts, which Bundy mocked and manipulated to his own mad ends. Ted presented the kind of prerational problem solved in the past by expedients of equal finality: public stoning, the stake, or lynch mobs. In earlier worlds, the notion of irredeemable evil was widely appreciated. In a more advanced, secular society, such ideas are anathema. The appropriate resolution for Ted Bundy, it was decided, was to warehouse him until the day that 1,200 volts of electricity could be shot through him, thus exacting society's price for the wanton murder of twenty to forty women. By his own lunatic testimony, Bundy *likes* Death Row, and is unconcerned about his prospective execution.

Ted himself no longer reflects upon the meaning of what he did, except to view it as far less rare than people like to imagine. He understands as well the utter hopelessness of trying to stop the dedicated psychopath, and once went so far as to acknowledge to me that this was a lesson gleaned from personal experience.

"Since my name came before the police within a matter of weeks after the Lake Sammamish thing," Ted said, "I suppose they can be faulted for not actually coming out to talk to me. But on the other hand, they can't be faulted because they were working from a huge list. They had hundreds and hundreds of leads. Which one do they pick? Do they pick the law student with no criminal background who was probably even known by some of the prosecutors working on the case? Or are they going to go after the 'types,' you know. The guys in the files, the real weirdos. Perhaps the manpower limited them, but for that kind of case they would probably need a thousand investigators."

He was even more candid with Hugh in their last interview. "The crimes are a bit unusual," he said, "but the really scary thing is that there are a lot of people who are not in prison, a *lot* of people who are not in prison, who were *far* more successful than I."

*Who were far more successful than I.* The remark was unequivocal.

Hugh expressed doubt at Ted's thesis, taking as an example the as yet unsolved Atlanta murders of young blacks, which clearly lacked the subtlety of Bundy's hunting trips. The killer or killers called attention to the homicides.

"But you see," Ted answered, "someone is being *so* obvious and still getting away with it. There's a case now in southern Florida where they're digging up bodies on this man's farm. This man is in his fifties, okay? He's now in prison on sex offenses. But in all probability, he's been at it for twenty or thirty years and has never been caught until now."

"How do *you* know that?" Hugh asked.

"It starts early," Ted replied. "The problems may not manifest themselves until the twenties. I'm talking about the kind of thing where a man secretly goes around abducting girls and disposing of them secretly. In every case I've read about—without exception, Hugh—that behavior started somewhere in the twenties."

Ted understands the mass killer as a phenomenon occurring with statistical regularity. "There are any number of people capable of it," he told me. "Somebody that was truly shrewd, with a little bit of money, could probably avoid detection indefinitely. It has always been my theory that for every person arrested and charged with multiple homicide there are probably a good five more out there."

There is no catalog or file on the killers who aren't caught. If Ted, who is in a position to know, is right about these unseen murderers, then society's true state of enlightenment about them probably matches what we know about other lethal diseases such as cancer. That is, very little.

Psychopathology may appear randomly, distributed among the population without regard to sex, class, or intelligence. If so, Bundy would fall among the highly capable—but far short of brilliant—strata of killers, about as bright as anyone caught to date.

It would be reassuring to say with finality what caused Ted to kill, to establish a link the way cigarette smoking has been connected to lung cancer. But his case resists categorization. There is no evidence of overt boyhood trauma, of physical abuse from women, of injuries beyond what any normal child is apt to sustain.

The discovery of his illegitimacy certainly played a far stronger role in shaping him than Bundy today will admit. He probably did, as he says, "make a decision about who I was," a decision with terrifying consequences. But the incident could not have provoked such a profound warping of his psyche had Bundy not been predisposed to it by his deep inner sense of inadequacy and hostility.

This was his"flaw," Ted's emotional weak point that he believes was congenital. Blaming his genes is consistent with Bundy's understanding of himself; positing an inherited defect would help to explain why he felt so different. And he may even be right. The latest scientific evidence seems to show that behavioral predispositions—such as a tendency toward alcoholism—can be inherited. Not nearly enough is known about Bundy's maternal and paternal forebears to say this is the case with him, but the possibility is intriguing.

Whatever the mix of influences upon him, the critical effect was to truncate his emotional development. He retained through life his preadolescent concept of females—remote and unreal, objects of perfection as he saw them on television and magazines; it was a small step thence to viewing them as objects for exploitation and abuse once he began reading pornography. If he secretly blamed Louise for what he was, and if it was she whom Ted killed symbolically again and again, then what more convenient rationalization could there be than to say it was all a game and to deny that the victims had any concrete existence? It was like cowboys-and-Indians, or cops-and-robbers, where part of the game is to play dead.

If it was Marjorie whom Ted was killing, or another symbol of the favored class whose breeding Ted resented and emulated, then the same rationalization held. Politics, a game, was his principal vehicle for moving among them, and it wasn't hard for a mind such as his to project the sham of his own image upon those he would punish for their birthright.

But this still is not an answer to the *why* of Ted Bundy. Here, Ted offers an answer that argues the key is individual stress in a world running toward anomie. It is not the meek but the weak who, Ted believes, inherit in such a world, the chronic losers who take power when "The System" begins to break down.

Thus Ted becomes the cultural descendant of Lee Harvey Oswald, Sirhan Sirhan, Charles Manson, and the rest. "I would say," he explained, "that if we took this individual from birth and raised him in the Soviet Union or Afghanistan or in eighteenth-century America, in all likelihood he'd lead a normal life. We are talking about the peculiar circumstances of society and of the twentieth century in America. There are a whole host of things to which a person is exposed which he would not be exposed to in a more simple culture, a more restricting or puritanical culture.''

And when, as in Ted's case, the breakdown is masked, the preyedupon no longer can distinguish the predators.

"We've mentioned the cultural kinds of factors that contributed to this behavior,'' he patiently explained. "Both to its development and its alleged success. We talked about cultural attitudes toward women. And we talked about violence and pornography. But another factor that is almost indispensable to this kind of behavior is the mobility of contemporary American life.

"Living in large centers of population and living with lots of people, you can get used to dealing with strangers. It's the anonymity factor. And that has a twofold effect.

"First of all, if you're among strangers you're less likely to remember them or care what they're doing or know what they should or should not be doing. If they should or shouldn't be there. Secondly, you're conditioned almost not to be afraid to deal with strangers.

"Mobility is very important here. As we've seen . . . the individual's modus operandi was moving large distances in an attempt to camouflage what he was doing. Moving these distances, he was also able to take advantage of anonymity factor.''

But the "anonymity factor'' was also a product of his own sick mind. Once convinced that images, not people, were being destroyed, it was possible for Ted to assume his predations would go unnoticed.

"In his readings and his observations and what have you—in his fantasy world—he'd imagined for some reason people disappearing all the time,'' Ted told me during his "speculations.'' "He was aware of how people dropped out and became runaways and whatnot. In devising his scheme, he'd taken this somewhat unrealistic conclusion that under the correct circumstances he could select any person as a victim and that there'd be virtually no attention paid to that person's disappearance. People disappear every day. It happens all the time.

"He was always amazed and chagrined by the publicity generated by disappearances he thought would go almost totally unnoticed. Still, he would cling to that belief that there would be virtually no furor over it, notwithstanding the fact that he was proven wrong. For some reason, it was a necessary way of looking at things. I mean, 'There are so many people. It shouldn't be a problem. What's one less person on the face of the earth, anyway?' ''

Unless his death sentences are someday commuted or, as is even less likely, his lawyers can force two retrials and win them both, Ted Bundy faces probable electrocution within five years. His death could come much more quickly if Bundy is caught up in the expected tide of executions that proponents say should restore credibility to the death penalty in the U.S.

There are several rationales for finally making good on the nearly 1,100 death sentences now pending. Leaving aside the onerous past and future problem of the occasional execution of an innocent convict, many people feel that swift executions are a deterrent to would-be murderers. This is a difficult notion to demonstrate convincingly. Others believe that it is cruel and inhuman *not* to carry out a death sentence speedily because of the years of fear and anguish a condemned man suffers while waiting to be killed. Also, there is a strictly economic argument; it is obviously cheaper—in theory—to execute a person than to feed and house him or her indefinitely. But in fact, the death penalty has significantly boosted the number of enormously expensive appeals battles being waged in state and federal courts across the country.

Finally, there is the politically attractive revenge argument. An execution—even the so-called humane alternative of death by lethal injection—makes the murderer pay in kind for having taken a life. Some people find a seductive symmetry in such a quid pro quo treatment for killers.

But Ted Bundy can only be executed once, scant compensation for a society he brutalized for years. Nor is there an adequate measure for the agony he wrought. Death is tangible; grief is not. Each death he caused created indelible pain among the survivors, those families and loved ones of the girls Bundy snatched away and murdered. In the service of his savage "condition," Ted marked hundreds of people for permanent grief.

Among them are his own parents. All along, Louise Bundy had hoped that Hugh and I would find something to end her nightmare. She had watched her dearest child reviled and condemned for a brutal sex murder, a charge she could not accept. In the end, we had to tell her she was wrong; the charges weren't calumny; her boy was a killer.

Just before Christmas 1980, we flew to Seattle and met with the Bundys. We spent an afternoon with Johnnie in their small kitchen and played for him several segments of tape, including a number of Ted's "speculations." Johnnie did not ask many questions, but quietly asked us to return that night so Louise could hear what he had heard.

The four of us sat in their living room listening to their son's disembodied voice describing the rape and murder of the un-named girl in an orchard. Louise let out several sharp, involuntary moans as she leaned forward in her chair, pain etched across her face. Johnnie sat by her and held her hand.

When it was over, they both thanked us for coming. Neither Johnnie nor Louise spoke a word to us about what they heard Ted say on the tapes. And neither one has spoken to us since.

Their son destroyed dreams and canceled the future. Lynda Healy would not become a teacher. Susan Rancourt would not be a doctor. Debra Kent wouldn't survive to finish high school. Kimberly Leach died in the seventh grade.

But Ted's special cruelty was to offer no confession, no rationale for what he did, and thus no explanation of why these girls had to die. All he left was shock and wonder and, in a half-dozen or so cases, pain with a particularly insidious effect; these people's daughters have never been found. Their grief renews itself with every late-night telephone call or crank letter, any reminder of the vain hope that Donna or Georgann or Debbie or Julie might still be alive.

There surely are other women he murdered whose names have never surfaced, hitchikers or runaways whose bodies also have never been found, or lie like that of Denise Naslund in a police evidence locker against the day when the mysteries of their deaths might be solved. The thousands of such people, reported missing but never found, offer one of the few hints at what Ted and those like him can do with impunity.

The shadings of grief Ted caused seemed infinite. Joyce Healy, Lynda's mother, spoke with a dignified stoicism to Hugh. "I guess I was lucky to have her as long as I did," said Mrs. Healy. "Lynda was an awfully hard girl to lose."

Warren Hawkins, Georgann's father, developed an unreasonable guilt that he had not protected Georgann that June night she vanished outside her sorority house. He was helpless to save her, helpless to rescue her, and helpless against the sick schemes of anonymous callers and letter writers who offered, for a price, to return his daughter.

"You just want to reach out and do something," he told me quietly. "But you can't. You get so drawn out. You waste so damn much emotional effort trying to transfer your hate and bitterness. You get over the loss, then you keep getting reminded of it."

The families of Carol DaRonch, Cheryl Thomas, Karen Chandler, and Kathy Kleiner did receive the cold compensation of seeing Bundy tried and convicted for his unsuccessful attempts on their daughters' lives. By contrast to the rest of the families, they were the lucky ones.

Ted was convicted for killing Margaret Bowman, Lisa Levy, and Kimberly Leach in Florida, but for all the rest of the dead girls—the probable eighteen, and possible forty—Ted escaped prosecution. In a real sense, he got away with their murders.

The survivors have in some cases been broken by their grief. One dead girl's brother was driven to commit sex offenses himself, and another boy has refused to talk in anything but monosyllables since his sister was found slain. Several families have been split by their loss—some into divorce, others into unending cycles of fear and recrimination, a need to hurt and be hurt for what has happened.

We have felt Ted Bundy's leprous touch as well, and there is no anodyne. For four years, Hugh and I lived in intimate contact with all the waste and terror Bundy engendered. Over that time, we produced a volume of reporting sufficient to fill three or four books this length. We wore out ten tape recorders, five in conversations with Ted.

The pursuit of detail grew obsessive, as if in amassing a million little facts we'd somehow arrive at a core truth, a neat, rational summation of Bundy's story. We couldn't; we can only say what it was like, not what it was.

For us, the experience is remembered as a series of vivid, ineradicable images; the conversations with Bundy at the prison, his mad scene before Judge Cowart, the night we told Johnnie and Louise what their son was.

There was Carole Boone with her fevered loyalty to Ted; the earnest and frustrated Bob Keppel; Terry Storwick, sad and confused; and Vic Africano, Ted's last attorney, whose hopeless task it was to defend an insane client in an unwinnable case.

Both Hugh and I have been stunned by this collective despair, and we've grown too familiar with death and insanity. Ted's abstract "inappropriate acting out" as reflected in the concrete reality of Kim Leach's hideous autopsy photographs or in the coroner's stark description of Caryn Campbell's half-eaten face is so grossly anti-human that it overwhelms the mind. The result is not an indifference to other horrors and different tragedies, but an extreme sensitivity to them. We do not care to meet another killer.

In Ted's case, there remain hundreds of separate agonies too acute and too enervating to set down. Perhaps if a single person can speak for all, it is Eleanor Rose, Denise Naslund's mother.

Mrs. Rose lives in a tidy blue frame house in White Center, Washington, just south of Seattle. Three walls of her kitchen are covered with pictures of Denise. Outside, Denise's tan Chevy is parked at the curb where it has been since Kenny Little returned it from Lake Sam that night in 1974. Eleanor has lived in the house for twenty-six years. Denise grew up there, and since her murder, Eleanor Rose rarely leaves the front door. And never at night.

Mrs. Rose is a wraith. About five feet five tall, she weighs less than a hundred pounds. Once, after 1974, her weight dropped as low as seventy-four pounds; that was when she had malnutrition and her bones grew so brittle that they would break. Her sister tried to make her eat, "but I felt like I'd just choke on anything," she told Hugh. Denise inherited many of her mother's features. There are echoes of the daughter in Eleanor's dark complexion, the shape of her face, and her delicate frame. The eyes are similar, too, except that Eleanor's are cast in perpetual sadness, and they rest in deep sockets framed by blue-black circles.

Eleanor Rose has been hospitalized repeatedly; has attempted suicide several times; has received electroshock therapy. She still sees both a psychiatrist and a neurologist and, at the time when Hugh talked to her, was taking seventeen separate medications.

She is emphatic on the special quality of her suffering. In the early months of 1974, she had read of the other missing girls. "It didn't touch me," she recalls. "I thought, Oh, gee, that's too bad. Until it hits a person's home, they can't even imagine what it is like. I mean, they just do not realize the full impact of it. They don't picture it actually really happening to them. Then they say, 'Oh, are you still like that?' What do they think? Do you grow a daughter on a tree and that you can go get another one?"

She did try to meet with the families of the other missing girls, "But I just didn't feel right with them. I felt different.

"Don't get me wrong. I do not mean that I loved Denise any

more than they loved their daughters. But I just couldn't get out of these stages of acceptance. I mean, I could make my mind believe that it really didn't happen. To this day, I still open that mailbox hoping that someone might have Denise and that somehow she'd get a letter to me.''

Mrs. Rose received her share of mail from ghouls and telephone calls from people who would ask, ''Is Denise there? Is Denise there?'' She remembers receiving death threats. She bought a pistol and two tear-gas guns that she keeps by her bed. Richard Bozich, the widower she married several years ago, never leaves Eleanor alone in the house at night.

Denise's death broke her mother's faith in God.

''I was religious,'' she explains. ''I raised my kids all the way through as Catholics. But when that happened, I turned away from God because I blamed Him completely. Our priest came by for a year, year and a half, trying to tell me that God didn't do it. I wouldn't wear a cross or anything.

''Yet half of me had to believe for Denise. I had masses said every month, but I didn't believe for myself. That was a real struggle.

''Now, I want to believe. I want to believe that I'll see her again. But then the other day there was an article that Billy Graham wrote that God can stop these things, but that He doesn't for some reason or other. So I said, 'See! See! God could have prevented it.' ''

Mrs. Rose's capacity for pain is great; her withdrawal since her daughter's murder has been nearly total. She has but one consuming interest. ''I have to talk about Denise,'' she says. ''People tell me, 'Why do you have those pictures out for? She wouldn't look like that now.' I mean, they can be so cruel. I tell them, 'I'll put those pictures away when I want to.' But I know I never will.''

# Acknowledgments

SEVERAL PEOPLE devoted an enormous amount of effort to this book. Joni Evans, our editor, lighted the way. Hers are the considerable gifts of talent and wisdom, which Joni tirelessly applied to the completion of the text. It was a singular experience to work with such an accomplished editor. Marjorie Williams, our other editor, joined the process when her critical insights and genius for structure were needed most. Marjorie touched nothing in the book but to improve it.

Kathy Robbins and Richard Convey are our allies and advocates. Their advice was always sound, their judgment unerring.

We are also indebted to the hundreds of people who shared their knowledge and information with us. Among them are: J. Victor Africano, Joseph Aloi, Ira Beal, Charlene Blaylock, John Boutwell, John Henry Browne, Johnnie Bundy, Louise Bundy, Dr. Al Carlisle, Norman Chapman, Don Davis, George Robert Dekle, Warren Dodge, Roger Dunn, the Reverend James P. Fairbrook, Michael Fisher, Ben Forbes, Judge Stewart Hanson, Warren B. Hawkins, Joyce Healy, Mary Lynn Hinson, Dr. David Hubbard, Judge Wallace Jopling, Kenneth Katsaris, Don Kennedy, Robert Keppell, Patricia Lasko, Dr. Lowell Levine, Bruce Lubeck, John O'Connell, Eleanor Rose, Larry Simpson, Richard L. Stephens, Terry Storwick, Dr. Daris Swindler, Herb Swindler, Jerry Thompson, Lynn Thompson, Marlin Vortman, Sheila Vortman, Fred Wallace, David Watson, Dr. Jolyon West, Patrick Walski, and David Yocom.

Finally, there is our gratitude toward friends and loved ones who generously lent their support over several years. We thank Allysa, Allyson, H. Grant, and Martha Aynesworth, Jennifer S. Boeth, Mike Cochran, Emmett Colvin, F. Philler Curtis, Susan Dahl, Peter Dearing, R.B. Denson, Charles Eaton, Bill Gilliland, Dewey Gram, Bill Gurvich, Cathy Halstead, Peter Halstead,

Lloyd Harrell, Robert W. (Editor Bob) Henkel, Jr., Lucy Anne Calhoun Howard, Annabeth Irwin, G. Brockett Irwin, Frank Jackson, Joseph D. Jamail, Jan Johnson, Susan Kamil, Laura Kavesh, Pam Leven, Char Macdonald, Dan McCrary, Buster McGregor, David McHam, Katherine Michaud, Joe Miller, Susan Murray, Isabelle Nicholson, Tom Nicholson, Marion Olson, James E. Parks, Penelope Percy, Roger Percy, Sally Powell, Michael Ruby, Robert Schulman, Merrill Sheils, Michael Sheldrick, Jerome Storvick, Luanne Tierney, Tom Tierney, Ruby Trujillo, Karen Turok, Sally Vandevanter, Carol Wolf, and Jeffrey Zeiler.

To Susan Harper Michand we owe a special debt. Susan was entrusted with the most sensitive and painstaking work on the book, and in Susan we found out surest believer. Her contribution is measureless.

# About the Authors

Stephen G. Michaud is a veteran journalist who was formerly a staff editor and reporter for *Newsweek* and *Business Week* magazines. He has written and reported on subjects as diverse as politics and physics, including religion, medicine, law, the arts, and national security. Mr. Michaud lives in New York City.

Hugh Aynesworth, who has worked for more than thirty-three years as editor, reporter, and consultant for newspapers, magazines, and television, has received four Pulitzer Prize nominations for his investigative journalism. He has been an investigative reporter for ABC's *20/20*, a bureau chief for *Newsweek*, an editor on such daily newspapers as the *Dallas Morning News* and the *Dallas Times Herald* and has written for the *Washington Post*, the *Los Angeles Times*, *The* [London] *Times*, the *Pittsburgh Press*, and the *Boston Globe*, among others. He lives with his three teenaged children in Dallas.

# CREDITS FOR PHOTO INSERT

Page 1: photos courtesy of Wide World
Page 2: photos of Denise Naslund, Janice Ott, and Caryn Campbell courtesy of Wide World; remaining photos courtesy of UPI
Page 3: bottom photo courtesy of UPI
Page 4: top photo courtesy of UPI; bottom courtesy of Wide World
Page 5: photos courtesy of UPI
Page 6: photo of Carole Boone courtesy of Wide World; remaining photos courtesy of UPI
Page 7: photos courtesy of Wide World
Page 8: top photo courtesy of Wide World; bottom courtesy of UPI